NATIONAL Health & Wellness CLUB®

Fit for Life

Exercise for Everyday People

NATIONAL Health & Wellness CLUB®

Health & Wellness Reference Library™

About the Author

Lynn Madsen specializes in writing for consumers about health and wellness topics.

In addition to her award-winning writing for *Today's Health & Wellness* magazine, Madsen has also written for periodicals such as *Family Day Caring, Mature Outlook, Mayo Clinic Health Letter, Truly Yours* and a wide variety of other publications, and Web sites including *CBS HealthWatch, Epotec, KidsHealth* and *MayoClinic.com.*

Madsen has authored all or portions of numerous books: *Family Health Organizer, Looking After Your Body: An owner's guide to successful aging, Mayo Clinic Guide to Self-Care, Mayo Clinic on Arthritis, Mayo Clinic on Digestive Disorders, Mayo Clinic on Prostate Health* and other Mayo health titles.

An honors graduate of Valparaiso University, Madsen is a core-curriculum certified member in good standing of the American Medical Writers Association and a regular attendee at Mayo Clinic's annual Family Practice Clinical Reviews.

Madsen enjoys an active lifestyle that includes regular walking, swimming and biking, and playing volleyball and softball with family and friends. She also enjoys canoeing and cross-country skiing as weather and schedules allow.

Fit for Life
Exercise for Everyday People
Printed in 2005.

The nutritional and health information presented in this book is based on an in-depth review of the current scientific literature. It is intended only as an informative resource guide to help you make informed decisions; it is not meant to replace the advice of a physician or to serve as a guide to self-treatment. Always seek competent medical help for any health condition or if there is any question about the appropriateness of a procedure or health recommendation.

National Health & Wellness Club
12301 Whitewater Drive
Minnetonka, MN 55343
www.healthandwellnessclub.com

3 4 5 6 7 8 9 10 / 08 07 06 05
ISBN: 1-58159-198-5

Tom Carpenter
Creative Director

Heather Koshiol
Managing Editor

Laura Holle
Assistant Book Development Coordinator

Teresa Marrone
Book Design & Production

Photo Credits
Phil Aarrestad Photography 89, 97, 98, 112, 120, 121, 132, 133, 134, 135, 137, 138, 139, 140, 212, 213, 214, 215, 288, 289, main cover; **Dan Marshall Photography** 192; **Ted Wentink Photography** 70; **Layne Kennedy Photography** 169, back cover (top).

Page 32, photo provided courtesy of **Health and Human Performance Department, University of St. Thomas.**
Page 80, photo provided courtesy of **Life Measurement, Inc.**

Bill Reynolds, Illustration

Contents

Foreword

The lifestyle problem of physical inactivity is prevalent in a majority of our population, both in America and worldwide. A sedentary lifestyle provokes and aggravates risk factors for both cardiovascular disease and stroke. Physical inactivity coupled with the overweight state and obesity is constantly providing a negative impact on the future health of billions of people.

FIT FOR LIFE addresses many issues related to importance of an active lifestyle with regard to both cardiovascular health and health in general. The book emphasizes that humans are "designed" to be active as early as the age of two years but often subsequently become victims of an inactive, unhealthy lifestyle environment that kindles both risk factors and disease.

Physical activity has been widely researched and supported by evidence-based studies regarding benefits to cardiovascular and overall health. A life of physical activity begins with a proper mental attitude and continually setting goals and tracking methods of exercise and physical activity. The issue of finding time for physical activity is important and the actual motivation of "getting started" is often problematic for many individuals. These problems may occur not only in the initial phase but also in long term maintenance.

FIT FOR LIFE further emphasizes that there are many roads to a healthy lifestyle. Such can include regular daily activity performed as yard work and housework to various types of more intense activities such as running, brisk walking, bicycling, recreational sports, and certain types of individual or group games.

Of essence in an exercise program is avoiding injuries particularly in the aging population. This should evoke interest in having advice on physical activity from an expert in the field and considering a proper type of warm up and cool down activities to surround a session of exercise. The effects of aging on the cardiovascular system can be delayed significantly in those who are physically active.

Adjusting goals to keep momentum or maintenance in exercise is vitally important and this book clearly emphasizes the importance of a long-term plan in keeping one in a regular program of physical activity regardless of the busy day, the lack of time and other realistic issues encountered on a daily basis. Obstacles are always of concern; particularly financial resources, uncooperative weather, lack of energy and boredom.

FIT FOR LIFE should be an asset to those interested in cardiovascular health and overall better health derived from an improved level of physical activity and exercise capability. Such physical activity benefit goes beyond that of cardiovascular and stroke health and includes the musculoskeletal system, certain neurological disorders, mental depression and other chronic diseases. This book should have an important place in the library of individuals who are becoming health-conscious and who have had the interest "kindled within" to become physically healthy and enjoy a better lifestyle.

As we continue in the new millennium, individuals must assume self-responsibility for cardiovascular and overall health. Medical and health professionals can do diagnostic testing, surgical procedures and prescribe highly effective medications for the care of an individual. However, it is up to the individual to have adherence to medications, control calorie and salt intake, be physically active, and abstain from tobacco. This process of self-responsibility is "in its infancy" but will hopefully improve as we evolve more incentives and rewards to individuals and groups who assume "self-control" of their health.

Gerald F. Fletcher, M.D.
Mayo Clinic Jacksonville
Jacksonville, Florida

Introduction

From its inception, this book was written for you—if you're an adult with an interest in getting into better physical condition. The central idea throughout the entire process of outlining, researching and writing this book was that, like the author, many people have an interest in this topic, would appreciate having additional accurate information and could use a gentle nudge in order to take some concrete steps to improve personal fitness.

While there are already many books and articles about fitness, this book approaches the topic in several unique ways. It presents the opinions or knowledge not of one person, but of many experts. It recognizes and presents varied kinds of information, from facts well documented by scientifically based research to theories that are just beginning to be tested. And it provides first-hand information based on the anecdotal experience of individuals.

You're the Expert

Unlike many books and articles, this book is based on the premise that no one knows your body better than you do. When it comes to you—you're the expert.

Fit for Life affirms the value of your personal experience, relative to your own health and fitness, and fosters a renewed sensitivity to what you know about yourself. In this way it seeks to empower you to understand—and act upon—the fact that you are the primary player when it comes to your own health and fitness. While the experts can share their valuable experience—and do so generously in these pages—they cannot sense what you perceive in your own body, they cannot force you to judge what action is needed, and they certainly cannot make you get up and active in order to improve your health and fitness.

About This Book

In an effort to share with you the value of personal experience—and perhaps, to motivate you to see that your own actions really can affect outcomes—this book presents a variety of information in sidebars. You will find two distinct types of sidebars in *Fit for Life:*

■ **Informational sidebars**—containing capsules of information relating to copy in the body of text. These sidebars are shown in boxes.

■ **Sidebar vignettes**—in which recognized experts, other individuals and the author share their personal experiences and efforts regarding physical activity and the topics under discussion. These sidebars will be treated with graphics like those below.

The author has sought out individuals who are recognized experts in the areas under discussion, and had them share their knowledge. Their words and advice appear throughout this book. Likewise, at the end of each chapter, you can read about the professional who reviewed the content before publication. The author reminds you that no information gleaned from a book should replace the valuable information derived from an ongoing relationship you have with the individual or individuals who provide your healthcare. There is simply no substitute for the cooperative relationship between you and a well-qualified healthcare provider.

An Ongoing Process

As I began work on this book, I set out to present information that was both known and still being learned about physical activity. I believed that I'd probably be close to finishing the project as soon as I found answers to most of my own questions.

As I spoke with an ever-widening circle of experts, I came to realize anew how much we still don't know and how many areas are still somewhat controversial when it comes to our bodies and physical activity. I have attempted to present a variety of viewpoints, sometimes in disagreement with one another. As is true in many aspects of life, you must look at the evidence and judge for yourself where you'll stand.

What I can say, however—with a stronger conviction than ever before—is that there's one thing on which the experts are unanimous: the belief that our bodies were designed for physical activity. I hope these pages will nudge and empower you to come to that conviction yourself—and to take the moves it implies to increase the activity level in your own life.

CHAPTER 1

What's This Book About—And Why Should I Care?

"Watch a two-year-old child for a while," suggested a Mayo Clinic physician. "Notice the activity level. It's amazing! You see how much our bodies were designed to move—throughout our entire lives."

The Mayo doctor was responding to a specific question about the level of physical activity she'd recommend for someone with arthritis. But if you talk with qualified experts about almost any aspect of personal health, the inherent truth behind her statement becomes increasingly clear.

Whether your questions concern the "big" killers you want to avoid—heart disease, cancer or diabetes—or even less deadly conditions—backaches, headaches or arthritis—the answers you'll get will often have one thing in common. And that same piece of advice surfaces quickly if you investigate how to live better with just about any health condition—or if you ask a bunch of experts in various fields for their kernel of advice that can make the biggest difference in anyone's long-term health.

Whether they use exactly the same words or not, the experts speak in unison. Their common message is, "Get moving!" The more researchers study the human body and its functions, the more they are convinced that our bodies were designed for physical activity—and lots of it!

Why Did You Open This Book?

Chances are, you're a busy person, with many time pressures. Yet, you've at least gotten as far as opening a book about fitness. Why?

Perhaps you're curious about exactly what "fit for life" means—and whether you qualify. Is there a quick test here for you on the first few pages to see how you rate? Or maybe you've given the subject a lot of thought—and even some energy—and want to improve your fitness level. Or are you getting older and want to learn more about making those "golden years" healthier?

You may be looking for information that will help you cope better with the cards you've been dealt, health-wise. Perhaps you have a family history of heart disease and you're wondering—apart from a genetic transplant—whether you can do anything to avoid it, or at least put it off for a few years. Or perhaps you already know that you have diabetes and want to stay as well as you can, for as long as possible. Are you spending more time in a doctor's office than you think you should, for a variety of reasons? Maybe you're "down in the dumps" a lot and wonder if physical activity could pick you up.

You may feel "out of shape," compared to your younger days, and wonder how hard it would be to become fit. Or perhaps you've never been very fit, but you're wondering what it would take to get there—or at least, to be closer to being fit.

If any of these descriptions seem appropriate—this book's designed for you. It aims to help you get moving.

What This Book Definitely Is Not

This book is not an encyclopedia on all aspects of physical health and conditioning. Nor is it a manual on how to train for the Olympics—or how to become a personal trainer or fitness instructor. Although the book contains authoritative and accurate information to get you started in a variety of activities, it doesn't provide the definitive word on any one activity. But it helps point you in the right direction.

It's not an attempt to enroll you in a cultlike program that's "way out" and takes control of your time, your pocketbook—your entire life. Nor does it seek to alienate you from the people with whom you want to spend time.

Not a "One-Size-Fits-All" Recipe

This book is also not a "one-size-fits-all" recipe for fitness. You are unique in many ways that affect your fitness—and your fitness program should reflect that:

- Your body functions in ways that may differ from those around you. Perhaps your friend can maintain a stable weight and eat huge meals, while you would balloon on such a diet. Someone else you know may jog five miles a day without any knee problems, while you may be sore for several days if you attempt it.
- Your genetic makeup matters. If you have one or more family members with diabetes or heart disease, for example, you should be particularly careful in controlling your risk factors.
- If your neighbor, with whom you

Darby: Look What 2 Years Can Do!

Two years ago, Darby, a sales specialist in occupational health for Kaiser Permanente, moved from the city's outskirts closer to her job in Portland. It seemed a good time to make some changes in her fairly average, basically sedentary lifestyle.

Darby knew it would be a real hassle to bring her car along when she moved. The aging vehicle needed extensive repairs, and Darby's new home was only half a mile from work—a distance she thought she could get used to walking. Besides, Portland had excellent—and inexpensive—public transportation that could take the place of a car in many instances. So she opted for life without a vehicle.

The results of Darby's decision have been dramatic.

Darby now walks a lot. She's never tracked her mileage with a pedometer, although she's considered doing that. Besides walking to work, Darby walks to the grocery store half a mile away and carries her groceries home—and up two flights of stairs. Last summer her initial attempts at organic fruit and vegetable gardening were successful beyond her expectations. A plentiful harvest enabled Darby to cut back on grocery purchases. She's also eliminated many fats and "extras" from her diet.

Darby frequently walks to the library and to other shopping areas. "I always need a destination, or it feels like a chore," she says. Some days she walks downtown during her lunch hour—and takes public transit back to work. Darby also walks or takes the bus to her classes on Saturday mornings at the local community college.

What about Portland's rain? "It doesn't bother me much," says Darby. She particularly appreciates the hassle-free time during her morning walk to daydream and organize her thoughts. Although both her apartment and her employer are in Portland's "Fareless Square," an area where there's no charge to use the public transit system, Darby says she's less prone to wait for a bus if walking looks like a better option. "If the bus is coming in 30 minutes and it takes me less time to walk where I'm going, I just walk there."

Although Darby never weighs herself—and has no idea how much weight she's lost—she does know she's dropped four or five dress sizes. And her 21-year-old daughter, who lives with her and is much more athletic, now enjoys walking with her mom because she no longer needs to slow down her pace to match her mom's.

So, what's next? Darby doesn't expect to invest a lot of time or money at a health club, but now that she can kneel and squat she wants to work on her upper body flexibility. She'd like to take a yoga class. Darby's also considering joining Portland's FlexCar program for the rare times when a car would be handy—when it's time to get the Thanksgiving turkey home from the store, for example.

plan to start walking every morning, functions at an entirely different level of cardiovascular fitness than you do, you may need to plan other physical activities as well, in order to meet your fitness needs more completely. Hint: If possible, don't eliminate such an otherwise beneficial activity simply because it doesn't meet all your needs. Try to add what's missing into the mix somewhere else.

■ Family circumstances differ greatly, and so do individuals' activity needs. Caring for a young or elderly family member or a partner may limit your ability to be away from home, so you may need to make the best possible use of resources at home rather than getting out alone for a fitness fix as often as some of your friends can.

■ Financial constraints may force you to look for low-cost ways of getting fit rather than simply joining a health club or Y.

■ Perhaps affording childcare while you take a fitness break isn't the problem—you just can't find the time to do it.

Once you start nudging your lifestyle toward improved fitness, the rewards may surpass your expectations. You may even find yourself becoming more fit than you'd ever imagined.

Basically, the closer you look at it, fitness involves a lot of common sense—and listening to your own body. Mom may have been much smarter than we thought when she told us to "just go out and play."

Cut Your Healthcare Costs—Some Serious Numbers

There's no longer any doubt about it: lack of physical activity costs most Americans a lot of money. The most comprehensive study, the *National Medical Expenditures Survey,* which studied 35,000 people, labeled as physically active anyone who got half an hour or more of moderate to strenuous physical activity three or more times a week.

If you're physically active, you have lower annual direct medical costs than people who are inactive—to the tune of about $330 per person, per year, according to The Centers for Disease Control and Prevention. The agency also estimates that increasing the level of regular, moderate physical activity of the more than 88 million inactive Americans over the age of 15 could reduce direct medical costs nationally by as much as $76.6 billion a year, with the biggest benefit going to women aged 55 or older. Another study showed that if only 10 percent of currently inactive adults began a walking program, the U.S. could save between $4.3 and $5.6 billion per year in medical expenses.

Employers are beginning to see the value of fostering employee health, as well. The U.S. Department of Health and Human Services reports that in 1998, 93 percent of employers had at least one program designed to improve employee health. Typical programs offer help in smoking cessation, managing stress, prenatal care, nutrition and fitness. The Department reports studies showing that physical activity programs in the workplace can reduce short-term sick leave by 6 to 32 percent and healthcare costs by 20 to 55 percent—while increasing productivity by 2 to 52 percent.

Trim Your Transportation Expenses

Darby isn't the only one saving money these days on transportation while becoming fit. Consider, for a moment, how many short trips of a couple miles or less you take in an average week with your car. Those short trips add up, expensewise. You and others in your family can save money by taking an extra 5 to 10 minutes to walk or bike to the store, library, post office, local school, bank or a friend's house. And, if you live in an urban area served by a program called FlexCar, the opportunities are even greater.

Running errands—or walking—not only saves gas, but can add healthy exercise to your day.

Save on Yard Work or Housecleaning Costs

Maybe you never thought of yard work or housecleaning as exercise. But it certainly can be! If you're physically able, becoming more fit may encourage you to do more of your own yard work, snow removal, cleaning and other household chores that require physical exertion. Although costs vary widely from one community to another, it doesn't take long to realize that, over time, your savings could be substantial. For example:

- **Typical Minneapolis Urban Area Charges** *(Assuming an average city lot size)*:

lawn mowing	$12 to $20
leaf raking	$15 and up per hour
snow shoveling	$15 to $25 per half hour
house cleaning	$25 to $40 per hour

- **Chicago Suburban Area Charges** *(Assuming average lot size)*:

lawn mowing	$20 to $40
leaf raking	$15 and up per hour
snow shoveling	$15 to $40 per half hour
house cleaning	$20 to $40 per hour

Trim Entertainment Costs While Trimming Your Waistline

Try this. Instead of parking right next to the theater for a night of snacks and a movie, park a few blocks away, walk to the theater and skip the expensive snacks. You'll not only save yourself money, you'll feel better, as well. Do you generally sit most of the day? Why not try an inexpensive activity that involves exercise in the evening or on the weekend for entertainment—and invite friends to join you! If you go out to

FlexCar: The Right Program at the Right Time

FlexCar is a car-sharing program offered in six cities in the United States: Seattle, Washington; Portland, Oregon; Long Beach, San Jose and Palo Alto, California; and Washington, D.C. Membership is over 7,000 and growing. It's tailored after programs in Canada and one which has thrived in Europe for 20 years.

"When buying a car, the typical American deals with most of the real cost of having that car up-front," says Steve Gutmann, business accounts manager for FlexCar Portland. "Once you acquire the car—whether it's with cash, a loan you pay off each month or a lease—the only other expenses for quite a while are occasional insurance payments, gas and oil. It's like walking into an all-you-can-eat buffet. You have no immediate incentive to drive less. When it's only the incremental cost of gas to consider as you use your car, you don't even think about it. Yet, the American Automobile Association estimates that the average American spends about $7,500 a year to own and operate a Ford Taurus. An average FlexCar member spends about $100 a month."

How is this possible?

"People in the program have a car when they need one. But when they see, as they go along, what it costs them, they drive about 67 percent less," says Gutmann. When people realize the cost of driving, they're ready to drive less, walk or bike more, use annual transit passes and do more things in their own neighborhoods—like shopping. And, in the process, they become more fit.

Here's how FlexCar works. You pay $25 to become a member, which covers the cost of a background check for insurance purposes. Once you're approved as a good driver, you have access to the program's cars, nationwide.

In Portland, the organization's roughly 1,300 members share about 40 leased cars—a number that grows by one with every 30 new members. And FlexCar's membership has nearly doubled every year.

Cars are assigned on a first-come, first-served reservation basis. Although you can reserve a car up to a year ahead of time, Gutmann reports that the overwhelming majority of users make their reservation the day they use the dinner, take a walk in the restaurant's neighborhood afterward—or at a nearby park. Or arrange to meet a few friends or coworkers in the evening at a local community open-gym night for a game of pickup basketball. Is there a tennis court in your neighborhood park that sits unused in the evening? Why not give it a try with your partner? Once you start looking around, there are many active things you can do in place of inactive entertainment. They don't need to cost any money, and you'll feel much better afterward.

car. Members can almost always schedule a car at their first-choice pick-up location and seldom have to opt for one at an alternate spot—usually just a few blocks farther away.

Cars are placed at strategic locations around town near members, who walk or bike an average of five blocks if they live downtown—slightly more if they live in less dense areas—to the vehicle they'll use. Every location has a bike rack, frequently near public transit.

Lock boxes are on a wall or post next to the car. After using the car, you fill out a trip ticket. Each month members receive a computer-itemized bill, averaging about $6 per hour of use. In exchange for a small credit on their monthly bill, members fill gas tanks when they're three-quarters empty, using a credit card in the glove compartment.

Although some members use FlexCar to replace a second car in the household, Gutmann reports that half of the members don't own a car. He acknowledges that the program is most viable in urban or close-in suburban areas, where population density means cars can be placed within a convenient walking distance for most users. Many members say FlexCar enables them to either sell a vehicle or avoid buying another one.

Members who take a road trip benefit from FlexCar agreements with two rental companies for corporate rates on longer-term rentals. And, notes Gutmann, having access to cars in all the cities that have FlexCar programs gives you new options when you travel. For example, some Portland FlexCar business commuters take advantage of FlexCar's discounted Amtrack rates and travel by train to Seattle, where they pick up a car for local use.

Gutmann and his wife—members of FlexCar for over 4 years—bike to work most days. Now that they're new parents, they've found childcare within a few blocks of home. They'll bike to and from work and coordinate dropping off and picking up their child each day, using a child trailer and eventually a bike seat. And it'll be surprising if their child doesn't become a cyclist, as well!

Fitness Is a Lifestyle!

One of the biggest roadblocks to an active lifestyle is the chair, according to fitness experts at the Cooper Institute in Dallas, Texas. The U.S. Surgeon General and the National Center for Health Statistics see disturbing downward trends in Americans' physical activity levels. And things don't appear to be improving in the younger folks, either. For example, according to government statistics, from 1991 to 1995 alone, enrollment by high school youth in daily physical education classes dropped from 42 percent to 25 percent.

The decline in physical activity worsens with age for both sexes. The federal government defines regular, leisure-time physical activity as light to moderate activity for at least 30 minutes five times a week or vigorous activity for at least 20 minutes three or more times a week.

Bob: Working on Year-Round, Active Options

Years ago—27, to be exact—my husband Bob began coaching and playing on a men's recreational church-league softball team. After several enjoyable, active softball seasons, he wanted to add something active to his off-season schedule. He was tired of "vegging out" on Friday nights. Meanwhile, I—a new mother—was ready to join him for an active night out. Volleyball seemed like a natural—participants could join at any skill level, indoor play could continue through winter and folks could consider it a night out, equivalent to a night at the movies, but more relaxing and invigorating. A number of other couples and singles agreed that it sounded like fun.

With a few phone calls to the local school district, Bob arranged to rent an elementary school gym for 2 hours on Friday nights throughout the school year. Because he advertised the activity through our church—and was able to use the church's certificate of insurance—the school district charged only a minimal fee, which Bob covered by charging players $1 to $2 each night. People came whenever they could. When our own kids were small, Bob arranged to use space at our church across the street from the school for child care and hired neighborhood teenagers to look after the youngsters. Parents pitched in to cover that cost, as well.

Over the years, Friday night volleyball has become a tradition. Pickup games every week are strictly recreational and now intergenerational, as the group includes adult children of some of the original players—and their friends. Players get as much of a workout as they like, as the mixed teams that form each week give the more able players an opportunity to compensate for those who are less able. Although it takes some organizing, Bob figures that over the years he's not only gotten good exercise, but also saved a fair amount of money ($2 per person is much cheaper than a typical movie on a Friday night). And we've made lifelong friends, as well.

By age 75, about one in three men and one in two women engage in no regular, leisure-time physical activity.

What, Specifically, Does "Fit for Life" Mean?

"Being active not only helps you feel good physically, but it gives you time to yourself to sort through your schedule and prepare for the pressures of your day," says Hall of Fame pitcher Nolan Ryan. "The better you feel about yourself, the more productive you can be—at work and at play."

To most people, according to the President's Council on Physical Fitness and Sports, fitness means meeting the demands of everyday life without becoming overly tired—and handling the occasional fastball that comes your way. The Council officially defines physical fitness as:

> *The ability to perform daily tasks vigorously and alertly, with energy left over for enjoying leisure-time activities and meeting emergency demands. It is the ability to endure, to bear up, to withstand stress, to carry on in circumstances where an unfit person could not continue, and is a major basis for good health and well-being.*

So much for the official definition of fitness. What does fitness specifically mean for you?

Fitness: It's Different Things for Different People

Just as each person is different, so is each individual's definition of fitness. You are the one who best knows what fitness means for you, and that definition may change over time. Now it's your turn to reflect about what fitness means to you—and capture some of those thoughts.

Take out a pencil and paper, or turn on the computer and start jotting down some of your ideas. Scan the following suggestions, noting things that particularly resonate for you. Some things you list may be things you hope to attain—others, things you've achieved and want to maintain. Don't try to get too detailed right now—there's time for that in later chapters. This is the time to dream, and capture some of those dreams.

The balance of this chapter introduces some of the possibilities you may consider, as you reflect on becoming fit. Think about what you've done—and what you've only imagined being able to do. Some things may sound interesting, while others may totally turn you off. That's fine. You'll also think of things you want to include, beyond those listed. At this point, simply capture your thoughts. This isn't meant to be a definitive list, but only an effort to get you thinking about what to include in your fitness trek.

- **Do things with kids!** They're great, active companions. Think of ways you can interact with young people—whether it's your own, your friends' or your neighbors' children or grandchildren, or kids at a local school, day care center or community center.

Take a peppy stroll with your kids or grandkids, letting them choose whether to walk or ride.

Look particularly for active things you can do with them. For example, volunteer to accompany a class on a field trip to the zoo, a bike hike, an inline skating or roller skating outing, canoeing or bowling. Some states require children to spend several days at a nature center at some point in their education, learning about the environment—and those days generally have lots of activity built in. Teachers frequently welcome adult volunteers who offer to go along. You may find yourself joining the kids in learning how to snowshoe or hike in the woods, while gaining new insight and awareness of the natural habitat around you.

But when it comes to kids, toddlers are the most active. "If you want a good workout, baby-sit a two- or three-year-old," suggests Vern Gambetta, who has coached sports at various levels for over 30 years and has served as the conditioning coach for professional athletes and teams. "First watch, then mimic, what they do. You'll be exhausted in no time!" Take a tot for a ride in the stroller while you walk, jog or skate behind. Or—if you can do it safely and have appropriate protective gear—take a youngster for a bike ride.

■ **Walk! It's the easiest exercise there is, and one of the very best!** Many professional athletic trainers, who have ready access to the very best and latest equipment, urge you to skip the fancy equipment and get out and walk. And many top-flight cardiologists and conditioning experts agree that it's the best exercise there is.

Maybe you'd like to be able to walk several miles without becoming winded.

Have you wanted to get a pet and considered the decent exercise you could get, simply by walking a dog every day?

Perhaps you live close enough to work to consider walking once a week or more—or use public transportation on the way there and walk home. If you're retired, perhaps you could find time to walk a lot more—to the library, bank or your place of worship.

Is your doctor's or dentist's office close enough to walk there for a check-up? It may surprise your doctor—it's not something many people do. Some people walk to and from the grocery store several times a week, bringing groceries home by hand, in a cart or in a backpack. Others get to know their area—and the folks who live in the community—when they join a walking or hiking club.

■ **Compete in amateur sports.** Whether you've ever been on a team or not, you can usually find one that competes at a level that's comfortable for you—even if you're just learning a sport. And don't be afraid to try something you've never tried before. Teams form through park and recreation departments of cities, at workplaces, through places of worship—and informally, among friends or neighbors. Depending upon the sport, fees and equipment needs are usually fairly minimal. Some places ask you to register an entire team (look for friends, relatives, neighbors, coworkers who might be interested—or post a notice at the grocery store or library), while others form teams after everyone signs up. Check newsletters you receive or look for postings at public libraries, sporting goods stores or grocery stores for details. Teams commonly form around these and other sports:

- basketball
- bowling
- broomball
- football (touch or flag)
- golf
- hockey
- soccer
- softball
- volleyball

■ **Swim laps at a community pool.** You don't need to join a fancy health or fitness club—or even your local Y (which may offer financial assistance). You often can find affordable open swim hours at local schools, community centers or colleges. And, depending upon where you live, in warm weather you may enjoy free access to lakes, rivers or the ocean.

■ **Learn how to skate with inline skates or roller skates.** Check community newsletters for inline skating trail information and local roller rinks for hours and rates.

■ **Learn how to canoe or kayak.** Again, your best bet may be a local newsletter—or stop at a local sporting goods store or rental facility and inquire about lessons or trial outings.

■ **Learn to dance or schedule a regular time to go dancing several times a month.** Many school districts and cities offer inexpensive lessons—or even free trial lessons. You may not even need to bring a partner.

■ **Try an activity you've always wanted to try—whether it's a short triathlon (AARP sponsors them around the country throughout the year), a hike up a midsized mountain or rock climbing.** You can frequently find information about such activities in the Sunday newspaper

Newly Defining a Trip to the Grocery Store

During the past year, as I increased my level of biking and walking, I became interested in eliminating some of my frequent car trips to the grocery store. I occasionally wore a backpack, and found it offered a comfortable way for me to carry groceries the mile home without ending up with the sore neck, back or arm that I got from carrying bags home by hand.

When my first bone density scan revealed that at age 52 I hadn't begun to develop the osteoporosis to which I'm genetically entitled, I realized I might benefit in several ways from the weight-bearing activity of walking and carrying groceries home in a backpack more often. I could strengthen my bones, my heart and the muscles in my trunk and spine—all at the same time. Several experts I queried about this agreed that it might be beneficial. However, it's not something experts recommend for everyone, according to Ray W. Squires, Ph.D., director of the cardiovascular health clinic, Mayo Clinic, Rochester, Minnesota, who expressed concern about the possibility of knee or hip joint soreness or injury that the added weight might bring. For the same reasons, Squires generally doesn't recommend using weighted vests or backpacks, except for hiking.

Now I challenge myself to see how few times I actually need to use the car when I buy groceries. Admittedly, I usually just buy food for two, and the task would be much more challenging if I still had ravenously hungry kids at home. Much to my husband's surprise, I've already carried a medium-sized frozen turkey home in the backpack with no problem. But so far I haven't carried an entire watermelon, and I also frequently use the car when I buy canned goods on sale. But it's an interesting challenge to try if you live fairly close to a grocery store. Again, it's important to remember to listen to your body. If it hurts—don't do it.

You'll need a decent backpack, with padded and adjustable straps. For me, there's a certain optimum height to wear the backpack, which can be comfortably loaded with a fair amount of weight for the walk home. And I usually don't actually notice the added weight on my walk home—after all, I've dragged around that much and more body weight day after day for years, until fairly recently. But I do find removing the backpack when I get home a rather exhilarating sensation.

sports pages, community education mailings or posted at sporting goods stores.

■ **Lose some of that extra weight you've been carrying or park those cigarettes for good.** If these are goals—whether you've tried many times before or not—physical activity can help you achieve them.

■ **Avoid spending so much time on the disabled list.** If you end up with aches and pains for several days every time you take on a moderately active project, it may be due to deconditioned muscles. Undertaking a modest program of regular activity that uses and tones those muscles can enable you to enjoy extra activity without paying for it for days.

■ **Avoid many chronic health conditions that sideline people as they get older.** Chapter 2 discusses the health benefits you can attain by becoming reasonably fit, especially relating to diseases of the heart and blood vessels (high cholesterol, high blood pressure, angina, heart attacks and stroke), diabetes, osteoporosis, some types of cancer and depression.

■ **Live a better life with health conditions that you already have.** Having heart disease doesn't mean you should become inactive—just the opposite. But purposefully improving your fitness level, whether you're dealing with heart disease or any other chronic health condition, can improve your quality of life—and prolong it.

■ **Enjoy sex more.** You'll derive more enjoyment from sex and be more sexually active if you're physically fit. If you exercise regularly, you're more likely to experience increased desire and

Regular activity can help you avoid time on the disabled list.

sexual confidence—and enjoy having sex more frequently. Studies show that regular physical activity enhances your ability to become aroused sexually and achieve orgasm—regardless of your age.

Aerobic activity—it doesn't seem to matter which kind—is apparently a real libido booster. Scientists don't know exactly why, but they suspect this may be due to a release of endorphins, the opiate-like chemical your brain produces. Endorphins may create a sense of well-being and make you more receptive to your partner's sexual overtures.

■ **Sleep reasonably well.** Regular moderate physical activity can help you sleep enough to be well rested, according to Timothy Roehrs, Ph.D., director of research, Sleep Disorders and Research Center, Henry Ford Health System, Detroit, Michigan. "Although regular exercisers don't necessarily sleep differently than nonexercisers, increased physical activity promotes a deeper, slow-wave sleep that is highly restorative," he says. "Furthermore, people who have difficulty sleeping frequently find that exercise has a sleep-enhancing effect. They experience a more rapid-onset, deeper sleep—as long as the exercise doesn't occur too close to a major sleep period." Roehrs recommends exercising—but not to the point of pain—no less than two or three hours before you want to sleep.

The amount of sleep required varies from one person to another, but you'll know it's the right amount if you feel energized and renewed when you awaken in the morning and don't feel tired or sleepy by midday or toward the end of the day. You may also find that becoming fit will mean you'll awaken free of many of the aches and pains you've come to expect with each new day.

Save any notes you've made so far, so that you can look back at them a few months down the road and see how you've progressed and changed. Don't worry about whether or not you'll meet

Physical Activity Can Often Help Cure Sleep Apnea

It's true. About 3 percent of American adults—twice as many men as women—have sleep apnea, a condition in which soft tissue in your airway collapses as you breathe, limiting your ability to inhale as much oxygen as you need. Sleep apnea becomes more common as you get older.

The most common symptom is loud snoring at night, often accompanied by dangerously long pauses in breathing. Doctors frequently treat sleep apnea by prescribing a continuous positive airway pressure (CPAP) machine during sleep. The machine comes with a mask that you wear over your nose and mouth while you sleep. The machine pumps air through the mask, keeping your airway open with air pressure slightly higher than the air pressure around you. Surgery is also possible, but less often successful.

You can often cure sleep apnea by losing 20 to 40 pounds and exercising, according to Timothy Roehrs, Ph.D., director of research, Sleep Disorders and Research Center, Henry Ford Health System, Detroit, Michigan. "Just as sleep apnea accompanies a rapid increase in body weight of 20 to 40 pounds for some people, a similar reduction in sleep-disordered breathing can follow a loss of the same amount of weight, probably due to a tightening of the muscles in the airway and neck," says Roehrs. He estimates that regular physical activity and weight loss of at least 20 pounds could resolve close to half of all sleep apnea cases—if people who lose the weight manage to keep it off.

your goals—just start aiming toward something positive. And, as you progress, you'll have ample opportunity to refine and change your targets.

Not a Test, but a Way of Life

Physical fitness isn't tied to a formal test, and you don't really need anything—other than your body, gravity and a place to walk. Being physically fit means having enough energy to perform the activities of daily life—whatever that means for you. The possibilities depend upon where you are right now and what sorts of fitness activities you undertake. It may mean you'll be able to vacuum your own rug or go up and down the stairs in your house without getting winded—or easily manage several flights of stairs in public buildings or at work.

Becoming physically fit may enable you to carry in your own groceries—or those of an elderly neighbor—possibly even up several flights of stairs. It may mean you can walk to the bus stop. Or perhaps you'll plant and maintain a small—or large—garden.

In fact, getting physically fit may enable you to undertake numerous yard projects on your own: mowing your own lawn (perhaps even with a push-type mower), painting or roofing your house, trimming your shrubs and trees and sawing the pieces into firewood-sized lengths. If you're fit, you may seed grass or lay sod in your own yard, rather than paying a professional to do it. Or, you may save a fair amount of money by doing part or all of a landscaping project yourself.

Fitness may mean being able to rake the leaves from your lawn or shovel the snow from your own sidewalk or drive-

Stairs as a Fitness Tool

Stairs, with the option to use an elevator, can be a wonderful fitness tool. In fact, if you're frequently in a building with several flights of stairs, you can use them in a variety of ways to increase your fitness.

If you're not used to taking stairs, try this. Get off the elevator one floor before your destination and take the stairs up the last flight—once a day, at first. When that becomes easy, add another flight, challenging yourself by increasing the number of flights every few weeks. Or simply increase the number of times you use the stairs throughout the day. Take the stairs down, if it doesn't cause knee pain. Otherwise, take the elevator.

Variations include taking a flight of stairs backward—up and down, holding onto the railing—which works different muscles than going forward, or using the bottom step for timed "step-ups" or for "jump-ups" (jumping, with both feet together, first up the step and then down, repeatedly, holding the railing, as needed).

way—something you should work up to gradually. If you already do that, perhaps you'll consider getting a bit more exercise by helping a disabled or elderly neighbor—producing a "win" for both of you.

Fitness may mean walking the golf course (starting with nine holes, first), rather than riding a motorized cart, either taking your bag on a pullcart or—if you're already fairly fit—shouldering the bag yourself. Maybe it means joining a group of coworkers or neighbors for a daily jog.

If you plan to travel, fitness may mean touring an area on foot, rather than taking a tour bus. Or maybe you'd like to bump your fitness up and try an active vacation—there are many available to suit a variety of budgets and ability levels (more on that in Chapter 7).

Fitness Means Being Active—in Your Own Way!

The physical activity experts at the Cooper Institute recently completed a study called Project Active. Half of the people in the study worked out in a gym using a standard routine, three to five times a week. The other half, called "the lifestyle group," met in small groups to discuss and work on ways to incorporate routine physical activity, like walking and stair climbing, into their daily lives. After two years, both groups realized the same health benefits: their average blood pressure, body fat, caloric expenditure and general fitness all improved similarly.

Participants who were moderately fit were half as likely to die prematurely as those in the lowest fitness category—and

Trying Our Hands at Landscaping

The landscaping in our yard was long overdue for an update. My husband and I knew the project would be costly, especially if we got the top-notch professional design assistance we wanted.

However, more confident of our physical capabilities because we'd made a concerted effort to improve our fitness level in the past year, we decided to ask about doing some of the "grunt" work on the project ourselves. The company we used quoted the project with numerous options, and we ended up opting to dig a trench for drainage pipes, spread 28 yards (two truckloads) of black dirt and do all of the planting ourselves, with some help from our adult kids.

Several years ago we probably would not have even considered taking on such a project. However, having a hand in actually accomplishing it not only helped us add value to our home, but also made us realize the success of our recent fitness efforts—and, enabled us to save several thousand dollars in the process, as well.

only 10 to 15 percent more likely to die prematurely as those in the highest fitness category. "There is a consistent gradient across activity groups indicating greater longevity and reduced risk of coronary heart disease, cardiovascular disease, stroke and colon cancer in more active individuals," the report notes.

"The magnitude of reduction in mortality across fitness groups is substantial," the Project Active report continues. "Essentially all analyses show at least a 50 percent lower mortality rate in the high-fit as compared with the low-fit individuals. In some studies, the difference in mortality rates between the most and least fit individuals was on the order of three- to four-fold."

A Self-Help Manual

Use this book to help you get and remain as fit as you'd like to be, in order to fully participate in life. The book offers help gauging how fit you are now, not in relation to others, but relative to your personal activity and health goals. Pause for a few moments to consider:

- What would you like to change?
- What's your dream or vision?
- What are the incremental steps you need to achieve that vision?

This book can help you improve your current level of fitness and make fitness a lifestyle choice. It can help you find your favorite fit way of life and overcome obstacles like time limitations, injuries, lack of visible progress, lack of

Shovel the Snow—Carefully!

Shoveling snow is great exercise—if you're up to it. But every winter about 1,200 Americans die from a cardiac event during or after a big snowstorm, frequently as a result of shoveling snow. But don't let that stop you—people die from falling out of bed, too! Just shovel it carefully.

Upper body exercise strains your heart more than leg exercise. And snow shoveling is also largely an isometric exercise—exercise in which your muscles work, but there's little actual movement until you finally lift the snow up onto the bank. Isometric exercise causes your heart rate to rise, your blood vessels to constrict and sends more blood to the straining muscles—all of which works to increase your blood pressure. In addition, you may find yourself frequently holding your breath as you bear down on the snow shovel, which can lead to sudden blood pressure and heart rate changes. And, if that's not enough reason for caution—stress hormone levels in your blood are higher in the morning and the platelets in your blood are stickier, which can contribute to a heart attack.

So, if you're up to the challenge and in shape, shovel away! But rest often and push the snow as much as possible, rather than lifting it. But if you're concerned that it may be a bit too much, hire a younger person to help out!

financial resources and uncooperative weather.

As you consider your fitness level, you need to dispel five common myths about exercise:

■ **Myth #1: Exercise makes you tired.** Actually, it helps reduce fatigue and manage stress. Increasing your regular activity level makes most people feel more energetic rather than tired.

■ **Myth #2: Adding exercise to your schedule takes too much time.** Just adding minutes of activity every day can increase your productivity.

■ **Myth #3: All exercise provides the same benefits.** While moderately intense daily exercise provides substantial health benefits and lowers your risk of heart disease, only regular, brisk and sustained exercise—that of a brisk walk, jog or swim for 30 minutes, for example—improves the efficiency of your heart and lungs and burns substantial extra calories. And we don't even know a lot yet about the benefits of low-intensity activity.

Golf can provide decent exercise—if you carry your clubs and walk the course.

■ **Myth #4: The older you are, the less exercise you need.** Regular physical activity is vital, as you age, in preserving your capacity to perform activities of daily living.

■ **Myth #5: You have to be athletic to exercise.** Not so! Many activities don't require special skills, which is one reason many people who didn't excel in school sports enjoy becoming active adults. Walking, for example, requires no special equipment or skill.

Now that we've covered the myths, let's get on to the truths about exercise.

Ray W. Squires, Ph.D., reviewed Chapter 1. He is the director of the cardiovascular health clinic at the Mayo Clinic in Rochester, Minnesota.

CHAPTER 2

Does Fitness Really Matter?

This chapter seeks to convince you that it's worth getting fit. Although there's been a lot of research on the effects of physical activity on the human body—and some recently on its effects on the mind—there's still much that's unknown or not yet understood. This chapter lays out the results of the research—and answers the question of whether or not it really matters if you're fit. Even if you know it's important to be fit, you may find some surprises here.

In 1996, the U.S. Department of Health and Human Services released *Physical activity and health: A report of the Surgeon General,* a comprehensive document that outlines reputable research concerning the effects of physical activity on health. That report, which very thoroughly reviews relevant research, forms the backbone of this chapter, with additional information included as updates.

Your Own Executive Summary

Here are the key messages of the Surgeon General's report mentioned:

1. Physical activity provides substantial benefits—even if the activity isn't strenuous.
2. A plethora of research points to the value of a moderate amount of daily physical activity for people of all ages, whether the activity is moderately intense for an extended period of time—a brisk, 30-minute walk, for example—or more intense for a shorter period—15 or 20 minutes of jogging or playing basketball.
3. Greater amounts of physical activity provide additional benefits, up to a point. Excessive activity can produce injuries, stress your bones and cause menstrual abnormalities.

The report details how Americans could reduce health burdens by increasing physical activity levels—a fact more recent information confirms.

The Challenge

Among Americans:

- 13.5 million people have coronary heart disease
- 1.5 million people have a heart attack and nearly 1 million die of heart disease—each year
- 8 million have adult-onset diabetes—a number that's growing alarmingly fast
- 95,000 people are newly diagnosed with colon cancer each year
- 250,000 people fracture a hip each year
- More than 50 million people—about a quarter of American adults—have high blood pressure, defined as higher than 140/90 millimeters of mercury (mmHg) on at least three readings
- More than 64 percent of Americans are overweight or obese

The Solution

The Surgeon General's report also details how regular physical activity can improve your health by:

- reducing your risk of dying prematurely from heart disease and other causes
- lowering your risk of developing diabetes
- helping lower your blood pressure, if it's high
- decreasing your risk of developing colon cancer
- reducing your feelings of depression and anxiety
- helping control your weight
- helping build and maintain healthy bones, muscles and joints
- promoting psychological well-being
- helping you, as you get older, stay strong and able to move about without falling

Since the report was issued, important new information appears to show that physical activity can prevent breast cancer and improve cognitive skills—especially as you age.

Lyn: Using the Luck of the Draw to Beat the Odds

Lyn, who wasn't in particularly bad shape, didn't consider her risk of early death before her dad died 2 years ago of heart disease. When he died, in his 60s, he'd had heart disease for over 20 years. After his death Lyn decided to lower her own risk of becoming an early fatality.

She signed up for a short-term health club membership and—before she had decided whether to extend it—won a drawing for an entire year's membership. It was the perfect opportunity to sample a variety of activities. Lyn soon found that she thoroughly enjoyed a spinning (cycling) class, has continued with that group of people now for several months and intends to continue after her free membership expires. After taking a weight training class, she now regularly works out with weights, as well.

With increased physical activity, Lyn has shed the few extra pounds she'd carried recently. And the most dramatic difference Lyn has noticed is that she awakens in the mornings feeling great. "Before, I used to wake up feeling like a truck had driven over me," she says. "Now I feel terrific in the morning, and I have a lot more energy all day long." Plus, Lyn realizes that she's reduced her chances of early-onset heart disease.

Physical Activity Reduces Overall Mortality Rates

Studies investigating the difference physical activity makes show that sedentary people—both men and women—experience a 1.2- to 2-fold increased risk of dying during the studies' follow-up periods, compared to their more active peers. And the association is even stronger when actual cardiorespiratory fitness is factored in than when reported physical activity is simply considered. Clearly, physical activity levels—regardless of whether activity is begun at a younger or older age—affect death rates. Here are some examples.

One study followed nearly 10,000 men, aged 30 and older, for 27 years. At age 50, moderate and intense activity levels reduced overall risk of death equally. The protective effect of moderate activity went well beyond age 80, while the highest levels of activity were less protective after age 70.

One recent 6-year study tracked over 6,000 men averaging age 59 (both with and without known or suspected heart disease). Capacity for exercise was the strongest predictor of death—even more accurate than blood pressure levels, smoking or diabetes history. Men who could do the least amount of exercise faced a risk of premature death more than four times that of men who could do the most.

Another 14-year study of over 30,000 people, whose ages ranged from 20 to 93, found that highly active folks were about half as likely as inactive people to die during the study, and those who were moderately active were about one-third less likely to die.

Two studies of people moving from a low level to a higher level of physical activity are particularly interesting. One study of sedentary, middle-aged male Harvard alumni, some of whom took up moderately intense sports activities during an 11-year follow-up, found that:

- Active participants experienced a 23 percent lower death rate than their sedentary counterparts, although not as dramatically lower as the 41 percent reduction realized by those who quit smoking during the study.
- All age groups who initiated moderately intense sports activities increased their life spans, including those aged 75 to 84.

Healthy men, ages 20 to 82, participating in the Aerobics Center Longitudinal Study, also reduced their death rates by improving initially low levels of cardiorespiratory fitness. Nearly 10 years after the study began, men whose fitness initially ranked in the lowest 20 percent but who had improved to at least moderate levels of fitness saw a 44 percent lower death rate than their peers who stayed in the lowest ranking.

Results Categorized

The following pages summarize the most pertinent results of a wealth of research on how physical activity affects your health. The information is organized by conditions—heart disease, diabetes, cancers, obesity, and so on.

Sifting Through Media Reports—and Dealing with Conflicting Results

Nearly every day, you hear news reports about how various aspects of physical activity affect your health. Some reports are well-documented and reputable, while others are of questionable value. Wise consumers question research that sounds suspicious. Don't overemphasize one study, especially if it's small. Some research—and a lot depends on who sponsors it—uses very small samples or is anecdotal, based heavily on the recollections of participants rather than on something measurable.

Much research linking physical activity and health focuses on endurance activities involving repetitive use of large muscle groups—walking and biking, for example. So, it's not surprising that most information available—and probably, the best—focuses on the effects of endurance activity.

Until recently, most studies used primarily white male participants. While many outcomes may be similar for women and cross racial lines, you can't always make that assumption. The Surgeon General's report reviewed a large number of studies and compared them more evenhandedly than you could even if you were to read about them one-by-one in your daily paper.

Cardiovascular Disease

Heart disease kills many people every year and is the focus of much research surrounding physical activity. Therefore, this part of the chapter is, by far, the largest.

Your heart, veins, arteries and capillaries make up your cardiovascular system. Your blood vessels—some as big as your thumb and others barely visible—form a continuous network carrying your nutrient-rich blood to your body's tissues. As blood returns to your heart, it has less oxygen (some has moved into your cells) and more carbon dioxide (a waste product from those cells). Like other muscles in your body, your heart gets stronger with regular exercise.

Dynamic exercise that involves the large muscles of your body enables you to increase your exercise intensity with less load on your heart. As your heart becomes stronger it pumps more efficiently with each beat. In fact, a well-conditioned heart pumping 45 to 50 times a minute moves as much blood as an inactive person's heart pumping 70 to 75 beats. Thus, if you're inactive, your heart may pump as much as 36,000 more times in a day—or 13 million more times in a year—than it would if you were well conditioned.

Exercise helps increase the blood flow to your heart and can improve the efficiency with which your blood vessels and the cells of your heart muscle exchange oxygen. Exercise also helps your body form new capillaries and other small blood vessels. As you continue exercising strenuously and the blood flow increases throughout your muscles, blood flow to and from your heart can increase as much as five times above its resting level. But if your blood vessels are obstructed—as they are in one type of heart disease—a problem arises.

Physical Activity & Heart Disease

Inactivity is now considered a risk factor for heart disease, and many studies have explored the relationship between the two. Over 40 studies establish a direct relationship between physical activity and a healthy heart. According to the most recent expert statement on standards for testing and training in exercise, the least fit men and women faced an increased risk of death from heart disease more than five times that of the most fit individuals.

One study followed 9,376 men (ages 45 to 64), who had no history of heart disease, for over 9 years. The 9 percent who either participated in vigorous sports frequently, did a considerable amount of cycling or who walked over 4 miles a day faced less than half the fatal and nonfatal heart disease other men in the study faced. If you already have heart disease, physical activity can lower your risk of death by 20 to 25 percent over your inactive counterparts.

Aerobic activity is continuous activity that uses your large muscles, making your heart beat faster and your lungs work more efficiently, increasing your endurance. According to the American Heart Association, exercises particularly beneficial to your heart include brisk walking, hiking, stair climbing, aerobic exercising, jogging, running, biking, rowing, swimming, and playing sports that include continuous running—soccer and basketball, for example. Moderate- and low-intensity activities that can provide long-term health benefits and help

What is VO_2max?

When you begin to exercise your large muscles, the rate at which your body takes in and uses oxygen from the air you breathe increases rapidly. The term VO_2max refers to the maximum amount of oxygen your body can take in from the air you breathe while you perform dynamic exercise. It's also called your aerobic capacity. Researchers consider it a good measure of your heart and lung function and your capacity for physical activity. However, most people don't have easy access to machines that measure VO_2max.

For most people, VO_2max peaks between the ages of 15 and 30 and generally declines after that. After age 30, the VO_2max of sedentary adults typically drops 9 to 15 percent per decade. By age 60, a man typically loses about a third of the VO_2max he had at age 20. A woman's VO_2max is generally less than that of a similarly sized man, probably due to differences in body structure and previous peak efficiency. (Incidentally, the American College of Sports Medicine reports that there doesn't appear to be a difference in magnitude of the improvement in VO_2max that's possible with endurance training. It will be interesting, considering the increase in women's athletics over the past 15 years, to see how comparative numbers change.)

While VO_2max decline appears to be age related, physical activity can affect it. Three weeks of bed rest can reduce a healthy man's VO_2max by 25 percent. On the other hand, as you start exercising, your body's rate of extracting and its efficiency of using the oxygen from the air you breathe increases rapidly and generally remains steady after 2 minutes.

Endurance training appears to help you reduce VO_2max decline by about 5 percent per decade. In one study, adults aged 60 to 69 realized a 12 percent improvement in their VO_2max after 6 months of moderate-intensity walking, and another 18 percent improvement after 6 additional months of jogging. And the improvement offered by endurance training apparently isn't gender sensitive.

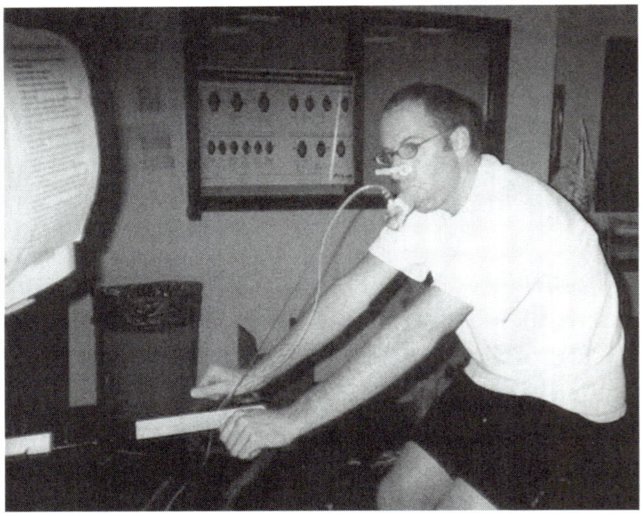

Few people have access to a machine to gauge VO_2max.

lower your risk of heart disease include walking for pleasure, gardening, yard work, housework, dancing, exercising at home and playing tennis, racquetball, soccer and touch football.

High Blood Pressure: a Major Contributor to Heart Disease

High blood pressure affects about 50 million Americans—including about 2.8 million youth, ages 6 to 17. Approximately one in four Americans is hypertensive.

If you don't exercise, you're nearly twice as likely to develop heart disease as someone who's active, and your risk of developing high blood pressure is 30 to 50 percent greater. But even a single episode of physical activity immediately and temporarily dilates your blood vessels, thereby lowering your blood pressure.

Most studies have evaluated fairly intense aerobic training, done three or four times a week, for 30 to 60 minutes

My Husband—Walking Proof

"Basically, you bought yourself 20 years by your healthy lifestyle," said the cardiologist who did my husband's angiogram. "And," he added, "it probably helped you avoid a massive heart attack."

As I worked on this book, my husband Bob, 59 years old, became a walking poster child for both the American Heart Association and the U.S. Surgeon General's report. Bob knew that genetics increased his risk for heart disease. He's the child of parents who both had heart disease. His older brother had his first heart attack at age 40, followed by a second heart attack and bypass surgery at age 50.

So 5 years ago, when Bob learned that his cholesterol was elevated, he began aggressively treating it with diet and exercise. Within the past year he added medication, and a month before his mild heart attack, his cholesterol levels tested well within the normal healthy range. Besides controlling his cholesterol, blood pressure and weight, Bob was also very active, walking at least 2 miles every day at a brisk 4-miles-per-hour pace, playing softball or volleyball weekly, tennis once a week and recently, full-court recreational basketball. A month before his heart attack he and his son "ran" their first 5K race.

After his heart attack, an angiogram—the gold standard for diagnosing heart disease—showed that Bob had one artery that was 100 percent blocked and four or five others that were blocked 70 to 80 percent. Apparently, collateral vessels had developed that were helping supply his heart, which was, the doctor said, apparently undamaged and very strong. Had Bob's lifestyle not been as healthy, the doctor believes the outcome would have been much worse. Now, following bypass surgery, Bob expects to be back at his full range of activities in several months, motivated by the very real knowledge that being active may buy time.

Isn't Heart Disease a "Man's Disease?"

Definitely not! Although many American women worry much more about breast cancer than heart disease, heart disease kills many more of them than does breast cancer. And heart disease also manifests itself differently in women than in men.

Nearly two-thirds of women who die suddenly from heart disease have had no previous symptoms. And women who have bypass surgery are nearly twice as likely as men to die as a result of the procedure—besides getting less symptom relief and requiring a second operation more frequently than men do.

A recent study of nearly 74,000 women, ages 59 to 79, showed that women who sat for at least 16 hours a day had a 68 percent higher risk of heart disease than women who sat for less than 4 hours a day and that walking briskly at least 2.5 hours per week cut heart disease risk by about a third. In fact, women who exercised most intensely, based on energy spent—regardless of the type of exercise—faced the lowest risk of heart disease.

Taking a brisk walk over your lunch hour can help ward off the #1 killer of women: heart disease.

a session. The studies show that this type of exercise reduces both the top (systolic) and bottom (diastolic) numbers of your blood pressure reading by approximately 6 or 7 mmHg. The least active men faced a 30 percent increased risk of hypertension over the most active men. Playing vigorous sports can help you lower your risk of developing high blood pressure by 19 to 30 percent. In fact, the most active 55- to 69-year-old women who were tracked for 2 years also lowered their risk—by 30 percent.

There's some evidence that you can achieve a similar, or even greater, blood-pressure-lowering effect with moderately intense activity. But if physical activity, weight loss and a reduced-sodium diet don't do the trick, you may need medication to control your blood pressure. If you do have high blood pressure, doctors frequently recommend that you avoid heavy weight training, as it can dangerously increase your blood pressure.

Are You Sure You Don't Have High Blood Pressure?

I found out less than 2 years ago—quite by accident—that I have heart disease. I was shocked, to put it mildly. I was fairly active, although most of my exercise was at moderate, rather than vigorous, levels. Admittedly overweight, I'd slowly whittled away extra pounds for several years.

Apparently hypertension, a key contributor to various types of heart disease, was a problem for me. Although my blood pressure was occasionally elevated at the doctor's office, readings were generally fairly average at home. I attributed the high readings to "white coat hypertension," a term used when nervousness raises your blood pressure at the doctor's office. But, regardless of the cause, heart clinic staff found my blood pressure simply too high too often. I had to do something about it.

Hypertension is associated with a notable list of conditions, including:

- various forms of heart disease, one of which is left ventricular hypertrophy (my diagnosis), which can eventually lead to congestive heart failure
- strokes, whether caused by a ruptured blood vessel (hemorrhagic) or by a blood vessel that's blocked (ischemic)
- kidney failure
- retinopathy, a disorder of the eye that can cause blindness
- peripheral vascular disease, meaning that blood vessels in your arms and legs are unable to adequately supply those areas

Fortunately, with a combination of medication, stepped-up weight loss, added strenuous exercise and relaxation activities, my health picture has improved. However, you don't get over heart disease. And I was shocked to learn that over 50 percent of the other adults in the study who, like me, had virtually no symptoms, had one or more early markers for heart disease. Elevated blood pressure topped the list.

High Cholesterol: Another Heart Disease Risk Factor

Risk factors for heart disease that appear in childhood—including elevated cholesterol levels—persist into adulthood. Cholesterol is a waxy material that insulates your nerves and helps produce hormones and digest the food you eat. But an overabundance of cholesterol in your blood builds up on the walls of your arteries, eventually causing hardening of the arteries and blocking the flow of oxygen-rich blood to your heart.

Your heredity, age and gender, diet and exercise determine how much cholesterol your body makes. Most lab results list total cholesterol, HDL (good) cholesterol, LDL (bad) cholesterol and triglyceride levels. For most people, optimal levels of each are:

- total – less than 200 mg/dl
- HDL – more than 40 mg/dl
- LDL – less than 130 mg/dl
- triglycerides – under 150 mg/dl

Your target numbers can change if you have risk factors for heart disease or have vascular disease (difficulties caused by obstructed, hardened or narrowed blood vessels). In these cases, ceilings for total cholesterol and for LDL are lower. You should discuss with your doctor what your individual targets should be, taking into consideration your health and health history.

The Surgeon General's report evaluated 95 studies that used various methods to look at a variety of populations for different lengths of time. It concludes that exercise can produce these desirable results: a 5 percent increase in HDL, a 6.3 percent reduction in total cholesterol and a 10.1 percent reduction in LDL cholesterol levels. In fact, even one episode of physical activity can improve your blood lipid profile for several days.

Some experts suggest that the most important number of the four is the LDL level and that reducing elevated LDL can cut heart attack risk by 40 percent. If you also want to lose weight, adding exercise to a diet produces significant reductions in LDL that diet alone won't produce.

HDL protects you against hardening of the arteries by transporting cholesterol to your liver for elimination. A National Institutes of Health Consensus Development conference concluded that men and women (middle-aged and older) who are regularly physically active have significantly higher HDL than their sedentary counterparts, and that a 12-week program of physical activity can improve HDL. Endurance-trained athletes generally have 20 to 30 percent more HDL than their healthy, sedentary counterparts. However, you probably don't need intense activity to see modest HDL level improvements.

But most people who inherit the tendency to have high cholesterol aren't able to bring their levels down sufficiently with exercise alone. However, eliminating saturated fat and cholesterol and substituting monounsaturated or polyunsaturated fats in your diet—in addition to increasing physical activity levels—can help. If this doesn't bring cholesterol levels down sufficiently, you may need medication.

Research continues to explore other factors besides cholesterol that may have some importance as cardiac risk indicators—for example, levels of homocysteine and C-reactive protein. Whether or not you need these tests is a matter you should discuss with your physician.

Other Cardiovascular Killers

Exercise can also help reduce your risk for **stroke**, the third leading cause of death among Americans. A recent study of 72,000 women (ages 40 to 65) showed that 30 minutes nearly every day of exercise that was at least moderate cut the risk of ischemic strokes by 30 percent and hemorrhagic strokes by 20 percent. Endurance training enhances your body's ability to use enzymes to break down blood clots. It also prevents formation of blood clots by making your blood less "sticky."

Even people with **heart failure** benefited from 30-minute workouts on a stationary bike three times a week. In fact, if you have heart failure and experience sexual dysfunction, you're probably better off working out than using potency drugs. Exercise can be just as effective and avoids potentially dangerous interactions with nitrates and other heart failure medications. An 8-week study that looked at the effect of moderate biking on sexual performance of men with heart failure concluded that the bikers saw a 77 percent improvement in their relationships with their partners and quality of their erections, while a control group noted no change. Incidentally, the partners of the biking group reported a nearly 100 percent improvement in their partner's sexual activity.

A physically active lifestyle may also reduce your risk of sudden cardiac death—even if you have heart disease. Although people with heart disease have an increased risk of **ventricular fibrillation**—a life-threatening disturbance in the heart's rhythm—during very strenuous exercise, this risk does not exist for

George: Neither Rain, nor Sleet, nor Snow

Studies show that occupational activity—if you get enough of it—can protect you from heart disease. George is a mail carrier who spends most of his day sorting and delivering mail on foot. While standing hasn't been shown to be protective, walking for long periods of time—an hour or more each day—is protective.

However, many people whose work involves physical activity don't get enough activity to reap these benefits, and thus, should supplement their work activity with leisure-time exercise. Because George, who's been a mail carrier for 18 years, walks about 5 hours each day, he does get a fair amount of exercise. However, he's never worn a pedometer to clock the number of footsteps he takes in a day.

Although he doesn't really consider himself active, George played on a softball team for many years and always biked a lot with his wife and kids. Now, at 55, he's still fairly competitive on the volleyball court, even after a full day of walking. So, if he can avoid the dog bites and slippery sidewalks—and stays active—George is likely to remain fairly healthy.

people with healthy cardiovascular systems. But whether you have heart disease or not, exercise can improve your heart's oxygen supply and reduce your risk of ventricular fibrillation.

Physical activity is inversely related to heart disease risk. If you are inactive but start exercising, potential benefits far surpass any risk of a coronary event. But how intensely you need to exercise for heart protection varies with your age and physical condition. For example, a brisk, 3-mile-per-hour walk is considered light exercise for a healthy 20-year-old, but vigorous exercise for most people who are 80.

Incidentally, it's important when you do exercise—whether you have heart disease or not—to slow down gradually as you finish your activity session. Some healthy people experience dangerous drops in blood pressure if they stop exercising suddenly. And it's even more important, if you do have heart disease, to increase your exercise and conditioning level gradually.

Whether you're a man or a woman, a growing body of evidence shows that regular, moderately intense activity reduces your risk of dying of heart disease. And, although you may need to reach a certain level of intensity to reap the cardiovascular benefits, that level still isn't firmly established and may vary among individuals. The Surgeon General's report recommends a minimum of 30 minutes of moderately intense physical activity—either continuously or in increments of at least 10 minutes—on most, if not all days of the week to reduce your risk of heart disease.

Diabetes

About 3 percent of Americans have been diagnosed with diabetes mellitus. But experts say that about twice that many have it and don't realize it. More than 169,000 deaths each year are attributed to diabetes. It's the seventh leading cause of death in the United States. The numbers are much higher if you include deaths resulting from complications of diabetes—like heart disease, stroke and heart failure.

Insulin is a hormone that regulates how your body uses blood sugar. Your body's ability to control the level of sugar in your blood is called glucose tolerance. When your glucose tolerance goes down, the concentration of sugar in your blood increases and so does your risk of developing diabetes. Exercise improves your body's ability to use insulin and maintain normal blood sugar levels.

Today, over 90 percent of Americans with diabetes have non-insulin-dependent diabetes mellitus (NIDDM), also called type 2. This type of diabetes occurs either when there's a problem with your body's production of insulin or if insulin levels are elevated but ineffective in normalizing blood glucose levels because of insulin resistance (decreased sensitivity to insulin). You're much more likely to develop insulin resistance and glucose intolerance if you're overweight—especially if your extra fat tends to accumulate around your waist, abdomen and upper body.

Societies that discontinue their traditional, physically active lifestyles have seen major increases in the prevalence of type 2 diabetes. You can observe this phenomenon if you compare a group of people who migrate to a technologically advanced environment with their ethnic counterparts who remain in the native land. Researchers also report that rural dwellers have a lower prevalence of diabetes than their urban counterparts.

One study of women, ages 55 to 69, who were physically very active, found that these women were only half as likely to develop type 2 diabetes as were same-aged women who were not very active. Exercise is especially important for men at high risk of developing diabetes: those with a high body mass index (BMI), a history of high blood pressure or a diabetic parent. (BMI is a general indicator that links weight to height to determine if you're overweight. For more information on BMI, see pages 77 to 78.) Each 500 kilocalories of added leisure-time physical activity per week offers a 6 percent reduction in the risk of developing type 2 diabetes —vigorous sports more than stair climbing or walking.

In one study of female registered nurses (ages 34 to 59), those who engaged in vigorous physical activity at least weekly had a 16 percent lower risk of developing type 2 diabetes during the 8-year follow-up than did women who reported no vigorous physical activity. A 5-year study of male physicians (ages 40 to 84) showed similar results. The Surgeon General's report concludes that diet and exercise are most effective in controlling type 2 diabetes in mild cases that don't require medication.

Physical activity seems to prevent diabetes by increasing your sensitivity to insulin—especially if your abnormal glucose tolerance is caused primarily by insulin resistance rather than by a deficiency in the amount of circulating insulin. Thus, physical activity is most effective in stopping the progression of type 2 diabetes in its early stages, before you need medication management. If you do require medication to manage your diabetes, diet and physical activity interventions are less likely to improve your diabetes—although you can still gain the other benefits.

Physical activities like biking can help you avoid having diabetes—or slow its progress.

According to cross-sectional studies, endurance athletes have greater insulin sensitivity than someone who's sedentary. Furthermore, men who have diabetes and are fit are half as likely to die prematurely as those with diabetes who are not fit. You can greatly reduce your risk of developing diabetes if you can avoid becoming overweight.

Cancer

Cancer is the second leading cause of death in the United States, accounting for a quarter of all deaths. **Colon cancer** is the most thoroughly investigated cancer in relation to physical activity. Whether you have an active job or are active during your leisure time—or both—research strongly suggests that physical activity lowers your risk of developing colon cancer. In fact, a study in Norway found that women who biked moderately—just 4 hours per week—reduced their colon cancer risk by nearly 40 percent.

Some experts believe that physical activity is protective, in part, because it reduces the amount of time that food spends in your gastrointestinal tract, thus limiting the amount of contact between the lining of your colon and potential cancer-causing chemicals. This may help explain the fact that physical activity may help reduce colon cancer, but not necessarily **rectal cancer**. While activity may shorten the time it takes partially digested food to move through your colon, waste material is generally only in your rectum briefly before you eliminate it. Thus, experts believe rectal cancer risk may be unrelated to physical activity levels.

Physical activity appears to be protective against **breast cancer**. When the Surgeon General's report was issued, studies showed "limited support to the hypothesis that physical activity during adolescence and young adulthood may be protective against later development of breast cancer." Since that time at least one study of 1,233 women with newly diagnosed breast cancer showed that the greatest breast cancer risk reduction appears to be with moderately intense everyday activity. While recent studies show that physical activity may be protective against **endometrial cancer**, researchers don't yet know how much activity you need and how intense the activity must be in order for it to be protective.

The second most-frequently studied cancer, relative to the effect of physical activity, is **prostate cancer**. However, results are mixed, and researchers can't say for sure whether or not physical activity has an effect on this cancer's occurrence. Results are similarly mixed for **ovarian** and **testicular cancer**, as well.

Obesity

You've heard the numbers: nearly two-thirds of Americans are overweight. The most recent study published by the National Center for Health Statistics reports that 64 percent of adults (aged 20 and over) are overweight, defined as having a BMI of 25 or greater. The same study reports that a significant number of those people—nearly 59 million Americans—are obese (BMI of 30 or greater), a rate that has doubled over a 20-year period since 1980.

Active infants and toddlers become couch-potato adolescents. Girls become less active than their male counterparts. Health care providers, now alarmed at the obesity rate among young people, term it an epidemic.

Basic Math: Physical Activity + Caloric Control = Reduced Obesity

Although the human body is complex and there is still a lot experts don't understand about weight gain and weight loss, the basic facts are not rocket science. You gain fat mass and become obese when your energy intake exceeds your total daily energy expenditure for a prolonged period of time. While you need energy simply to maintain basic bodily functions, like digesting and absorbing nutrients and breathing, the biggest variable is how much energy you spend in physical activity. For each excess 3,500 kilocalories of energy you take in, your body stores 1 pound of fat energy.

Recent studies suggest that physical activity and reduced caloric intake are well-matched teammates in the fight against obesity—and that, over the longer term, neither can do it alone. The

Increased treadmill time allowed study participants to reduce age-related weight gain.

Surgeon General's report notes that physical activity is an important contributor to weight loss, although its effect varies greatly. "It is not clear how much exercise is required to prevent weight gain or 'repeat' weight gain, although it has been suggested that the levels may be much higher than the currently recommended doses of physical activity," the report notes in a hint predictive of the latest recommendations.

Studies show that physical exercise alone without dieting has only a modest effect on total body mass and loss of fat mass. An interesting, although fairly small study at the University of Alabama compared caloric intake and exercise habits of 61 women for 1 year—both those who maintained their weight and those who gained weight. The difference between the two groups came down to 275 calories per day or 1 hour and 20 minutes of low-intensity daily exercise—walking, for example. Studies also show that only 30 percent of those who lose weight strictly by reducing calories manage to maintain that weight loss over time.

Clearly, for long-term weight management, the most successful combinations mix diet with exercise to use the resulting energy deficit efficiently and to help maintain weight loss. Endurance training, in particular, effectively reduces total body mass and fat mass, while maintaining constant or slightly increased levels of fat-free mass.

A more recent study followed over 5,000 middle-aged men and women for 7.5 years. Those who increased their treadmill time minimized weight gain, while those whose fitness levels remained unchanged slowly gained weight with age. For each minute they increased their treadmill time, participants reduced their weight gain by 1.3 pounds over those whose treadmill time stayed the same. Some researchers have concluded that it may be necessary, as we age, to increase physical activity levels simply to maintain a constant body weight.

Physical activity can account for as much as 15 to 40 percent of the calories you burn each day—and the more vigorous the activity, the higher the rate. The Surgeon General's report also notes that physically active men and women have a more favorable waist-to-hip ratio (less obesity near the waist, where it's more predictive of heart disease) than sedentary people have. And regular physical activity also helps control appetite.

Osteoporosis

Osteoporosis, which primarily affects older people, occurs when you lose bone mass, causing your bones to become fragile and fracture easily. While osteoporosis can affect both women and men, it becomes particularly serious for women when they lose bone mass at an accelerated rate after menopause. One of every six of the 1.5 million hip fractures in the United States every year is attributed to osteoporosis, and hip fractures are associated with a 1-year mortality rate of 15 to 20 percent. A third of the women and a sixth of the men who reach age 90 will have sustained a hip fracture.

The Surgeon General's report describes bone as "dynamic tissue that is constantly remodeling its structure by resorption and formation." In other words, the cells in your bones are con-

Can Exercise Help You Lose Weight Following a Pregnancy?

The short answer is "Yes." Most women struggle with their weight following pregnancy. Although the average postpartum weight retention is 2.2 pounds, women who are overweight before they become pregnant and who gain more than the recommended amount of weight during pregnancy are more likely to retain the extra weight after their babies are born. A recent study found 70 percent of women unhappy with their appearance at 6 months postpartum. It also found that women lose the most weight in the first 3 months after giving birth. Furthermore, women who haven't returned to their pre-pregnancy weight by 6 months postpartum are likely to retain that added weight for a long time.

But exercising can help you avoid being part of that statistic. You should begin gradually and set reasonable goals. (See pages 241 to 243 for tips on overcoming challenges that you face postpartum as you resume physical activity.)

tinually being renewed. The report further says that, "physical activity, through its load-bearing effect on the skeleton, is likely the single most important influence on bone density and architecture." Bone cells respond to having weight (load) placed upon them by altering the balance between your body's system for forming new bone and breaking down and reabsorbing existing bone, in order to build greater bone mass. "The higher the load, the greater the bone mass; conversely, when the skeleton is unloaded (as with inactivity), bone mass declines," the report states. So if you want stronger bones, weight-bearing activity is a critical part of the answer.

Most people don't think of osteoporosis as being a problem among younger adults, but research shows that athletic young adults already have a higher density of bone minerals than sedentary young adults have.

Prolonged bed rest or immobility causes rapid and marked decline in bone density. More-active women generally face a lower risk of hip fracture than less-active women. Resistance exercise (weight training) may have more pronounced effects on bone density than endurance exercise. And you can significantly reduce your chance of falling and breaking a bone with exercises that improve your balance and gait.

One study compared 25 healthy postmenopausal women (ages 58 to 75) who did back-strengthening exercises for 2 years with a control group of women who did not do the exercises to strengthen their backs. Even 8 years after they'd finished the exercises, researchers found that the exercise group retained a significant advantage both in back strength and in bone density over the control group. Ten years after the study began, members of the control group were nearly three times more likely than members of the exercise group to have compression fractures of the spine.

Gladys: Full Speed Ahead—Again—at 91

Gladys was always quite active, until osteoarthritis struck when she was about 70. Before she realized what was happening, she was confined to a wheelchair and unable to do many things she'd enjoyed for years. She seemed to be rapidly wasting away.

With the help of her husband and friends, who came in and massaged her hands and feet, and with aloe vera, which she considers a miracle drug, Gladys gradually started walking. Before long, she was taking regular, daily walks. The wheelchair's been gone for years now.

After her husband's death a decade ago, Gladys moved into a senior building, where she's flourished. She enjoys socializing with friends, walks at least a mile a day and does some serious fishing with relatives on an annual week-long fishing trip. As near as anyone can figure, what's kept Gladys going all these years is exercise, friends and—she'd add—aloe vera.

Osteoarthritis

Osteoarthritis is the most common form of arthritis and is the leading cause of limited activity among older adults. It's characterized by both the degeneration of cartilage and new growth of bone around a joint. The question of whether exercise is protective against osteoarthritis or makes it worse has been rather controversial.

According to the Surgeon General's report, there's apparently a difference between recreational and competitive levels of physical activity when it comes to your joints. While competitive running at high levels is associated with the development of osteoarthritis seen on X rays, research suggests that if you do recreational running over long periods of time you have no more risk of developing osteoarthritis of the knee or hip than sedentary people do. The report also notes that there's currently no evidence that walking increases your risk of osteoarthritis if you have normal joints.

Problems appear to cluster around joints that see excessive use and injury in competitive athletes. For example, although osteoarthritis of the elbow and shoulder joint is more common among professional baseball pitchers, it's not certain whether this is because of injury or due to excessive physical activity. And osteoarthritis is no more common among soccer players who have never suffered knee injuries than among

How Much Physical Activity Is Advisable if You Already Have Osteoarthritis?

The Surgeon General's report strikes a fine balance between the value of physical activity in helping you retain function in a joint and the possibility of accelerating damage by using injured joints. Research on animals in which osteoarthritis has been experimentally induced suggests that using injured joints inhibits tissue repair. However, the report is very supportive of reasonable levels of physical activity for people with osteoarthritis. It reports that after regular, moderate physical activity you're likely to see a significant reduction in joint swelling if you have arthritis. Other studies show that increased levels of physical activity are also associated with improved mood, ability to carry on activities of daily living and physical fitness.

Clearly, if you want to preserve the function in a joint, you need to move it. The Surgeon General's report describes the process by which cartilage in your joints is nourished by movement and says that disuse makes them more vulnerable to injury and eventually results in loss of normal joint function. The report concludes by saying that, "regular physical activity of moderate intensity has been found to raise the pain threshold, improve energy levels and improve self-efficacy among persons with osteoarthritis."

sedentary people who don't play soccer. The Surgeon General's report concludes that, "regular, noncompetitive physical activity of the amount and intensity recommended for improving health thus does not appear harmful to joints that have no existing injury."

More recent studies show that if you're overweight, you can cut your risk of osteoarthritis in half by losing just 11 pounds. And strengthening your quadriceps muscles (located at the front of your thighs) can reduce your risk of developing osteoarthritis by 20 to 30 percent.

Fibromyalgia

Although experts don't know a lot yet about the effects of physical activity on fibromyalgia, two small studies seem to indicate that exercise is probably the best thing you can do for yourself if you have this condition. One study found an improvement in stiffness, pain, fatigue, anxiety and depression among subjects who participated in a 20-week, well-balanced fitness program. In another study, participants felt and slept better after 8 weeks of twice-weekly workouts on weight machines.

Glaucoma

Intraocular pressure, a symptom of glaucoma, improved in nine sedentary subjects who were suspected of having glaucoma, after 3 months of aerobic exercise training. At the end of the 3-month period their mean aerobic capacity improved 30 percent, while intraocular pressure was reduced by 20 percent. However, a word of caution: just 3 weeks after the exercise training ended (and subjects presumably returned to their sedentary habits) intraocular pressure returned to preconditioning levels.

Cognitive Skills

Currently, the relation of physical activity to cognitive skills is the focus of some very interesting research. Animal studies suggest that exercise may stimulate the growth of new brain cells that can enhance memory and learning. Scientists also now believe that regular physical activity may reduce the risk of cognitive decline in older adults.

About 6,000 women, age 65 and older, participated in a study of cognitive decline at the University of California at San Francisco. The women's cognitive skills were tested as the study began and again, 6 to 8 years later. Researchers found that women who walked less than one-half mile per week were the most likely to experience cognitive decline (averaging 24 percent), while women who walked about 2.5 miles a day (18 miles a week) averaged 17 percent cognitive decline.

Another recent study followed 4,615 men and women age 65 and older who had normal thinking, learning and memory skills as the study began. After 5 years, those with the highest levels of physical activity had the lowest risk of developing cognitive impairment, Alzheimer's disease or dementia.

Have you ever wondered if physical activity could enhance creativity? An interesting, although, admittedly, extremely limited, British study observed a group of 60 volunteers participating in a 25-minute aerobics class one day and watching a 25-minute video on archaeology and rock

Physical activity builds fitness and brain power, at any age.

formations on another day. After each 25-minute period, they took creativity tests— for example, brainstorming, for 5 minutes about all the innovative or unusual uses they could devise for a common object. Testers found that suggestions offered after the exercise sessions were much more creative than those that surfaced after participants watched videos—although it would be interesting to know if using videos selected by the individuals would have produced a different outcome.

Carla Hannaford, Ph.D., author of *Smart Moves: Why Learning Is Not All In Your Head,* describes a 4-month aerobic training program of brisk walking for men and women in their 50s and 60s that increased their performance on mental tests by 10 percent. Furthermore, when she examined 13 different studies linking exercise with brainpower, she found that exercise stimulated the growth of developing brains and prevented the deterioration of older brains. She believes recent research helps explain this phenomenon. "Muscular activities, particularly coordinated movements, appear to stimulate the production of neurotrophins, natural substances that stimulate the growth of nerve cells and increase the number of neural connections in the brain," she writes, noting that a University of California researcher found that rats exercising on wheels had more neurotrophins than did sedentary rats.

Mental Health & Mood Disorders

At the time of the Surgeon General's report, mental health disorders cost the American economy $148 billion per year. Nearly a third of Americans ages

15 to 54 report having had a mental disorder during the past year, most frequently mood or anxiety disorders. Fully 10 percent of all adults suffer from a depressive disorder in any given year, women more often than men.

Although the Surgeon General's report acknowledges that the effects of physical activity on most mental disorders is not well studied, research suggests that physical activity may be associated with reduced symptoms of anxiety and depression, as well as with improvements in well-being. If you're inactive, you're twice as likely as an active person to have symptoms of depression. Although a single session of physical activity frequently causes transient mood improvements and temporary reductions in muscle tension, it takes regular daily physical activity to experience this calming effect on an ongoing basis.

Two Canadian surveys of nearly 50,000 young people and adults found that physical activity is associated with fewer symptoms of anxiety and depression, a more positive mood and feelings of general well-being. Having little or no recreational physical activity was significantly predictive of greater-than-average depressive symptoms. However, the amount of exercise you need to realize psychological benefits is not necessarily the same as the amount of exercise you need to improve your cardiovascular fitness. Men with no hours of sports play per week showed similar rates of depression as men with 1 to 2 hours, while those with 3 or more hours weekly had 27 percent less depression than the least active group. One word of caution: some

Another Reason to Get Your Kids Moving!

In her book, *Smart Moves: Why Learning Is Not All In Your Head,* Carla Hannaford, Ph.D., describes several projects that demonstrate the possibility of improving learning with physical activity. A Canadian study of over 500 kids, for example, found that those who spent an extra hour each day in gym class performed notably better on regular school exams than their less active counterparts.

Hannaford is a proponent of the specific Brain Gym exercises developed by Paul Dennison, Ph.D., who has a background in curriculum development and experimental psychology. "Movement is the door to learning," says Dennison, who designed these exercises in the 1970s as he struggled to find a way through his own dyslexia and visual difficulties.

When Hannaford used these exercises for 5 to 10 minutes each day with 19 special education students in grade 5, she found that in 1 year's time, average gains on reading and reading comprehension tests ranged between 1 and 2 years, and that half of the kids saw an average gain of 1 year on math tests.

endurance athletes experience mood disturbances with over-training. But clearly, regular, reasonable levels of physical activity reduce anxiety and depression, improve self-esteem and help you better manage your stress.

Colds & Flu

The Centers for Disease Control and Prevention estimates that Americans experience 425 million colds and flu cases each year, and that the total cost of these illnesses, in lost school and work days and medical expenses, is about $2.5

Bobbi: Did Exercise Really Help Her Quit Smoking—After Decades of a 2-Pack-a-Day Habit?

Bobbi wasn't sure that bumping up her walking program several notches would help her stop smoking, having failed at numerous attempts before. But now, it finally appears she has succeeded. She's been smoke free for 2 years.

A recent study of 281 sedentary adult female smokers supports her hunch. The smokers were assigned a cognitive-behavioral group that either included vigorous exercise or did not. The exercise consisted of three supervised sessions per week, while the control group had three supervised health education lectures per week. Abstinence was measured 1 week after quit day, at the end of treatment (week 12) and at weeks 20 and 60.

At each measurement point the gap widened between members of the exercise group, who achieved a significantly higher level of continuous abstinence, and the control group. In addition, by the end of the program members of the exercising group had achieved, on average, significantly greater functional capacity (or fitness) and had gained less weight. When the study ended, 11.9 percent of exercising participants and 5.4 percent of the nonexercisers were still abstinent.

A Brown University study found that exercising vigorously three times a week throughout a smoking cessation program doubled a woman's chances of quitting successfully. Furthermore, the women who exercised only gained half as much weight as other participants in the study who quit.

Exercising while you're trying to stop smoking can help you breathe easier, go farther without becoming tired or winded and manage your weight. Initially it can also help reduce nicotine cravings.

Bobbi, whose stress level zoomed last spring when her husband broke his back in a workplace accident, also found that exercise lifts her mood and helps her deal with life's stresses. She's tried kicking the nicotine habit before, but she's convinced that this time is finally the charm. And she plans to continue her daily 3-mile walk.

billion. Although the average adult has between two and five colds a year, one study of 547 healthy adults (ages 20 to 70) found that the most active adults experienced 25 percent fewer colds than the least active adults. In two other studies, women of various ages walked briskly for 35 to 45 minutes, 5 days a week, for 12 to 15 weeks. Walkers in both studies experienced only about half as many days with cold symptoms as their sedentary counterparts.

It's worth noting, however, that the edge in immune function seems to disappear when training ramps up. Among runners preparing for the 1987 Los Angeles marathon, those who trained at levels over 60 miles per week were sick twice as many days as those who trained at less than 20 miles per week. And a study testing immune systems of marathon runners before and after 2- to 3-hour runs found that the runners experienced a steep drop in immune function that lasted from 6 to 9 hours after they stopped running.

Regular Physical Activity Pays Off!

While you may never participate in formal studies that track the improvements fitness can bring to your everyday life, you'll still notice the improvements. You'll have more energy and endurance to deal with your everyday tasks. You'll find it easier to get dressed with your newly improved balance and flexibility. It'll be easier keeping up with your kids' or grandkids' activity—and you may even welcome it, rather than simply find it exhausting.

As you move your trunk muscles, thereby nourishing the blood vessels and nerves that serve your back and neck, you'll see increased mobility and reduced back and neck pain. If you've experienced knee or other joint pain, exercise may actually reduce your pain as you strengthen the surrounding supportive muscles and tissues.

You may be surprised when others notice your improved appearance. You'll actually look healthier! In the process you may acquire an improved self-image and your mood may be enhanced, as well. Not only will you relax and sleep more easily, but you'll sleep more soundly. You'll cope more easily with everyday stress—as well as with the big stressors—if you can stay as active as possible through stressful times. And your fitness quest may even bring you into new relationships that you'd never imagined with friends and family.

Walter A. Hinck, M.D., reviewed chapter 2. He is the chair of the Family Practice Department, vice president of the Bloomington Lake Clinic, and clinical associate faculty at the University of Minnesota Family Practice Department.

Gerald F. Fletcher, M.D., reviewed the 1st half of chapter 2. He is a professor of medicine at Mayo Medical School and a cardiologist at Mayo Clinic, Jacksonville, Florida.

CHAPTER 3

Fitness Begins In Your Head (Or, Start Seeing Yourself as an Active Person)

Let's get down to the personal level now—beyond all the studies and statistics of the last chapter. After all, you didn't participate in those studies. It doesn't really matter if physical activity is great for someone else—if it doesn't work for you. What motivates you?

It's Your Call

You *do* have the power. Clearly, no one but you can decide to move toward becoming fit. It's strictly a personal decision. Yes, your partner may beg you to do it. Your kids or grandkids may try every imaginable way to nudge you to take that first step. Your friends may tell you they hope to enjoy your company for many more years yet. Maybe your boss has even begged you, whether it's because he or she values you as a person and a key contributor to the organization or for more mundane reasons, like the hit the insurance premiums take when your group's healthcare usage goes up, or because it's difficult to cover your work when you're out ill. Perhaps you've watched friends tangle with chronic health conditions. Maybe you're not even that "unfit."

It's your decision. No cajoling or pleading can change that fact. Do you want to become fit or not? You need to realize, to believe, that you're worth it and that you

Mia: Realizing She's Not Like Some of Her Friends

Mia recalls that when she was a freshman in college she was typical—hopping into cars and running around with classmates, eating whatever junk food struck her fancy. While many of her friends, who were doing precisely the same thing, remained thin, Mia didn't. Suddenly she was gaining weight at the rate of about 10 pounds a year.

"I watched the weight going on when I was 20, and then gained another 10 pounds when I was 21. I don't think I realized, even then, that my metabolism was different than that of many other people I knew," she says. "But I began to realize that eating wouldn't be where I could get most of my pleasure. But that's not terrible."

Mia, who's 5 feet, 4 inches tall, tried to control her weight by more careful eating. But she became seriously concerned, when she weighed in at 160 pounds at age 22. Finally, with resolve, she lost about 20 pounds in less than 9 months of carefully monitoring everything she ate. But when she was 29, a light went on.

"Perhaps I could eat more if I exercised. I have no health issues, and I thought running might be easy and interesting." Mia began jogging alone at a lake near her home, trading "war stories" with a coworker who also ran. Finally, after a year, she could run all the way around the lake—2.8 miles.

Mia gradually ran farther and in her 30s became interested in long-distance running, motivated chiefly by the realization that if she ran more she could eat more. Soon she was running marathons. But after doing that for a while, Mia concluded, for a variety of reasons, that she probably wouldn't continue running marathons all her life. She cut back to simply running a moderate amount 6 days a week, monitoring more closely what she ate. "Otherwise, it was easy to go on a 10-day vacation—and come back 5 to 7 pounds heavier," she says. "I realized I can't just play around with it. I need to stay on top of it."

Mia, now 51, never weighs herself. However, she notices how her clothes fit each time she puts them on. "I still have to watch what I eat, and I exercise 6 days a week," she says. In the morning Mia gets up at 5:30, so she can run 4 to 5 miles before work, regardless of the weather. But she says, "I may stop after 2 miles if it's 20 below." Mia says keeping a running log book—available at book stores or sporting goods stores—has helped her. She jots a few notes each day she runs, including a comment on the weather, the time she starts, how far she runs and how she feels afterward—and has done it since 1983.

In the summertime Mia bikes, but says biking isn't her primary exercise, because it's weather dependent. Although she can put her bike on a trainer indoors, she doesn't find that particularly enjoyable. Although Mia biked over 2,000 miles one year, she now averages about 1,000 miles a year.

Running and biking has led Mia to many treasured friends. She joined her state's running and biking associations and has traveled with biking groups to Death Valley, Baja, Hawaii, Costa Rica and the Yucatan Peninsula. Most trips enroll 10 to 30 people, many over age 40, and many trips offer a selection of distances you can cover in a day—beginning at 20 miles. (See Chapter 7 for more information on biking.)

Mia rounds out her fitness program with 20 minutes of free-weight exercises for upper body strength three times a week. "You can see results quickly with weights," she says. Mia admits she's somewhat haphazard with flexibility work, saying "If I was injured more, I'd take it more seriously." Fitness is now a lifestyle for Mia. "It's a kind of peer pressure thing," she says of her supportive biking and running friends. "If I'm not out there, people wonder what happened." Weekends frequently find Mia and her friends meeting for a run and going out to breakfast afterward. Now, Mia can't imagine life without exercise. "I can't feel good, unless I get up and exercise right away," she says.

personally can positively influence some outcomes in your life, by living an active life.

Don't focus on fear—the fear of dread diseases, the fear of what you're doing to your body, of dying young. Fear only motivates when it's no more than a moderate level, when you sense that you still have some control over your situation. Excessive fear tends to make you overly anxious and paralyze you. Focus instead on the benefits of being fit.

According to the National Institutes of Health, you're more likely to start—and stick with—a program of regular physical activity if you:

- see a tangible benefit from doing so
- choose an activity you enjoy
- can become proficient enough that you feel competent doing your chosen activity
- feel safe as you do it
- have regular access to your chosen activity
- fit it into your daily schedule
- don't incur excessive financial or social costs
- don't experience a lot of negative consequences, including injuries, wasted time, negative peer pressure or self-identity problems as a result of your activity
- see a need to balance your use of labor-saving devices—like golf carts and cars—and your sedentary activity—watching TV or using the computer—with activities requiring higher levels of exertion
- are encouraged by your healthcare provider to become active

Employers can help by providing encouragement, opportunities for activity, reminders and rewards for taking a step that benefits both you and the employer. Some employers designate an indoor area for lunch-hour walkers, while others construct trails on their grounds and encourage employees to walk or jog on them. Something as simple as placing a sign near the elevator encouraging people to use the stairs and indicating where the stairs are located is helpful. Some employers discount parking fees for workers willing to park farther away and walk to the building.

Find a friend or colleague with whom you can share some physical activity—all you need is a pair of good shoes and the clothes you have on.

You *Can* Change

One of the most powerful predictors of behavior change is believing that you have the skills you need in order to succeed. Clearly, even a small amount of activity is better than none. You may not think about it often, but you have already made changes in your life. Consider, for example—or make a list of—things you've already changed to improve your odds of staying healthy.

For example, you probably use seat belts, which were unknown just a generation ago. Perhaps you've switched from the full-fat homogenized milk you drank as a child to low-fat or skim milk. Over the years a few speeding tickets and hikes in your insurance rates may have convinced you to drive more slowly. Perhaps you have preventive medical care at regular intervals: cholesterol testing, dental and eye exams, mammograms or PSA tests.

Just as you've made these changes, you can also decide to make a notable change in your activity level. Surely, this can become an important milestone in the list of decisions you make that affect your health.

Change Your Mental Image

Start mentally picturing yourself as a fit person. After your image comes into focus, capture it somewhere—either with words or with a more visual depiction on paper, on the computer or by speaking into a tape recorder. Describe what you see.

What activities are you doing? Where? When? With someone, or alone? How does being active affect what you do during the day? Your appearance? Your attitude—and the way others see you? How does it affect your relationships? How does your new lifestyle affect the people around you, whether family, friends or coworkers? What do you look like and what are you doing 10 years from now?

Experts Check In

The number one barrier to becoming physically active, according to most experts, is lack of time. (See Chapter 5 for more information on finding time to be active.) Another problem inactive people frequently encounter is lack of a person or persons with whom to share an activity, according to Bess H. Marcus, Ph.D., professor of psychiatry and human behavior and director of physical activity research at Brown University Center for Behavioral and Preventive Medicine at Miriam Hospital, Providence, Rhode Island, and coauthor of *Motivating People to Be Physically Active.* "It's a lot easier to sell exercise if we can make it fun for folks." Marcus recommends finding an activity you enjoy and finding someone with whom you can enjoy sharing it. "Maybe you can connect with your teenage kids by sharing a walk after dinner. Or walk with a colleague or friend to lunch, talking as you go. Or try something different—being active in a beautiful place, perhaps."

When people say they don't know how to be active, Marcus stresses walking. "Everybody can do it. All you need is a comfortable pair of shoes and a safe place to walk. If you don't feel inspired by walking in your own neighborhood, drive to another

Enjoy an "Activity Snack"

"You don't need to restructure your entire day. Just take a little activity snack," says Bess H. Marcus, Ph.D., professor of psychiatry and human behavior and director of physical activity research at Brown University Center for Behavioral and Preventive Medicine at Miriam Hospital, Providence, Rhode Island, and coauthor of *Motivating People to Be Physically Active.*

"If you haven't had a health issue wake-up call, you probably don't want to hear about adding another priority in your life. Grab an activity snack—a short walk or a climb up and down a flight of stairs. Everyone can fit in a 10-minute activity snack now and then. And once you're doing that, it's much easier to bump it up to a longer period, or do it more often."

neighborhood to walk. It doesn't need to be a place where you have to pay something to go there. If the weather's bad, walk at the shopping mall or turn on the music at home and make up your own step aerobics or dance routine."

Think you're too tired to exercise? "Adding activity gives you back much more than you invest in energy—and it improves your quality of sleep," says Marcus. "If 30 to 60 minutes of activity drains you, 10 to 15 minutes here and there can dramatically boost your energy, especially after lunch, for example."

Marcus notes that, if you're older and often alone, you may be more motivated to exercise if you can find ways to incorporate social time into the scheme. Perhaps you have a friend who would enjoy taking a morning exercise class with you and going for coffee afterward. Before long, an exercise partner becomes a confidant and friend, someone who expects to see you and nudges you if inertia is tempting. "And your

Dealing with the Hurdle of Fibromyalgia

As I researched this chapter, trying to discover what motivates people to start moving toward becoming fit, one friend was foremost in my mind. She's in her early 40s, a generous friend, a wonderful teacher and loving wife and mother. Unfortunately, she suffers greatly from fibromyalgia. She's rather obese and, beyond the physical activity required by her profession as a school choir director, she gets very little exercise.

Fibromyalgia is a chronic condition that causes fatigue and widespread pain in the fibrous tissues of your muscles, ligaments and tendons. I've looked for some effective way to encourage this friend and help motivate her to move toward fitness. I've asked for advice from several experts. Another friend who's tangled previously with quite disabling fibromyalgia is now very active and enjoys a full life—a result, she says of educating herself about fibromyalgia, coming to the understanding and acceptance of the fact that she's the only one who can manage her condition, being willing to take amitriptyline (a non-steroidal antidepressant) and helping on the local hospital's Warmline, a service for people dealing with fibromyalgia. But clearly, fibromyalgia places quite varied limitations and degrees of disability on the people it strikes.

After I discussed my concerns about my young friend and what might be helpful for her with my friend and family physician, Marvin Brooks, M.D., he thought about it overnight. The next day Dr. Brooks suggested a visualization exercise that may be helpful—probably for anyone who struggles to take that first step toward fitness. He shared it with me, and calls it, "Recipe for saving a friend." I thank him for letting me share it with you.

First, picture in your mind a three-dimensional solid—I prefer a rectangular one, but cylindrical is fine. Picture it clearly in your mind. Then, name

time together ends up being a special time."

"Exercise is so important that you should probably need a doctor's permission to be sedentary," says exercise psychologist Andrea Dunn, Ph.D., of the Cooper Institute in Dallas, Texas, paraphrasing a comment by Bengt Saltin, M.D., exercise physiologist, professor and director of the Copenhagen Muscle Research Center. But Dunn also notes that it's important for people in her field of work to be extremely patient.

She tells of one participant in the Cooper Institute's Project Active scientific study, for which 235 relatively inactive people were recruited. This man sat in the corner during numerous sessions, arms crossed, glowering. "He was a difficult participant for us," she says. "Eventually he stopped coming. But we continued sending him the material he'd missed with a nice note saying, 'Sorry we missed you. If you can make it next time, please come. Here are the materials we discussed.'"

---

that space with your name—Lynn-space, for example. Think of this as the space you have carved out of the time-space continuum. This is your space, it's who you are. It's your very own space, and through it you are connected to the world around you.

Now visualize your physical body—in this case, an obese body—inside your space, filling the space. Notice that it takes up a significant part of the volume of your finite space. Look at whatever space is left as your opportunity. It's not much, at this point.

Now, picture in your mind what you want that space to look like. What other things would you like to have in there, filling your Lynn-space? Perhaps a picture of you swimming strongly against an ocean tide. Or directing a children's choir in a premier performance of a piece you composed. Or an image of you canoeing with your son. Maybe another one of you and your family or friends enjoying an active outing together. Or a picture of yourself simply enjoying a day's activities and then climbing into bed for a good night's sleep. Then, picture your hand on the plug to the drain that empties your space. See your hand, pulling the plug to open the drain and letting part of your body—the overweight part—flow into the drain. As the excess weight leaves and your body changes, allow those things you pictured wanting in your space with you to fill that space. Do you like your space better now?

Make it happen! Believe in yourself! You are powerful. You have the ability to change your space. Repeat this exercise daily, until you're comfortable with your piece of space-time. This visualization exercise can help you change your life. You can define your destiny and avoid becoming a victim of external circumstances.

The challenge—and the solution—lie within your reach.

I've shared this exercise with my friend and now I hope, one way or another, she finds it possible to break fibromyalgia's grip on her life, one small step at a time.

"So we were very surprised, 3 years later, when we held a debriefing meeting for study participants, and he showed up. His wake-up call was being diagnosed with diabetes. He looked at his materials and things clicked. People aren't always on our timeline. They'll move at their own rate. Sometimes it takes a very long time. Meanwhile, it's important to keep sending positive messages their direction."

Getting Started Needn't Be Drastic

Small, short spurts of activity have documented value. Practice being active for short periods of time, in safe environments, where you won't be harmed physically or psychologically. Start in places where you won't be embarrassed, teased or criticized, and where it's okay to look silly as you learn something new.

If going to a fitness center feels awkward, ask a friend to go with you.

"Remember that doing something is better than doing nothing," says Beth Warren, manager of Mayo Clinic's Dan Abraham Healthy Living Center for employees, affiliates and retirees. "Small steps are important. I urge people to try just 1 day a week, or one 10-minute walk. People don't know how to incorporate physical activity into their lifestyle, because it's never been a priority. If it becomes a priority, it can change your behavior.

"You probably won't change overnight, and it's not the end of the world if you don't always manage to fit in your activity session. Even the most dedicated exercisers don't feel like exercising some days—and sometimes they don't exercise. You may not notice immediate improvements on the scale, but you probably will notice, early on, that you feel better.

"It's frequently difficult for a person to go into a fitness facility for the first time," she continued. "You don't know how to use the equipment, and everyone may appear to be in better shape than you are. It helps if you have a friend who can go in with you, at least until you're comfortable with the setting and the equipment. But, if you don't want to do that, just try walking a bit one day this week—and then do it again next week. After a few weeks, try adding a second walk."

Progress usually occurs gradually. Everyone has occasional setbacks. A big difference between you and a pro is that you have many other facets to your life. Don't let setbacks destroy your effort. It may take many tries, just as kicking a nicotine habit can take 10—or even 20—tries. But each time puts you that much closer to making active living a part of your lifestyle.

As you think about becoming more active, perhaps you'll feel a greater sense of commitment if you sign a contract with yourself. It helps even more if you can share with someone else your desire and commitment to act. Pick a start date and start planning for it.

An interesting study of the process people go through when making lifestyle changes found that you can dramatically increase your likelihood of success simply by resolving to change. At 6 months, 46 percent of people who had made a resolution to change were successful—not bad, when compared to the 4 percent success rate of those who made no resolutions. Three things predicted a positive outcome: believing that you can do it, having the skills necessary to make the change and being ready to change by the start date.

Start Setting Goals

If you haven't already, get a paper and pencil or sit down at the computer to start formulating goals. First, write or type your answer to this question: What do you believe will happen if you increase your level of physical activity? Jot down which benefits listed in the last chapter you'd like to realize: help with managing your weight, controlling your blood pressure or cholesterol, firming up flabby areas, sleeping better, thinking

Dan: Starting Is the Hardest

"Whether you're a couch potato or an endurance athlete, like I once was, the hardest part about getting fit is starting!" says Dan, who happens to be blind. "It's so much easier to sit on the couch and have a beer and watch TV with family or friends." Although he's relatively deconditioned, compared to the several times he's competed—and won gold medals—in international Paralympic swimming competitions, Dan still tries to exercise regularly.

"Once you start working out, that same half-hour or hour really gets into your blood. I used to smoke a bit, and the things they tell you about smoking are all true—except they leave out the part about it feeling really, really good. But after you get into an exercise routine, you find that the exercise produces those same, little, feel-good endorphins in your brain. And, of course, it's a much healthier way to get them. You can get the really happy, exhilarating feeling without coughing and lung cancer.

"Last year I took 29 trips for my job, and I always put the running shoes in my bag. However, they rarely came out of the bag. I find that the best solution is to find an exercise partner. Then, if you don't get up and get going, you let the partner down, because that person assumes you're going to be there. Whether it's coworkers, friends, neighbors or family—you can motivate each other."

more clearly or being depressed less often and so forth.

Now consider how increasing your physical activity will influence people around you who matter the most to you. Talk to those people and encourage them to share their opinions with you. How do they think your increased activity will affect them? Are they supportive—or will they be, when they learn of your plans and goals? If they're not supportive, how will you deal with them?

If they are supportive, can they help you find the time you need to do what you want to do? Can your partner get supper ready while you exercise, for example? Or help keep you motivated by regularly walking with you in the morning or evening? Help people who want to be supportive of your effort think of ways that they can help you. Would a close friend or loved one be willing to walk with you regularly, for example? Acknowledging and dealing with the impact your behavior will have on your life increases the likelihood you'll succeed.

You're more likely to make a commitment to change if you have positive expectations. For now, goals can be small and specific. Setting—and achieving—small goals will help motivate you to reach for larger goals. You'll define and fine-tune your goals more fully in Chapter 4. For now, a goal like, "I'll walk the dog 10 minutes every day," is better than a general statement like, "I'll be more active every day."

One of the best predictors of your success is whether or not you believe that you've mastered the skills and have whatever else it takes to succeed. This

Years of Xs Finally Ease Up

I've tracked my swimming for many years—probably 20 or more, by marking my mileage on a chart. I've done 2.5 miles a week for longer than I can recall. Initially, I did it in about three sessions per week, but after I suffered a nerve injury, I was forced to alter my regime.

Yet, I continued, one way or another, to get in my 2.5 miles—simply kicking my legs while hanging on to a kickboard, when I had to limit my arm strokes. And, no matter what, I stayed at the 2.5-mile rate, year-in and year-out. If I fell behind, I'd make it up within a week or so. And for many years I've routinely done half a mile five times a week, one way or another.

As I worked on this book, I found that I'd come to a turning point: I wanted to swim farther sometimes. Previously, when I'd feel like doing that, I'd mark it down, and sooner or later, I'd have to miss a swim, so it all ended up evening out. Not now. Sometimes I just wanted to go an extra time, simply for the break and refreshment I felt I gained from a swim. So, for the first time in many, many years, I no longer keep track of my swimming on paper. Swimming has become as natural a part of my life as brushing my teeth, and I don't track that, so it seems pointless right now, to continue to track my swimming.

also means eventually becoming less dependent on external factors to keep you going—a friend or loved one who's urging you to start, for example.

Listed below, just to get you thinking, are some examples of specific goals. Write down—or type—some goals that specifically meet your needs. Start where you are and work from there to increase the intensity, frequency or length of what you decide to do. For example, you may set walking 1 mile as a goal. As you accomplish and master doing that, you can adjust that goal in a number of ways: walk a mile in 20 minutes, or walk 2 miles or walk 1 mile twice a day. Some of these goals are short-term, others longer-term:

- swim 2 lengths of a pool
- ride my bike 5 miles
- lose 5 pounds
- take the stairs at work up one floor once this week
- firm up my flabby torso before a coming class reunion or family reunion
- learn to dance before my daughter's wedding
- learn how to inline skate
- get half an hour of vigorous exercise at least 4 days a week
- share active time with my children or grandchildren once a week
- eliminate 1 hour of TV viewing or computer games each week and use the time for physical activity
- obtain a local trail map (check with your town's park and recreation department) and start walking or biking—and marking—all the trails shown there
- get a dog and walk it once a day

Consider Including Doable, Long-Range Goals

Be realistic. Don't set a long-range goal that you're sure you can't achieve. But do consider including "stretch challenges" that you think you possibly can achieve. List those under a separate heading for long-range goals. They might look like this:

- participate in next year's 5K fun walk/run
- walk 500 miles next year
- lose 20 pounds or get my BMI (body mass index, see page 77) in the healthy range
- adopt an eating style that helps manage my weight more effectively
- speed up my walking so I can keep up with my grandkids
- swim a quarter mile three times a week
- walk a nine-hole golf course and pull or carry my own bag, rather than renting a motorized cart
- find and become active in a community hiking club
- join a recreational tennis, racquetball or handball league
- quit smoking
- participate in a physically active outing at work, with neighbors or with a seniors group—whether it's a fun run or hike, or a softball, touch football or volleyball team
- substitute some sort of physical activity daily for 1 hour of TV viewing or computer activity

Don the Trail Walker: All Because of a Dog

Sometime during the first year after Don's retirement, his wife brought a dog home from work. The frisky, 55-pound golden lab needed a new home—and someone to walk it regularly. Don, who was fairly sedentary, volunteered to walk the dog to the nearby park. So he and the dog began walking. Today they routinely walk 4 to 5 miles a day, sometimes as much as 8 miles.

And now, 7 years later, Don's name surfaces quickly when you talk to the folks at Portland's Transportation Options Group. He's become a leader in developing and mapping Portland's trail system, specifically in the southwest part of town, where paths and walkways were randomly scattered and disconnected until a few years ago.

"I live about a mile and a half from the Willamette River, and the elevation changes 500 feet between here and there," he says. "I started exploring various ways to walk to the river. There were a lot of streets in the valley, most of them running parallel to the slope. But they were entirely disconnected. Developers hadn't done much to help walkers get around. So I went to a meeting to talk about it."

Soon the retired civil engineer was organizing a committee that joined a neighborhood coalition. He built an e-mail list—now numbering over 700 names—and sought political support. Under Don's leadership the Southwest Community Planning Group eventually got a master plan approved for an urban trail system, and has been constructing trails on a voluntary basis ever since. They got the mayor's attention when, for under $300, they finished a portion of the trail estimated to cost $90,000, thanks to the group's volunteer efforts. Don knows how to get results by working the system. "Sometimes the city kicks in just to get rid of me," he says, noting that Portland contributed gravel to the most recent project and regularly contributes staff planning time.

This group has now developed a walking map, available for $6, of all the walking routes of southwest Portland—about 40 miles in all. Income from map sales supports the group's trail building and reconditioning projects. "We just finished reconditioning 800 feet of trail in one day." Over 100 workers volunteer, 15 quite actively.

"All you need to get started," says Don, "is a good pair of walking shoes—something that holds up and feels comfortable at both the beginning and end of your walk." And it all started, he says, "when my wife brought home the dog."

Facing the Obstacles

Consider what obstacles you'll face in your efforts to get fit, and start writing them down. Ask yourself, "What keeps me from being active?" According to the Centers for Disease Control and Prevention, these are the most common barriers people identify:

- lack of time
- influence of peers discouraging physical activity
- lack of energy
- no willpower
- fear of injury (which is, in reality, a much smaller risk than that of inactivity!)
- lack of skill
- lack of financial resources

Clearly, you'll need to overcome the obstacles you've identified, and this book can help you do that. It's important to realize, however, when it comes to changing your lifestyle, that it's not all or nothing, and it may take a while.

Find an Activity You Enjoy

If you don't know how to do an activity that interests you, so-called guided practice may help—taking a class, getting feedback. It gives you a chance to try a new behavior and see if it's something you could continue on a regular basis. If you don't like it, there's no need to feel guilty. You haven't invested a lot of time or money. Just keep looking and trying different activities until you find

Guided practice can help you try a new activity.

one that fits. Eventually, you'll want to master the activities you select well enough to do them on your own with confidence.

Cities frequently offer short walks or bike rides. Many health clubs or recreation centers offer free trial days, and some employers partially underwrite their employees' health club joiner or monthly fees. Look for free introductory classes—in dancing, step aerobics or swimming—at the beginning of seasons or during traditionally slow times of the year. Perhaps a short-term investment—whether it's for three introductory golf lessons (using rented or borrowed equipment) or a three-month membership at a rec center—will help you find an activity you enjoy. Inquire during slow times at rental vendors about opportunities for free or reduced-price trial use of paddle boats, canoes, tandem bikes or inline skates. Some facilities also offer occasional or annual free family days when you can try something new.

Another serious obstacle you may encounter as you seek to become active and fit is inertia in those around you. In fact, you may encounter it in your friends or loved ones, who tell you, "You don't need that much activity. You're doing too much." But you likely know better than anyone else how much activity it takes for you to become fit and feel healthy. Gently explain to those around you that it's a priority of yours and that you need—and want—to do it.

Seek out people around you who model the kinds of behaviors you want to incorporate into your lifestyle. Ask how they got started. Their stories may resemble yours—and may help you see activity as a realistic possibility. Get rid

Carrie: Kicking the Habit, Gradually

Twenty-something, and working in a primarily sedentary job, Carrie decided to try again to kick the smoking habit. "I was sick a lot. It was very expensive—and kept getting more expensive. Plus, I just didn't like to stink," she says. "And I knew, deep down, that smoking was lousy for my health."

When she signed up for a kickboxing class, Carrie knew she could handle the demands of the class better if she wasn't smoking—and she didn't smoke for the 6 months' duration of the class. Although the class is over, Carrie refrains from smoking most of the time and is now busy coaching a high school girls' swim team. "I occasionally swim with the girls," she says. "But they're too fast for me now."

Although Carrie still smokes occasionally, she hopes to be totally tobacco free soon and realizes that she needs to get back into a regular exercise routine. Now she's motivated primarily in order to lose weight. "I know that it's healthy for me to exercise at least three times a week," she says—and she's making plans to do exactly that.

of those mental tapes that say, "You've tried this before," or "You can't possibly find time for that amount of activity." Once you decide it's a priority, you will find the time. More on that later.

Anticipate lapses. You'll inevitably reach plateaus in your progress. Everyone does. But plateaus don't mean failure, and you may be able to shorten them by anticipating and planning for them. According to the Centers for Disease Control and Prevention (CDC), about half of the people who start an exercise program drop out in the first 3 to 6 months. If this happens to you, it doesn't mean you're a failure. Ask yourself if you need to try a different activity. Some people who find that they hate running, for example, end up thoroughly enjoying walking. Sometimes success only comes after many failed attempts. These are steps along the way to success. Recall what motivated you in the past. Explore whether it can motivate you again, and if necessary, re-think your motivation, goals and strategies.

Many people find it more helpful to acknowledge that this is not just an activity change, but a lifestyle change. Tell your friends and family what you're doing, and ask them to help you stay committed—perhaps even to join you. And plan a specific time in your day for activity.

You're more likely to stay active if you can build in variety with new twists. If you're walking, try doing a block or two backward (in an area without traffic and with a flat, smooth surface). It works different muscles than walking forward does. If your plan includes a new eating style, look for a recipe that uses a vegetable you seldom eat. If you're swimming lengths of a pool, swim one or two with all-out effort. Go up the stairs at home backward once or twice a day (holding the railing for safety).

If you're biking or walking, look for a new destination that you can visit once a week—a library, video store, grocery store, discount store or friend's house—and build that into your routine. If you normally read the paper at home, could you save some money and walk to a nearby library to read it several days of the week?

If you have a competitive spirit, challenge yourself to something that's doable—but a reach—and build in some prizes for steps along the way. How about offering a challenge to your family, neighbor, friend or partner? Prizes can be as simple as a cup of coffee, a T-shirt or a walk together in a local garden or architecturally interesting area. If the challenge is longer-term, how about a half-day at a spa? Just be sure that the prizes don't undermine the challenge—like splurging on dinner for a weight loss challenge.

Start Documenting Your Progress—Right Now!

It's important that you notice every single bit of progress. How you document that progress depends on the types of goals you set. Keep it simple—perhaps with a notebook in your car, near the door at home, in your desk at work. It can be as simple as a piece of graph paper with Xs on it for each mile—or quarter mile—you walk, bike or swim.

If you walk the same route every

day, drive it once to clock the mileage—or wear a pedometer. If you swim laps, ask the lifeguard or look on the wall for a sign that indicates how many pool lengths constitute a mile. Record your activity every day, and you'll be surprised at how quickly it adds up!

If your long-term goal is to be able to walk the golf course for an 18-hole round, inquire at the course as to the distance involved, and start building up to walking that distance, perhaps pulling a cart or wagon with groceries to build your strength. Time yourself on your walking or biking route (not on Monday, if you haven't done it over the weekend) and check and record your time once a week or once a month to see if it's improved. If you want to lose weight, start weighing yourself and recording your weight once a week, at the same time of day—again, probably not after a couple days off from your usual routine.

If you want to start a weight-lifting program, record the weight you use for each lift and your maximum number of repetitions and gradually increase one or

Bob Goes for the Gold

My husband Bob always thought he'd be a good runner but never got around to trying it while he was in school. But when our son Dan, who had recently lost 80 pounds and was starting to enjoy more physical activities, decided to run the 5K "Turkey Trot" on Thanksgiving morning, Bob's ears perked up. Although it was chilly, Dan and a friend of his completed the race through town. When he came over to show his dad his T-shirt, Dan challenged his dad to join him in 10 days for another 5K race around a scenic city lake. Bob took the bait.

Although he'd done considerable walking and picked up his level of exercise in several sports recently, Bob didn't specifically train for the race, beyond his usual walking, which looked like an acceptable alternative to him. He figured he could walk 5K in the same amount of time our son had jogged his first race. He was psyched and ready to go when Dan and his girlfriend picked him up Saturday morning.

At the site, Bob was glad for Dan's help getting registered and ready to go. What Bob hadn't expected, though, was the irresistible urge, shortly after the race began, to sprint past a group of people. And that's just what he did. After he sprinted, full speed ahead, for a brief while, he returned to his healthy walking pace until he felt the urge to sprint again. And thus he completed the race—a sort of interval training exercise, sprinting as he felt able and then walking until he felt like sprinting again. Each time he passed a large group of people, he experienced a real "high." Our son, meanwhile, who'd hoped to set a steady pace for the race, found his father's on-again, off-again style disconcerting. But they both completed the race, had fun and plan to do it again.

the other as your routine becomes easier. If you want to lower your blood pressure, buy a home monitor and take your blood pressure once a week before you exercise. (Note: Only take it once, sitting, with your legs uncrossed, breathing normally.) If your goal is to manage stress better, jot down a few lines once a week to describe how you're doing.

Getting to Know You!

As you track your progress, note the times of day that are best for you to be active. Are you a morning or an evening person? You're probably wasting your time if you're fighting your natural rhythms. However, you may be surprised to see how much more energy you have throughout the entire day once you start becoming active and more fit. Keep track of how your priorities—and goals—change, record your progress toward those goals and note how you overcame obstacles you encountered.

Keep a record of the people and resources around you that support your intention to change. If a friend you meet for coffee regularly encourages your efforts, ask if the two of you could substitute a walk once a week during coffee time. (Some people carry their coffee in insulated, covered mugs on a "talking walk.")

Make Fitness a Habit!

Habit, according to Stephen Covey, author of *The 7 Habits of Highly Effective People*, is the intersection of knowledge (the "what to do" and the "why"), skill (the "how-to") and desire (the "want to"). If you want to make something a habit, it helps to be proactive, rather than reactive. As you start tracking your activity, you'll become more aware of your current behavior patterns.

Anticipate, from the outset, that fitness activities will become a regular part of your daily schedule—and plan around that. Build into your daily schedule tangible reminders to be active—putting the remote control out of sight or keeping your walking shoes by the door at home, in your car or at your desk as a reminder to take a walk.

If you hope to stick with activities and do them frequently and consistently, they should be activities you enjoy. You can opt for primarily one activity or a variety of things. Perhaps it's something

Bob: Plugging the Meter to Walk

Shortly after he acquired a treadmill and determined to walk more regularly, Bob found an interesting device for tracking and rewarding his walking—a parking meter. This meter is attached to a glass-enclosed wooden bank that offers 15-minute time segments in exchange for quarters. Bob decided to start "pay-as-you-go" walking, taking a break several times a day, plugging the meter with a quarter and walking for 15 minutes, until the red flag pops up.

Don: I Hit Rock Bottom

Shortly before I finished work on this book, a friend, Don, decided to take the plunge and get back into shape after a few years of being sluggish. "I had to reach the bottom," he said, as he told me of his decision to turn things around as he neared 60. "I've had no motivation. But last weekend did it for me. I knew I couldn't spend another weekend like that again. I had nothing to do from noon until midnight both Saturday and Sunday. I tell myself that food is wonderful, and so is sleep, so that's all I do. I have no commitments, no motivation. And as I think about retirement—" he stopped. "I'm not going to spend every single day like that. I just can't do that."

Realizing he was depressed, Don searched for a place to go. His daughter, soon to be married and concerned about Don's health, asked him if he wanted to live long enough to see his grandkids. "I can see how depression can kill a person. If I didn't have healthy friends and family and had nothing to live for, it would be real hard. At least I'm healthy enough to redirect my energy. But I feel guilt, anger, shame."

Don ended up making an 18-month commitment to a health club. "I knew if I didn't have money invested, I wasn't going to do it. I've always been a quitter," he said about his previous attempts to dig out of his hole of depression. He still struggled with the question of whether he was worth that much money or not.

But he began to go. And he began to define goals. "I want to lose weight and relieve my stress. Originally I wanted to lose weight and have a social outlet. I guess now my main goals are to lose weight and gain muscle." Noting that the exercise equipment at his home sat unused, Don concluded that he needed the social contact and the motivation he gets from seeing others sweating and working hard. He met with a trainer, who helped him devise his own program, and he got off to a good start by working out 10 of the first 14 days.

And already, he found it easier to walk up a flight of stairs.

you enjoyed in your youth, that's adapted to your current skill level. If you were on a swim team, perhaps you'd like to swim laps now—or join a Master's swim club. If you played a team sport in school, perhaps you'd enjoy playing on a recreational or senior league team of the same sport or a similar sport that's easier at your current age and ability level. In any case, it's helpful to attain some level of proficiency in your chosen activity.

Should You Consider Hiring a Personal Trainer?

Most people don't need to hire a personal trainer in order to become fit. You can do a good job yourself, if you learn to listen carefully to your body and use a well-balanced program that includes cardiovascular conditioning, strength building and flexibility activities. On the other hand, you may decide that, since you spend money on a lot of other things, it's worth spending this money on your health. And a good personal trainer can help you design a well-balanced exercise regime that's suited to your specific needs.

If you have medical problems, you may be better advised to work with a good physical therapist. They're medically trained (at least a master's level degree) and must pass national exams and be registered by the state to practice. They're also legally limited from practicing outside their field of expertise. On the other hand, personal trainers aren't required to have any medical training.

A personal trainer's time generally costs from $30 to over $100 per hour. If you have a chronic health condition, you can probably expect the cost to be toward the high end. However, you may be able to get the costs down to a more affordable level if you can space out your sessions with the trainer. Personal trainers' fees are usually not covered by your health insurance, although it's worth investigating whether or not that's true in your case. Some insurance plans cover an exercise evaluation and prescription done by a personal trainer. Or, if you have a flexible spending account, the rules may cover the services of a personal trainer if lifestyle modification counseling costs are covered.

It may be challenging to find a good personal trainer. Ask for recommendations from your doctor or people you know. Personal trainers may work out of health clubs, studios or their home—and they may, or may not, have flexible hours. Don't be afraid, if you have special needs, to ask about a trainer's experience in that area. Consider it a red flag if people who work with a trainer you're considering using frequently end up at the doctor's office with musculoskeletal injuries.

There are no state or federal licensing regulations that uniformly govern personal trainers. In fact, there are at least 10 national and over 100 local organizations that certify trainers. Unfortunately, studies show that many personal trainers are not well qualified for their jobs. The University of California at Los Angeles tested 115 fitness professionals in a variety of areas. Most had been certified by at least one organization. The results are startling:

- Those who had a bachelor's degree

in exercise science or were certified by the American College of Sports Medicine (ACSM) or the National Strength and Conditioning Association (NSCA) had scores that averaged above 70 percent.

- Everyone else scored less than 40 percent.
- Those who had both a college degree and either ACSM or NSCA certification had the highest scores.

Clearly, it's worth checking a personal trainer's credentials. It's also advisable to ask whether the trainer carries liability insurance. Personal trainers can help assess where you are, in terms of strength, flexibility, body fat and balance. They can also help you establish an exercise plan, including exercises that increase your cardiovascular fitness, strength and flexibility.

A qualified personal trainer may be helpful in setting up your program, but check his or her credentials.

If You're Motivated—Then DO It!

If you've gotten this far in the book, you're probably motivated and just need to get going. Do it! Share your vision, as you've begun to develop it, with a friend or partner. Maybe that person will even join you in an effort to become more fit. The following chapters help you get started and provide valuable reference information. You can influence your health. Now do it!

Bess H. Marcus, Ph.D., reviewed chapter 3. She is an author, professor and director of physical activity research at the Brown University Center for Behavioral and Preventive Medicine at The Miriam Hospital.

CHAPTER 4

Planning Your Approach, Setting Goals & Tracking Your Fitness

When the National Academies' Institute of Medicine (IOM) announced new recommendations for physical activity levels recently—an hour of accumulated physical activity per day—the national groan was audible. Whatever happened to the U.S. Surgeon General's recommended half hour of exercise on most days of the week—which, alone, seemed hard enough to reach? Unfortunately, some people threw their hands up in resignation. There would be no pleasing these so-called experts, they said. You might as well just flop down on the sofa and give up.

Don't do it yet! There is a reasonable explanation, and the outlook isn't as hopeless as you might think. "The Institute of Medicine's recommendation (which is not a national recommendation, nor is it issued by the federal government) has a more specific focus on the amount of physical activity necessary to prevent weight gain or to maintain current weight," says Gregory W. Heath, D.Sc., M.P.H., lead health scientist at the Center for Disease Control and Prevention's Division of Nutrition and Physical Activity. "The Surgeon General's recommendation, on the other hand, addressed the minimal amount of physical activity necessary to accrue some health benefit—a more general outcome."

Actually, the two recommendations aren't contrary—they're just recommendations for different goals. "Ideally, physical activity would be prescribed for a specific individual, based on personal needs and interests," say the authors of an explanatory report issued by the President's Council on Physical Fitness and Sports. "The basic recommendation of the 1996 report suggested all American adults accumulate at least 30 minutes of moderate physical activity equivalent to brisk walking on most, if not all, days of the week ... The physical activity promotion strategy behind the Office of the Surgeon General's guidelines was to encourage the greatest benefit for the greatest number of people. They were designed to help people do some physical activity rather than none ... The guidelines [from the Institute of Medicine] were actually prepared by the Food and Nutrition Board of the IOM ... The media failed to report the basis for the IOM's recommendation, which was primarily based on the amount of activity necessary for body weight management ... The public should view them as complementary rather than competing."

The new number is also cumulative. It includes both low-intensity activities of daily life, like cleaning your house or sweeping the sidewalk, as well as more vigorous activities. And you can shorten the time you need by increasing the intensity of your activity—jogging for 20 to 30 minutes, rather than walking 4 miles in an hour, for example. The Surgeon General's recommendation, on the other hand, is based on the amount of activity that studies show it takes to reduce your risk of dying prematurely or having a chronic condition—like heart disease or diabetes.

The harsh fact is that nearly two-thirds of Americans do not get any regular physical activity, and 25 percent are completely sedentary. Those who monitor our health at the national level are becoming alarmed—with good cause. But fear can be paralyzing. Fortunately, you're reading this, so you're not paralyzed, but you want to know what to do.

Where Are You Starting?

While you could spend days figuring out where you are along the fitness continuum, you don't need to. Yes, it's good to know where you start, in order to detect progress. But we're all different—and starting at different points. We also have different goals, and you'll find that your progress will differ from that of a friend or family member. The important thing is to get started—and get moving!

Plan to start gently and increase your level of activity as you become more comfortable with it. Starting too quickly can leave you injured and discouraged.

A variety of tools can help you know where you're starting. We'll discuss some of the tools briefly here, and if you know of others that you wish to use, that's fine. The main reason to assess where you start is to be able to see your progress over time. It's not important how you stack up, compared to someone else. What is important is to see positive changes in yourself; knowing where you started helps you do that, especially if the changes are gradual. It also helps you to know how vigorously you can safely plan to exercise. It's important to work from where you are now, not where you wish you were or where someone else is. And it's important to remember that others don't have the same health issues that you may have. Truly, the only valid comparisons are those with yourself at various stages along the way.

Should You Check In with Your Doctor First?

If you're under age 35 and in good health, you probably don't need to see your doctor before undertaking a reasonable exercise program. If you're older than 35, have been inactive for a number of years and anticipate starting a rigorous exercise program, it's probably a good idea to check with your healthcare provider first. If you have a heart condition or a family history of early stroke or heart attack deaths, you should have medical supervision until you've established a safe level of activity.

You definitely should talk with your doctor first if you:

- have high blood pressure (regularly greater than 140/90 mm Hg)
- have type 1 diabetes
- feel pain in your chest, the left side of your neck or your left shoulder or arm when you participate in physical activity—or immediately afterward
- become extremely breathless after exerting mildly
- often feel faint, have spells of severe dizziness or frequently lose your balance
- take prescription medications—especially if you have been told by your doctor to take medication for high blood pressure or a heart condition
- have severe muscle, ligament or tendon problems
- have bone or joint problems, such as arthritis, that could be aggravated by exercise
- are over age 65 and not accustomed to exercise

Vigorous exercise presents minimal health risks if you are in good health or following a doctor's advice—much less risk, in fact, than habitual inactivity or obesity. Unfortunately, although studies show that you're more likely to engage in physical activity if your physician recommends it than if it's not discussed, your physician may be one of many who don't specifically encourage their patients to exercise. But don't let that stop you from bringing up the topic! And if your physician lacks the up-to-date knowledge to be helpful in this area, look for a physician who is, or seek out either a physical therapist with experience in this area or an experienced exercise physiologist (preferably with an advanced degree or certification by the American College of Sports Medicine or the National Strength and Conditioning Association) or an athletic trainer.

A brief note of caution: If you were quite active in your school days and haven't been very active for a number of years recently, it may not be a good idea to compare your fitness level now to what it was then. If you were an active 18-year-old, kept fit by consecutive athletic seasons at school, your risk of injuring yourself then by setting the bar too high was much less than it may be now, after a few—or more—years of inactivity. Don't beat up on yourself now for not being able to lift anywhere near what you did then—or do the number of pushups, or run the mile in anything near the amount of time it took you then. This is an especially important caution if you have chronic conditions or are at risk of having them now—especially heart disease and diabetes. And, if you're tempted not to be reasonable, your body will surely remind you!

You know where you want to be, and you alone know how you feel at any given moment. Listen to your body. Adjust your program in response to what your body tells you. Here are some ideas to get you going.

Assessing Where You Are Now

You can design your own assessment that takes into account the types of activities you enjoy and actually hope to participate in on a regular basis. Think of the things you do—and want to be able to do more easily—and start to measure them today. Use the goals you began to define in the last chapter, or develop them now. Don't think of your goals as set in stone. Plan to adjust them as you go, to meet your changing needs.

Designate a start date and record what you do now as your baseline. If you wish, use several different indicators to gauge different aspects of your fitness. The key is to record where you start, so that you can detect progress. Keep it simple, so you can easily recheck yourself at the identical task periodically.

Here are some additional ways to assess where you are now that may or may not be relevant to your personal goals. Consider these idea starters. Use one or more of them or make your own short list. Be sure you warm up your muscles with gentle activity before you begin to time or measure what you do.

- How far can you walk in 5 minutes, or how long does it take to walk 1 mile? (See instructions in the sidebar.)
- How long does it take to climb a flight of stairs—or two flights?
- How long can you stand on one foot without support? (Be sure to time yourself on each foot, and don't be surprised if they're different.)
- Holding a known quantity of weight (cans of food work fine—or, if you can't manage that, use the weight of your own arms), how many times can you raise your arms with that weight? Or how long does it take for you to lift that weight 10 or 15 times?
- How many times can you get up from a kitchen chair in 2 minutes, without using your hands?
- How much do you weigh? Note: weigh yourself about the same time of day, always on the same scale, wearing little or no clothing (no shoes) each time, with the scale on a solid surface (not carpeting).

Gay: Meeting Some Goals & Working Toward Others

Seeing the big 5-0 looming on the horizon, watching her parents and their friends in their 70s and 80s become overweight and disabled—and having the encouragement of a friend—finally got Gay moving toward fitness over 2 years ago. "I write life and health insurance policies, so I know it's a big deal," says Gay, who owns an insurance company with her husband.

"If I can do it, anybody can," she continues. "Before, I wouldn't go shopping, because I didn't want to walk in the mall. If I had to go, I'd park in the space closest to the store. I had tried a few things without much success in the past, but was never very committed. But now I wanted to try getting off the blood pressure medications I was taking, and I wanted to avoid osteoporosis. I knew it was time to take care of myself. And I finally got the message that if you want to stay healthy, exercise must be a part of your life."

Gay thought of exercise as a chore and figured that committing to 30 minutes a day would be a major undertaking. However, her friend spurred her on to commit 1 hour 5 days a week—and to make it a #1 priority. "I've never been a morning person, but this makes me feel so good, that I don't mind getting out of bed at 5:15. My family can't believe I'm still doing this," she says. And on weekends, when she doesn't walk with her friend, Gay frequently walks by herself—often farther than she goes on weekdays.

Gay and her friend began regularly walking 3 miles a day on weekday mornings in the summer. When the kids went back to school, schedules became more complicated, but the morning walks remained a top priority. "Exercise was a chore at first, but now it's something I want to do," says Gay. "I'm the one who reaps the rewards. My hair and my skin are better—which I can only attribute to eating right and exercising. I decided it was time to start taking care of myself and not just everyone else. And once I started feeling better, why would I want to go back to my old ways?"

Gay still wants to add in some weight training to tone her arms, and feeling so much better has encouraged her to try some new sports. "I haven't played tennis in years and would like to take it up again," she says.

Recently, exercise proved to be a great stress-releaser that helped Gay make it through some tough times as she helped her failing mom, who lived nearby and eventually died. And Gay still harbors a secret fantasy—her "hidden side," as she calls it: getting back to tap dancing, which she did—and loved—while she was in school and right after she finished college.

■ How long does it take you to bike 1 mile?

While these indicators needn't be highly detailed, it's good to have some measurable way to gauge your progress. You'll probably find yourself adding new ways to check yourself as you move along in your program. That's fine! The key point now is to start tracking your progress. Use a piece of paper you keep handy—or a notebook or the computer—to record your numbers at regular intervals.

Components of a Good Fitness Program

Although nearly any lifestyle change that gets you moving is worthwhile, you can plan your activity to maximize your benefits and minimize your risk of injury. Researchers tell us, for example, that if one of your goals is to increase your endurance, you really need to move around more than 1 or 2 days a week. They also know that active periods should last at least 10 minutes to improve your VO_2max, the rate at which you extract oxygen from the air you breathe (see explanation of VO_2max, page 32), a good indicator of cardiovascular fitness.

Most experts describe a good fitness program as including components in several key areas:

- cardiorespiratory endurance
- muscular strength and endurance
- flexibility

Many fitness programs also include balance and some recently include core stability, as well. And body composition—how much of your body is lean tissue (muscle and bone, for example) and how much is fat—is another item experts also suggest you consider. We'll discuss each of these in the pages that follow.

It's up to you—preferably, in consultation with your physician—to decide what to include in your fitness program. Think about what you'd like to be able to do, but currently find difficult. What

Track Your Progress with a Walking Test

Use a simple walking test to follow your improvements. Here's how:

1. Find a 1-mile track or map out your own 1-mile route near your home or work (using your car to gauge the distance initially).
2. Walk slowly for a few minutes to warm up.
3. Time yourself as you quickly walk the mile. Just for comparison purposes, you may also want to take your heart rate immediately when you finish—if you didn't smoke or consume caffeine for at least an hour beforehand (because they can affect your heart rate).
4. Repeat this test every 3 months to track your progress.

health issues do you want to avoid? What bad habits do you want to kick? Use this information to firm up your fitness goals and develop methods to judge progress. Expect these lifestyle changes to become a permanent part of your new, physically active lifestyle.

Besides deciding what activities to include in your fitness program, you should consider how frequently, for how long and how intensely you want to do them. If you want to improve your cardiovascular fitness, for example, experts recommend planning to be

What's Your BMI?

Here's how to find your body mass index (BMI):

1. Weigh yourself on a scale.
2. Measure your height in inches (without shoes).
3. Find your height in the column on the left.
4. Follow that line with your finger, until you find the weight closest to yours.
5. Go to the top of that column to read your BMI. On average, healthy BMI ranges from 18.5 to 25.

BMI	**19**	**20**	**21**	**22**	**23**	**24**	**25**	**26**	**27**	**28**	**29**	**30**	**35**	**40**	**45**	**50**
HEIGHT	WEIGHT IN POUNDS															
58″	91	96	100	105	110	115	119	124	129	134	138	143	167	191	215	239
59	94	99	104	109	114	119	124	129	133	138	143	148	173	198	223	247
60	97	102	107	112	118	123	128	133	138	143	148	153	179	204	230	256
61	100	106	111	116	122	127	132	137	143	148	153	158	185	211	238	264
62	104	109	115	120	126	131	136	142	147	153	158	164	191	218	246	273
63	107	113	118	124	130	135	141	147	152	158	163	169	197	225	254	282
64	111	116	122	128	134	140	145	151	157	163	169	174	204	232	262	291
65	114	120	126	132	138	144	150	156	162	168	174	180	210	240	270	300
66	118	124	130	136	142	148	155	161	167	173	179	186	216	247	278	309
67	121	127	134	140	146	153	159	166	172	178	185	191	223	255	287	319
68	125	131	138	144	151	158	164	171	177	184	190	197	230	262	296	328
69	128	135	142	149	156	162	169	176	182	189	196	203	236	270	304	338
70	132	139	146	153	160	167	174	181	188	195	202	207	243	278	313	348
71	136	143	150	157	165	172	179	186	193	200	208	215	250	286	322	358
72	140	147	154	162	169	177	184	191	199	206	213	221	258	294	331	368
73	144	151	159	166	174	182	189	197	204	212	219	227	265	302	341	378
74	148	155	163	171	179	186	194	202	210	218	225	233	272	311	350	389
75	152	160	168	176	184	192	200	208	216	224	232	240	279	319	360	400
76	156	164	172	180	189	197	205	213	221	230	238	246	287	328	369	410

active at least 3 to 5 days a week for at least 20 to 60 minutes each day, depending on the intensity of your activity. Activities can vary, as long as they use your large muscles, are rhythmic, can be maintained continuously for at least 10 minutes at a stretch and can get you breathing heavily. Plan strengthening activities for your muscles, on the other hand, 2 or 3 days a week for each area of your body. And, although you can retain or build flexibility with just 2 or 3 days a week of appropriate exercise, most experts recommend moving all your muscles through their complete range of motion most days. And your program will be most helpful, if it's well rounded.

Body Composition

Research shows that your body weight and composition can affect your health and fitness. A common tool for determining a healthy weight for someone of your height is the body mass index, or BMI (see sidebar, page 77). People in the range termed healthy (BMI from 18.5 to 25) are at the weight that statistics show is most healthy for someone of that height. If your BMI is from 25 to 30, you are considered overweight, and if your BMI is 30 or above, obese.

Keep in mind that these indicators are simply a statistical look at BMI. If your BMI is a bit below 18.5, you may be quite healthy, unless the lower weight results from illness. And some people who have a great deal of muscle mass may show up with unusually high BMIs, which doesn't necessarily mean they're not healthy. Clearly, BMI doesn't tell the whole story, because fat weighs less than muscle. Someone in the healthy range may still have more fat than is healthful and little muscle. Similarly, someone who's very fit may actually weigh as much as someone who's overweight. So use the BMI chart as just another helpful tool in determining whether or not you may be healthier if you lost some weight.

Researchers use several other indica-

Ditch the Jelly Belly

A key reason for the new waist-measurement test is that the intra-abdominal fat that's stored deep within your abdomen around the organs there increases your risk for many chronic diseases. And exercise does a great job of reducing that fat!

In a recent study of previously sedentary, overweight women, ages 50 to 75, half of the group exercised in various aerobic activities for about 45 minutes a day, 5 days a week for a year. More important than the modest 3 pounds, on average, that they lost, was the reduction of up to nearly 7 percent of the fat in their midsections. Nonexercisers, not surprisingly, lost neither.

tors to evaluate body composition, including:

■ **Waist measurement**—Fat around your waist can be more dangerous to your health than fat around your hips. Your health risks are statistically higher if you're a woman whose waist measures more than 35 inches or a man whose waist measures more than 40 inches.

■ **Girth measurements**—You can track changes resulting from weight training by measuring your biceps muscle, for example, and noting changes in its size as it becomes more fully developed.

■ **Underwater weighing (hydrostatic weighing)**—Considered the "gold standard," this method accurately shows percent of body fat. It requires special equipment and trained personnel, and is usually found at universities and upscale health clubs. It costs about $30.

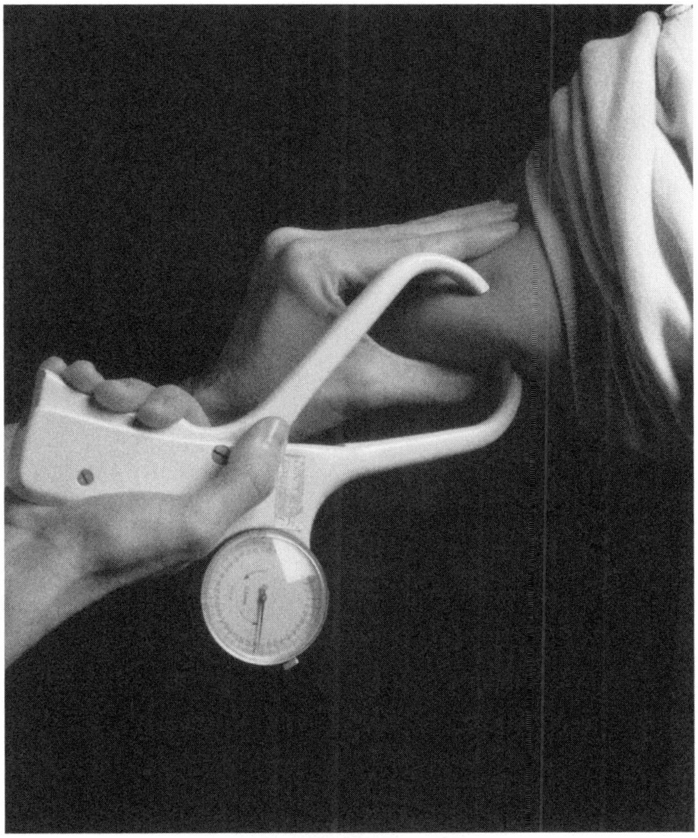

One way to judge body composition uses a special caliper to measure amount of fat in several places.

■ **Dual x-ray absorbiometry (DEXA)**—About as accurate as hydrostatic weighing, this 20-minute procedure uses low-energy X rays to scan your entire body. A computer then calculates your body composition. This procedure is usually done at hospitals or major research institutions. The bed used for the procedure may not accommodate large people. It costs around $60 to $70.

■ **Skinfold measure**—A professional does this test, using a special tool to measure the amount of fat several places on your body. Accuracy is not as good as hydrostatic weighing or DEXA. Costs range from $5 to $30.

■ **Bioelectrical impedance (BIA)**—Based on the fact that fat resists the flow of electrons, this method involves passing a low dose of current through your body. Although many health clubs offer this test, results can vary widely, depending on when you last ate, how well hydrated you are, stage of your menstrual cycle (for women), when you last exercised and when you last urinated. Costs are about $5 to $10.

■ **BOD POD (air displacement plethysmography)**—A process similar to hydrostatic weighing, this process uses air rather than water. The test is

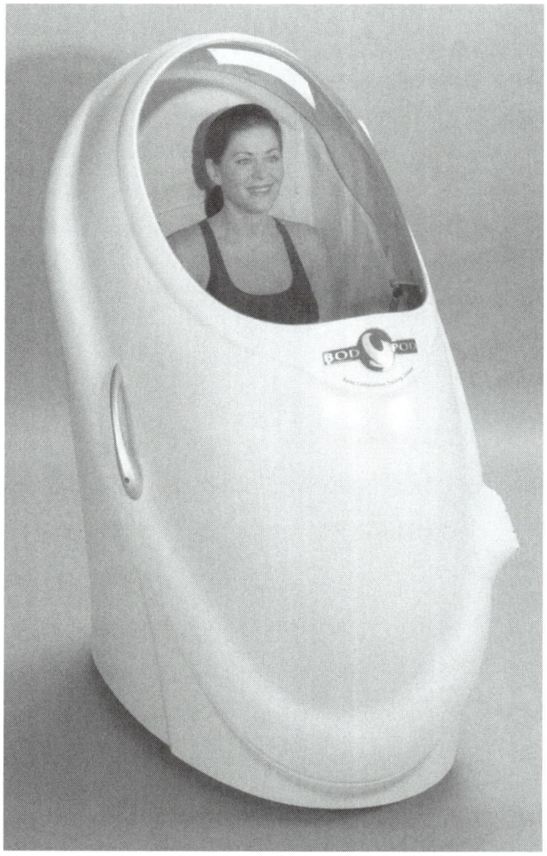

Air displacement plethysmography uses air to measure percentage of body fat.

conducted at research institutions as well as at some fitness centers and weight loss clinics. Costs range from $50 to $75.

Many experts don't think most people need a sophisticated system to evaluate their body composition. "I'd recommend disrobing before a mirror and noting how you look," says Heath. Chris Bopp, a graduate research assistant at the University of South Carolina, who works with these sophisticated techniques, agrees. "Most of us can look at ourselves and know where we need to firm up or take off weight," he says.

METs: Energy Costs of Various Physical Activities

Scientists describe how much energy various activities require by using the term METs, which stands for metabolic equivalent. One MET (scientifically described as 1 kilocalorie per kilogram per hour, or 1kcal/kg/hour) is roughly equivalent to the energy it takes to sit quietly. A MET also refers to the amount of oxygen your body at rest consumes in 1 minute (milliliters per kilogram per minute, or ml/kg/min). One MET is roughly equivalent to 3.5 ml/kg/min.

While you don't need to understand how METs are calculated, it's helpful to know how various physical activities compare, in terms of the energy you expend while doing them. Here's a list of common activities and their metabolic equivalents. Note how some activities you may not have considered to be exercise actually require a fair amount of exertion. Also note the difference it can make if you simply pick up the pace of an activity.

This table also helps you understand how much fuel (food) it takes to do common activities, compared to sitting quietly, which is 1 MET. Consider these differences, as you select your daily activities.

Energy Costs of Various Activities

METS	Description
8.0	**BICYCLE, GENERAL:** 12-14 m.p.h., moderate effort
4.0	bicycle: <10 m.p.h.
6.0	bicycle: 10-12 m.p.h.
10.0	bicycle: 14-16 m.p.h.
7.0	**BICYCLE, STATIONARY:** general
3.5	bicycle, stationary: very light effort
12.5	bicycle, stationary: very vigorous effort
5.5	**CONDITIONING EXERCISE:** health club exercise, general
2.5	conditioning exercise: stretch, hatha yoga
3.0	conditioning exercise: lift weights, light or moderate effort
3.5	conditioning exercise: calisthenics (e.g., home exercise), light or moderate effort; row, light effort
4.0	conditioning exercise: water aerobics
6.0	conditioning exercise: lift weights, vigorous effort; slimnastics; jazzercise
7.0	conditioning exercise: row, general; ski machine, general
8.0	conditioning exercise: calisthenics (e.g., push-ups, sit-ups, jumping jacks, circuit training), heavy, vigorous effort
8.5	conditioning exercise: row, vigorous effort
9.0	conditioning exercise: stair-climber, treadmill, general
3.0	**DANCE:** ballroom, slow (waltz, foxtrot, tango, cha-cha)
4.5	dance: fast (disco, folk, square, line, polka, country); hula; belly; swing
4.8	dance: ballet or modern, twist, jazz, tap, jitterbug
5.0	dance: aerobic, low impact
5.5	dance: ballroom, fast
6.5	dance: aerobic, general
7.0	dance: high impact
8.5	dance: aerobic, step, with 6- to 8-inch step
3.0	**FISH:** general

Energy Costs of Various Activities *continued*

METS	Description
2.5	fish: from a boat, sitting
6.0	fish: in a stream in waders
2.0	fish: ice fish
5.0	**HUNT:** general
3.0	**HOME ACTIVITIES:** general cleaning
2.0	home activities: prepare food, hang or fold laundry, make bed
2.3	home activities: wash dishes, standing
2.5	home activities: put away groceries, shop without a grocery cart, carry packages, water plants, sit and play with children
3.0	home activities: heavy cleaning (e.g., wash car or windows, clean garage), carry small child
3.3	home activities: sweep floors
3.5	home activities: vacuum
3.8	home activities: scrub floor or bathtub on hands and knees
4.0	home activities: sweep garage; walk/run and play with children, moderate; walk/run and play with animals, moderate
5.0	home activities: walk/run and play with children, vigorous
6.0	home activities: move furniture, carry boxes
7.5	home activities: carry groceries upstairs
9.0	home activities: carry boxes or furniture
3.0	**HOME REPAIR:** repair car, general carpentry, paint or paper inside home
5.0	home repair: clean gutters, hang storm windows, paint outside of home
6.0	home repair: install rain gutters, build a fence, roof
7.5	home repair: carpentry, saw hardwood
0.9	**INACTIVITY:** sleep
1.0	inactivity: sit quietly and watch television, listen to music, lie quietly, lie and talk on the phone, recline and write, watch a movie in a theater, meditate

Energy Costs of Various Activities *continued*

METS	Description
1.5	**LAWN, YARD AND GARDEN:** stand and water lawn or garden
2.5	lawn, yard and garden: mow lawn with riding mower; apply fertilizer or seed a lawn, walking
3.0	lawn, yard and garden: pick fruit or vegetables
3.5	lawn, yard and garden: use a leaf blower or edger
4.3	lawn, yard and garden: rake and bag grass or leaves
4.5	lawn, yard and garden: operate snow blower, walking; plant seedlings, shrubs or trees; trim shrubs or trees manually; weed garden
5.0	lawn, yard and garden: spread dirt with a shovel, carry or stack wood
5.5	lawn, yard and garden: mow lawn with power mower
6.0	lawn, yard and garden: chop wood, haul branches, dig or spade garden, mow lawn with hand mower, shovel snow by hand
1.3	**MISCELLANEOUS:** sit and read book or newspaper
1.5	miscellaneous: sit and talk or talk on the phone, sit at a sporting event, sit and play cards or board games
1.8	miscellaneous: sit and write, do desk work, type, stand and talk, read or talk on the phone
2.0	miscellaneous: sit and do arts and crafts, moderate effort; travel or tour (involving walking and riding)
2.0	**MUSIC:** sit and play classical guitar, play cello, flute, horn, woodwind
2.5	music: play violin, trumpet, piano
3.0	music: play guitar, standing (rock and roll band)
3.5	music: marching band (walking)
1.5	**OCCUPATION:** light office work, meetings, lab work, watch repair, light assembly (sitting), farming (milk by machine), data entry, type
2.0	occupation: direct traffic, walk on the job (less than 2.0 m.p.h.) in office or lab, police (drive a squad car)
2.3	occupation: stand (bartender, store clerk, assembly, filing)
2.5	occupation: nursing; custodial work (clean sink, dust, vacuum), light effort; farming (drive harvester or tractor, cut hay); machine tooling; ride mower or forklift, operate crane; teach stretching or yoga (sitting)

Energy Costs of Various Activities *continued*	
METS	**Description**
3.0	occupation: custodial work (buff floor with electric buffer, take out trash), farming (milk by hand), stand (weld, repair autos, patient care nursing)
3.5	occupation: general carpentry; custodial work (general clean or mop), moderate effort; electrical work or plumbing; farming (chase cattle on horseback), moderate effort; locksmith
4.0	occupation: baker, moderate effort; farming (feed small animals); masseur or masseuse (stand); police (make an arrest); lift 10- to 20-pound items continuously with limited resting or walking; paint; hang paper; walk 3.0 m.p.h. and carry light objects or push wheelchair; teach physical education or exercise class
4.5	occupation: farming (feed cattle or horses, haul water)
5.5	occupation: outside construction and remodeling, farming (shovel grain)
6.0	occupation: build roads (includes haul debris, drive heavy machinery), groom horses, use heavy tools (jackhammers, etc.)
6.5	occupation: mine coal; truck driving, load and unload
7.0	occupation: move or push heavy objects (75 pounds or more)
8.0	occupation: carry heavy loads (such as bricks), carry moderate loads up stairs; move boxes (16 to 40 pounds); farming, (bale hay, clean barn), vigorous effort; forestry (general); race horses; use heavy, nonpower tools (shovel, spade)
8.5	occupation: dig ditches
12.0	occupation: fire fighter, general
6.0	**RUN:** jog/walk combination (jog component less than 10 minutes)
7.0	run: jog
8.0	run: 5 m.p.h.; run in place
9.0	run: cross-country
10.0	run: 6 m.p.h.
11.5	run: 7 m.p.h.
13.5	run: 8 m.p.h.
15.0	run: up stairs

Energy Costs of Various Activities *continued*	
METS	**Description**
16.0	run: 10 m.p.h.
1.5	**SELF CARE:** eat (sit)
2.0	self care: groom (wash or shower, shave, brush teeth, apply makeup)
2.5	self care: dress or undress (stand or sit)
1.3	**SEXUAL ACTIVITY** (moderate effort)
2.5	**SPORTS:** billiards, croquet, darts (wall or lawn), play catch (football or baseball)
3.0	sports: bowling, play Frisbee, golf (miniature, driving range), pitch horseshoes, shuffleboard, volleyball
3.5	sports: archery, golf (using power cart)
4.0	sports: coach football, soccer, basketball, baseball, swimming; ride horseback, ping pong, T'ai Chi
4.5	sports: badminton, social singles or doubles; basketball, shoot baskets; golf (walk and carry clubs)
5.0	sports: children's games (e.g., hopscotch, dodge ball, tetherball); skateboarding; softball or baseball, fast or slow pitch
6.0	sports: basketball, nongame; fencing; tennis (doubles)
7.0	sports: broomball, kickball, racquetball, soccer, roller skate, tennis
8.0	sports: basketball game, football (touch, flag), handball (team), hockey (field or ice)
10.0	sports: karate, kick boxing, jump rope
12.0	sports: handball, inline skating (rollerblading)
1.0	**TRANSPORTATION:** ride in car, truck or bus
2.0	transportation: drive auto or light truck
2.5	transportation: ride motor scooter or motorcycle
2.0	**WALK:** around house, less than 2 m.p.h.
2.5	walk: push or pull stroller with child or walk with children, bird watching
3.0	walk: downstairs, walk the dog, walk 2.5 m.p.h.
3.5	walk: carrying infant or 15-pound load (suitcase); walk 3 m.p.h., moderate pace

Energy Costs of Various Activities *continued*

METS	Description
4.0	walk: pushing wheelchair, nonoccupational setting; walk to work or class
5.0	walk: carrying 1- to 15-pound load upstairs; walk 4 m.p.h., very brisk pace
6.5	walk: march rapidly, race
7.0	walk: backpack; climb hill with load up to 9 pounds
8.0	walk: carrying 25- to 49-pound load upstairs; climb hill with load 21 to 42 pounds; walk up stairs or climb ladder; walk 5 m.p.h.
3.0	**WATER ACTIVITIES:** canoe or row, 2 to 4 m.p.h., light effort; sail; surf (body or board)
4.0	water activities: paddle boat; swim (tread water), moderate effort; water aerobics
5.0	water activities: kayak, snorkel
6.0	water activities: water ski, swim (lake, ocean, river) or leisure
7.0	water activities: canoe or row, 4 to 6 m.p.h., moderate effort; canoe with portages; scuba dive; swim freestyle or backstroke laps, slow, moderate or light effort
8.0	water activities: swim crawl slow (50 yards/minute), moderate or light effort; water jog
10.0	water activities: swim freestyle laps, vigorous effort; swim breaststroke
11.0	water activities: swim butterfly; swim crawl fast (75 yards/minute), vigorous effort
12.0	water activities: canoe or row, >6 m.p.h., vigorous effort
3.5	**WINTER ACTIVITIES:** snowmobile
6.0	winter activities: ski downhill, moderate effort
7.0	winter activities: ice skate, ski jump (climb up carrying skis), sled, toboggan
8.0	winter activities: ski cross-country (4 to 5 m.p.h.), moderate speed and effort; snowshoe

Adapted from "Compendium of Physical Activities: Classification of Energy Costs of Human Physical Activities" by B.E. Ainsworth, W.L. Haskell, M.C. Whitt, M.L. Irwin, A.M. Swartz, S.J. Strath, W.L. O'Brien, D.R. Bassett Jr., K.H. Schmitz, P.O. Emplaincourt, D.R. Jacobs Jr. and A.S. Leon. Published in Medicine and Science in Sports and Exercise, *volume 32, pages S498–S504. Used with permission.*

Cardiorespiratory or Endurance Activity

Although many people call it cardiovascular conditioning, this dynamic activity actually involves not only your heart and circulatory system but also your lungs and respiratory system. These two systems continuously work together both to deliver oxygen and nutrients to your body's tissues and to remove wastes from those tissues. As your large muscles engage in rhythmic, repeated movements—when you walk briskly, jog, inline skate, climb stairs, do aerobic dance movements, swim, ski cross country, cycle, play racquet sports or jump rope, for example—your body depends mainly on the energy it gets by consuming oxygen.

Your blood delivers oxygen throughout your body. As your pace quickens, your body requires more oxygen and is challenged to meet this need. Your heart beats faster and you breathe more rapidly. As your heart becomes more adept at meeting this challenge, it can become stronger and operate more efficiently. One way to demonstrate that you're working these systems is to measure your pulse rate, which indicates the number of times your heart beats in 1 minute. Compare your pulse rate before and after you exercise. The more demanding your workout, the more your pulse will increase. You can also judge your level of exertion by noting how hard you're breathing.

Monitoring Your Level of Exertion

Although some trainers and fitness experts suggest using your heart rate as an indicator of your exertion level, many cardiologists prefer a so-called rate of perceived exertion scale. This tool helps you determine the intensity of the effort, strain and/or discomfort you feel when you exercise—without any positive or negative value attached.

"People, in my opinion, should pay less attention to heart rates and more attention to how they feel," says Paul Thompson, M.D., director of preventive cardiology at Hartford Hospital in Hartford, Connecticut, and professor of medicine at the University of Connecticut School of Medicine. Cardiologist Gerald F. Fletcher, M.D., professor of medicine, Mayo Medical

Heart Doc Heeds His Own Advice

Claiming to be "a little over age 65," cardiologist Gerald F. Fletcher, M.D., professor of medicine, Mayo Medical School, Mayo Clinic, Jacksonville, Florida, heeds the advice he and other experts give by fitting running into his busy schedule nearly every day. Whether he runs with his wife—his nurse—or alone, Fletcher manages to do 15 miles a week.

What keeps him committed to exercising? "I want to stay healthy, so I can enjoy life," he says.

School, Mayo Clinic, Jacksonville, Florida, and lead author of the American Heart Association's recent scientific statement on exercise standards, agrees. Incidentally, cardiologists also note that, because beta blocker medications lower heart rates, a simple heart rate calculation is not an accurate indicator of exertion rate for people taking these drugs.

Studies clearly demonstrate that rate of perceived exertion is a reliable way to judge your effort. This method also takes into account individual differences, unlike the simple formula for heart rate levels (see sidebar). Furthermore, individuals are fairly consistent from one time to another, when they're tested, in indicating their rate of perceived exertion.

While some trainers suggest using a scale of 1 to 10, the standard scale recommended by Fletcher and others is the Borg Scale, developed by Swedish psychologist Gunnar Borg, which ranges from 6 to 20 points. A rating of 6 indicates no exertion and 20 indicates maximum exertion. Stages of light exertion range downward from 11, with exertion becoming somewhat hard at 13, heavy at 15 and very hard at 17. Generally, experts say aerobic conditioning starts when the perceived level of exertion is from 12 to 14.

Aerobic activity—that which is rhythmic, at least moderately vigorous and continues for 10 minutes or more at a time—can help strengthen your heart and improve the ability of your body to use oxygen from the air you breathe. But you needn't become an Olympian. Studies show that your greatest improvement occurs as you move from sedentary to moderate levels of aerobic activity, training at least 2 days a week for a cumulative 20 to 60 minutes. Interestingly, people who train much more than 5 days a week don't see a dramatic improvement—and sometimes none at all—as higher levels can increase your risk of injury. However, some people still train nearly every day, in order to maintain their weight or to lose additional pounds.

Quick Walking Pace Check

Want to know if you're walking briskly enough to benefit your heart and lungs? Here's a quick way to tell, offered by the American College of Sports Medicine.

Count the number of steps you take in 1 minute (step with the right foot, then left foot = two steps). For most people, walking 30 minutes at a rate of 125 steps per minute is a good aerobic workout. One mile equals approximately 2,000 steps.

Other experts say that if you can't carry on a conversation, you're walking too fast, but if you're able to sing a song, you're moving too slowly.

Determining Your Target Heart Rate

Although many cardiologists would like to dissuade you from using your target heart rate to gauge your level of physical activity, many trainers still use this system. Generally, they recommend exercising at 50 to 75 percent of your maximum heart rate for optimum benefit to your cardiovascular system.

Find your heart rate by placing the tips of your forefinger and middle finger lightly inside your wrist, just below the base of your thumb, over a blood vessel. Count the number of beats in 15 seconds and multiply by four to get your heart rate in beats per minute. Generally, your heart rate rises as you start exercising vigorously.

Your so-called maximum heart rate is 220 minus your age. For example, if you're 50, your maximum heart rate is 170 and your target range for aerobic training (multiplying by 0.5 and 0.75) is 85 to 127. Incidentally, according to the American College of Sports Medicine, aerobic activity at 50 percent intensity for 30 minutes burns between 200 and 250 calories, while aerobic activity at 75 percent intensity for 30 minutes burns approximately 300 to 350 calories.

However, this general method doesn't take into account individual differences or adjustments that your doctor may recommend. If you take beta blockers or any other heart medications—or if you have a heart condition—ask your doctor for a recommendation on exertion levels.

You can also monitor your heart rate with a monitoring device that you wear. Some monitors strap across your chest, while others strap to your wrist. Numbers appear on a digital display. Heart rate monitors are more commonly used by competitive athletes or people whose doctors have specifically advised them to monitor their exertion during exercise.

Take your pulse with your fingertips lightly over a blood vessel just below the base of your thumb.

If you want to gauge your level of activity with a heart rate monitor, wear it all day for several days to get an idea of your normal heart rate range. The monitor can also show you how long it takes, once you stop exercising, for your heart rate to return to normal, a period of time that will probably go down as your fitness increases.

Are you curious about how weight affects your heart rate? Find out, by walking a given distance, both with and without 7.5-pound weights around each ankle.

Choose Your Aerobic Activities

If you select aerobic activities you enjoy or want to learn, you're more likely to stick with them. Eventually, you may include an increasingly wider assortment of activities. This so-called cross-training can work a variety of large muscle groups and provide a more well rounded effect. On the other hand, if you concentrate on one activity, you'll probably see your skill and endurance improve more rapidly and you can more easily see progress. Researchers say which activities you choose matters little to your overall cardiac conditioning—there's benefit in just about anything that gets you moving your large muscles continuously and rhythmically for a period of time.

Think about activities you've enjoyed before—and some you've wanted to try. Look for things you can do frequently—or combine several activities that you can't do as often. If you enjoy cross-country skiing, plan other activities for times when you can't ski—perhaps inline skating, for example. If you like to canoe or row a boat, find other activities for times when you can't get out on the water, maybe a community center where you can use a rowing machine during the cool weather, for example.

If you're elderly or overweight, remember that activities requiring lots of running and jumping cause more injuries than low-impact and non-weight-bearing activities. Experts repeatedly recommend walking—it doesn't require special skills or equipment and has a very low injury rate.

A good aerobic workout starts with 5 to 10 minutes of warm-up activity, then picks up to at least a moderate level of exertion and finishes with another 5 to 10 minutes of cool-down activity and stretches. The middle section with more exertion is the part you will alter as you become better conditioned, either lengthening the time you exert at that level or increasing the intensity. Or perhaps you'll add an additional day of exercise during the week or another exercise break during the day. As you get older it may take longer to increase your level of exercise endurance. Again, listen to your body, and remember that no one knows your body better than you do.

Once you start regular cardiorespiratory activity, it's smart to stick with it. Experts report that missing sessions now and then or reducing the frequency or duration of your sessions for as long as 15 weeks doesn't appear to adversely affect VO_2max, muscular strength or endurance, as long as you maintain your activity's intensity.

However, studies show that your fitness level will drop significantly, if you totally miss just 2 weeks of activity. Missing 4 to 12 weeks will cost you fully half of your original improvement in VO_2max. And, after 10 to 32 weeks of inactivity, you're back at square one.

Resistance or Strength Training

Having strong muscles is another important component of fitness. Even if you don't want bulging muscles—which is called hypertrophy and, incidentally, isn't a necessary outcome of strength training—you probably appreciate it

Special Considerations for Women

Since women's bodies differ from men's bodies, it's not surprising that exercise affects women differently than it affects men. Some differences are probably due to fundamental differences in body composition and structure. For example, Mayo Clinic reports that:

- Women's bodies have, on average, about 11 percent more body fat and about 8 percent less muscle mass than men's bodies have.
- Women's lower average lung capacity is probably due to women having smaller rib cages than comparably sized men have.
- Women's wider pelvises (suited for childbirth) means their femur bones (between hip and knee) are angled differently than men's femurs, altering knee alignment and possibly making women more susceptible to knee pain.
- The typical male's advantage in many aerobic activities may occur because men have greater muscle strength and longer arms and legs.
- Reliance on fat metabolism probably contributes to women's superior endurance in events of longer duration.
- Women also frequently have lower blood pressure and faster heart rates than men.
- And, although women often sense pain sooner than men do, they generally have more coping strategies to better deal with pain.

Although experts really don't know why, rigorous cardiorespiratory conditioning can sometimes cause menstrual irregularities. But it doesn't appear to affect fertility, unless ovulation and menstrual periods completely stop.

If you're pregnant, discuss your activity level with your healthcare provider. While there are some special considerations for pregnant women (see Chapter 8, page 221), it's wise to stay as active as possible throughout your entire pregnancy.

Although there have been comparatively fewer long-term studies to date of menopausal women and exercise, experts haven't found that menopause alters VO_2max or strength responses to exercise training.

If you're female and just beginning an exercise program, you should know that women who initiate activity by participating in high-impact exercise experience more orthopedic injuries of their lower extremities than men do. In fact, these injuries occur about twice as often in younger women and as much as four times as often in older women, when compared to same-aged men. Again, experts believe this may result from differences in body structure. And regardless of whether you're male or female, injury risk increases when you participate in high-impact activities if you're overweight or if you've previously injured the part of your body subjected to added stress.

when you can carry your own groceries into the house and your laundry basket to the washing machine. And, although you may not have to wrestle your dinner entrée to the ground any more, it's helpful—though admittedly not vital—if you can manage to lift or pull your own suitcase with relative ease when you travel.

Modern technology has dramatically reduced your need to use much strength in day-to-day living. Consider the ease with which you bring groceries home from the store or mow your lawn. And when was the last time you had to actually push open a door at the grocery store or get up from your chair to change the TV channel? Yet most experts consider strong muscles an important component of a healthy body. The exercises in this category—called strength or resistance exercises or training, weight training or weight-lifting exercises—can make you stronger and increase your stamina.

With today's modern conveniences, people usually don't think much about strength until they consider whether or not they'll eventually need assisted living or nursing-home care. And truly, at that point in your life, having done resistance exercise can make a huge difference. It may be what enables you to continue living independently.

Secrets of My Favorite Nonagenarian

When Helen died recently, just 2 days shy of 91, I was negotiating with the publisher about writing this book. Helen immediately came to mind as a person who exemplified the lifestyle this book promotes.

I'd interviewed the spry and independent Helen 2 years earlier for another assignment, to glean her sage advice on healthy aging. To my surprise—after all, Helen didn't sport bulging muscles—her recipe included a strength training component, in addition to pulling her own golf cart, which she did at least once every week until she was 90. A widow and cancer survivor, Helen willingly shared her advice, but only reluctantly divulged her age. Here are the highlights of her recipe for successful aging:

Every single morning—without fail—I do exercises for 10 to 15 minutes. I sit in the chair and do scissors with my feet. Then I take the dumbbells in my hands and move my arms up and down, back and forth and in circles. Then I stand and do larger circles. Finally, I stand and hold onto a chair with one hand and move first one, then the other leg, up and down.

I make sure I talk to someone every day, and I try to see people at least three times each day. Every morning I stop at a nearby restaurant for breakfast and coffee.

I take classes through the school district and Elderhostel, and I volunteer at church every week. I've also done a lot of substitute teaching in elementary schools. Until recently, I volunteered weekly in a kindergarten class. I also tutored reading a lot and volunteered for many years at a

Researchers now understand that doing resistance exercise dramatically increases your chance of entering old age with healthy bones. Strength training can help you maintain or lose weight, have stability in your core—or central—muscles and lift your mood. It also enhances your speed, balance, coordination, jumping ability and flexibility.

As resistance exercise improves both your strength and endurance it can also help prevent injuries, especially to your arms, legs and back. Muscular strength enables you to exert force for a brief period of time, something you can measure easily by monitoring your progress in weight-lifting exercises. Muscular endurance, on the other hand, allows you to repeatedly contract or continue to apply force against a fixed object with one or a group of muscles. You can demonstrate this, for example, by doing a number of push-ups to gauge the endurance of your arm and shoulder muscles. Clearly, as you age you can benefit a lot from weight or resistance training, because strength is so crucial to functioning independently.

---

school for delinquent boys.

I'm an active member and have had leadership roles in numerous academic, church and civic organizations. I'm in a golf league, and I play in four bridge groups.

My family is very close knit, and we do many things together. My husband and I had three children and eight grandchildren.

Attitude means a lot to me. I always look on the good side and try to put stress in the back of my mind. Sometimes I have a talk with a real good friend, and I pray a lot. I love to travel.

I keep my mind busy. I read a lot—mostly fiction, and the daily paper, as I have time. I listen to the news, but don't watch a lot of TV. I simply don't have the time.

In order to remember things, I have notepads everywhere, and I always put my keys and other things in the same place, so I can find them easily. I carefully watch the calendar.

When I last spoke with Helen, I inquired about her travel plans—not imagining she'd die in a day or two. She hadn't picked her next destination, she said. On the day she died Helen begged off her weekly golf game, feeling a bit under the weather. After returning several phone calls at her apartment, Helen sat down to rest and died peacefully in the chair.

Given the choice, who wouldn't pick such a last day? Looking back, I have to believe that Helen's active lifestyle enabled her to have more choice in the matter than most of us may have.

Do You Need Those Fancy Machines at the Gym?

Definitely not! There are various ways to do strengthening activities, each with its advantages and disadvantages. Some experts recommend machine training, especially if you're older. They believe the machines make it easier to know how much weight you're moving and to avoid injuring yourself by adding too much weight too quickly.

Some trainers, like Vern Gambetta, who has coached at various levels for over 30 years and has served as the conditioning coach for several professional sports teams, recommend that you train with integrated movements, rather than isolating individual muscles. "Remember that your body is the ultimate free weight," says Gambetta. "Before you add external resistance (weights), you should be able to handle your own body weight in exercises like pull-ups, dips, lunges and step-ups.

"Most machines are designed to isolate muscles and work in single joint, single plane movements," says Gambetta. "That type of strength isn't readily transferred to actual sports and can interfere with your coordination patterns and predispose you to injury. Train integrated movements, not isolated muscles."

You can design an effective strengthening program without machines.

Incorporating Weight Training into Your Program

Regardless of the weight-training program you select, it's important to progress gradually and systematically. Continue your aerobic exercise as planned, but on days when you do both strength and aerobic exercise, save time warming up and cooling down by following your aerobic exercise with strength training, and then stretching. Sports medicine experts note that it's not the amount of weight you move that matters as much as how many times you can move it, and trying to lift too much can easily injure your muscles or make them sore.

You can design your own resistance program at home, using your own body weight and free weights (dumbbells and ankle weights; see pages 145 to 146 for information on selecting this equipment)—or make your own weights by partially filling milk jugs with sand or water or old socks with sand. Or, use the facilities of a nearby gym or health club. You may also find classes through community education programs. If you'd prefer to work alone, it's worth investing in an illustrated weight-training guide or video to work you through the proper positions for each basic exercise.

An important safety note before you begin: the single greatest cause of musculoskeletal injury that occurs with resistance training is a previous injury. If you've been sedentary until now, it's especially important to go slowly to avoid excessive strain on under-worked muscles and joints—especially if you have arthritis, according to Robert J. Dimeff, M.D., medical director of sports medicine at The Cleveland Clinic. Dimeff notes that arthritic joints that aren't painful with minimal activity can flare up with strength training, so if you have osteoarthritis it's best to check with your physician before you begin.

Plan to include exercises targeting your major muscle groups—your back, shoulders, chest, abdominal muscles, thighs, hamstrings, buttocks, triceps, biceps and calf muscles. Begin with the large muscles first (chest, back, quadriceps), then progress to the smaller muscles. Eventually, you may build up to sessions of 20 to 30 minutes two or three times a week, giving your muscles time to recover on the days between workouts. Many people alternate days between areas of the body—focusing on the upper body one day, lower body another and abdominal or trunk muscles on the third day.

Yes, Women Need Resistance Training, Too

Women need resistance training as much as men do—if not more. Because osteoporosis causes women to lose bone at an accelerated rate—and because after menopause, women have heart disease rates equaling those of men—weight or resistance training is very important for women.

Resistance training can stimulate bone growth, promoting activity in the bone cells as the contracting muscle causes the tendon to which it's attached to pull on the bone. As you target your workout, be sure to include those bones most likely to be fractured: the hips, spine and arms. Resistance training even increases cardiovascular endurance.

Flexibility Training

Flexibility simply describes how far and how easily you can move your joints, and it's closely linked to the tightness of your muscles. When you talk to experts about flexibility training, it doesn't take long to find some key differences of opinion. Here again, it's good to know what the experts say, but ultimately base your decisions on your experience with your own body, which no one knows as well as you do.

Few people dispute the idea that you should move your joints and muscles through their full range of motion—that is, the distances and directions that you can move them—every day, if possible. If you neglect to do that for a long enough period of time, chances are good that your range of motion will decline. "Move it, or lose it" is definitely true, when it comes to flexibility and range of motion.

The experts agree that it's important to warm up before you work on flexibility. Stretching cold muscles can actually damage them. Experts are unanimous in saying that stretches should be gradual and gentle, not bouncing, and that you should only stretch to the point of resistance. If it hurts, you're pushing too hard.

If tight muscles inhibit your range of motion in a joint, other muscles attempt to compensate. Unfortunately, muscles and tendons frequently lose their elasticity with age. Gambetta lists five factors that determine your flexibility:

- the elasticity and length of your muscles and tendons—which is partly genetic, but also something a well-designed training program may alter
- a joint's structure—your shoulder is inherently more flexible, for example, than your knee or hip
- your basic level of coordination and motor control of your joints
- your fitness level
- your psychological or emotional state—you're usually less flexible when you're "up-tight" or tense

Gambetta further stresses the importance of comparing both sides of your body—and comparing yourself only to yourself, as your training progresses, rather than comparing yourself to others. The goal he emphasizes in flexibility training is to move your joints through as great a range of motion as you can control. He also believes there's little correlation between static flexibility—being able to touch your toes, for example, which is often recommended as a test of flexibility—and dynamic performance. Incidentally, Gambetta notes that excessive looseness can be a liability in sports requiring rapid changes of direction and acceleration: basketball, tennis or soccer, for example.

The greatest controversy arises when you consider whether or how much flexibility training can reduce injuries or muscle soreness. In a recent report, Australian researchers who reviewed seven studies on flexibility discovered that stretching before or after a workout had such a tiny effect on alleviating muscle soreness that it was too small to be considered worthwhile for preventing muscle soreness. They conclude that, "the average subject would need to stretch for 23 years to prevent one injury."

However, Stephen Rice, M.D., Ph.D., a primary care sports medicine specialist and spokesperson for the American College of Sports Medicine, notes that even if it doesn't prevent soreness and injury, "flexibility is an important part of being fit, just like muscle strength, endurance and aerobic capacity." And Rice, who's 56 years old and plays recreational softball, notes that he always stretches before games and hasn't yet injured a muscle.

American College of Sports Medicine experts offer several possible explanations for the Australian study's results. First, being flexible doesn't mean that a muscle can absorb greater force. Many sports injuries don't result from over-stretching a muscle, but occur while a muscle is moving within its normal range of motion. Because stretching may also increase your tolerance for pain, you may not heed the pain warning that normally might cause you to stop stretching a muscle far enough to injure it. And, they say, mild stretching also weakens a muscle for about 15 minutes, during which time you may be at greater risk of injury if you stretch it.

Balance—It's Part of Every Step You Take

You probably never stopped to consider how vital balance is, but remember that a large part of your walking gait is one-legged—that is, you're standing on one leg, while the other is moving. "Think of your body as a pin balancing on its tip," says balance expert, physical therapist Robert H. Whipple, M.A., clinical assistant professor, University of Connecticut Health Center and physical therapist at Bethel Nursing and Rehabilitation Center. "Your body is constantly falling. When you stand, you're in perpetual motion. When your brain gets the message from sensors throughout the skin on the soles of your feet and strength receptors in the muscles of your calf that you're falling, it sends commands to your muscles to contract and halt the tipping. It takes less than a split second for a message to get to your brain and be acted upon by your highly responsive, workhorse calf muscles at the back of your legs to pull you back up into a neutral position."

Of course, the process of maintaining your balance is more complicated and involves your eyes as well as your ears. And numerous medical conditions, herbal preparations and medications can also affect your balance. If you experience a sudden change in your balance, contact your healthcare provider. Be sure to mention any medications, herbal products or supplements you use.

How to Keep—Even Improve—Your Balance

Here's how to quickly check—and improve—your balance. Stand near a counter, table or chair to steady yourself as needed.

■ Raise one leg off the ground slightly as you balance on the other leg. Time how long you can stand on each leg (balancing ability isn't necessarily symmetrical). Try the same thing with your eyes closed.

■ Stand with your feet side by side, touching. Now slide one foot forward half the length of your foot (called a half-tandem), with the heel of your forward foot pressed into the instep of your back foot and the bulge behind your big toe on your back foot touching the instep of your forward foot. Time how long you can hold this position.

■ Now time yourself standing with one foot directly in front of the other, toe to heel (called a tandem and much more difficult).

Walking is one of the best ways to improve balance and it strengthens many of the muscles you use for balancing. These two exercises can also

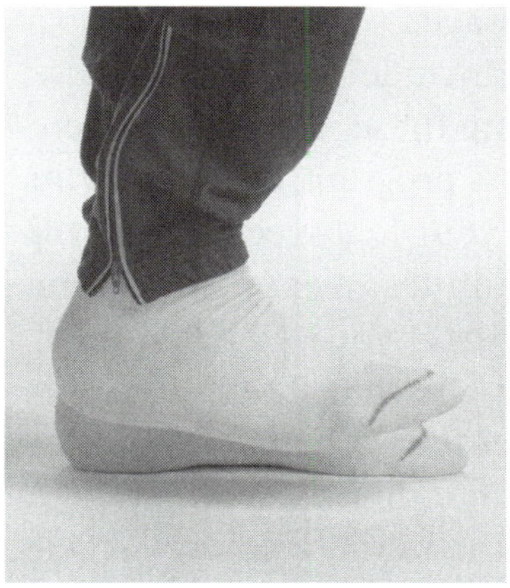

Time yourself balancing on each leg.

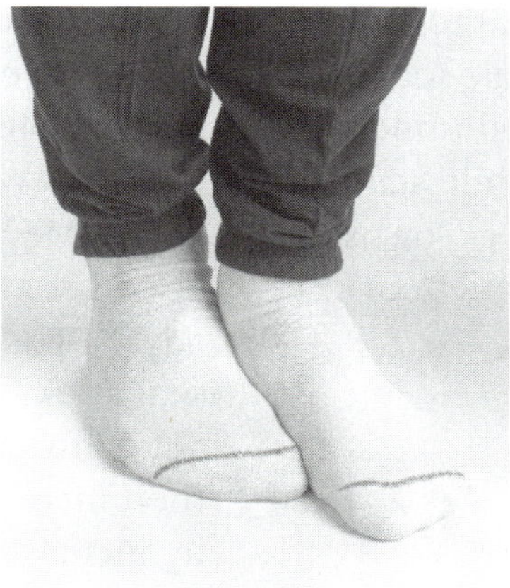

The half-tandem is slightly more challenging.

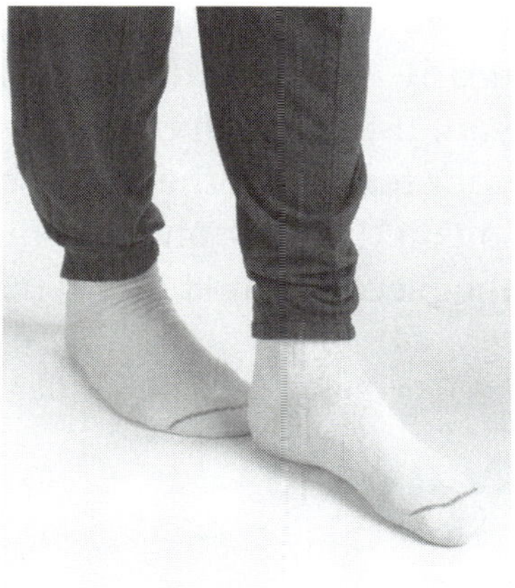

Stand near a table or chair to attempt the tandem.

improve your balance.

1. Toe raises (to strengthen muscles in your shin that keep you from falling backward or from tripping, if your toes lag behind the rest of your foot as you walk)—Stand near a corner wall, with your heels 6 to 8 inches from the wall. Simultaneously lift the fronts of both feet as high off the floor as possible—probably 2 to 4 inches; then lower them. Do 2 sets of 20 reps nearly every day. If this becomes simple, add resistance by pushing down on the tops of your toes with a sponge mop.

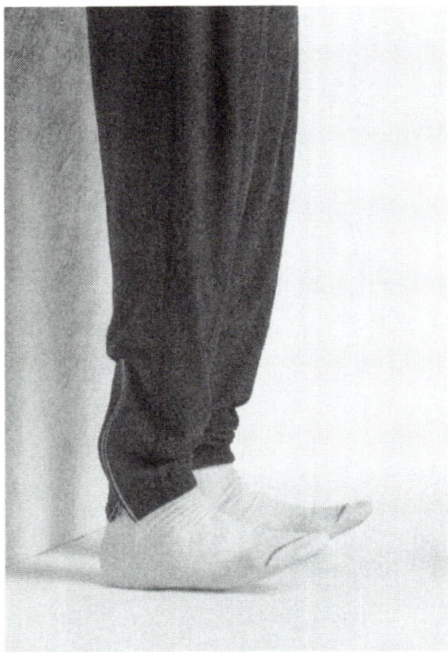

Stand near a wall for toe raises.

Daily heel-ups can ease pain and improve balance.

2. Heel-ups (to strengthen the calf muscles that propel you forward, give spring to your knee, support your ankles and enable you to climb stairs)—Place your hands above a counter, tabletop or chair back for support. Slowly rise to your toes, keeping your body straight. Hold for a count of 3 and then slowly return to a normal standing position. Relax your muscles completely between repetitions. Repeat, with your eyes closed. Gradually build up to 20 reps nearly every day. If this is simple for you, use a 2-inch piece of wood under your toes or do the exercise while standing on the floor on only one leg—or use the piece of wood under that one foot.

Make Your Goals Specific—Now

You've had the opportunity to think in general terms about your goals. Now make sure your goals are specific and recorded. Ideally, your goals will include something that focuses on aerobic activity, at least one kind of resistance work and ongoing ways of building flexibility. Allow space to add others as they occur to you. The more specific your goals, the more likely you'll achieve them. Some goals should be long-term—wanting to lose a specific amount of weight in time for your reunion next year, for example. Or you may want to lower your blood pressure or cholesterol levels, in an attempt to reduce your medication dosage.

Be sure to include short-term goals, as well. Meeting these, especially when you're new to a program, will keep you going. Maybe your first week's goal will be to get 10 minutes of exercise on one day—a good goal if you've been quite sedentary, and one that should look doable now. Meet that goal several times, then increase it, either by adding time or by increasing the number of days you'll do it. When you break your goals down into manageable pieces, you set yourself up for success, which keeps you going in a program.

Goals often include measurable details. This makes it easier to know when to move your goal up a notch, gradually increasing the pace of activity, the number of repetitions, length of your session or the number of sessions per week. Don't expand your goals too quickly, but listen to your body. You'll know if you've done too much too soon, and you should avoid injuring yourself.

Tracking Your Progress

It's helpful, especially early in a new fitness program, to track your progress. Records can be as detailed as you like and kept in a book or on the computer—or even jotted on a piece of paper. You can also use a book like *Active Living Every Day: 20 Weeks to Lifelong Vitality* to outline your program and track your progress. Consider including:

- your goals

What's Core Strength?

Core strength or stability is a trendy topic among some trainers. The term refers to strength in your spine and the large muscles in the center of your body. However, although Ray W. Squires, Ph.D., director, Cardiovascular Health Clinic, Mayo Clinic, Rochester, Minnesota, doesn't find the term itself of particular interest, he does believe it's important to strengthen your abdominal and back muscles.

Core conditioning focuses on strengthening the various muscles in your torso, back, hips, inner and outer thighs and chest, rather than focusing on strengthening individual muscle groups (abdominal muscles or biceps, for example). Conditioning the muscles in the center of your body can help treat or prevent back pain and improve posture, balance and stability. It can even help you generate more power, as you use your central muscles more effectively. Core training is based on the concept that when you build a strong core it becomes a sturdy platform from which your arms and legs work, enabling you to walk farther and faster, be a better swimmer or runner or hit a tennis ball more effectively. Core training also emphasizes the role of proper breathing and posture, and seeks to reduce the likelihood of injury.

Exercises to strengthen your core muscles can be as simple as pulling your navel back toward your spine, which strengthens the deep transverse abdominis muscle—whether you're sitting, lying or standing—a classic core exercise. Squires notes that you can also strengthen many of those muscles in your trunk with walking, running, swimming and biking. Core strength may also be improved by other types of exercise such as Pilates and yoga, as well as by weight training.

■ your starting point on any mini-tests you decide to use

■ statistical information—your weight, blood pressure, cholesterol levels, current medications

■ your activity, including the date, type of exercise, distance or duration, how you felt before and afterward

■ names and contact information for people whom you consider resources or boosters

■ obstacles that you may—or do—encounter, and ideas for handling them

Don't let record-keeping enslave you. And don't exercise when you feel you really shouldn't or exceed the amount your body tells you is reasonable. If you need to miss a day—for whatever reason—don't double up on the amount you do the next day. Instead, try to find a time when you can add another session, perhaps on a day

Shaping: Small Steps on the Way to Something Better

"Focus on doing small pieces of something on the way to doing something bigger," urges Bess H. Marcus, Ph.D., coauthor of *Motivating People to Be Physically Active,* clinical psychologist, professor of psychiatry and human behavior and director of physical activity research at Brown University Center for Behavioral and Preventive Medicine at Miriam Hospital, Providence, Rhode Island. Marcus finds this strategy from Learning Theory quite helpful as she works with sedentary people.

"If I suggest that people take 5-minute walks the first week, they'll more often than not come back having taken 10-minute walks," she says. "It's much better than asking them to do 30 minutes and having them come back having done only 5. I'm not asking them to restructure their day." She compares it to suggesting that a smoker switch to a lower-tar-and-nicotine brand or reduce the number of smokes in one day, rather than the "Just do it" message, which Marcus finds less helpful.

And, she says, coercion doesn't work. Being active should be a free choice, not something you do just to please someone else. "Face it. You may need to reengineer your day. You may start with 2-minute walks, building up over time to 5 minutes, then 10. Set realistic short-term goals. Perhaps you can manage 10 minutes of physical activity on three different days this week. If you don't already get that much activity, it's a good goal. Achieving it gives you a sense of mastery and accomplishment—and sets you up for future successes. If you set the bar too high and something causes you not to meet the goal—a cramp, becoming winded or being uncomfortable, perhaps—you may become discouraged and give up. "

when you normally wouldn't exercise as much. Everyone misses planned exercise sometimes. Just continue at your normal pace the next day.

Reward Yourself

Rewards can help propel you toward your fitness goals. One reward will be feeling better when you're more active. Clothes will fit better. You'll have more energy. You may be rewarded when you step on the scale. People will notice at some point and tell you that you look healthier.

But more tangible rewards can help, too. On days when it's hard to see small improvements, something tangible may just keep you going. Just make sure your rewards are consistent with your goals and support you in achieving them. If you want to lose weight, don't reward a week of biking with a big meal.

Marcus recommends giving yourself points for every half hour of activity, with the opportunity to trade points for exercise clothes. Or if you like to read, do it only after you've had a targeted amount of physical activity that day. Congratulate yourself for exercising four of the last six days and treat yourself by calling a special friend who lives elsewhere. Or put a coin into a large jar every day you meet your exercise goals. When the jar's full, use the money to buy yourself something special.

You may also enjoy crossing things off a daily "to-do" list, notes Marcus. "Track your time or your goals," she says. "Meeting goals can be very satisfying. And find someone you care about to be a cheerleader with you—a family member, friend, child or coworker."

Here are some other reward ideas:

- a stop for your favorite gourmet coffee, after a week of walking every morning
- a new T-shirt
- a weekend walk with a special friend on a nearby nature trail
- a dollar in the kitty for a new outfit you'll buy when you lose 10 pounds
- a new pair of walking shoes
- a step counter (it needn't be fancy)
- flowers
- dance or tennis lessons or an aerobics class—or another active class
- $5 toward a special outing or vacation after you've met a monthly goal
- a new CD or tape or player to use as you walk or jog
- a half-day at a spa for a massage and pedicure
- a new haircut at a special salon
- a 3-month membership in a health club, Y or local recreation center

Don't be timid about rewarding yourself—or arranging a reward system with an exercise buddy—you're worth it!

Gregory W. Heath, D.Sc., M.P.H., reviewed chapter 4. He is the lead health scientist, Division of Nutrition & Physical Activity at the Centers for Disease Control in Atlanta.

CHAPTER 5

Finding Time to Get Fit

This chapter is brief, and it has one purpose: helping you find ways to squeeze physical activity into your busy schedule. Keep these two key facts in mind from the outset:

Fact #1: A day is 24 hours—for every single one of us.

Fact #2: The only way you'll find time in your busy schedule to squeeze in physical activity is to make it a priority.

Lack of time is the number one barrier that people mention, when asked why they don't manage to fit physical activity into their schedules. Clinical and health psychologist Bess H. Marcus, Ph.D., professor of psychiatry and human behavior at Brown University Medical School and director of physical activity research at the Brown University Center for Behavioral and Preventive Medicine at The Miriam Hospital, is a great example. She's coauthor with LeighAnn Forsyth, Ph.D., of *Motivating People to Be Physically Active,* and has published over 100 papers and book chapters. If that doesn't sound like enough to keep one person busy, you should know that she's also a wife and mother of two kids, ages 9 and 11. How, you may wonder, can such a busy young woman manage to wedge in any physical activity at all—other than dashing from one place to the next? Here's what she says.

"You have to make time to be more active. Yes, many

people don't necessarily have time to drive to a gym, put on special clothes, exercise for 30 minutes or more, then take a shower and change clothes again. But I don't believe they lack time to accumulate three 10-minute periods of activity in one day. And that's all it takes to have a very good start. If people tell me they don't have time to do that, I ask them if lack of time is truly a barrier—or, perhaps, an excuse."

Marcus talks of "activity snacks," and suggests that you squeeze them in much the same as you squeeze in a mid-afternoon snack of food. To make that easier, she suggests keeping an extra pair of sneakers handy in the car or in your desk. "Make sure you always have the ability available to be active. And the more you can do to be ready for it, the better. Get in 10-minute snacks of exercise throughout the day. When you go to the doctor's or dentist's office, ask how long the wait will be. If it's more than a couple of minutes, go out for a walk rather than sitting and reading magazines in the waiting room. Do the same thing if someone who has an appointment to meet with you cancels or doesn't show up or if you're waiting for a table at a restaurant. Those are often bits of time when you can't really do much of anything else, and you won't work up a huge sweat in a 10- or 20-minute walk. Sure, it's easy to talk yourself out of it, but if you're on the lookout for the spare minutes and have your shoes handy, it's easy to do." Need to get to the airport early to check in? Wear your walking shoes, because airports usually offer great indoor walking spaces. The cumulative effect of several bits of time like that can be significant.

It's also curious, says Marcus, that some people see their children as a hindrance to activity—especially considering how much time they spend chauffeuring them to their physical activities. "How about a brisk walk around the soccer fields, while your

Marcus Juggles Physical Activity in the Mix

Although sometimes it's a real challenge, busy mom and wife Bess H. Marcus—Ph.D., professor and director of physical activity research at the Brown University Center for Behavioral and Preventive Medicine at The Miriam Hospital—manages to squeeze physical activity into nearly every day. Frequently her physical activity schedule revolves around her children's schedules. "My 11-year-old child leaves for school about 45 minutes before my 9-year-old child goes to school," she says. "That's when I use the treadmill or exercise bike. On weekends I try to go to the gym, and I also take classes in weight training."

But Marcus, who particularly enjoys walking or taking an aerobics class with her friend, has learned to be flexible—an approach she recommends. "This weekend, for example," she said, "my kids have three soccer games on one day. But I'll find a way to fit something in, even if it's just walking around the field."

child's team warms up?" she suggests. "While they're at a 30-minute piano lesson, why not walk around the neighborhood near the piano studio?"

Another strategy that works for many of the clients that Marcus has is to pair a sedentary activity with being active. For example, many people find ways to read the paper, a magazine or a book—or watch TV—while getting physical activity. Others don't allow themselves to do that sedentary activity—reading or opening the mail, for example—until they've gotten their physical activity for the day. "If you pair exercise with a leisure activity you perceive as important or enjoyable, it helps make it something you look forward to all day long, rather than one more thing to cram into your busy schedule." An interesting study Marcus and Forsyth mention found that kids who were obese were willing to pedal a stationary bike in exchange for access to their favorite sedentary behavior, usually video games or movies on the VCR. And by putting the stationary bike near the TV set, it's possible to watch a video or your favorite TV show while cycling.

Some turn a sedentary activity into an active one—renting books on tape and only allowing themselves to listen to the tapes when they walk or jog. Or why not use a portable or speaker phone—or one with a long cord—and move around while you talk?

Some people need a daily news fix and discover that, instead of sitting for half an hour or longer in front of the TV, they can listen to the news on the radio while they take their daily walk in the morning or evening—or both. "If you work from 8 in the morning until 8 at night," says Marcus, "you may need to invest in equipment to use at home. If you have exercise equipment, get it out of the spare bedroom and put it near the TV."

Track Your Physical Activity

Tracking your activity may sound tough, but it isn't necessarily. It can be as simple as getting a pedometer and wearing it for a few days, recording the number of steps in a day. If it's tough to imagine how you'll find time to fit in more—or more vigorous—physical activity, Marcus and Forsyth recommend doing your own brief time-and-motion study. This can help you see where you spend your time and where you may find small bits of time you can dedicate to activity. You can do this in a variety of ways. Here's a suggestion, adapted from Marcus and Forsyth.

Track four days: pick two typical days during the week as well as Saturday and Sunday. Use a form like that shown on the following page, making one copy for each day you'll track. Keep the form and a pencil or pen with you, so that you can fill out the form as the day goes on.

Make a slash mark in the appropriate box for each 10 minutes of activity, as shown. At the end of the day, tally the total minutes in each category. If it's too difficult to fill this in throughout the day, pause at midday and at the end of the day to do it. Here are some typical activities of each type:

■ Light: walking a mile in 30 minutes, sweeping the floor or sidewalk, dusting furniture, grocery or window shopping, picking up twigs in the yard, bowling, playing pool or shuffleboard, walking up a flight of stairs at a leisurely pace, yoga

- Moderate: includes many house and yard activities, such as vacuuming, scrubbing floors, washing windows, raking leaves, mowing the lawn, weeding the garden; walking a mile in 15 to 20 minutes; ballroom dancing, playing volleyball or table tennis, golfing without a cart, biking (less than 10 m.p.h.), horseback riding, low-impact aerobics or playing Frisbee, baseball, softball or tennis doubles
- Vigorous: includes running (5 m.p.h.)—whether for a given distance or, for example, to catch a bus, walking uphill, climbing stairs, shoveling snow, chopping wood, shoveling dirt, loading and unloading a truck, laying brick, using heavy tools, pop dancing, playing singles tennis or racquetball, doing dance aerobics, climbing rocks or mountains, jumping rope, playing basketball or soccer, biking (12-14 m.p.h.) or skiing (downhill or cross-country)

Then, when you've tracked at least four typical days (two weekdays and two weekend days), total the amount of light or moderate/vigorous activity in the columns on the next page and calculate the total minutes of activity throughout the day. Use the comments area to note places where you could possibly move activity from light to a more vigorous level or where you could pair activities in order to make room for more vigorous physical activity.

Daily Activity Tracker

Activity	Intensity	10-Minute Periods	30-Minute Periods	Total Minutes
House & Yard Work	Light			
	Moderate/Vigorous			
Occupation	Light			
	Moderate/Vigorous			
Sports & Leisure	Light			
	Moderate/Vigorous			
Walk/Jog	Light			
	Moderate/Vigorous			
Stairs	Light			
	Moderate/Vigorous			

This type of study helps you find what Marcus calls "pockets of time" where you can add activity. "If you sit at your desk for most of an hour and then take 5 minutes to walk to the desk of a colleague, could you combine that with walking an extra loop to the drinking fountain?" Marcus suggests. "Or if you stop at the desks of two different colleagues in two short trips, could you combine those two stops and walk for a longer period of time? Instead of walking to a lunchroom, eating and then walking back—how about walking to pick up lunch and bringing it back to eat, so your walking time is all in one block?" If you walk to mail a letter in the mailbox two blocks away, could you walk six more blocks to the next mailbox?

"Many people simply don't realize they know how to be active," says Marcus. "But if they see their own data they can become quite creative, turning, for example, a window-shopping stroll through a shopping mall into a moderate-activity walk in the mall or a routine ride on an elevator or escalator into stair climbing. Many people have difficulty trying to think of how to add an hour, or even half an hour, of activity to their day. But it's much easier, if they look for ways to expand their shorter activity periods or increase the intensity of their activity."

If your schedule is heavily predetermined during the week and more flexible on the weekends, Marcus suggests looking to the weekends for larger chunks of time to devote to physical

Weekly Activity Tracker

Day of the Week	Date	Minutes of Light Activity	Minutes of Moderate or Vigorous Activity	Total Minutes of Activity	Comments
Sunday					
Monday					
Tuesday					
Wednesday					
Thursday					
Friday					
Saturday					
Weeky notes:					

activities you enjoy. "For many of us, weekends have a different structure," she says. "It may be possible to plan and take a half-hour walk. However, if you're a parent of school-age kids and on duty 24 hours a day on Saturday and Sunday, weekends may be the most difficult time to find time for exercising alone. If that's the case, look for active things you can do together." Many times getting your kids to do active things with you simply requires that you figure out which activities may spark the interest of the kids.

For some people looking for time to exercise, weekends really warrant a second look. Perhaps you enjoy sleeping in on Saturday or Sunday morning, and would only reluctantly give that up. But, just once, try splitting the difference and getting up a little bit earlier to exercise, still sleeping longer than you do during the week. Toss in a load of laundry, and head out the door for a walk or bike ride while that first load washes. You may be surprised how much more alert and energized you are when you return—and you've already started the day's work. Or get up early enough to enjoy the sunrise from a bike or on a jogging path near your neighborhood—it can add a new dimension to your day and energize you at the same time.

The key to finding the time, says Marcus, is that "you need to feel that you're choosing to be active and not doing it only to please someone else. If you feel that you're being coerced, you won't manage to find the time to change to an active lifestyle." And,

Bumping It Up a Notch

As I worked on this chapter I found myself making good use of Marcus's advice. One day, in particular, was jammed with people to contact, lots of work to do and little time to do it. When I first looked up from my computer, five minutes of the hour I had set aside in the middle of my day for biking was already gone. I was torn about whether to even bike at all, knowing that I would need to spend extra time working to catch up for several unanticipated interruptions that had required my attention that morning.

But I only deliberated very briefly, reminding myself that my health is a priority that supercedes work and that missing a few minutes didn't mean I had to skip the rest of the hour I had set aside for exercise. I hurriedly donned my bike shorts, bundled up and headed out on my bike, determined to go as far as I could in half of the time that was remaining and then head back. I rode as quickly as I could, getting extra "push" from an invigorating morning of work. My mind helped drive my legs to pump faster.

Much to my surprise, I ended up biking the distance that usually takes me an hour to ride—in about 52 minutes! Yes, I was sweating and had to wash up and apply deodorant before getting back to work. But I'd used some of my biking time to plot my afternoon work, and I was more efficient, alert and energized after the change of pace the physical exercise brought. And I was pleased that I had just proven to myself that it was possible to compress time and bump my activity level up a notch when I needed to.

Marcus reminds us, it's important to see some short-range benefits when you do squeeze in some activity—like being energized and realizing that you're being a good role model for your friends or family.

Make an Appointment to Exercise—and Keep It!

"Now that my career doesn't depend on physical conditioning, I find it challenging to find the time to exercise," says Nolan Ryan. "My strategy is to write it into my calendar and not book anything to interfere with those times."

The President's Council on Physical Fitness and Sports suggests these techniques for working exercise into your day:

- Get up a little earlier for a physical activity you can enjoy doing in the morning.
- If possible, walk to work—and walk some more, once you get there.
- Use the stairs whenever possible, even if just for part of the distance you're going up (taking the elevator or escalator the rest of the way).
- Walk during your lunch break.
- Catch a ride or take the bus to work—or wherever you're headed—and walk back.

Don't use the closest bathroom, but

Conquer Mt. Everest

Here's a fun challenge, mentioned by Marcus and Forsyth, for you to try, either solo or with friends.

Mt. Everest is 29,028 feet high. Most office buildings have 13 feet between floors. (Or, you can pick another large mountain or building—or a local landmark.) Once you know the distance between floors, calculate how many times that distance goes into the number of feet of the object you've selected to climb. You can also do this in your home, measuring the height of one step in your staircase and multiplying by the number of stairs to calculate the number of feet between floors; then divide that distance into your target structure.

Set a target date for your trek to arrive at the summit, and calculate how many flights of stairs it would take to get there by that date. You can use this with friends, neighbors or people at work—either individually or by forming teams. Or, simply challenge yourself. Track ongoing progress on a chart.

A team of four, for example, would take 93 days to reach the summit of Mt. Everest, climbing six floors per person per day, if one person climbs an extra floor just one day. (29,028 feet ÷ 13 feet = 2,233 floors; 2,233 floors ÷ 4 teammates = 558 floors per member; 558 ÷ 6 floors per day = 93 days + 1 additional floor) opt for one that requires you to walk a bit. If you care for children or grandchildren, take them with you to a high school track and let them play in the center of the track while you walk, jog or bike. Before you take out the car for a short trip to the store or library, pause to ask yourself if you could find the few extra minutes it would take to walk, jog or bike there.

Double Up for Twice the Bang

Some people find it stressful to double up activities. You may, for example, want to listen very intentionally to the birds, stream or other sounds in the natural environment around you as you walk—and not have headphones or a cell phone at your ear. And some research shows that when people attempt to do two things simultaneously, they frequently don't really save time—or they may not do either very well. And be aware of safety concerns that may enter in, as well—especially, for

---

It Truly Is a Matter of Priorities!

My friends David and Carolyn Poulter, both very busy people, manage to fit a fair amount of physical activity into their lives. When I asked David how a busy person finds time to exercise, his reply was, "How can anyone *not* find time to exercise?"

Although he works full time as a physical therapist and clinic director—and teaches internationally—David puts exercise high on his list of priorities. He's often up very early so that he can work out 45 minutes before work, while viewing the tape of an hour-long TV program that aired as he slept the previous night (fast-forwarding through the commercials). At work he carves 40 minutes out of his lunch time to exercise at a nearby health club, and frequently takes his bike out for a ride when he gets home from work or on the weekends.

David also manages to bike a fair amount in distant locales, when he travels to give his seminars. "I usually choose hotels with gyms, and many have pools, as well. The last hotel where I stayed had a poor gym, but I used the stepper machine. If I don't have facilities at my hotel, I usually run up and down the fire stairs or I run outdoors. And, if nothing else is available, I find a local gym."

Carolyn, a nurse and personal trainer, says she uses a lot of psychological trickery to coax herself into activity when she might not feel like exercising. "I tell myself that I'll just work out for 10 minutes. Invariably, I end up working out a lot longer," she says. "Sometimes, when I think I don't have time or I'm not motivated, I just put my workout gear on, not planning to work out, but I usually end up doing it, anyway.

example, if you're wearing a headset and can't hear traffic while you jog in the streets.

However, other people find that doubling up activities makes time for exercise in a day where it doesn't look like there will be time. For them, it's a two-for-one exchange. Instead of choosing between touching bases with a close friend or taking a walk, they do both—either in person or by cell phone. (It's even easier to walk and talk on the phone if your phone has a headset.) If you're just getting used to thinking about exercising, why not try doing exercises just during the commercials of your favorite TV shows? Marcus suggests inventing your own impromptu aerobic dance routine in front of the TV.

Or, if you ride the bus, subway or train, here's a wonderful balance exercise you can do as you travel. This suggestion comes from balance specialist and physical therapist, Steven L. Wolf, Ph.D., Catherine Worthingham Fellow of the American Physical Therapy Association and professor in the department of rehabilitation medicine, Emory University School of Medicine. As you ride, stand near a vertical pole and try to

---

"I know that, even if I don't have the time, I'll get a lot more done if I work out. On days when I don't work out, I seem to get nothing done. I eat more. And I feel like doing nothing. In fact, the less I do, the less I want to do. But my health is more important than just about anything. If I'm not balanced, no one else around here will be, either."

Sometimes Carolyn pencils her workout times into her calendar, just like a business appointment. When her workday starts at 6 a.m., Carolyn frequently gets up very early, so she can exercise before work. "I often hate getting started, but afterwards I'm really glad I did it," she says. She also notes that most people find it easier to get their exercise first thing in the morning. "Otherwise, too many things come up that provide excuses for not finding the time."

Carolyn's games also show up in her approach to housework. "Sometimes I try to do things at fast speed. Or, if I have several things to take upstairs and put away, I'll take them one at a time, so I end up making a number of trips up and down the stairs."

Carolyn frequently exercises while doing household tasks. She may perform squats or lunges or rhythmically pull her navel in toward her spine while she does dishes or talks on a mobile phone, going to the refrigerator to do 10 biceps curls with a gallon of milk, first in one hand and then the other. Carolyn also has a magazine rack near her workout area. She says she reads a lot while working out and enjoys accomplishing two things at once.

Although Carolyn and David model active lifestyles for their two children, they don't coerce them. Lauren, a junior in high school, hasn't really found a lot of ways to fit exercise into her busy academic, social and work schedule—right now, it's not a priority. Nathan, now 12, on the other hand "is never still," his mother says.

Practice balancing while riding a bus or train.

keep your balance without holding on. Keep your hand poised to grasp the pole if you need to, in order to remain upright. Challenge yourself to see how long you can maintain your position unaided by the pole. If that's too simple for you, try it with your eyes closed. If it's too difficult, try it with your feet a little farther apart, which increases your foundation, hence your stability.

Stuck in your car in traffic? Make good use of that time, as well. Some people keep hand weights in the passenger seat just for such occasions. Others work on the abdominal strengthening exercise Carolyn Poulter mentioned: slowly pulling your navel in toward your spine, hold briefly, then release. You can also use the time to work on your relaxation breathing, slowly inhaling, then exhaling. Try to work up to a 10-count each way. It also can make dealing with traffic much less stressful.

If the transition from your daily activity to your evening activities usually leaves you shortchanged for exercise, try taking half an hour before making supper to go for a walk or a bike ride. And, if you have kids or grandkids, take them along or encourage them to join you. If they're not interested in walking or biking with you but are old enough to help out, ask them to start supper while you walk or bike.

Restructure Your Weekend

Does your weekend begin with an inaudible "crash" on Friday? For many Americans, Friday night marks the start of a weekend slide from health, highlighted by overindulgence in food and drink and a shortage of physical activity. You can change the tone of your entire weekend—and feel much better by Monday morning—if you build your weekend around activity, or at least incorporate activity into your other weekend activities. If you want to get together with friends, why not ask them to join you for something active? Or, if you're going to a movie, concert or play, why not go for a walk beforehand?

Many families make an effort to spend some time together on one weekend day. Instead of renting a video or doing something else sedentary, why not spend that time doing something active together? Depending upon the age and ability levels of your family members, a number of options might be doable and fun: taking advantage of family night at a local pool, getting together with another family to play ball, taking a bike hike, going dancing or roller skating. Or how about a picnic and swim at a nearby beach? Or a cross-country ski outing—or snowshoeing in an area park preserve? If you have friends over for dinner, how about suggesting that they bring walking shoes for a pleasant walk either before or after dinner? Is the basketball court at your neighborhood park empty? Why not challenge friends of the family or neighbors to a friendly basketball game? None of these options need to consume a lot of money or prep time, and they serve a social function as well as getting you moving.

Your Employer May Be Willing to Help You Find Active Time

Employers can be supportive of their employees' efforts to get physical activity in a number of ways. Some employers compensate employees for health-related activities, whether it's a membership at a health club that your doctor recommends or weekly Weight Watchers meetings. And you may find, when you talk with your employer about your desire to fit in more activity, that there are more options for flexibility in your schedule than you'd imagined. If you work away from home, consider for a moment your transit time to and from work. If you usually commute during rush hour, think about whether you could buy some time by slightly altering your routine. Could you get a jump on the rush, arrive there earlier by heading in before the traffic rush, and then use the extra time for a walk near work? Or, at the end of the day, how about getting some exercise before you start driving, enabling you to unwind a bit and miss the worst of the traffic?

Some people work out at a health club near their place of work. Others go for a walk or bike ride immediately after work and then head home. Still others may take a break from work late in the afternoon to work out, returning to

Friday: Cook's Night Out

For years Friday night has been "cook's night out" at our house. If we have other plans, my husband and I may grab a quick bite beforehand, or if there's more time, we may enjoy a more leisurely supper at a local establishment.

Since we've tried to "up" our activity level the past several years, we've added a new dimension: during the months when daylight and the weather allow, we often plan our supper destination within biking distance of our home. After we've biked there, we not only enjoy lighter fare if we know we'll need to bike home afterward, but we also feel better when we get home. We've eaten supper—and shared a pleasant bike ride, as well. And we enjoy it even more when friends join us for the ride and supper.

work for an hour or two before going home. Or perhaps there's flexibility around the lunch hour. Can you drive in and start working earlier, in order to take a longer time for both exercise and a light lunch in the middle of the day?

Some companies encourage employees to jog together over the lunch hour. Or they suggest that employees hold "walking meetings" when only two or three people are involved, using a tape recorder, if needed, for note-taking. If you normally take a taxi or bus to meetings nearby, allow a little extra time and

If You Want to Get Something Done, Just Ask a Busy Person

When Lana, now 33, accepted a job in corporate tax preparation 2 years ago, it was the first full-time indoor desk job she'd had. Previously she'd had major responsibility for a shipping and receiving department and spent a fair amount of time outdoors moving around: running forklifts, loading machinery onto flatbed trailers and handling incoming and outgoing shipments. "I've always needed to be moving," she said. She was nervous about accepting a job that would require her to sit indoors for 8 hours a day.

However, Lana manages to find ways to move around, even in her sedentary job. "As I work on each form that I must complete, I need to get up and make two trips to the copier. And I use every other opportunity I can find to move around in the office," says Lana, who often opts for a walk up a nearby hill over her lunch break rather than eating lunch, especially during the summer months.

Realizing that she'd miss being outdoors, Lana signed up as a volunteer for a home and outdoor maintenance service, sponsored by the United Way and her state, that enables elderly people to stay in their homes. She's assisted 10 ladies for 2 years now—mowing lawns, raking yards, shoveling snow, trimming shrubs and handling other miscellaneous tasks, in addition to caring for her own home and yard. Last year she also played in a weekly volleyball league, and some weeks plays volleyball one additional night, as well.

When she married Greg last summer, Lana also became a part-time mom to his two kids. But that hasn't meant she's given up her active lifestyle. "I try, in the evenings, to get out before dark and walk," she says, noting that she prefers the serenity of the cemetery nearby over the city noise to which she hasn't yet grown accustomed after moving to the city from a more rural area. "It's 1.2 miles from my house to take one loop around the cemetery. So, if I do that twice, I'm walking a couple of miles," she says. "And, as I walk through the cemetery, if I see that a wreath or vase has toppled over, I'll pick it up and set it back where it belongs."

walk there, saving some money—and maybe even some time.

Other employers purchase small lockers and place them near a restroom, so that employees who work out before beginning—or in the middle of the day—can freshen up before returning to work. Still others encourage heavy-duty workouts, like the National Institutes of Health, which installed showers for employees to use.

Some employers encourage bikers in a variety of ways, realizing that each employee who bikes in to work means there's one less space filled in the parking lot. If there's no bike rack at work, ask if one could be installed in a lighted area near a door (some are placed in covered employee parking ramps). Some employers encourage bikers to adjust their working hours, so they can arrive and depart at the times that are not peak times for car traffic coming and going. And now more cities make it possible to use the bus or rail car one way and bike the other direction by providing bike racks on transit vehicles. If you don't want to bike to work, you can ride the bus in and take your bike, bringing along a change of clothes for the bike ride home.

Think Outside the Box

If you care for children during the day and are exhausted by suppertime, why not take turns swapping child care with a neighbor or friend so each of you can exercise? Or look for an active tot-adult class you can take with your child or grandchild. Letting kids see you being active models an active lifestyle. That's the best way you can teach children to be active.

If you have teenagers who simply aren't interested in joining in on something active, ask them to help by taking on more of the household tasks, giving you more time for exercise. Ask what else your kids treasure and would be willing to barter with you to get—perhaps greater use of the car?

Bess H. Marcus, Ph.D., and Marvin A. Brooks, M.D., reviewed chapter 5. Marcus is professor and director of physical activity research at the Brown University Center for Behavioral and Preventive Medicine at The Miriam Hospital. Brooks is a family practice physician.

CHAPTER 6

Getting Started

If you're this far into reading this book—or even just skimming it, chances are good you're at least curious about whether you can and will follow through to attain some reasonable level of fitness. You realize you'd benefit by improving your fitness level. It's great if you've formulated at least a few goals to get you going. You realize that fitness is multifaceted and that various types of physical activities have specific consequences, and you may have given at least some thought to finding time to devote to improving your fitness level. So, let's get going. Remember, there's benefit to any level of exertion, as long as you keep the first rule in mind: listen to your body!

Maybe you've stumbled at this point before and find the next step just too big. You can't fathom an entire program. Well, don't worry. You don't need to think in terms of an entire program. And even if you had a complete personalized program, it would inevitably need changing and adjusting along the way. And don't assume you need to go right out and buy a lot of equipment or invest significant resources in membership, classes, trainers and clothing.

Start Where You Are

Start by making the most of any activity you already have in your repertoire—today! If possible, just bump up the level a bit. When you do something active, try to do a little bit more—or do it a little longer or with a little more intensity. Just activate!

If your activity level truly is next to zero (you did get out of bed, didn't you?), try for a 5-minute walk today. When you pick up the paper at the front door or bring in the mail, walk to the end of your block and back—or up and down a flight of stairs in your building. Don't worry about going fast. If doing that doesn't cause any pain or other bad effects, could you make it a habit? After you do that for a while, maybe you could go all the way around the block or up and down several flights of stairs.

If you don't live someplace where you can walk around the block—for whatever reason—how about adding that little bit of walking when you go somewhere else to do something regularly? Could you add the walk before you go into the grocery store or work—or any other place that you visit at least once a week? You'll find, once you start looking for times to add in a little bit of exercise, that they're there.

If you already get activity somewhat regularly, tweak it a bit. If you're a walker, take one block at a faster pace or, if you walk on a track, do half a lap backwards. Find a flight of stairs—at your house or apartment, work or a public building nearby—that you can go up backwards once today or tomorrow. If all the activity you get focuses on your lower body, try doing something with your arms—even if it's just standing up and pretending you're the conductor for the next piece of music that plays on a radio station you enjoy.

Meanwhile, this chapter gives you a number of tools to ease into a lifestyle that's more fit. It will guide you through some activities you may want to incorporate into your normal days and weeks. If you're debating whether or not to buy some exercise equipment, it will help you decide whether you should do that—and how. If you're considering joining a health or fitness club, it will give you a few pointers. As you read this chapter, you'll see that it seeks to be respectful of your time, for you—like most people—have a lot going on in your life.

Workout Schedules

If you flinched or cringed when you read that word "schedules," you're not alone. You can find some very good books that go into a lot of detail proposing schedules for a workout. But becoming fit doesn't require that you have a fancy schedule. It does, however, mean that you'll need to include a variety of activities. Limiting your focus to one type of activity—aerobic conditioning or muscle strength building, for example—means that you'll be well conditioned in one area, but may fall short in others.

Your personal workout schedule (if it can be called that) should be determined by:

- your personal fitness goals
- your present level of fitness
- your health picture
- your interests

Although there's a great deal of variability within any age category, your age may also influence some of the decisions you make about your workout schedule. For example, as you get older you often need to begin new activities more slowly than you could when you were younger. And, of course, because you're not a professional athlete, your personal schedule and convenience are also key considerations in scheduling your physical activity.

Let's get specific and talk about some weekly and daily fitness targets. Given a perfect world, experts say what's best for most people is getting at least half an hour of aerobic activity nearly every day, resistance training 2 or 3 days a week and flexibility exercise and the opportunity to move all of your muscles and joints through their full range of motion every day.

But for now, think about where you are and your vision of where you want to be. Imagine a line from here to there—and start taking incremental steps to get there. Work through the various components of this chapter to give structure to your approach. Remember, it's your body and you're in charge. And, enjoy!

Begin with a Warm Up, End with a Cool Down

Warm Up. Whenever you start moving your body before your muscles are warmed up, it's best to start gradually and build up slowly. When you warm up with moderate activity, your heart rate, breathing rate and body temperature all gradually increase, preparing your body for more vigorous activity. Contrary to what many people formerly believed, this doesn't simply mean doing a few stretches, although once you have your muscles warmed up, stretches can certainly be a worthwhile part of a warm-up regimen. The movements you use to warm up should resemble those you'll use for the activity that follows and should at least warm the muscles that the activity will use. Even if you want to develop your use of explosive energy, you'll reduce your likelihood of injuring your muscles and connective tissues if they're warmed up before you put sudden demands on them.

Plan at least a couple of minutes to warm up—most experts suggest 5 to 10. Gradually pick up the pace as your warm-up progresses, so that you're operating near the level you'll sustain by the time your warm-up is finished. In addition to low-intensity motions simulating those that you'll use in the activity to follow, general warm-ups frequently include movements such as walking or slow jogging, knee lifts, arm circles and trunk rotations.

Cool Down. When you finish the activity you've chosen to follow your warm-up, don't just stand still or sit or lie down right away. Slowing down your rate of exertion gently gives your body time to adjust gradually and helps your heart and blood vessels return to their normal function. It also prevents possibly dangerous drops in blood pressure and pooling of blood that can occur if you suddenly cease activity. Cool-down periods should last at least several minutes, preferably 5 to 10. You can begin by simply slowing down the aerobic activity that preceded your cool-down

Warm-Up Routine

Eventually you may develop your own routine for warming up. Try to include something for all your major muscles and limbs, once a day, if possible. Here are a few examples:

1. **Neck flexion and extension:** Tuck in your chin and bend your head forward, shoulders relaxed; return to upright. Then look to the ceiling and stretch your neck back; return to upright.

2. **Neck rotation:** Without moving your shoulders, chin tucked in, turn your head first to look over one shoulder, then the other.

3. **Ear to shoulder:** Without moving your shoulders, pull your ear to your shoulder, first on one side, then on the other.

4. **Shoulder shrug:** Lift your shoulder straight up toward your ears, tighten, then relax, keeping your neck and head erect.

5. **Thigh front stretch:** Holding a chair or counter for support as needed, use your other hand to pull your foot straight back and up toward your buttocks, without arching your back or bending at your hip. Switch sides and repeat.

6. **Hamstring stretch:** While seated upright, extend one leg and pull your toes toward you, then relax.

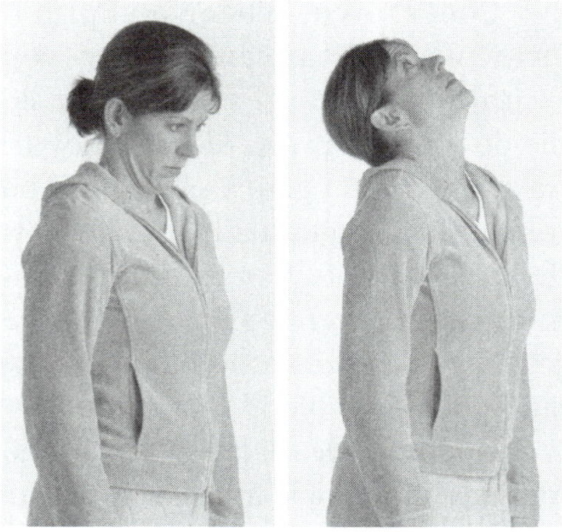

Neck flexion and extension.

Neck rotation.

Ear to shoulder.

7. **Knee hug:** Lying on your back on the floor, use both hands to gently pull one knee to your chest as you bring your forehead toward your knee, then ease back down. Repeat with the other leg.

8. **Lower back relaxation:** From a kneeling position (tops of your feet touching the floor), gently lower your buttocks between your feet, bending forward to extend your arms straight ahead of you on the floor. Hold for 20 to 30 seconds.

Lower back relaxation.

A routine that you do prior to a weight-training workout could add slow movements of the type you'll use, but with only your body weight. A warm-up routine before running could include walking for 2 to 5 minutes, jogging for 2 to 5 minutes and then running full speed briefly.

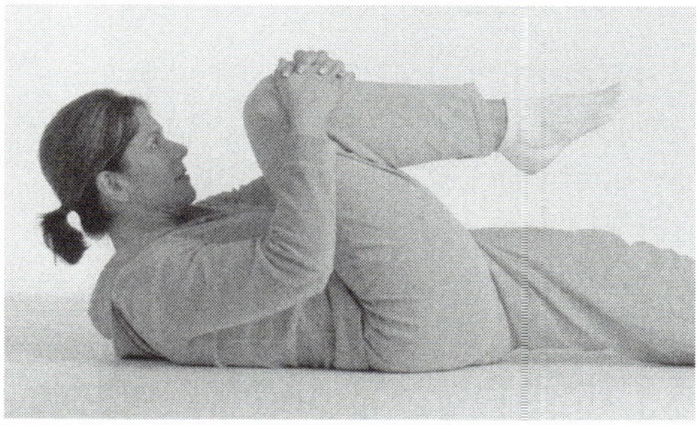

Knee hug.

Shoulder shrug.

Thigh front stretch.

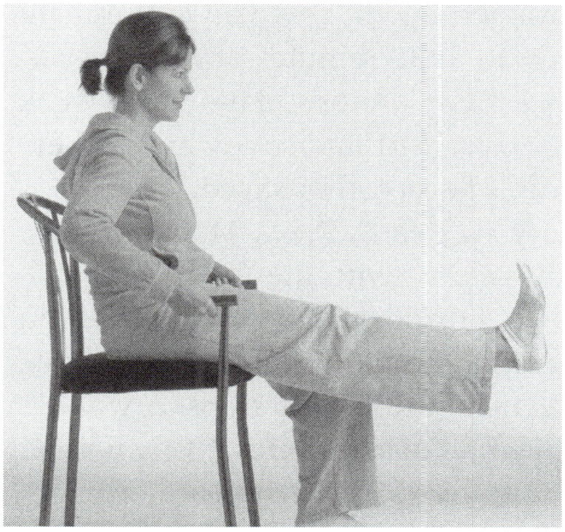

Hamstring stretch.

time or by slowly walking or doing a low-level exercise. Ideally, stretching is best included either just before or after the cool-down period.

Try to warm up and cool down whenever you exercise. It's not necessary, or even desirable, to always include all the components of a good overall fitness program in each activity session. But somewhere in your weekly schedule try to build in time for physical activity that targets cardiorespiratory endurance, muscular strength and endurance and flexibility.

Cardiorespiratory Endurance Activity

Try to find time for at least three sessions of cardiorespiratory endurance activity each week. It would be great if each would last at least 30 minutes. But since even 10 minutes of continuous, rhythmic activity can improve your cardiorespiratory fitness, you can accumulate 10-minute sessions that add up to meet your goals. However, many experts do strongly suggest that you accumulate at least 20 to 30 minutes of cardiorespiratory activity on most days of the week.

"Remember that activity and its benefits can't be stored or saved," says Gregory W. Heath, D.Sc., M.P.H., lead health scientist with the Centers for Disease Control and Prevention Division of Nutrition and Physical Activity. "The benefits tend to be very transitory and you need regular stimulus." When asked how many days a week of cardiorespiratory activity he recommends for most people, Heath doesn't hesitate. "The minimum should be most days of the

Heath: Another Researcher Who Practices What He Preaches

Running—or "some movement faster than a walk"—is generally the activity of choice for Gregory W. Heath, D.Sc., M.P.H., lead health scientist with the Centers for Disease Control and Prevention Division of Nutrition and Physical Activity, who aims to meet the goals he recommends for others. Heath, who's 52, brings a small bag lunch to work, opting to use the bulk of his lunch time to change into running clothes and jog on one or more of the four or five jogger-friendly routes in metropolitan Atlanta that he and others from his office frequently use.

"I run most days—probably 5 or 6 days a week, on average," says Heath. "I go 3 to 10 miles, depending on how much time I have and how well I feel." In nicer weather Heath jogs to the small university campus that's near his office and runs faster intervals on the general athletic fields there.

Weekends usually find Heath running in area parks or from his home and he frequently walks with his family. He usually rests one day each week.

week. You need it every day," he says with conviction. "Would you think about brushing your teeth only 3 days of the week? Benefits are best maintained with regular stimulation. Preferably, you'll stimulate your cardiorespiratory system with regular activity every 24 hours." Heath recommends at least moderate activity most days and suggests going for more vigorous activity on 3 of those days—"a walk-jog combination, vigorous swim or more intense cycling for 20 minutes of sustained activity."

Heath notes that you can be very creative, once you look for ways to weave activity into your routine: walking to public transit or to work or getting together on a regular basis with friends with whom you can share a walk or another aerobic activity you both enjoy, for example.

Noting that the benefits of aerobic exercise go beyond keeping your heart and lungs healthy, Janie T. Clark, exercise physiologist, host of the PBS television series *The Wellness Workout* and author of numerous books on exercising, including *Full Life Fitness: A Complete Exercise Program for Mature Adults*, urges

Betty: Living Her Dream at 81

As a youth, Betty yearned to try numerous activities that were out of reach to her. Although she grew up on the shores of Lake Superior, the lake was too cold for swimming. Schools didn't have swimming pools in those days, and her family never had the funds to explore other options for swimming. She never had a bike, but Betty does remember having a pair of well-worn roller skates.

When she was about 50, a friend asked Betty if she'd ever consider taking swimming lessons with her. Although Betty worked full time and had a family, she quickly accepted. Soon the two pals were joined by other friends who also wanted to swim, and the group met at a local YMCA to swim several times a week. Betty also purchased her first bike as an adult and enjoyed riding it for many years.

Betty, now 81, misses the friends who've dropped out of her group of regular exercisers, but she's determined to keep her own activity level high. Although she doesn't walk as far as she did years ago, when she frequently walked several miles downtown to work, Betty still walks quite a bit—indoors and out-of-doors.

Three days a week Betty faithfully rises quite early and heads for the Y, where she first walks in the gym—one mile in 20 minutes—and then heads for the pool, where she swims 10 lengths, practices water aerobics exercises and strengthens her upper body by doing chin-ups from a swim team diving stand.

The secret of her healthy longevity? "Easy," says Betty. "It's all the activity I get: walking and swimming—and I love working in my yard."

readers to aim for getting aerobic exercise at least three times a week. "When you're just getting started, you may feel much more comfortable with shorter exercise sessions at first, and that's fine. Just plan an easy schedule and stick with it. You'll gradually make gains in endurance and can lengthen your sessions accordingly. Build up to a 20- or 30-minute aerobic segment in small increments as you grow stronger.

"The person who completes 4.5 miles in a workout twice a week is not likely to lose much fat, while the person who completes 3 miles in a workout three times a week will grow lean. Both exercisers are doing 9 miles a week, but the more-frequent exerciser gets a better return for his or her efforts," she says.

What Kind of Cardiorespiratory Activities Should You Select?

It depends a lot on what you like to do and will actually do with some degree of regularity. There are many different activities from which to choose, although some will better suit your individual needs and goals than others. Experts frequently recommend walking briskly, jogging, swimming, cycling, jumping rope, rowing, cross-country skiing, or playing continuous action games like racquetball, handball, basketball or tennis.

Think about activities you've enjoyed in the past and whether or not you may enjoy doing them again, perhaps adjusted somewhat for your age or health status. If you enjoyed swimming or playing basketball on a team during your school years, for example, perhaps you'd like to give one or more of those sports a try again. Check out adult activity options through your area park and recreation department. Or if there's something you've always wanted to do but have never gotten around to actually doing, this is a good time to find out if it's a good activity fit for you.

If you want to improve your cardiovascular fitness or control your weight, use the chart on pages 81 to 86 to consider activities in light of your interests and their MET rate. Note how you can improve the aerobic nature—and caloric expenditure—of various activities by picking up your pace. Or, if you want to try something different, look in Chapter 7 for activities you've considered trying. Read how to get started in an activity and give it a try.

Muscle Use & Energy Expenditure

As you consider various cardiorespiratory activities, think about which muscles the activities use. Activities like swimming and simulated skiing (using a machine) extensively involve both upper and lower body muscles, which is great. You may assume, since these activities use a wider assortment of muscles than running, that it also takes more calories to do them than you if you run at the same level of exertion. However, according to Heath, running recruits a greater muscle mass than swimming or cycling, and therefore can consume more calories at the same exertion rate. This is due, in part, to the effort your body must spend overcoming gravity as your muscles propel you through space when you run. "Antigravity muscle recruitment is significant," says Heath, who notes that the equation also involves your body's biomechanics.

Therefore, although you may use a greater variety of muscles to swim or cycle, running at the same level of intensity actually expends more calories. This may make it a more desirable option for you—if your body doesn't balk at the additional pressure running puts on your bones and joints, compared

Is Faster Always Better?

You can, indeed, ramp up your energy expenditure by increasing the amount and intensity of most aerobic exercise. But it's a mistake to think that faster is always better, when it comes to exercise. Here's some advice from the American College of Sports Medicine.

1. For maximum cardiovascular benefit, select a variety of activities that stimulate your heart, lungs and other muscles.

2. Some activities—walking, cycling, jogging or climbing stairs, for example—have a fairly consistent intensity and energy expenditure that's not dependent on your skill level.

3. Some activities can vary greatly, depending upon your ability level. If you're highly skilled, you can work harder and longer and burn more calories. Examples of this type of activity include aerobic dancing, bench stepping, hiking, swimming and water aerobics.

4. Other activities vary greatly in energy expenditure, as well, depending upon the performance level that's required of you. Energy required for basketball, racquetball, tennis and volleyball can be quite different, depending upon the skill and number of the competitors you face, the pace and the size of the space involved.

5. For many activities you can safely gain additional benefit as you increase the amount and intensity of your exercise. Vary only one thing at a time. If you walk outdoors or on a treadmill, for example, find a hill or increase the grade or resistance. If you cycle, always try to maintain 80 to 100 revolutions per minute; once that's easy, you can safely increase the pedal resistance. If you step up and down a stair, pick up your pace or add a riser to increase the distance you step.

6. Faster is not better, when it comes to flexibility conditioning. In fact, you can injure yourself, simply by progressing too quickly through a stretch.

7. While speed may improve power when you train muscles for strength, it is not helpful when you want to improve muscle endurance.

to swimming or cycling. In general, given the same level of exercise intensity, you'll use more calories performing weight-bearing activities than non-weight-bearing activities. And don't forget, weight-bearing activity helps maintain your bone mass and prevent osteoporosis.

Clark notes that aerobic exercise can be more effective than sit-ups for flattening your abdomen and better than leg lifts for slimming your hips. And she points out that it's not necessary to invest any money or buy any equipment. She suggests designing your own simple aerobic dance workout that you can easily do at home. Here's how:

1. Find some music you like. Change movements according to the number of beats (every 4 or 8 beats, for example) or with each song change (typically about every 3 minutes for pop music).

2. Put together your own routine, beginning with leg movements. Start by walking or marching in place, progress to running in place, doing knee lifts or high kicks, stepping across and in front of (or behind) one foot with the other, touching your heel or toe in front or back, sidestepping.

3. Mix and match arm motions to go with your leg movements: swing your elbows forward and back with a march step; reach out toward the front, side or ceiling; do a front crawl, backstroke or breaststroke motion; add punches (controlled, not just flinging your arms) with an opposite leg motion; push first to one side, then to the other with both arms; do

Blocking Out Daily Exercise Time

When I decided to extend my exercise time a couple of years ago, I found it much easier to stick with a plan if I scheduled three blocks of time for exercise on most days. Otherwise, I seemed to run out of time each day before I got my targeted amount of exercise. I remind myself frequently that this doesn't exclude exercising at other times or substituting a different time when it works out better for me.

Family members know that most days I rise early in the morning while they're still asleep for my first exercise, generally swimming or biking. My clients and other regular business contacts know that I block out time in the middle of my day for exercising, as well. If I haven't gotten in my morning swim, I may do it then. Or I may take out my bike for a refreshing ride to the river trail or to run errands. I may also walk outdoors or, if the weather is lousy or I'm awaiting a callback from someone, I'll use a stationary cycle indoors.

And each evening, regardless of the amount and type of exercise we've gotten during the day, my husband and I end the day by briskly walking 2 miles. (This is contrary to the advice of sleep experts, who caution that exercising close to bedtime may delay falling asleep. We haven't found that to be the case for us.) I find it easier to establish these fixed blocks, filling them primarily with aerobic activities and adding in flexibility and strengthening activities as the day goes on, than to start totally from scratch finding time for and selecting exercises each day.

a jumping-jack arm motion; add claps; raise one hand overhead while touching your heel with the opposite hand.

Don't hesitate to select several kinds of cardiorespiratory activities. Assume it's a given, on any day, that you'll exercise. It's just a question of what sort of activity you'll do and when. And feel free, like Heath, to vary the amount you get from day to day. Getting physical activity into your schedule will be easier if you can find one or more blocks of time during your typical day when you—and the people around you who might be affected by your schedule—know that you plan to exercise.

Muscle Strength & Endurance Training

Helen, the 90-year-old woman you met in Chapter 4, illustrates perfectly how simple muscle strength and endurance training can be. Clearly, says Squires, you need resistance training in order to increase strength.

The older you are, the more benefits resistance training offers—simply because strength is so vital to being able to function independently. Besides making your muscles stronger, strength training can help you burn calories more efficiently and may increase your metabolism while it improves your body's muscle-to-fat ratio.

Actually, resistance training only gained popularity and acceptance in the last 30 years or so, according to Jay Hoffman, Ph.D., associate professor in the Department of Health and Exercise Science, College of New Jersey, Ewing, New Jersey, member of the American College of Sports Medicine and the National Strength and Conditioning Association and author of *Physiological Aspects of Sport Training and Performance* (Champaign, Illinois: Human Kinetics: 2002), an excellent book for learning more about the science behind resistance training.

Before that, resistance training was discouraged, as it was thought to limit range of motion and decrease athletic performance. However, in addition to simply enabling you to do everyday tasks, strength training is helpful for many activities or sports, although some may only use a limited range of motion for the sport. You still need to put your joints through their full range of motion, in order to improve joint strength and muscle flexibility. And one key benefit of resistance training is that it helps prevent injury.

You don't need a gym membership or to invest in fancy equipment to do strength training. You can do some strengthening exercises using only your own body weight (for example, the crunch, shown on page 132). You may decide to purchase some weights (see page 145 to 146 for advice), but that's not even required. You can use cans or bags of food, socks with sand or other weight in them—or plastic milk or detergent containers partially filled with sand or water. Another option is to use resistance bands or tubing (see page 145).

Some experts recommend machines, which not only help you know how much weight you're lifting and which muscles you're challenging, but also reduce the likelihood of injury. Others dislike the fact that machines may only work one muscle at a time and don't necessarily train you in "functional" fitness—that is, in everyday motions that require strength and endurance. Many of these experts prefer free weights, which are weights that you hold and for which you determine the movements. And other experts say you can develop decent muscle strength and endurance programs by primarily using your body weight and gravity.

Regardless of the method you use for resistance training, there's one important key to gaining maximum benefit and minimizing the chance of injury: controlled movement.

Starting a Strength-Training Program

If you opt for machines as you first begin weight training, you may appreciate the fact that machines are easy to use (as long as you use them properly) and can be very safe. However, some experts recommend combining free weights with machines even as you begin weight training and then, as you advance, moving totally to free weights. However, if you get into heavy-duty weight lifting with free weights, you'll also need a buddy who can serve as your "spotter," someone who can help you avoid injury if you lose control of a weight you're using. That's why many people find a partner with whom to lift.

Because developing muscular strength and endurance is worthwhile—by whatever means you select—this section includes some brief introductory material on developing your own program. If you have osteoarthritis in any of your weight-bearing joints—especially your knees, hips or shoulders—discuss a weight program with your doctor before you begin. Arthritic joints that may not be painful with minimal activity may flare up painfully if you start weight training too aggressively. Also be sure to discuss a

What About Circuit Resistance Programs?

In a circuit resistance training program you move through a series of different exercises (10 to 15 reps each) with very little rest between them. Circuit resistance training programs have a very modest effect on cardiovascular fitness as seen in VO_2max, the maximum amount of oxygen your body can take in from the air you breathe. Studies of such programs, lasting 8 to 20 weeks, show that men gain about 4 percent in VO_2max, while women gain about 8 percent—far less than the 10 to 15 percent you can gain in the same amount of time with a traditional aerobic training program. However, a circuit resistance program can have a valid role as a component of an overall cardiovascular conditioning program. Research also shows that resistance training either slightly improves or has no effect on flexibility, regardless of your gender.

Common Resistance Training Terms

Here are some of the most common resistance training terms:

- **Structural** or **functional** training—which requires the coordinated action of many muscle groups (squat, for example); **body-part** training—in which you isolate and train a single joint or muscle group (knee extension or biceps curl, for example)
- **Repetition** or **rep**—one complete movement of an exercise; in a lifting exercise, this includes both lifting and lowering the resistance
- **Set**—a group of reps done continuously before stopping, typically somewhere between 1 and 15; the number of sets in your program depends on your goal; although a typical program may include three to eight sets, novices can gain strength in as few as one or two
- **Intensity** or **training load**—the amount of weight you lift per repetition
- **Rep max (RM)**—the maximum number of reps you can do with a given amount of weight or resistance, using proper technique; **1RM** is the maximum amount of weight you can lift 1 time
- **Frequency of training**—the number of sessions per week; although novices can make significant improvements in strength with two to four training days per week, athletes already at a high level tend to need more; if time constraints make more sessions difficult, be sure you include the work on your central or core muscles as often as possible or design a program with numerous multi-joint exercises
- **Progressive overload** or **progressive resistance exercise**—a continual increase of stress placed on a muscle, whether with increased load or reps, as your muscle becomes capable of producing greater force or having more endurance; if the load on a muscle is unchanged, no further strength gains occur
- **Training volume**—total amount of weight lifted or reps performed in a workout session; if you want to increase strength and power you'll lift heavier loads few times (low training volume) and if you want to increase muscle growth, you'll use a lighter load but lift it a greater number of times (high volume)
- **Rest period length**—the length of rest between sets is important as it relates to the recovery of one type of energy source before you do your next set; rest periods under 1 minute appear related to the development of high-intensity muscular endurance and hypertrophy (increase in the size of your muscles)

weight-training program with your doctor before you begin if you have heart disease, as there will be some important safety precautions you need to take.

Becoming stronger doesn't require lifting heavy weights. It's not the amount of weight that matters as much as how many times you can lift it. Start with an amount of weight you can comfortably lift about 8 times, or 8 reps. Squires notes that the appropriate amount of weight can vary greatly from one individual to the next. "When it comes to lifting weights by hand, 1 pound may be appropriate for someone at age 80, while a 25-year-old person may start with 10 pounds," he says. "Don't compare yourself to someone else. Start out conservatively to avoid injuring yourself. You can always increase the amount of weight you use."

If you can easily lift a weight more than 15 times, move up to one slightly heavier. Note that different parts of your body will be able to lift or move different amounts of weight. Therefore, you'll need to vary the amounts you use accordingly.

Lift the weight slowly (2 to 3 seconds), pause for 1 second, then lower it again slowly. Breathe normally the entire time, exhaling as you lift or push, inhaling as you lower or ease off of the weight. After you've lifted the weight 8 to 15 consecutive times (a set)—or nearly to the point of exhaustion, rest for at least 30 to 60 seconds, and then lift it again—probably for fewer reps this time, as you'll tire more quickly. Stick with about 8 to 15 reps, adding weight when an amount becomes easy to lift. It's safer, as you get older, to use lighter weights and lift them more times. Never continue lifting to the point of pain.

Include exercises (perhaps 6 to 8 different ones) that target the major muscle groups in both your upper and lower

Don: See What Just 1 Month Can Do!

Don, whom you met in Chapter 3 as he began his program, has stuck with it doggedly. Much of his effort has been devoted to strength conditioning. He's worked with a trainer to develop his own program, which includes, among other things, free weight arm exercises that he does while balancing on an exercise ball. A big guy, he knows he's become stronger as he's worked up to balancing and exercising with 20 pounds in each hand.

When Don was 35, he could easily do push-ups—50 regular and 10 one-handed. When he began his program, nearing the age of 60, he could barely do three regular push-ups. He was determined to regain the ability to do them easily—a clear goal. He also wants to lose weight—another clear goal. And he and my husband set a joint goal of running a 5K race together next fall.

About a month after he began his program Don offered to demonstrate his progress with a push-up demo. The week of his demo, Don was up to doing 10 push-ups several times a week, and he offered to show me a set of 10. However, spurred on by pride in his accomplishment, Don didn't body. Include exercises for the muscles in your abdomen, legs, chest, back, shoulders and arms. Be sure to work both sides of your body evenly. Some experts suggest working your larger muscles first and then your smaller muscles, while others say it really doesn't matter what order you use. Judge by what your body tells you. Doing weight-training exercises while standing, rather than sitting helps improve the strength of your skeletal muscles. When you're finished working one group of muscles, stretch them briefly before moving on to avoid unnecessary soreness later (10 to 15 seconds—not as long a stretch as you'd use for a regular flexibility exercise).

It's also not necessary to do strength training for all parts of your body on the same day. You may prefer working your upper body one day and your lower body the next, allowing the muscles in your upper body to rest and recover. You can maintain your level of strength by working each muscle group twice a week and build strength by working muscles three times a week.

Change only one thing at a time: increase your load (weight), add reps, alter the speed of your lifts, shorten or expand your rest period between sets or increase your overall volume of work. When you make these changes, do it methodically and gradually—and record them. And again, never increase more than 10 percent in one week.

Don't try to increase the load equally on all your muscles at the same time. Increase the load in greater increments for large muscles than for small muscles. You also don't need to do the same number of reps or sets for each exercise. Here again, tracking what you do makes it easier to keep your program progressing.

---

stop at 10, but went on to do 20! Not surprisingly, 2 days later, when he tried to do them again, he was still sore from overdoing it, and was reminded to limit his increases to 10 percent a week.

Into his fifth week Don clearly saw progress. He was committed. In fact, when an out-of-town trip caused him to miss 2 days in a row, he rearranged his schedule so he could stop on the way back into town to work out. "It's that important to me now. I'll figure out some way to get there," he said.

He's gone beyond the initial quick changes he noticed—easier stair climbing and getting in and out of cars—to some more concrete milestones, including 10 push-ups, 2 sit-ups and 10 to 15 seconds of balancing on one foot. But he hasn't lost any weight yet, and is a bit discouraged by that, although he reminds himself that he may have lost some fat and turned the weight into heavier muscle. "I keep looking at my belly and wondering when," he said. "I think my muscles are toning up, and my face seems longer, my shoulders more muscular. And now I can run a quarter mile." Don's also ventured out into the dating world and is considering signing up for some aerobics classes soon.

Different Approaches Produce Different Outcomes

Training for muscular strength focuses on lifting larger loads fewer times, with longer rest periods (often several minutes) between sets. Muscular endurance training, on the other hand, focuses on lifting lighter weights more times, with shorter rest periods (less than 30 seconds) between sets.

Increase power by either producing the same amount of work in less time or doing more work in the same amount of time. Increase your muscle size by lifting moderately sized loads as many times as you can, resting briefly between sets.

Your greatest increase in strength comes in the first 4 to 8 weeks of training. Then, progress usually slows down. Experts recommend that novices increase dynamic muscle strength by using loads about half the size of the maximum load they can lift. If you've been lifting for a while and are trained, you'll probably need to use at least 80 percent of your maximum load to produce changes in your nervous system that lead to increased strength. You'll see the greatest increases in strength if you train at a moderate speed.

Simple Resistance Exercises

These exercises, selected to condition various parts of your body, can get you started in a resistance program. No weight amounts are given (for those exercises that use added weight), because you should use an amount to suit your ability. You can make your own weights, using milk, water or detergent bottles partially filled with sand or water—or you can purchase hand weights (see pages 145 to 146). Start conservatively, adding weight as you become stronger. There are also no numbers of repetitions given, so that you can work at your own ability level. If no health conditions limit you, you may continue an exercise nearly to the point of fatigue, but not to the point of pain. When you can do an exercise 12 to 15 times, increase the weight you use for that exercise. Again, note that some of these resistance exercises don't require any weight beyond your own body weight. Hoffman recommends that for additional "how-to" information you read Thomas Baechle and Barney Groves' latest book, *Weight Training: Steps to Success* (Champaign, Illinois, Human Kinetics, 1999).

Crunch.

1. **Crunch** (tones your abdominal muscles): Lie with your back on the floor, knees bent and feet flat on the floor. Place your palms on your thighs. Slowly raise your head and shoulders as you slide your hands toward your knees. Hold 2 seconds and slowly return to the start position. Be sure not to hold your breath while you do this exercise.

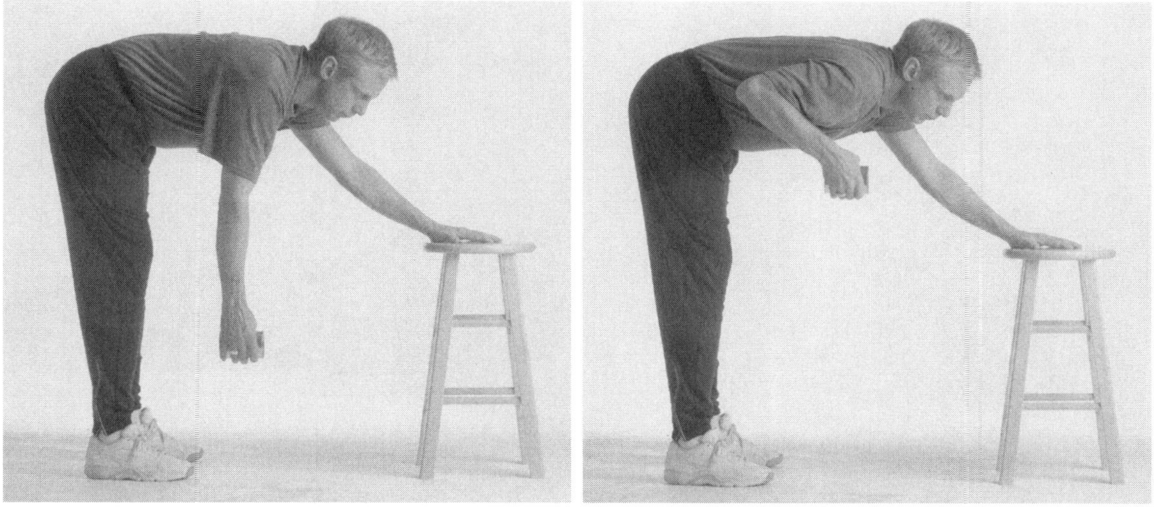

Bent-over single-arm row.

2. **Bent-over single-arm row** (tones your upper and middle back muscles): Stand, feet about 12 inches apart, knees slightly flexed, facing a chair or table. Bend over from your hips, with your back flat, your abdominal muscles pulled in, squeezing your shoulder blades together, with your left hand on the chair or table for support. Hold a can or weight under 1 pound in your right hand, hanging straight down at your side. Keeping your arm near your body, slowly raise the can straight up to your trunk. Ease the weight back down with a controlled movement. Switch arms and repeat.

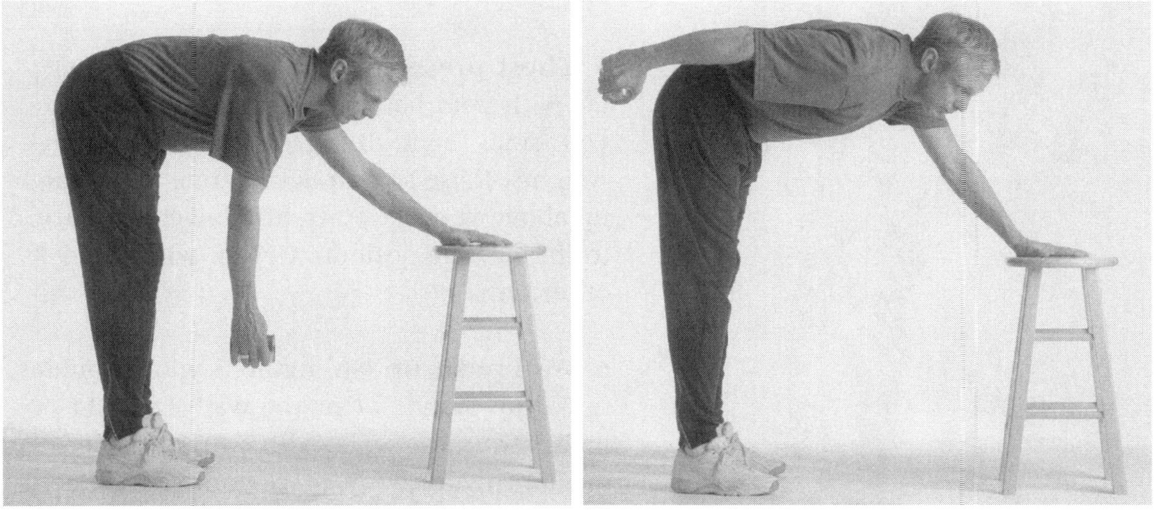

Bent-over single-arm kickback.

3. **Bent-over single-arm kickback** (tones your upper arm triceps muscle): Stand, as you did for #2. but keep your upper arm aligned with your torso and stationary. Moving only your forearm, slowly lift the weight up and slightly behind your hip, without locking your elbow. Slowly lower the weight to the start position. Switch arms and repeat.

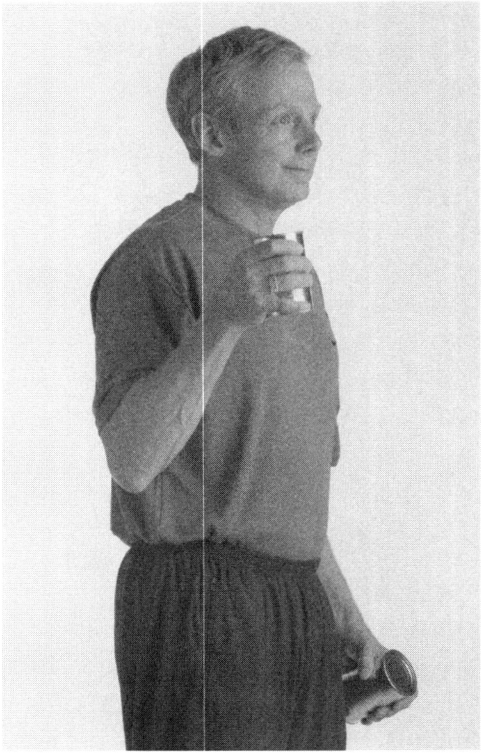

Arm curl.

Chest press.

4. **Arm curl** (tones your forearm biceps muscle): Stand, with your feet shoulder-width apart, knees slightly flexed, arms at your sides. Hold a weight in each hand, palms facing in. Alternating arms, lift the weight (with your hand and forearm) up to your shoulder in a smooth motion, keeping your elbows close to your sides. Slowly ease the weight back down, allowing your elbow to extend to its beginning position.

5. **Chest press** (tones your chest muscles): Lie with your back on the floor, elbows at your sides (bent 90 degrees), hands holding weights. Raise and straighten one arm straight up above your chest. Gently lower your arm to the starting position. Repeat with your other arm.

6. **Wall push-up** (strengthens your shoulder muscles): Stand, facing the wall, 18 to 24 inches from the wall. With your arms perpendicular to your body, place your palms flat on the wall, fingers pointed up. Use both hands and arms to push your body away from the wall, then slowly lower your body to the wall.

Wall push-up.

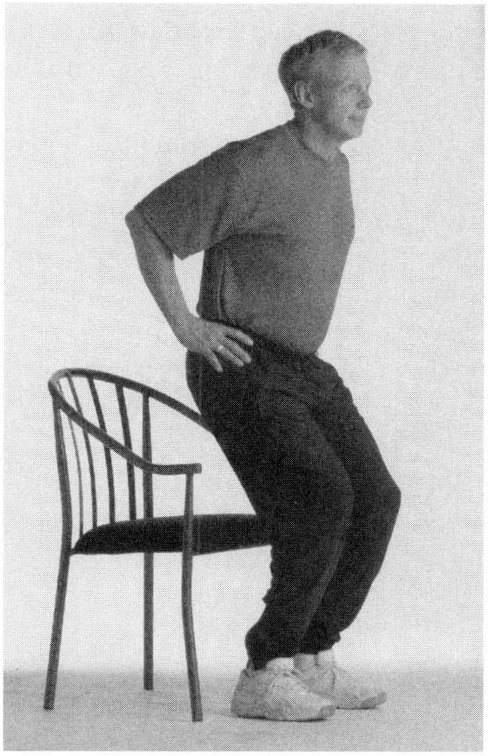

Quarter squat.

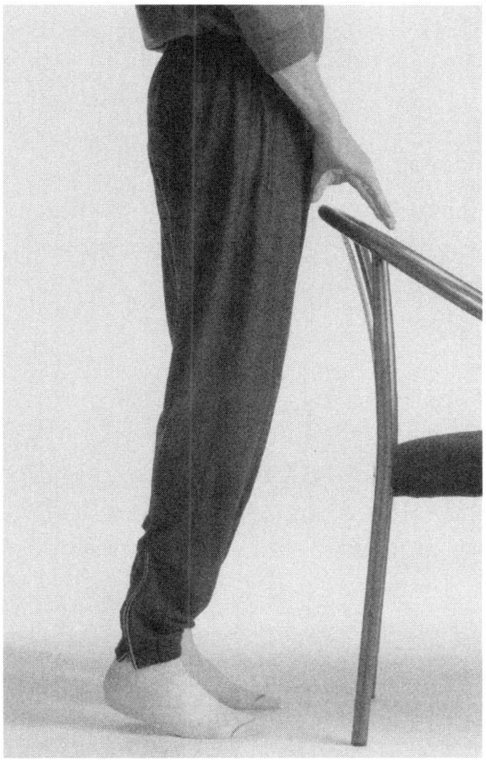

Standing heel raise.

Upper torso lift.

7. **Quarter squat** (tones your thigh muscles): With a chair behind you and keeping your feet flat on the floor, bend at your knees into a squat position. Don't bend beyond 90 degrees. Return to an upright position.

8. **Upper torso lift** (tones the muscles of your lower back): Lie face down, arms at your sides. Raise your head and upper torso. Ease back down.

9. **Standing heel raise** (tones your calf muscles): Stand facing the back of a chair, hands resting on the back of the chair for stability. Raise your heels to stand on your toes. Lower your heels gently to the floor.

The American College of Sports Medicine specifically recommends avoiding several common strengthening exercises, because they tend to either strain muscles or are ineffective. They include: deep knee bends, full or straight-leg sit-ups, double leg lifts and squat thrusts.

Building Strength with Resistance Bands or Tubing

They look like huge rubber bands or stretchy ropes with handles. They're called resistance or stretch bands, and they provide varying amounts of resistance. You can use them quite effectively to tone many of the same muscles you tone with weights. Although they don't work as well as weights for leg and arm curls and you don't have the feedback of a number on the weight to tell you how much you're lifting, resistance bands can produce good results—especially in strengthening your upper body. And they're easy to pack up and take with you—wherever you go.

Before you begin, examine the bands carefully to make sure they're free of nicks or tears that could cause them to break. Also be sure that you control the bands in both directions, in order not to injure yourself. As with weights, it's best to exercise a variety of muscles, repeating on one side what you've done on the other. You can work most muscles by securing one end of the band under your foot, holding it in both hands or tying it to something stationary.

Squires: Longer Stretches Are Better

Many experts suggest routinely holding a stretch for 10 to 30 seconds, while you relax and breathe freely through your nostrils. But for Ray W. Squires, Ph.D., director of the cardiovascular health clinic, Mayo Clinic, Rochester, Minnesota, 10 seconds—even 30—isn't long enough, simply because stretching makes him feel so good. "When you stretch, there's something that basically helps you feel good," he says. "I can't exactly tell you why—it's probably part physical and part mental. Endorphins are probably a small part of the puzzle."

Squires tries to hold a stretch for at least a minute and says that most athletes suggest holding a stretch even longer and doing many reps. Although Squires agrees that stretching offers the most benefit at the end of your workout, he routinely stretches both before and after, just to fit more stretches in.

It doesn't take long to discover that Squires loves many different forms of exercise. Despite a very busy schedule, he builds in time for plenty of activity. In bed by 10 p.m., he usually leaves the house by 5:30 a.m. for his run to work, which means anywhere from 2.5 to 10 miles, depending on how he feels and what the weather's like. Minnesota winters don't even slow him down much—although, "if the wind chill's 80 below or there's a thunder or ice storm, I don't run," he concedes.

Sometime before he heads home for the day Squires takes advantage of the excellent weight-training equipment at the cardiovascular clinic's exercise area. Squires is active at least 5 days a week—often 7, with hiking, skiing, biking and basketball topping his list of preferred activities.

Flexibility: Another Key —but Oft-Neglected— Component

While experts may debate whether stretching appropriately prevents injuries—after all, says Squires, who's going to tell athletes in a study's control group that they can't stretch?—experts don't dispute the value of stretching for flexibility. Authors of the book, *Treat Your Own Strains, Sprains and Bruises,* give these pointers on appropriate stretching:

1. Always warm up your muscles before stretching.
2. Never bounce up and down while stretching.
3. Stretch firmly, but not to the point of pain.
4. Begin slowly, and once you feel a firm stretch, relax and hold that position briefly. Then try to stretch a bit more until you again feel a firm stretch. Release slowly and rest before you repeat the stretch.
5. Do this at least three times a week, preferably daily.

The same authors also note that most sports and recreational activities use a limited range of motion. Exceptions to this can include aerobic workouts, ballet, gymnastics, martial arts and yoga. So, depending upon the activities you choose to include in your exercise regime, you'll probably need to include additional stretching exercises in your plans in order to maintain your body's optimal flexibility in all directions.

Experts don't recommend that you simply stand and reach for your toes to increase flexibility, as it can strain your lower back. Here are some helpful stretches you can safely do several times a week, if not daily. Be sure to breathe normally as you do them. Holding your breath while exerting can dangerously raise your blood pressure.

Calf muscle and Achilles tendon stretch.

1. **Calf muscle and Achilles tendon stretch:** Stand with your palms on the wall (fingers up), arms parallel to the floor, feet a shoulder's width apart. Step forward with your right foot and, with both feet flat on the floor, bend at your knees and shift your weight to your forward foot. Slowly lower your hips to the point of feeling a gentle stretching sensation in your lower leg. Hold for 20 to 30 seconds, then repeat. Switch legs and repeat.

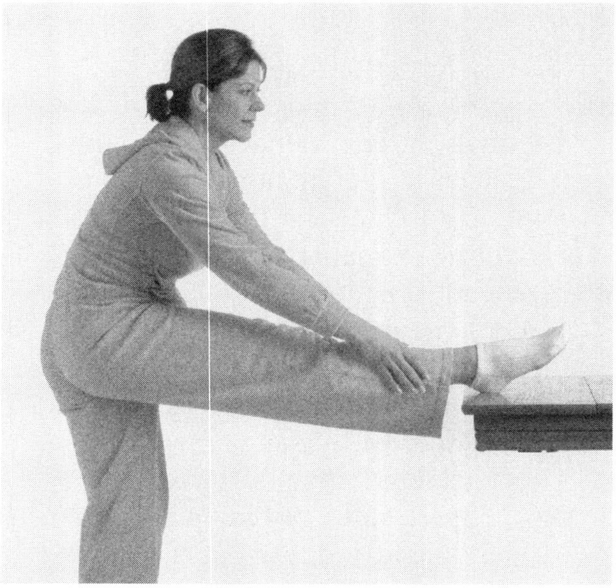
Thigh back stretch.

Thigh front stretch.

2. **Thigh back stretch:** While standing, extend your leg and rest one heel on a chair or table. Keeping your back straight, gently lean forward, flexing the other knee to increase your stretch. Repeat, with your other foot.

3. **Thigh front stretch:** Holding a chair or counter for support as needed, use your other hand to pull your foot straight back and up toward your buttocks, without arching your back or bending at your hip. Switch sides and repeat.

Hip flexor muscle stretch.

4. **Hip flexor muscle stretch:** Step forward with your left leg about one shoulder's width and flex your knee until it's directly over your foot. Then, with both feet pointed straight ahead, keeping your left foot flat on the floor and your right leg straight, slowly bend your left knee to lower your body weight until you feel a gentle stretch (don't worry about keeping your right heel on the floor). Switch legs and repeat the exercise.

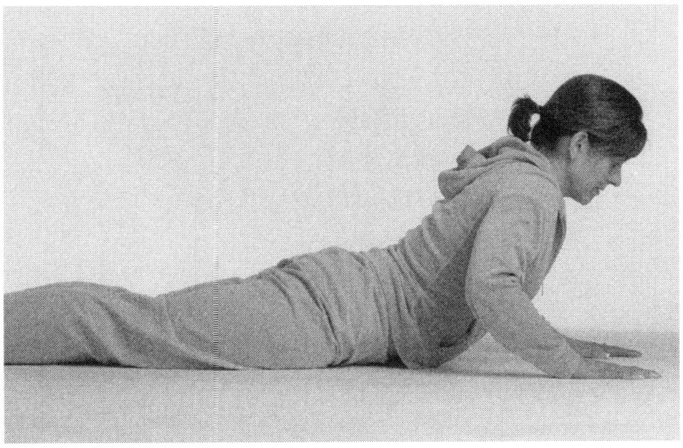

Back extension stretch.

5. **Back extension stretch:** Lie on your stomach on the floor, palms flat on the floor at your shoulders. Straighten your arms to slowly push your head and torso up until you feel a firm stretch in your lower back, keeping the muscles in the lower half of your body limp. Hold briefly, then gently lower your upper body and repeat.

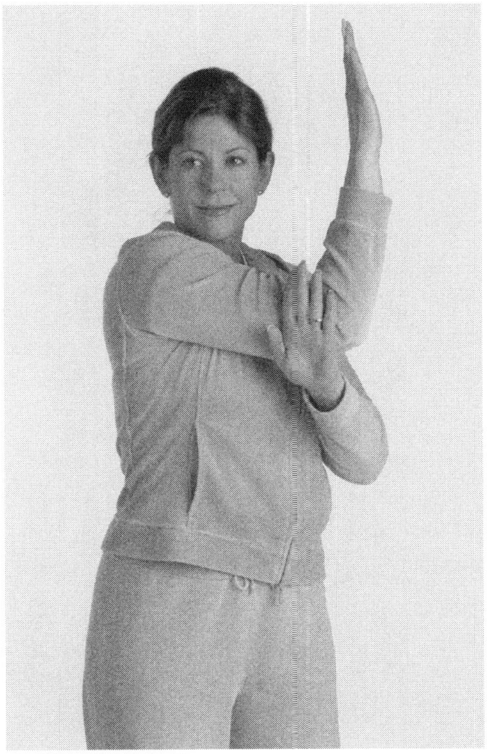

Shoulder and upper arm stretch.

6. **Shoulder and upper arm stretch:** Extend your right arm in front of you, upper arm parallel to the floor, elbow bent at a right angle. Place the back of your other hand outside your elbow. As your outer hand attempts to pull your elbow toward you, resist with the other arm. Repeat, with your right arm in several positions across the front of your body and at several heights. Feel the stretch between your shoulder blades.

7. **Shoulder and chest stretch:** Stand with your arms behind your back and fold your hands together, fingers interlocking. Keeping your head erect and without leaning forward, with your elbows straight, slowly raise your arms.

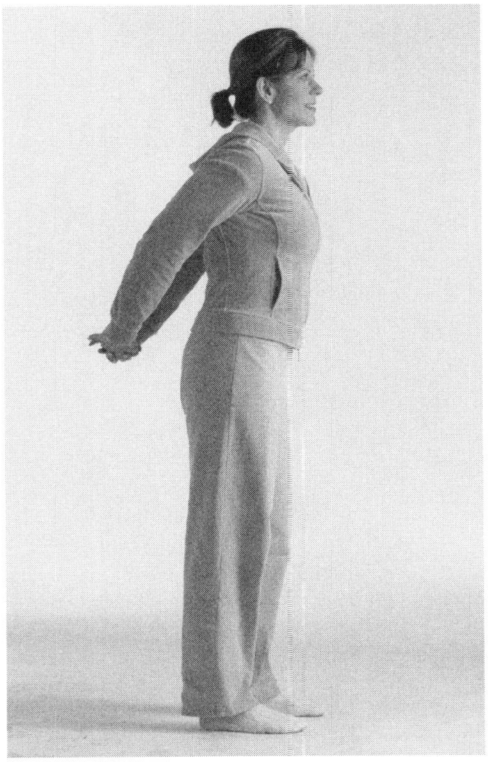

Shoulder and chest stretch.

Neck rotation stretch.

Pectoral wall stretch.

8. **Neck rotation stretch:** Sit or stand upright, chin tucked in, looking straight ahead. Turn your head to look to one side to the point of a gentle pull and hold briefly. Then turn your head toward the other side until you feel a gentle pull and hold briefly.

9. **Pectoral wall stretch:** Clasp your hands behind your head. Spread and stretch your elbows back as far toward your shoulders as possible.

What About Joining a Health Club or Using a Public Gym for Exercise?

Although none of the material you've read so far requires or encourages you to invest in a membership at a health club or Y or to use a public gym, you may wonder if that's necessary. No, it's not. This book begins with the premise that you don't need to join a health club to find ample opportunities to be physically active and fit. That's one reason the book has numerous examples of activities and individuals that don't require fancy equipment or facilities.

However, as you become more active and want to explore a variety of opportunities, you may debate about whether you'd enjoy joining a club, or perhaps would prefer investing in some equipment that you can use at home. It's not a decision that you should make hastily. Here's some help.

What's Involved with Joining a Health Club?

Picking a place where you'll regularly exercise can be as simple as buying a pack of tickets to a nearby school gym that's open for community use at night through your city's park and recreation department or local school district. Or, it can involve paying a joiner's fee and agreeing to have a facility withdraw monthly payments from your bank account. Beware, however, of so-called "lifetime memberships," as they're often very pricey and once you've paid the large chunk of money, you have no leverage to receive customer service—or guarantee that the facility will remain open. But there are many options available to most people between those extremes.

Be very cautious before you make any long-term commitment. At the very least, visit a facility you're considering before you commit to a longer term. Here are a few questions to consider, if you're looking at a membership organization:

1. Do you enjoy working out with others and find a social environment a "plus"—or are you intimidated or rattled by the presence of others?
2. What about the location? Is it close to your home or work? Will it be convenient for you to use, or does it take a major effort to get there? Is the facility clean? Is it safe, with well-lighted exits and parking areas? Is there adequate parking, or can you get there by other means—walking, biking, using mass transit?
3. Is it well equipped, and is the equipment well maintained and adequate to serve the people who use the facility when you'd be there?
4. Do the hours suit your schedule?

Include Rests in Your Resistance Training Program

During resistance training a chemical change takes place in your muscles to produce energy. In order to let your muscles fully recover and regain their balance before being challenged again, it's important to rest them adequately between sets.

Studies by the American College of Sports Medicine show that, while much of the chemical balance is restored in 1 to 3 minutes, some of the processes that take place in your muscles to help them fully recover may take as much as 6 minutes. With light activity between sets—perhaps brief range-of-motion exercises without resistance or intermittent walking—you can help your blood bring the necessary oxygen to your muscles and remove lactic acid that accumulates. Preliminary evidence suggests that adequately allowing for this recovery enhances the process of increasing your muscular strength and endurance.

Are the specific facilities you'd use there available for your use when you'd expect to use them? How many other people use them at that time? Be sure to visit at the time you expect to come, and consider it a red flag if visits are discouraged.

5. Is the staff helpful and well qualified for what they do (licensed and credentialed)?

6. Do you have to sign a contract? If so, what's included? What's not included?

Look for stability in a facility and its management. Check with the Better Business Bureau for records of complaints about a place you're seriously considering. Don't allow yourself to be pressured into signing something you haven't carefully reviewed, and make sure that all oral promises are written into any document you sign. Consider carefully your assorted payment options. Is there a trial period, during which you can withdraw without losing a major investment of funds? Unless you're sure that this facility will meet your needs, ask about a 1- or 3-month trial membership. Most health clubs also have promotional periods, when you can join without a fee or for a reduced monthly payment. Ask how often those come. They're often scheduled during low-use periods—perhaps when school starts in the fall or during the months when people are outdoors more.

As you consider your options for physical activity, look for a variety of ways you can be active. If exercise opportunities are convenient and accessible, you're more likely to actually use them. Many people—nearly two-thirds of those who join health clubs—also work out on equipment they have at home.

Is Resistance Training Gender-Neutral?

Although, on average, women's mean total body strength is 63.5 percent that of men's, the two are much closer if women and men of comparable relative body mass are compared. Research shows that body composition changes that occur with weight training are fairly comparable between women and men. Men tend to experience greater muscle hypertrophy (increase in size) than women, which researchers suspect may be due to women's lower levels of testosterone.

Experts say women and men can easily share the same weight-training programs. Women may opt to work their upper bodies more, because that's where the greatest difference in strength appears between women and men—possibly because women have a lower proportion of their lean body mass in their upper bodies. Although women in resistance-training programs gain strength at least as quickly as men, women's rate of gain, unlike men's, tends to plateau after 3 to 5 months.

Can You Set Up Your Own Gym at Home?

You don't need a gym to get plenty of physical activity, but you may find it easier to stick with a regimen if you dedicate some resources to acquiring equipment to use in your home. It can become difficult, however, to stay in the habit of using equipment that you need to set up and take down each time you use it.

If you have some space available to consider dedicating to your fitness activities, ask yourself these questions before making any decisions:

1. What activities do you enjoy and want to incorporate into your fitness program for an extended period of time?

2. What kinds of equipment would you need to continue doing those activities, and is it likely you'll want to use that equipment for a long time? Does the equipment you're considering have only one function, or is it something that you can use for a variety of conditioning activities? How would buying that equipment line up with your long- and short-term fitness goals, especially as you seek a well-rounded program that includes all aspects of fitness? Have you tried that specific type of equipment before—perhaps at a health club?

3. Do you have space available—with the appropriate electrical power source (if required) and floor surface to accommodate this equipment? Is adequate lighting available? Who else uses that space, and will that use be compatible? Be especially cautious in placing equipment where small children can be injured. Is anyone else likely to use the equipment for its intended purpose?

If you decide to set up an exercise area in your home, you'll use it more regularly if it's comfortable and inviting. Mirrors can not only make a space seem larger, but can also help you check your form and posture as you exercise. If you want to read while you ride a stationary cycle, be sure lighting is adequate. You'll also need air moving, once you start picking up your pace (portable fans can help here). And, if you live with or near others, consider whether you'll affect their space and privacy, as well. This can be especially important if you intend to watch TV or listen to music while exercising, as you may need to turn up the volume or use earphones to hear it. Is a telephone nearby, or can you use a portable phone?

Floor coverings can make a big difference. Some equipment is difficult to use if it's placed on carpeting that has a thick pile or padding. Hardwood floors provide an ideal surface for many activities, but can be noisy and difficult to maintain. A rubber mat can protect the floor and reduce the noise.

Buying Athletic Equipment

Because this book is designed to be a "stand-alone" approach to fitness, you won't find a lot of information here about buying athletic equipment. Ample good information is available from a variety of places, including the American College of Sports Medicine Web site (www.acsm.org). There are several important things to remember, if you decide to purchase equipment. Douglas Brooks, personal trainer, author of numerous books—including *Your*

Personal Trainer—and international lecturer, recommends finding several activities you enjoy and purchasing the equipment required to cross-train indoors when necessary. He recommends the treadmill as a solid choice and suggests complementing that with a manual resistance bike, stair stepper or rowing machine. Here's some information to get you started.

Rule #1 when shopping for exercise equipment: **Assuming it's of good quality, exercise equipment is only good for your health if you use it.**

Keep these additional things in mind, when shopping for exercise equipment:

1. **Know what you're buying.** Try any large equipment before you buy it—for at least 5 to 10 minutes. Talk to people who have the equipment you're considering—sales staff may provide names of people to contact. Is the equipment made by a major manufacturer? Has that company been around for a while? How do you maintain the machine—and how much will that cost? Inexpensive machines are frequently flimsy and difficult to adjust. At your local library check *Consumer Reports* and other consumer periodicals for ratings of major equipment. What's the track record of the store or company where you plan to buy the equipment? At commercial equipment stores, the sales staff may be able to discuss differences between what they sell and equipment of lower quality. That way, if you do consider equipment that's not commercial grade, you'll at least be aware of the tradeoffs. Be skeptical of any claims that a piece of equipment is effective for spot-reducing—it's simply not true.

2. **Have a long-range plan.** If you plan to work out at home and buy equipment to do that, consider—before you make any purchases—what and how much you'll eventually buy, so that

Getting Equipment Inexpensively

The American College of Sports Medicine notes that more expensive equipment doesn't necessarily make you more fit. You don't need to break the bank to acquire decent exercise equipment. Alternatives may exist—as previously mentioned, substituting plastic milk or detergent bottles for free weights, for example. Carol Torgan, Ph.D., muscle researcher and spokesperson for the American College of Sports Medicine, notes that you can also substitute bicycle inner tubes for resistance bands—they're quite inexpensive, even when new.

If you've studied available consumer information and shopped new equipment, you may be able to pick up excellent values at used equipment stores, thrift shops, garage sales or from the want ads. You're safest doing this when you buy something without a lot of electrical features, because it's easier to test this type of equipment.

you can plan your budget and space accordingly.

3. **How will you learn to use the equipment?** Sometimes it's less expensive to enroll in a 3-month program at a facility where you can work under the watchful eye of a qualified trainer and decide after that whether you want to buy equipment—and which. Some equipment is much easier to use with personal instruction. Videotapes can be helpful—and some manufacturers provide them. Many manuals leave a large gap between the information they provide and the amount you need to know to maximize the value you can gain from a good piece of equipment.

4. **The nitty-gritty:** Will the equipment be delivered? If not, do you have means for getting it home? Inquire about assembly. Is it required? Can you do it yourself? What if you get stumped when trying to assemble it? What's the return policy? It's best if the company has a 30-day unconditional return policy. If you want to return it, who pays the shipping? If the equipment needs repair, who will do it and where?

Recommendations for Specific Equipment

Many of these recommendations come from the American College of Sports Medicine.

Jump rope—one of the best equipment investments you can make. (Your knees and back will be especially grateful if you can find a surface with some "give" for jumping—a foam mat, for example.) Buy a weighted rope with some outer protection at its center, where it repeatedly hits the floor.

Resistance bands or tubing—generally available in packages of three with varying tension: light, medium and heavy. They're usually sold with an instruction book or video that explains how to use them.

Step counter—another piece of inexpensive equipment that can motivate you to move more throughout the day. Experts recommend skipping the fancy features—which are frequently inaccurate anyway—and looking for one that you wear at your waist to simply count steps (by responding to vertical acceleration of your hip). They're extremely accurate under laboratory testing conditions, but much less so in actual life, where walking speeds vary and movements such as bending or shifts in weight may be interpreted as steps. But they do help you compare one day of your activity with another day. Expect to spend $15 to $30.

Physioballs—come in several sizes: typically 55 centimeters (cm), 65 cm (most common size) and 75 cm, and recommendations depend upon your size. Prices range from $10 to $60 and up. Some come with a hand pump, which is convenient for travel. You should be very cautious if you try these, warns David Poulter, P.T., Dip. M.D.T., as it's easy to injure yourself while using a physioball.

Free weights or dumbbells—are available in a variety of materials and sizes. Cast iron (approximately $0.50 per pound) and vinyl or neoprene (approximately $0.80 to $1.00 per pound) are the most common. Neoprene is less apt to chip than vinyl. You don't need a weight bench and barbells, because you can do a lot with a set of light handheld dumbbells (purchased in 1-pound increments, often in sets containing several different sizes).

Stationary bicycle—comes in either upright (like a regular bicycle) or recumbent models. Recumbent seats allow you to extend your legs directly in front of you while pedaling and are often preferred by people with balance or mobility concerns or low back pain. In upright models, get a seat that's large and well padded. Make sure you can adjust the handlebars and seat to comfortably accommodate your height and leg extension and that your weight is evenly distributed between the arms and seat. Try it long enough to be assured that you can comfortably use it, because one of the main reasons people stop cycling is that their machine is uncomfortable. The seat should be level, so it doesn't put too much pressure on your groin (if it's pointed up) or too much weight on your arms and shoulders (if it's pointed down). When your leg is at the bottom of a stroke, your knee should bend only slightly. If handlebars are at a proper height your back, arms and shoulders won't become fatigued (from having them too low) and you won't have excessive pressure on the seat (from having it too high). Make sure the cycle provides adequate resistance and that all the moving parts have good clearance (don't rub on one another). Also make sure you can get on and off easily. Look for a wide, stable base and a covered flywheel. Expect to pay from $450 to $1,500, more if you want fancy programming options.

Rowing machines—can provide an excellent overall aerobic workout, as well as strengthening your abdominal and back muscles. Make sure you have enough space to accommodate the machine as it's used (and to mount and dismount). These machines typically cost from $700 to $1,800.

Treadmills—are available in either motorized or human-powered models. If you're an experienced walker or runner, you may appreciate a treadmill with a variety of training programs—and may use it more often than one lacking those options. However, only about 30 percent of treadmill users actually use a programming device. If you buy a motorized one, the motor should be at least 1.5 horsepower, and shouldn't stall when you firmly plant your feet on the belt while it's running at a low speed. Check the voltage (110 is a typical home outlet, and you may need to alter your wiring to handle one that uses 220 volts, the amount used by many washers and dryers, for example). The belt should be at least 18 to 20 inches wide and 48 inches long to reduce your chances of tripping and falling as the treadmill runs. The platform should be low, and you should have enough space on the sides to straddle the belt. Also be sure, when planning a location for the machine, to allow enough space to move around it. Look for a speed range of at least 0.1 to 8 miles per hour. Check to make sure the speed increases gradually (not suddenly) and that the machine doesn't stall or grind under your weight as it's running. Ideally, you'll be able to adjust the incline, either manually or electrically, from 0 to at least 10 percent. Make sure the machine doesn't wobble at the highest incline setting. Also check to see whether you can use the treadmill while walking with your normal gait, and make sure that a bar or rails used for balance won't hinder you, if you swing your arms as you walk. If it's a manual machine, make sure it stops moving when you do. Also be sure you don't have to lean on the handrail or grasp the rails to use the machine, because this reduces your workload. It's better, once you're used to walking on the treadmill, if you can just place one finger on the rails to keep your balance. Expect to spend up to $1,000 for a good treadmill for walking, and up to $2,000 for one that's good for running.

Elliptical trainer—the latest rage, this is basically a cross between a treadmill, a stair climber and a cross-country ski machine— all excellent calorie-burners. Because your feet never leave the pedals, it's low-impact. You can adjust the resistance or incline to ramp up your workout—or switch directions to vary the muscles you use. Studies show elliptical trainers are equal to treadmills for cardiovascular conditioning and more strenuous than stationary bikes or stair climbers. Beware of flimsy and unreliable home models sold on TV. A decent home-quality machine will cost $500 to $1,000, and a commercial-quality machine at least $2,000.

Elliptical trainer. (Photo provided courtesy of Precor incorporated ©2002.)

Clothing

The most important clothing item you'll need is well-fitting protective gear appropriate to the activity you select. Don't skimp here. It may save your life.

Buy protective gear that's appropriate to your skill level. If you're a beginner, don't buy expert equipment. For a variety of sports, the most important protective gear you can wear is a helmet. According to Sheila Sobell, author of *Smart Guide to Sports Medicine*, helmets could prevent a third of all cycling injuries and at least one of every six snow skiing, inline skating and mountain biking injuries. Make sure that any helmet you wear is certified to meet ANSI, ASTM, SNELL or CSA safety standards. Helmets should fit snugly and allow you to have normal peripheral vision. Biking helmets should be worn flat on your head, not tilted back, as tilting a helmet back limits protection provided to the front of your brain (if you fly over the handlebars, for example). If you're wearing your helmet and have an accident, it's a good idea to have the manufacturer inspect the helmet for damage that may not be visible to an untrained eye.

The item of clothing most important for many people's fitness programs is shoes. Athletic shoes can protect your feet, ankles and knees from repetitive-use injuries, as well as from jarring and twisting. Besides having a spare pair of shoes that you can keep in your car or at work, it's a good idea to invest in a good pair or two, so that you can air them out between workouts. And experts also recommend using shoes specifically designed for your activity, especially if you participate in that activity several times a week. You can, however, use the same shoe for two sports that use the same surface. Although walking shoes are generally more rigid and last longer than running shoes, many people prefer using running shoes for walking, because of the additional cushioning.

Sobell recommends that you replace running shoes every 350 to 500 miles and walking shoes every 1,000 miles. She also advises unlacing and retightening new shoes weekly during the first month you own them. Sobell offers these sports-specific shoe tips:

- **Walking shoe**—Look for good heel support and flexibility at the ball of your foot to help give traction for forward motion.
- **Aerobic dance**—Because impacts

What Distinguishes a Good Shoe from One That's Lousy?

There's a considerable amount of research behind a decent pair of athletic shoes, according to Rob Johnson, M.D., primary care sports medicine physician, who suggests looking for a shoe produced by a name brand manufacturer like Nike, Adidas, New Balance, Asics, Reebok and others. Feet are as different as the individuals who walk on them, so it's not surprising that the shoe that's good for you might not suit someone else's needs at all.

The good shoe companies design shoes for at least three different kinds of feet, according to the type of arch you have. Flat feet benefit from a stable shoe with motion control, while high arches fare best with a shoe that has a soft midsole for a great deal of shock absorption. People with neutral arches (somewhere in the middle of the two extremes) can wear any type of shoe that's comfortable. Johnson recommends consulting Web sites for the shoe companies or *Runner's World* magazine to find the correct shoe for your type of foot, training at the distance at which you train. "If you have a high arch, look for a cushioned midsole. If your foot is slightly flat or rolls in, consider a shoe that's stable and has motion control," says Johnson. "Don't go out and buy a thin-soled racing shoe that even the champs don't wear for training."

can be severe, buy shoes with plenty of cushioning and shock absorption. Shoes should have good heel support, a high toe box and be securely fastened to your foot. Sobell cautions that running shoes are not appropriate for aerobic dance and increase your risk of injury. These shoes may need replacement every 6 to 12 months.

■ **Racquet sports**—Look for shoes that offer good support and enable you to move quickly without damaging your knees.

■ **Golf**—Get a shoe with good cushioning and arch support for walking.

■ **Cycling**—wear a cross-training shoe that supports your arch and instep and has a heel lift.

Buy shoes later in the day, because your feet generally swell throughout the day. Wear socks you'll wear for your activity when trying on shoes. Look for shoes with wide toe boxes and heels that don't slip. If you use orthotics, bring them along and try the shoes on with them inside. If your feet are differently sized, buy shoes to comfortably fit the larger of your feet. Women with wider feet may find a better shoe fit in a men's shoe (women's size 10 equals men's size 8). And don't buy any shoe that's not immediately comfortable.

Medications That Can Affect Your Activity

One last thing to double-check before you get started is the effect any medications you take may have on your body during physical activity, according to Rob Johnson, M.D., director of primary care sports medicine at Hennepin County Medical Center in Minneapolis, Minnesota. Some medications, for example, can affect your output or exertion level, while others can affect your fluid level. Your plans should take those things into account. You may also notice some differences in your ability to exercise if you begin taking a new medication. And, as you think about medications you use, don't forget to consider prescribed medications, as well as over-the-counter ones.

Here are some common medications that can alter your body's response to activity:

■ **Diuretics** like hydrochlorothiazide (Esidrix or HydroDIURIL) or furosemide (Lasix), for example, which you may take for high blood pressure and other heart-related conditions, have a tendency to cause your body to release potassium and can also make it more difficult to maintain your balance of fluids. "You won't get thirsty any sooner," says Johnson, who notes (in chorus with many other experts) that thirst is not a good indicator of how well hydrated you are. "Your fluid levels have to be down by about a third to stimulate your thirst."

■ **Beta blockers** like propranolol (Inderal) or metoprolol (Lopressor), according to Johnson, may also reduce your exercise capacity.

■ **Psychotropic** drugs for schizophrenia like chlorpromazine (Thorazine) can affect your ability to sweat, raising the risk of heat-related injuries during physical activity.

■ **Asthma** medications, now administered chiefly with inhalers, have greatly improved the ability of people with this condition to participate in physical activity more fully than they could prior to the use of inhalants.

■ **Ibuprofen** (Advil or Motrin), an over-the-counter medication, can reduce the blood flow to your kidneys and further complicate fluid losses that occur during exercise in the heat.

■ **Aspirin, acetaminophen** (Tylenol or Excedrin) or **ibuprofen**, all over-the-counter drugs, affect your body's natural thermostat (the hypothalamus) and can have an unpredictable effect on your body's ability to maintain or dissipate heat.

■ **Nonsteroidal anti-inflammatory drugs,** including aspirin, ibuprofen and naproxen sodium (Aleve) can raise your blood pressure.

■ **Some common, over-the-counter cold medications,** including Contac, Dimetapp and Sudafed can increase your heart rate, raise your blood pressure and make exercise seem like more of an effort than you'd expect.

If you have diabetes it's also very important to closely monitor your body's response to activity. If you have type 1 diabetes, this is especially critical, since your health is much more brittle if exercise causes dramatic swings in your glucose levels. This isn't usually a problem for people with type 2 diabetes, Johnson notes. For them, exercise is frequently the most important form of therapy, in addition to weight loss. Johnson urges people with type 2 diabetes to check blood glucose levels before each meal and after their largest meal of the day. He notes that exercise is likely to lower your blood glucose level, and if you're new to exercising, Johnson encourages you to gauge your body's response to exercise by checking your glucose levels during and immediately after exercise. If you have diabetes, he also recommends carrying some hard candy in your pocket and, if you anticipate a long period of exertion, a fluid containing glucose, as well.

Gregory W. Heath, D.Sc., M.P.H., and Rob Johnson, M.D., reviewed chapter 6. Heath is a lead health scientist, CDC Division of Nutrition & Physical Activity at the Center for Disease Control in Atlanta. Johnson is a primary care sports medicine physician.

CHAPTER 7

Many Roads Lead to Fitness

Opportunities for physical activity abound—at times, they seem endless. Once your life takes a turn toward an active lifestyle, you'll find that you can have lots of fun—regardless of your age or physical condition. You'll meet interesting people and be invigorated by activity. Instead of thinking of physical activity as something you "must" do, you can find a new "take" on it and realize that moving your body and growing strong is something you can celebrate.

This chapter seeks to give you a peek at the treasure trove of physical activity that's out there. It's not exhaustive. There are books written on many of the activities touched lightly in this chapter. And some of them aren't discussed at all. This is just a start, and you're certainly capable of finding more information on anything of interest. But it's designed to pique your interest and whet your appetite, to encourage you to give some of these things a try. Hopefully, you'll find some ideas here you hadn't considered—or something you've secretly yearned to do, but didn't know how to start doing.

Active Travel

When you return from a trip, is the main thing you talk about the food you ate? For some people, travel means going places and sitting—whether it's on a beach during a vacation, or at a business meeting if it's a trip for work. And in either case, the highlight seems to be what they ate.

Let's try a new approach. Travel presents a few interesting opportunities: for finding new activities in different places, for providing new settings in which to be active in ways already familiar to you and for presenting interesting challenges that tease you to be creative if you want to be physically active.

Making Moving Part of Business

Many people don't think "active," when they think of traveling on business. But if you make activity a part of your business travel, you'll enjoy your time away more and return home feeling better. Even if you don't get in your full regimen that you're used to at home, you'll feel a lot better when you get back home if you've gotten some activity. And, if you actually get more activity than you might have gotten at home—that's super!

Travel. Advance planning helps—even in the matter of which shoes you wear for travel. If you're flying and need to spend some time in an airport, wear walking shoes and either carry on or pack other shoes you'll need for business. Dress comfortably. If you're leaving from a larger airport, plan to arrive well ahead of your flight time. Check your bags or place them in a locker and then start walking. Skip the people mover—that's for people who are running terribly late, carrying more than they can comfortably manage or unable to walk well. If you're able to walk—do it! Airports can be very interesting places to explore. You may be surprised at what you'll find at the end of a long concourse or on a different level than you're used to seeing. You'll find things at the airport that you never knew were there—and you can put on miles in the process, all in a climate-controlled walkway. Incidentally, this type of physical activity around the time of travel also reduces your risk of developing blood clots as a result of sitting on the plane.

Although sometimes it's difficult, you may be able to get in some helpful movement while in the air or on a train or bus. Extend your legs, flex your ankles and rotate your feet, first in one direction, then the other. Walking the aisles can prove to be a very challenging balance exercise. Don't hold on if you don't need to, but keep your hands ready to grab a seat, if you need to steady yourself.

In your seat you can also pull in your belly button and relax, shrug and relax your shoulders, do some of the neck exercises mentioned earlier or do Kegel exercises (see page 243). This is also a good time to practice relaxation breathing. If this is something you've never tried, see *The Relaxation Response* by Herbert Benson, M.D., with Miriam Z. Klipper (New York, New York: Avon; 1990). You'll also feel better on your trip if you can stay well hydrated, which means avoiding caffeine and alcohol; drink water, juice and caffeine-free soft drinks when they're offered—or whenever you like if you bring your own.

If you're driving, you may have a lot more leeway to take your gear—including a bike or inline skates. Call bike shops ahead of time where you're going and inquire about paths, and print maps from Web sites. If you're considering renting a bike or skates when you get there, it's a good idea to reserve them ahead of time. If you'll be using the paths early or late in the day, make sure you have adequate light—on your bike, if you're riding, and a good flashlight, if you're rollerblading, running or walking. And, as you set out, it's a good idea to put the phone number and address of your hotel in your pocket, along with a small amount of cash and a cell phone, if you have one.

Lodging. Another consideration, as you plan your trip, is choosing your lodging. If you're required to stay at a specific hotel, call ahead to learn about its exercise facilities. Pack a swimsuit and comfortable exercise clothing. If the hotel doesn't have any facilities, ask about health centers in the area and either call them or check out their Web sites for information on hours, facilities, pricing, and so on. If you have a Y membership at home, it probably will be honored where you're going. If these options don't produce anything helpful, check with some of the area's colleges and universities, many of which have times when the public can use the facilities for a small charge.

If you still haven't found anything helpful, don't forget that you can always walk—it's just a question of where and when. Ask at the desk about the safety of walking in the neighborhood around the hotel and about other options that may be accessible by using the city's transit, whether it's a larger park or a pleasant residential neighborhood. If walking alone in the dark is the only option, walking in the morning before your business meetings is frequently a safer time than walking at night. And many cities are lovely at this hour, as they start to awaken. Conferences are increasingly scheduling morning walk/runs at an hour that leaves enough time to return and shower before meetings begin.

If your conference has scheduled a city bus tour, consider whether you could get to know the city just as well on foot—and get some good exercise in the bargain. You might also consider asking business associates in the city for recommendations, although it's not uncommon for folks who don't live right in the town or near the place where you'll be staying to have no idea what's available there. Another option, often overlooked, is to walk during part of the lunch hour, during a session you may not need to attend or during a snack break in your meetings.

No Such Thing as "Can't" Exercise!

Even if you must stay in a hotel without exercise facilities, or are involved in mandatory sessions from dawn to dusk and can't locate a nearby health facility, you can still get physical activity. In fact, it may be staring you in the face. Would a business contact be interested in sharing a walk while meeting? How about some fast dancing after the business day—or an evening of bowling?

Does your hotel have stairs? If so, you have all you need for a wonderful workout. Check with the front desk to find out if the stairs are lighted and safe. Failing that, walk the halls—something several source persons consulted for this book mentioned doing while traveling. You can also do some calisthenics—jumping jacks in your room, push-ups,

I Never Assume the Conference Hotel

When I've attended conferences, I've been amazed at both the exorbitant prices of rooms at the conference hotel and at some of the lovely—and much less expensive—options near there. You can learn about them in a variety of ways—from travel books at your local public library or by doing a quick Web search, pairing the name of the city and the words "inexpensive lodging," or seeing what the city's name and "bed-and-breakfast" turns up.

Sometimes—in New York and Philadelphia, for example—I've stayed at bed-and-breakfast establishments that were very reasonably priced and near my meeting site. In New York I stayed at a lovely Manhattan brownstone and in Philly at the home of a woman on Antique Row, where I had my own balcony. Neither was an elaborate, pricey establishment, but both were very comfortable and the innkeepers were very helpful. And, of course, the price of breakfast is included.

The real plum, something I learned from a traveler's aid information desk at the airport in Vancouver, British Columbia, was a lovely new Y hotel with accommodations just a few blocks from my conference, complete with a small in-room refrigerator and community kitchen facilities on several floors and—best of all—a daily pass to the Y's full health facilities (just a few blocks away). I had a lovely view of the city from my fifth-floor windows, and the only conveniences I sacrificed were a television (there were several big-screen TVs in sitting rooms, if I'd wanted to watch TV) and a private bath (I shared with a next-door neighbor whom I never met). Incidentally, that Y facility is available to families, as well as individuals.

I've also found that sometimes it's easier to look for lodging outside of the downtown, in an area where it's easier to get exercise. Several times I've still been able to save money and enjoy good options for physical activity by doing this, and renting a car or riding public transit into town for my business. And then there's always the possibility of staying with a friend or relative who's hospitable. Once, while staying with my parents in a Denver suburb, I biked into town for my conference each day. Denver buses also have the equipment to carry bikes, so sometimes I rode the bus one way and biked the other.

external frame pack for overnight camping. The American Hiking Society Web site also provides details on what to look for in any of these pack styles.

■ Aim for zero environmental impact, which includes following federal, state and local laws governing flora and fauna. Note that many plants are protected species. Capture the beauty with your camera, and leave it for those who follow you to enjoy, as well.

■ To keep raccoons and bears away from your food at night, hang it from the branches of a tree away from your tent.

Backpacking is an inexpensive way to enjoy the beauty of America's protected lands while enjoying physical activity that can be as strenuous as you'd like. If you decide to go with a group, keep the number of people below 10. Ask the person most familiar with first aid to bring up the rear and agree to wait for everyone to catch up at forks in the path. Also make sure everyone knows your destination.

Badminton

METs: 4.5

Badminton provides another inexpensive, fun way to get some physical activity—usually outdoors, and frequently at a picnic. Pack badminton gear, as well as a couple of flying discs (commonly known as Frisbees, see page 172) on your next picnic, and you'll have ready-made entertainment that's a lot less fattening than sitting around polishing off the food.

All you need to play it is another player—or three—a net, racquets and shuttlecocks, or "birdies," as many people call the feathered objects you hit back and forth over the net. It's available year-round and nationwide.

Find more information, including historic facts, details of record-holders and the rules of the game at: www.usabadminton.org. A badminton set costs around $20—less, if you buy it at a garage sale or from a thrift or second-hand sporting goods store. Or, check with friends—many folks have them stashed away somewhere in their garage or attic.

Baseball

METs: catch 2.5
game 5.0

Although there aren't a lot of nonprofessional adults playing "The Great American Pastime," there are some. Because a baseball moves a lot faster than a softball, you have to be quicker at starts and stops and have a faster reaction time in order to play without getting injured. Baseball is generally not a good aerobic conditioning activity, although a good, nongame, fielding workout can get fairly aerobic. But nonetheless, it can be a fun complement to a regular fitness program. Required equipment is a glove, bat, ball and a billed cap—as well as at least one companion with whom to play. You may have to hunt to find a team, though. Ask at sporting goods stores that carry baseball equipment.

Use a bat that's suited to your grip, and wear batting gloves to avoid blistering. Teams and leagues frequently separate younger players from older ones (age 40 is a good dividing point, it seems). Pitchers frequently see overuse injuries. Otherwise, injuries include being hit by a batted or pitched ball, sliding or colliding with another player. Warm up well before you try to either throw or hit a ball at full speed and run the bases. Find more information at: www.usabaseball.com.

Basketball

METs: shooting baskets 4.5
nongame play 6.0
game 8.0

A perennial favorite, basketball is quickly overtaking baseball as the great American pastime. In the past 15 years, participation by men ages 35 to 54 has more than doubled. Participation by women is up significantly, as well. You can play alone or with any number of people, and this game can be an excellent conditioner for aerobic fitness, coordination, balance and agility. Helpful skills also include good ball handling and jumping skills. Many communities around the country offer opportunities for adult play, both individually and as part of a team. Levels vary widely, so if you're overwhelmed the first time you try a group, look again for a group that plays at a level closer to your own. Check with park and recreation departments in your community or ask at work whether there's a group that plays. You can also start your own group, using a neighborhood park, or you may be able to arrange to rent the court of a community center or a school gym for a small fee. Fees are frequently based on the type of group, so investigate all the possibilities.

Injuries usually involve high-speed collisions with the ground or with another player, trauma injuries to the ankles, fingers and hands and overuse injuries of the knees and shins. The higher ankle support of a basketball shoe provides some stability to your ankle. You may need to tape your ankles and fingers if they're weak or have been injured previously. It's also helpful to strengthen your supporting muscles and ligaments with resistance training exercises. You can spare your feet, knees, legs and hips some trauma by playing on a variety of surfaces. Helpful activities as you learn the game include jumping practice, catching the ball while moving, side-stepping, back-and-forth running practice at an increasingly faster pace (with rapid starts and stops) and shooting baskets. Before you start playing at full speed, be sure to warm up the muscles in the lower half of your body, as well as your shoulders.

Bicycling

METs: under 10 mph 6.0
10 to 12 mph 10.0
14 to 16 mph 12.5

If you haven't biked since you were a kid, you may find that the bike scene has changed quite a bit. Right off the bat, you're faced with a lot of confusing choices: Do you want a road bike (skinny tires) or one of the several wider-tire models—mountain bikes, some with dual suspension shock absorbers; cross-trainers; the recumbent models that look like you're sitting on a lounge chair? Do you want to lean over the handlebars or ride more upright? Do you want one of those huge bike seats or one of the newer split models that are supposed to spare your private parts? Oh, yes, and by the way, they're now known as saddles, not seats. And how many gears do you want? By now, you're probably wondering if you need an advanced degree to even figure out how to ride the thing.

You'll be glad to know, it's really not that tough to ride a bike these days.

Your best bet, if you're interested in biking, is to try a few bikes and see what's best for you. Decent bike shops will let you ride bikes that you're considering; it's not a good idea to buy any bike you haven't ridden. If working with a decent bike shop doesn't help you know what kind of bike you want, try renting a few different kinds and riding them in the types of settings where you plan to do most of your riding.

One thing you'll be pleasantly surprised to discover is that it's not difficult to adjust to bikes with multiple speeds. And you'll also be pleased to discover that those multiple speeds make it much easier to ride a bike on varying terrain

No Hurdle's Too Great for This Enthusiast!

To say Becky Anderson's a biking enthusiast is a great understatement. A certified Effective Cycling Instructor by the League of American Bicyclists, she's half of the tandem Team Blueberry, based in Portland, Oregon. She and teammate Louie Martin, also a certified cycling instructor and bike mechanic for over 10 years, commute on a daily basis and lead rides throughout the year for a number of bike clubs in Oregon and Washington, biking between 10 and 100 miles nearly every weekend.

But don't let the fact that Becky's a serious cyclist put you off, because Team Blueberry provides some of the most helpful, accessible advice available, if you want to start biking—and it's free at their Web site: www.blueberryrides.com.

Although she has type 1 diabetes, Anderson has been a serious biker for 17 years—and has ridden as much as 9,000 miles in one year. She commutes to and from work on a daily basis, 6.5 miles each way. Most of the time, she and Martin are mounted on one of their five tandem bikes, each appropriately named—including the antique Gooseberry, an upright bike that Anderson can ride in her regular clothes for cruising around town and shopping, and two aluminum frame bikes, the Blueberry, for club rides, and the Raspberry, for commuting.

Sure she's noticed some major changes since she first started biking. "I don't have to wonder if @#$ biker! [expletive deleted] is my middle name," says Anderson, noting that automobile drivers are more used to having bikes on the road than they were a few years ago. Incidentally, you'll find some very helpful information at the Web site, when it comes to dealing with motorists. And, counsel the Team Blueberry experts, "In conflicts with motorists, the bicyclist usually looses out, both on the road and in court," so avoid these conflicts at any cost.

than it used to be—up hills and down if you're on the road, and over bumps and boulders if you're into mountain biking. It doesn't matter if you don't know how many speeds you have, or realize that the gears overlap—you just need to learn how to use them, and a lot of that is just a matter of getting used to the feel of it.

Whether you're new to biking or an old pro, you can find lots of helpful information at a great Web site: www.blueberryrides.com. This site, offered by the Oregonian duo of Becky Anderson and Louie Martin, has tons of helpful information, from suggestions for buying a bike and learning how to use the gears to knowing the rules of the road and how to change a tire.

Buying a Bike

Buy from a reputable bike shop and buy the lightest bike you can afford, advise Anderson and Martin. You can change a lot of the components as you go, but you'll always have to work with the frame you buy. While you can cover a lot more pavement a lot faster on a road bike, the hunched over position may be too uncomfortable for you, as a beginner, and the bike is definitely harder to control off-road or on sand and gravel. At the Blueberry Rides Web site you can find more information on pros and cons of various materials—including aluminum, carbon, steel and titanium—and styles of bikes—including mountain, road, touring, recumbent and tandem. You can also learn there how to know whether the bike fits you or not and how to adjust one so that it does fit.

"Don't skimp," when it comes to buying a helmet, advise Anderson and Martin. Never buy a used helmet, because you can't always tell by visually inspecting one if it's been in a crash and lost some of its protective characteristics. Incidentally, wear your helmet level on your head, not tipped back like a hat. If you say that looks silly, just consider for a moment, what would hit the pavement first if you took a header over the bike's handlebars.

Unfortunately, although 50 percent of riders report that they use helmets, observational studies put that number as low as 17 percent—and retailers haven't seen a boom in sales that the higher number would imply. At least 20 states have mandatory bike helmet laws—which now cover about half of the kids 14 and under in the United States. New helmets should have the Consumer Product Safety Commission (CPSC) sticker inside, and older ones should be certified by the American Society for Testing and Materials and/or the Snell Memorial Foundation. You may be more inclined to wear a helmet, if you realize that they prevent between 74 and 85 percent of brain injuries that bikers would experience in accidents.

And don't leave the bike shop without lights. Laws now require a headlight and rear red reflectors at night, but Anderson and Martin recommend opting for a blinking rear taillight, which can be seen from greater distances in lower light.

Getting Started

Anderson recommends starting out by biking on the streets of your neighborhood and getting used to the traffic. Be sure you stay an arm's length away from traffic and parked cars, and from

Riding on the road is actually safer than riding on sidewalks.

the outset you should know that the rules of the road apply to bikers. Because you're slower moving than other vehicles, stay to the right and ride in predictable patterns. The leading cause of accidents for bikers is a motorist at a stop sign or light who doesn't yield to the biker, say Anderson and Martin, who urge making eye contact before crossing in front of a vehicle stopped at an intersection, just to make sure the driver has seen you.

"Don't ride on the sidewalks, because they're more dangerous than riding on the road," says Anderson, who notes that bike lanes also can be fairly high-risk places to ride. "There's a perception of safety that isn't reality," she says, noting that bikers need to help motorists understand that bikes belong on the road. If this is new information for you, check out the Web site, where you can see good descriptions of where and how you should bike on the roads. And it's a good idea to check with your city about rules regarding riding on sidewalks—they vary greatly, even within one metropolitan area.

"Start slow and build up gradually," says Anderson. "Even if you're physically fit—if the bike doesn't fit you, or if you try to ride 100 miles without doing time in the saddle beforehand, or if the saddle isn't right for you, then you'll have 'bottom issues'," her term for the various discomforts you can incur by spending too much time right off the bat on a bike seat. Anderson recommends wearing bike shorts—only once between washings and without underwear. Some people wear two pairs of biking shorts for extra comfort on longer rides.

"Sore butt is inevitable, if you're just starting," says Anderson. "Limit your time in the saddle at first, and work up gradually." That's good advice, whether you're a novice biker, or just at the start of a new biking season, if you don't bike year-round. Anderson also mentions several products that can help prevent or treat saddle sores, including baby powder in your shorts to help keep you dry, and various products you apply to either your shorts or yourself, including Carmex, Bag Balm, Body Glide, Chamois Butt'R. Incidentally, some soreness is also a result of improperly adjusted bike seats and handlebars.

Using the gears on your bike correctly reduces the stress on your legs and knees and gives you a more efficient ride. It's best if you can keep the pedals moving at a pace somewhere in the range of 60 to 100 revolutions per minute (rpm) on the level—doctors who treat sore knees prefer the higher number. This helps you avoid knee problems that you may encounter by using a gear that doesn't allow you to spin at that pace. When you're learning to shift, learn to manage the gears in the back wheel first, and then the front—techniques also described well at the Blueberry Rides Web site.

Shifting gears and climbing hills is something you should master as you become comfortable on your bike, if you want to use biking for improving your fitness level. Without hills, biking is a moderately helpful cardiorespiratory exercise. But it can become a great aerobic exercise quite a bit faster if you tackle hills. And, of course, you might eventually want to take on the mountains!

Biking at higher altitudes doesn't necessarily mean the same thing as mountain biking. Some people enjoy biking over mountain passes. Doing so requires both a certain level of fitness and a bike with sufficient gears to enable you to keep your pedals moving at a speed you can handle. Needless to say, it also requires good brakes—and don't underestimate the challenge of riding down a steep mountain pass, often with switchbacks. Enthusiasts collect notches for their mountain passes—as in, "How many have you done over 10,000 feet?" If you're just starting, getting to this point may take a while, but it certainly can be a laudable goal.

What most people call "mountain biking," on the other hand, is much more popular—and responsible for a lot more injuries. It's off-road biking on challenging terrain. If you decide to go this route, you'll surely be able to find kids happy to join in. But do take these precautions:

- Always wear a helmet that fits properly.
- Always ride in control, which means practicing your off-road skills before you get to the challenging terrain. If you can't feel in control, simply get off and walk, but keep an eye out for bikers bearing down or coming head-on at you—and get out of the way to avoid a collision.
- Check your brakes before heading out—and use them before you turn, not as you turn, because at that point it's easy to apply them too hard and lose control in a skid.
- Remember that your front brakes have a lot more stopping power than the back brakes. That means it's easy, if you apply the front brakes too quickly or too hard on a steep descent, to flip the bike and take a header over the handlebars—not a recommended move—"called an 'endo,' with the 'o' being a long vowel," notes Anderson.
- A couple of skill tips: shift your weight to your back wheel on a steep descent to improve your balance; you may also want to learn how to "loft"—pull up on the handlebars and shift your weight to the back tire to get your front wheel over obstacles like rocks and logs.

If this sort of riding really appeals to you, and you get quite involved with it, you should know that so-called extreme biking—doing this type of biking more than 2 hours a day, 6 days and an average of 187 miles a week for more than 7 years—has recently been shown to increase the likelihood of male fertility problems, and possibly to increase testicular calcium deposits, which are linked

My Version of Mountain Biking

Since I'm originally from Colorado and my parents still live there, I often vacation and frequently bike in that gorgeous state. My own bike is a cross trainer, which means I sit upright, and it has wider tires than a road bike. It's not fancy, but I've put a fair number of miles on it in the 13-plus years I've owned it. I've biked around the Denver area and in the city a fair amount, and I've biked on some high, lovely paved trails in the mountains—mostly between mountains, actually.

When I was most recently in Colorado in the fall, staying about 10,000 feet above sea level in an inspiringly beautiful mountain ski area, I decided to rent a mountain bike for a few days from the Y there and try my hand at biking around the area. I thought the bike would be quite similar to mine. I had noticed a paved path on the road driving up, and I thought I'd see how far it went. I knew I couldn't do an entire mountain pass, as I'd often seen other bikers on the shoulder of the road doing—saying to myself as I drove past them that they must either be incredibly fit or nuts. But I assumed there would be plenty of relatively flat places to ride.

My first surprise came when I saw the bike. It had two shock absorbers and looked like it was made for a 15-year-old kid who was fearless: sturdy and ready for rugged wear. I knew my plans needing some tweaking when I got my first glance at the release I was asked to sign—a full page of very tiny type, which basically said I'd be responsible to finance a medical evacuation flight, should I become injured. I received a trail map and set out on what was reported to be the tamest of the area's off-road trails.

Within 10 minutes, my plans had totally changed. I quickly discovered that, even though I was relatively comfortable on this bike in the parking lot, what the folks there called a trail and what I was used to knowing as a bike trail were very different. I'm simply not into learning how to jump boulders and gullies while trying to figure out where the trail goes—and, oh yes, while also trying to stay on the bike, which was quite bouncy. If I wanted a relaxing—yet aerobic—workout, I decided, I'd need to get back on the pavement. And that's what I did.

The rest of the week I thoroughly enjoyed riding the bike. I found that the paved trail I'd seen went only a few miles, so I used the ample roadway shoulder. I rode each day, and became more acclimated to the altitude, as well. Some days I rode between several small towns, once partway up a mountain pass, and several times on a low-traffic, paved side road that followed a beautiful river valley. The rides were inspiring, sometimes challenging and something I looked forward to every day.

with increased cancer risk.

While it's important to understand that most bikers don't have long-term problems with pressure injuries to the crotch area, this is something that becomes more common among bikers who spend a lot of time in the saddle. If you spend quite a bit of time on a regular bike saddle and notice numbness, urinary difficulties or erectile dysfunction, try these things:

- Check to be sure your saddle isn't too high or tipped up at the front.
- Shift your position more often while riding, moving forward or back on the saddle and standing on the pedals at regular intervals. Get off the bike every few miles and walk around.
- When you anticipate going over a bump, stand and let your legs, rather than your bottom, absorb the shock.
- Consider trying a different saddle style. In a recent study, reported in *The Physician and Sportsmedicine,* an experimental bike seat significantly reduced numbness in that area.

If you do become an avid biker, remember that it's very important to replace fluids frequently as you bike. It's a good idea, if you're out biking for more than half an hour, to bring water. Numerous attachment devices for water bottles are available—or you can carry

Mia: Biking the World

Mia, whom you met in Chapter 3, is a single woman who's biked a fair amount around the world. She's biked with a number of groups, some through organizations set up to provide active vacations, others with groups of friends who've decided they enjoy biking together. You can also ride on a fundraiser bike ride, and many states have rides during the summer that cross the entire state.

Organized trips (you may have read about them in the travel section of this chapter), generally state up-front the minimum number of miles you should be able to ride in a day, in order to sign up for the trip. They also list, for each trip, the number of miles you'll actually ride each day, as well as the type of terrain you can expect. The trips have so-called sag vans that follow the route and help bikers whose bikes break down or who simply are tired and need to stop and get a ride.

Mia has found a group of bikers—many from Canada—who enjoy organizing their own trip to Jamaica every year. They stay in rustic places and enjoy food cooked by local residents for about $700 a week. Besides organized trips to Death Valley, Baja, Hawaii, Costa Rica and the Yucatan Peninsula, Mia's also done a mountain bike trip in South Dakota (200 miles, from Deadwood to the bottom of the state's George Mikkelson trail, with a lift back from a local resident who charged $20) and biked in Holland (where bikes rent "dirt cheap" and, Mia reports, everyone rides). Mia was recently disappointed, when she was in Ireland hoping to bike part of the time, but found that it's impossible to rent bikes out of season (she was there in March). She still hopes to do more biking in Europe, Peru and—a big-ticket destination—New Zealand.

plastic bottles or cans in a backpack or basket. Anderson notes that hydration and good nutrition become especially important in making your ride comfortable when you bike longer distances.

Anderson and Martin also suggest that you look into joining a local bike club, where you can get lots of helpful tips on biking, as well as information about group rides and updates on trails in your area. That—and by checking their Web site—is how most of the riders who accompany Anderson and Martin on the Blueberry Rides learn of upcoming trips. You can also ask for bike trail information from your city, county or state—or find it online. You may even choose to become a community activist, lobbying for a more biker-friendly community.

The Bike Buddy program in the Puget Sound area, for example, pairs experienced volunteers with novice bike commuters from the same area. The veteran helps the novice select a comfortable route, ride safely in traffic, learn how to fix a flat tire, rent a bike locker and learn to take the bus with a bike. There are nearly 2,000 members of the Bicycle Alliance of Washington, and between 4 and 8 percent of area residents bike or walk to work.

Yes, you can get a very good workout on a stationary bike, where you can monitor your pulse, time spent and resistance. For many people, a stationary bike enables them to get quick, easy access to aerobic activity, regardless of the weather. A cycling program can help rehabilitate aching knee joints, build thigh muscle strength, increase knee motion and reduce pain, according to Alison P. Toth, M.D., the orthopedic surgeon who directs Duke University's Women's Sports Medicine program. In an ideal world, you'll have both types of biking opportunities available.

Bowling

METs: 3.0

Broomball

METs: 7.0

Calisthenics

METs: 3.5 to 8.0

Canoeing and Kayaking

METs: 2 to 4 mph 3.0
4 to 6 mph 7.0

Croquet

METs: 2.5

Canoeing can be quite relaxing—and will also give you a great upper body workout.

Canoeing—I Love It. Kayaking—Here I Come!

First, a recommendation. You can find a lot of excellent canoe and kayak information at this Web site: www.paddling.net. For that reason, the information won't be repeated here. The site will help you know what to buy—and even features a want ad section—and how to rate both waterways and paddlers. It also features maps and information, by state, of good places to paddle.

I think I must have been a fish in a former life, because I love swimming and canoeing. And, since a couple of friends have kayaks, I'm hoping to try that soon, as well. Canoeing is a wonderful way to spend time, either alone or with one or two other people, enjoying the beauty of the country's lakes, rivers and waterways, whether it's the quiet, pristine beauty of a north woods or high mountain lake; a relaxing pastoral scene on a gentle river flowing through the countryside; or the towns, bluffs, locks and dams on the mighty Mississippi River.

Canoeing offers an inexpensive way to enjoy the water. We bought our aluminum Grumman canoe from an outfitter through a want ad in the Sunday paper. (Outfitters routinely recycle their stock every 3 years or so.) It has seen use, but is in fine shape, and we've added a few scratches and dents along the way. But it's none the worse for wear. You can also rent canoes many places, and it's a great way to spend an afternoon. Put on a life jacket, sunscreen and a hat, and you're ready.

You don't need to take a class—you can teach yourself to paddle a canoe, although I'm sure if I'd taken a class I'd be much more expert and proficient. There are many opportunities, if you wish, to join groups heading out for canoe trips of several days. Before signing up for that, though, you really should spend a few hours paddling, and check into the length of the portages—the spaces over which you may have to carry the canoe and your supplies between lakes, around rapids or through shallow or rocky passages. Portaging can be hard, heavy work.

Paddling the canoe, on the other hand, usually can be as strenuous as you'd like. If you're not sure how much you want to paddle, look for a modest-sized lake that doesn't have high waves—on a day when the weather is calm. If you travel a river route, you may hardly need to paddle at all, depending on the river flow and distance you want to cover. But don't forget that you need to have a way to get back to your vehicle if you left it where you put the canoe into the water.

It's law in most places that you have to either wear or have with you a personal flotation device (life jacket), as do the others in your boat. Also be sure to take an extra paddle, in the event that one slips out of your hand and you need to paddle to pick it up.

If you're paddling alone, position yourself in the middle of the canoe, on the floor. If there are two paddlers, each one sits on a seat at one end of the canoe. The function of the front person—in addition to paddling—is to look ahead, keep an eye out for rocks hiding near the surface of the water and warn the person in the back, who does most of the steering, of obstacles ahead. If you have a third person, that person should sit in the middle of the canoe on the bottom of the boat.

I've never been in a canoe that tipped, which isn't at all unusual for people who use canoes. The primary thing to know when you canoe is that the boat is quite stable if you follow a couple of basic rules—assuming you're not taking out a racing canoe. First, never stand in the boat, once you've set out. When you board the boat, the boat should be perpendicular to the shore, with the gear already loaded. The person who will sit in the back steadies the boat as the person who's going to sit in the front moves to the front seat, holding both sides of the canoe, feet always on the craft's centerline. Jerky motions aren't encouraged. When the first person is situated, the other paddler pushes the boat out and gently climbs aboard, again, keeping your feet in the middle of the boat and not making jerking motions.

Although you'll want to avoid learning to canoe when the wind and waves are high, the other important thing to know about canoe stability is that it's almost always better to meet a swell or wave at a perpendicular angle. If you're parallel to the roll of the water, it can roll the canoe much more easily. And always keep an eye on the weather, keeping in mind how far it is back to where you need to go. You don't want to be on the water in a storm, especially an electrical one.

Kayaking, while somewhat similar to canoeing, predominantly involves personal crafts. If you go with someone, it's likely that you'll each have a boat. Kayaking also requires some knowledge of righting a turned boat (that's the first lesson), and some people advise beginners to take instruction. Rather than sitting on a seat, as you do in a canoe, the only thing that separates you from the water in a kayak is the material of the kayak. Kayaks are generally covered; you sit with your feet extended in front of you under the cover. They carry much less gear than a canoe, and you propel them with a paddle that can be used on both ends. Again, personal flotation devices are a "must," as is keeping an eye on the weather.

Dancing

METs: ballroom 3.0 to 5.5
country, disco, line, polka, swing 4.5
jitterbug, tap 4.8

Fencing

METs: 6.0

Football

METs: play catch 2.5
coach football 4.0
play touch or flag football 8.0

Frisbee (Flying Disc)

METs: 3.0

Like badminton, volleyball and other games often played outdoors, spending some time with friends tossing a flying disc, also known as a Frisbee, can provide a fair amount of exercise. Although most people use the term Frisbee, that's actually the brand name of the flying discs produced by Wham-O Corporation, of California. Flying discs were first used for recreation in the early 1900s in New Haven, Connecticut, when the Frisbie Company supplied pie tins thrown and caught by students at Yale University. Plastic discs arrived after World War II, and the sport really took off after that, with international competition beginning in the mid-1970s. There are several world championship competitions each year, in both individual and team events.

Two of the most popular actual games currently played are ultimate and disc golf. Ultimate is a self-refereed team sport resembling football, with seven players on a team. The object is to pass the disc to a teammate, who must catch it in the opposing team's end zone. You can only advance the disc by passing, and you must stop running after catching it and establish a pivot foot before passing it on. No tackling is allowed, but defense tries to force the offense to turn over the disc—which occurs if it hits the ground, goes out of bounds or is dropped, blocked or intercepted.

Disc golf has rules similar to golf played with a ball and uses discs of varying weights and flight characteristics. Special green metal baskets on poles take the place of golf holes. There are hundreds of permanent courses in North America, Europe and Asia. You may be surprised to find them at a larger park near where you live, once you know what they are. You can learn about special tosses and other game variations at the World Flying Disc Federation Web site: www.wfdf.org.

Gardening

METs: 1.5 to 6.0

Golf

METs: miniature or driving range 3.0
with power cart 3.5
walk and carry clubs 4.5

The great thing about golf is that everyone can play and enjoy the exercise, as well as the social interaction. While golf is not famed for being a super aerobic activity for most people, you can greatly improve its conditioning value by ditching the golf cart and pulling or carrying your clubs. For a recent study, 55 middle-aged former golfers took up the game again—this time without carts. They played two or three times a week for 5 months, during which time they realized increases in aerobic performance and endurance, improved HDL cholesterol levels and lost an average of 3 pounds and 1 inch from their waistlines.

It's best, if you plan to start golfing, to take a few lessons to avoid some of the injuries that are common to golfers—especially golfer's elbow. And it's tough to break bad habits if you start with incorrect technique. The American Academy of Orthopaedic Surgeons has several exercises at their Web site (http://orthoinfo.aaos.org) that you can use to avoid golfer's elbow and low back pain caused by a poor swing.

"The golf swing is a motion chain that involves all parts of your body," says Edward Laskowski, M.D., co-director of the Mayo Clinic Sports Medicine Center. He notes that the force is transferred all the way from your ankles up your body through your wrists—the smoother, the better. A small study reported that the style of golf grip also greatly affects the amount of head and eye movement during putts. While the differences didn't appear to be very significant when golfers took 20 3-foot putts, it was much more noticeable on the 20 9-foot putts each right-handed golfer took: the conventional (right hand below left hand) grip elicited greater motion in the right shoulder, requiring more head and eye movement to stay focused on the ball, and the cross-handed grip (right above left hand) was much more effective on the 9-foot putts.

Gymnastics

METs: 4.0

Have you watched the Olympic gymnasts with amazement and always thought it would be fun to do some of those things? If so, you probably figured that, since you hadn't started gymnastics as a young child, you'd missed your chance. Not so!

A source person for this book, Ann Webster, Ph.D., health psychologist at the Mind/Body Medical Clinic, Beth Israel Deaconess Medical Center, Boston, and instructor in medicine at Harvard Medical School, has been active in the sport since she was young and has stuck with it. In fact, she's been going to the same gym for over 30 years, and noted that it's not all that unusual for a mature adult to be involved with gymnastics, a fact confirmed by the expert who owns and operates Drago's Gym, where Webster goes.

"I've had people start gymnastics at age 65 or 70," says former professional soccer player Drago Mehandzic, who immigrated to the United States in 1967 from Yugoslavia, and purchased the gym that bears his name today. Mehandzic, simply known as Drago, notes that most of the people who come as adult beginners in gymnastics are people who come with a friend, initially to observe. They decide they want to try it, and then they either take group classes or private lessons.

"It's a progressive thing, not that you'll be a competitor," explains Drago. Classes begin with about 15 minutes of stretching, and then proceed to work on the mat: headstands, handstands, backbends, eventually progressing to the rings and trapeze. "You need to come probably six times to start to be comfortable with it," he says. And, he notes, as other sports have become more popular, it's harder to find people who teach gymnastics well—especially to mature adults. "Look for an older instructor who understands adult learners," suggests Drago. And yes, according to Drago, leotards are optional. You can work out in a pair of shorts and a T-shirt. And you'll want to wear socks or tights, as well, suggests Drago. So, if it's always been a dream of yours—give it a try!

Handball

METs: team 8.0
singles 12.0

When you think of handball, you probably think of the indoor game played on a racquetball court, in which players smack a little black ball off of a wall with their hands. **Team handball**, played by about 15 million players on five continents but just emerging in the United States, is quite different. For one thing, the ball is not played off of a wall. First-time spectators describe it as playing soccer with your hands, although they say that some aspects of the game remind them of basketball, water polo or ice hockey. Interest in the United States was sparked by the 1996 Atlanta Olympic games, and players around the country now play the game year-round.

No special skills are required to start playing the game, but as you learn it, you'll become more skilled at dribbling, shooting and passing the ball. Most new players can be game-ready in a matter of weeks.

Team handball is played by two teams, each usually having six court players and one goalie. The court is larger than a standard basketball court, and can be located on sand or grass, or on an indoor floor. The object of the game is to throw the cantaloupe-sized ball into the opponent's approximately 7-foot by 10-foot goal while defending your own goal. Except for each team having a 60-second time-out, play is fast and continuous in two 30-minute halves, unless a referee stops the play. A point is scored with each goal, and game totals frequently run in the high teens to mid-twenties. The defense is similar to basketball, as defenders protect the goal area—a semicircle 18 feet from the goal—into which only the goalie is allowed. More contact is allowed: although you can't push, hold or endanger an opponent, torso contact is permitted. Excessive roughness results in a warning or 2-minute suspension.

Players primarily move the ball by passing it, and are allowed to take three steps with the ball before and after dribbling it. However, they can only stand still with the ball for 3 seconds. The offense looks for a way over, around or through the defensive wall protecting the goal area.

Players wear jerseys or shirts, shorts, socks and court shoes—and often knee or elbow pads. Goalkeepers wear brightly colored long-sleeved shirts and sweat pants to distinguish them from court players of both teams. Players can change roles if they change uniforms during the game. The only equipment needed is a ball (which usually costs $10 to $60) and a set of goals, although beginners can use tape to draw the goal on a wall.

Hiking (see Backpacking)

Hockey

METs: field or ice hockey 8.0

Field hockey is played by athletes all across the United States and is particularly prevalent in the northeastern and mid-Atlantic states, as well as in California, according to Howard Thomas of the United States Field Hockey Association. The sport is played year-round, both indoors and outside. Outdoor teams generally have 11 players, while indoor teams have six.

You can learn the required skills through community organizations, as well as at clinics. The equipment you'll need includes a field hockey stick, ball, shin guards and a mouthpiece. Goalkeepers also need pads, gloves, kickers and a helmet. Equipment is available at specialty field hockey stores.

Horseback Riding

METs: 4.0

"Try to find someone who teaches you to communicate with the horse," says Dan Ramberg, a horseback riding instructor who teaches riding instructors. Too frequently, people aren't given the opportunity to teach a horse or learn something from the animal, according to Ramberg.

Adult learners are not at all unusual in horseback riding. Ramberg says fear is the biggest hurdle to overcome when learning to ride a horse—regardless of your age. "Everyone's afraid, to some degree, although most people don't realize or admit it," says Ramberg. "Sure, I have a fear level, but it's probably different than 99 percent of the people out there, when it comes to horses. But when you're in control, your fear level goes down," he says. "Many people are spoiled by their first encounter with a horse, frequently due to poor instruction."

You can learn to ride a horse from a neighbor or friend, at a public facility or a private business. In most areas of the country you can rent horses by the hour for about $20 to $25. Ramberg recommends lessons, which you can find by looking up stables or horseback riding in the phone book. If you're not sure you even like horses, Ramberg suggests going on a public trail ride, hay ride or sleigh ride. He gives group lessons for up to eight people at a time. Many other stables only teach lessons privately, usually at the cost of about $30 to $35 per lesson.

Ramberg suggests steering clear of so-called breed barns—businesses that breed specialized Arab show horses or quarter horses. Lessons at those places, he says, are quite structured and high-powered. "You can learn at whatever level you'd like," Ramberg says. "Public trail riding is basically just sitting on a head-to-tail machine. If you take lessons, you learn to go up and down hills, maneuver separately, cross streams—and how to manage the horse."

Ramberg suggests most people need to be on a horse for a total of 8 to 10 hours before they feel comfortable riding. "Ride different horses. And ask if the place that offers lessons will teach you to put the saddle and bridle on the horse yourself and go for a ride. Places worth their salt will do that. You want an instructor who will teach you about horses. That's different than just teaching you to stay on a horse during a trail ride."

Horseshoes

METs: 3.0

Using many of the same skills as shuffleboard (and at the same MET rate), pitching horseshoes is another moderately active outdoor sport that's perfect for relaxing on a summer afternoon with friends. A set of horseshoes costs about $26, and in an hour of tossing horseshoes, you can work off one 3-ounce piece of barbecued chicken.

Ice Skating (Figure Skating)

METs: 7.0

Although you probably won't enter the Olympics, ice skating, or figure skating, can still be an enjoyable activity—year-round, if you live near an indoor ice arena. Time on the ice is often precious, so your best bet may be to look for times when schools are in session, as teams tend to schedule time on the ice when school gets out. Figure skating—a perennial favorite Olympic event—requires balance and coordination.

If you've never skated before, it's a good idea to rent skates and take some lessons as you begin. The United States Figure Skating Association has special curriculum designed for adult beginners, divided into four levels. The beginning level includes skills such as recovering from a fall, forward strides and glides, skating backward and snowplow stops. Check the Association's Web site (www.usfsa.org) for more information about classes and figure skating clubs in your area.

If you wear custom orthotics in your shoes, put them into the skates, as well. You can buy skates at sporting goods stores, as well as at thrift or second-hand sporting equipment stores.

Inline Skating (Rollerblading)

METs: 12.0

If you decide to join one of America's fastest-growing sports, you can gain cardiovascular benefits, as well as strengthen the muscles of your legs and buttocks, possibly also your shoulders and arms. These skates have a line of

Inline skating is great exercise, and lots of fun. But don't forget safety gear.

low-friction polyurethane wheels that enables an experienced skater to cruise at speeds of 10 to 17 miles per hour.

If you don't take a class—often available through community education, at health clubs and local Ys—at least get some information from a knowledgeable sales clerk about proper fit and safety guidelines. If you skate on the road, you're subject to the same rules as a biker or motorist. Skate to the right and pass to the left, and always yield to pedestrians—no matter if you're on the road or on a trail.

Protective gear is a must: a helmet, knee and elbow pads. The largest group of skaters to become injured in one study were in the 18 to 35 age category, and the most common cause of injury was loss of control, frequently leading to a fracture of the forearm or wrist. Most injuries involve either first-time, novice or occasional skaters, frequently due to lack of control and stopping skills.

Jogging (see Running)

Karate

METs: 10.0

A "grassroots, inexpensive way to obtain necessary conditioning for healthy living," is how Katherine Thiry, of the USA National Karate Foundation, describes the experience of learning the Japanese martial art of karate. For many people, this is a first exposure to the Japanese culture, yet it's not really a way to become familiar with Japanese social norms, and class practices are not reflective of social etiquette in Japanese society.

Karate is accessible to people around the country, year-round, and is best learned from an instructor at a dojo (the Japanese word for school). At first you don't need anything other than loose-fitting clothing (called "gi"), and you can expect to be barefoot, as it's customary to remove your shoes at the dojo entrance. Eventually, you will need protective gear, which includes a mouth guard and hand pads (costing approximately $150).

Instructors teach and demonstrate typical manners for the classes, including deference and respect, shown by bowing to the instructor and recitation of the tenets of behavior and expectations (called "kun"). You'll learn how to properly say "please" and "thank you" and when to do so, as well as appropriate care of karate equipment, belts and uniforms. Horseplay, profanity or unruly behavior is clearly not allowed.

Before you choose a karate school, visit and observe the student body and watch an entire class. Inquire locally about the school's reputation and trust your instincts.

Kayaking (see Canoeing)

Kickboxing

METs: 10.0

Pilates

METs: unavailable

Created in the 1920s by Joseph Pilates, according to Drago Mehandzic, owner and operator of Drago's Gym in New

York City, Pilates was first used by the German immigrant nurse to rehabilitate injured people in London hospitals. Originally developed by attaching springs to beds, the Pilates system today relies on specially designed resistance training devices and a sequence of exercises that emphasize core movements and body balancing.

According to the American College of Sports Medicine, Pilates is especially popular among dancers and has been shown to produce strength and flexibility gains. It may also be useful for knee rehabilitation. This technique focuses on concentration, control, a flowing movement, precision, body centering and breathing.

If you're interested in learning Pilates, Drago, who's certified to train Pilates instructors, recommends looking for a certified professional.

Ping-Pong (see Table Tennis)

Racquetball

METs: 7.0

Raking Leaves

METs: 4.3

Rock Climbing

METs: depending on the degree of difficulty 6.0 to 8.0

Bouldering, or climbing low, more horizontal rocky surfaces without ropes or gear is an activity some people enjoy, while many others want the more challenging thrill of a vertical climb. Climbing walls are going up at amazing speeds at sporting goods stores, community centers, fitness facilities, colleges and universities—even in high schools and junior high schools. It seems everyone wants to get into the act. You can probably find an opportunity near you, and age isn't a factor. In fact, personnel at a sporting goods store who were interviewed indicated that they regularly have people in their 70s and 80s climbing—and "somebody 4 years old can do it." Walls or pinnacles have areas with varying degrees of difficulty, and you can spend weeks just climbing every aspect of one facility's wall. You wear a special harness and are tethered by a dynamic rope that stretches and absorbs the force of the impact if you lose your footing.

It's probably a good idea to take a class when you first attempt this sport, and realize that different climbs require varying physical strength. Ask if the instructor is certified through your state's climbing association. "You get into shape by doing it—it builds endurance," says one expert, noting that you're most likely to notice the exertion in your hands and forearms. "Some people become expert very quickly, while others take longer." What usually holds someone back is a fear of heights.

Expect to sign a waiver. If you're under age 18, you'll need the signature of a responsible adult. Gear is provided and costs vary, with $10 being a fairly common daily rate. Some fitness clubs simply require a club membership and don't charge an additional fee. Find climbing walls in your area by checking a phone book or doing a Web search, under climbing associations.

Roller Skating

METs: 7.0

Rollerblading (see Inline Skating)

Rope Jumping

METs: 10.0

Rope jumping is a great cardiovascular conditioning exercise, if you can handle the impact of jumping. Wear shoes—cross-trainers or aerobic shoes—that are well-cushioned in the ball of your foot and have a reinforced toe. If you can, find a cushioned surface for jumping—a thick rubber mat (found in some offices) would work well.

Pick a lightweight rope with grips that won't slip when your hands get sweaty. Step on the center of the rope and if the grips come to the middle of your chest, it's the right length. As you jump, keep your back straight, head up, shoulders relaxed, elbows close to your body and knees slightly bent. You can reduce the impact on your knees if you

Nelson Takes to the Rocks

What kid doesn't love climbing rocks? If you want an activity that will interest your teenagers, here's a great one, says Miriam Nelson, Ph.D., director of the Center for Physical Activity and Nutrition, and associate professor of nutrition at the Friedman School of Nutrition Science and Policy at Tufts University, fellow of the American College of Sports Medicine and author of *Strong Women Stay Young; Strong Women Stay Slim; Strong Women, Strong Bones; Strong Women Eat Well* and *Women and Men Beat Arthritis.*

Nelson and her husband go rock climbing twice a week with their kids—ages 10, 12 and 14. Sound scary? Nelson says it isn't, and that it's something everyone can do together, regardless of your level of expertise. She insists that her family is incredibly safety conscious. In the winter you can find the family at a local indoor site, while you'll frequently find them outdoors on the real thing in the summertime.

Nelson considers herself fortunate for loving physical activity. In addition to rock climbing and hiking with her family, Nelson is an avid walker, squeezing in 30- to 45-minute walk/runs several times a week and lifting weights twice a week at home.

"I try to tuck in physical activity," says Nelson. "I walk on errands when I can, I take the stairs. I like being active. I find that when I'm sedentary I can go stir crazy and I need to move. Not surprisingly, I get more physical activity on weekends." Although she realizes that getting teens to do things with their parents is tricky, Nelson says that her family manages to go for a walk together at least once on a weekend. "You have to be willing to do what the kids like," she says, noting that soccer, theater and dance keep the kids busy, as well. "It's important to establish the habits early on."

jump low, as well. And, if you get bored, just try some fancy foot moves you may remember from your childhood.

Rowing

METs: 2 to 4 mph 3.0
4 to 6 mph 7.0

Running/Jogging

METs: jog/run combination 6.0
jog 7.0
run 5 mph or in place 8.0
run cross-country 9.0

Think you may want to try running? You don't need special facilities or equipment, and you can do it anywhere, at just about any time.

Incidentally, how many calories you spend running depends on your speed, as well as on how much you weigh. For example, for 1 hour of running:

- If you weigh 100 pounds and run 5.5 miles per hour (mph), you use about 440 calories, which rises to 610 at 7 mph.
- If you weigh 200 pounds, it takes about 880 calories to go 5.5 mph and 1,220 for 7 mph.

Go Ahead—Turn the Doorknob!

Interestingly, a lot of what some of the best trainers and runners tell you about getting started on a running program applies to folks who simply want to get a bit more fit, as well as to people training for the Olympics. What does a runner-turned-trainer consider her most important advice for beginning adult runners?

"The hardest thing about running is turning the doorknob," says Lorraine Moller, who competed in four Olympic games, winning the bronze medal in the 1992 women's marathon. "You need to be very conservative, if you're just beginning to run. Less is more," Moller says.

Some experts suggest building a program by beginning with a combination of walking and jogging or running.

"First, you need the platform of good health." Moller recommends that you clear any medical conditions you may have with your physician before starting a running program—"and your doctor probably needs to get an exercise program, too," she adds with a chuckle.

How to Tailor Your Program

"Go from running slowly to building distance, and then gradually go faster. Even if you can only walk for 10 minutes, that's a good start," she says, cautioning against trying to build speed too soon. Moller bases this recommendation on the belief that it's most important to build aerobic capacity first, boosting your circulatory system and enhancing your body's ability to use oxygen—what Moller calls "the health-giving nutrient."

Moller recommends combining walking and running, then gradually reducing the walking component until you can run comfortably for an hour. "Your aerobic system responds quickly and can build up quickly—in just a few months," she says. "If you can stick with it for 3 months, you will have developed an aerobic base that makes activity comfortable and pleasurable for you, and you will have established a habit."

As you begin, Moller suggests going out and walking for 10 minutes, then running gently for as long as you can, then walking for another 10 minutes. She also recommends listening to your body. "You'll know when you've had enough."

"Continue to sandwich your runs with at least a 10-minute walk," says Moller. Add 5 minutes a week to your exercise regimen by increasing the walk time on your first two workouts of the week and your run time on the third day.

Continue adding 5 minutes a week until you reach an hour's duration. "Once you can go an hour, you can continue to build time, if you're interested—and then work on speed," says Moller, who cautions against being a slave to your watch. "Don't measure how far and how fast—this just puts unnecessary pressure on you. Focus, instead, on enjoying it, and don't make it another stress in your life."

Moller recommends finding a training buddy who's well suited to your fitness level—"someone you enjoy talking with and someone you're not too competitive with." Then enjoy running leisurely with that person, talking as you run. "You're more likely to get out and do it, if a friend's waiting for you at the corner," she says. "And you're more likely to keep it aerobic if you talk." Moller suggests that all runners—

Each week*	Walk (minutes)	Run (minutes)	Walk (minutes)	Total (minutes)
Week 1—all 3 days	10	5	10	25
Week 2—				
Tuesday and Thursday	12.5	5	12.5	30
Saturday	10	10	10	30
Week 3—				
Tuesday and Thursday	12.5	10	12.5	35
Saturday	10	15	10	35

*on 3 nonconsecutive days, e.g., Tuesday, Thursday, Saturday especially if you sweat heavily—supplement their diets with a good electrolyte drink.

Moller and Nobby Hashizume both draw their recommendations from the techniques of Arthur Lydiard, the New Zealand coach who's worked with numerous Olympic gold medal runners from several continents over the years. Hashizume, founder and executive director of Five Circles, a nonprofit organization dedicated to enhancing and broadening the sport of running for the betterment of individuals in communities across the country, has been involved with running for 30 years in Japan, Australia and New Zealand, and in the states of Washington, Oregon and Minnesota. He was a professional running coach in his native Japan before coming to the United States. Hashizume studied under Lydiard, whom he periodically brings to the United States to conduct training seminars.

Lydiard attracted attention 40 years ago, when he took a group of 20 New Zealanders, ages 50 to 74, who had survived heart attacks and were getting back into shape, and trained them for 8 months, using his aerobic-building techniques. At the end of that time, he invited members of the press to observe the trainees running 20 miles. "News reporters, who showed up on their bikes, expected to see the joggers drop dead," says Hashizume. "Instead, they had a hard time keeping up with the runners. Eight of those runners later went on to complete full marathons—26.2 miles."

Build Your Aerobic Foundation

Here's how Hashizume recommends using running to build your aerobic foundation, keeping Lydiard's "train, don't strain" always uppermost:

1. Continually remind yourself to build up gradually.

2. First shoot for duration rather than speed—whatever works best for you, whether it's walking or running—until you can handle a 20-minute continuous block of walking and running.

3. Then start to pace yourself. Substitute running for walking until you can run 20 minutes continuously, on a flat surface. Then run 10 minutes, and turn around and go back. If it takes you 12 minutes to go back, you started too fast. If it takes you less than 10 minutes, you started too slowly. Ideally, you'll run at the same pace the entire time. It's not the distance, but the speed that stops you.

Hashizume notes that Lydiard's the-

Moller: Keeping Up with Children Is Tough Work

"Chasing a child is far more of a full-time job than I'd ever imagined," says four-time Olympian and bronze medal women's marathoner Lorraine Moller, who became a mother at age 45. Now, in addition to trying to keep up with her small child at her home in Boulder, Colorado, Moller runs up to an hour two or three times a week and coaches the Wings of Mercury, a group of 25 runners of all ages and abilities. A number of Moller's runners hope to make the Olympic trials.

ory is built upon the principle that longer periods of exercise develop the capillary system around the working muscles, improving VO_2max. But that doesn't necessarily mean doing long distances every day. In fact, Lydiard says he's seen the best results when athletes ran about 100 miles a week. To illustrate, Hashizume tells of when his wife, then a busy financial planner with little time to run during the week, decided to run her first marathon. She trained about 3 days a week, including one long run of 90 to 180 minutes. "It's the duration of training that builds up capillary beds and stamina," explains Hashizume. Incidentally, his wife finished her first marathon in 3 hours, 54 minutes—a better time than that achieved by a friend who ran 6 miles every day.

When you run "all out," you're said to be running in your anaerobic zone. Although Lydiard acknowledges that developing anaerobic capacity—in which you face a ceiling beyond which you can no longer function—is necessary for competitive running, he finds it harmful to do more anaerobic exercise than is necessary. This is due to a buildup of lactic acid and the body's difficulty in dealing in a positive way with the acidic state caused by anaerobic work.

"It's always much better to start out too slowly than too fast," says Lydiard. Every day you train, you should finish knowing that you could have run more."

Run Barefoot

"Don't be oversold on rigid, highly cushioned shoes for running," says Lorraine Moller, who competed in four Olympic games. "You want a shoe that allows your foot to move. Don't lug an army boot. Mechanics are much more important than cushioning."

Hashizume agrees, noting that you don't need the most expensive running shoe. He recommends looking for a mid-priced, sufficiently cushioned racing flat that's flexible and light. "If your shoes are rigid, it's like trying to walk or run in a cast," he says. "Thick soles keep you too far from the ground and unstable. Your body should learn to take away the impact of running with a smooth running style. Research shows that runners bounce more when they're wearing highly cushioned shoes, and they come down hard on the ground. That cushioning sends a false message to the brain.

"Bare feet or shoes that have less cushioning help you develop a much smoother stride—that's one reason why African runners are so good," he says. "You don't want to be bouncing. A good foot-strengthening exercise is to go to a grassy area once a week and run barefoot. Today's high-tech shoes, in the name of supporting our feet, actually end up making them weaker."

Safety: More Important Than Distance

Here are some safety tips from the American Academy of Orthopaedic Surgeons:

- Avoid running in heat or in high pollution.
- Drink 10 to 15 ounces of water 10 minutes prior to running and again every 20 to 30 minutes along your route. Weigh yourself before and after you run, and drink 1 pint of water for every pound you've lost.
- Allow time to acclimate yourself gradually.
- Tell others where you're running and stay away from traffic.
- Wear reflective material at dusk and dawn and avoid running in the dark.

Relaxing as you run is something Lydiard also emphasizes. "You must learn to relax," he says. "Relaxation is the key to good running."

Sailing

METs: 3.0

Scuba Diving

METs: 7.0

If you've always dreamed of going scuba diving, it may take some time to save the shekels, but you can make it a reality. It's not a cheap sport.

One good way to find out if you like it is to try a one-day resort dive, offered by many resorts in areas with dive destinations (see sidebar). You'll receive instruction and get a chance to become acclimated to the equipment, often in a swimming pool, before you go on a closely controlled, fairly shallow dive the same day. This will cost about $75 to $150.

Don't buy anything until you figure out if the sport is all you'd hoped it would be. Meanwhile, you can rent everything, and only buy it if and when you decide you're serious about scuba diving—and you have a better idea what you'd want.

You can't rent or buy equipment or get on a dive boat without certification. Before you take the certification course, you should be able to swim 200 yards without stopping, tread water 15 minutes and be comfortable in the water. While scuba diving is something you

Runner's High: Is It for Real?

Although researchers aren't sure, they now suspect that mood changes brought on by intense, usually aerobic exercise may be due to an increase in levels of the mood boosters (dopamine, norepinephrin and serotonin) in your brain, increasing body temperature, the calming effect of rhythmic exercise or simply the sense of control and accomplishment you feel when your exercise distracts you from your daily anxieties.

generally don't do alone, you don't have to provide your own "scuba buddy," because scuba shops put together groups of people to go on dives together. So, although it's not necessary to know someone else who wants to learn with you, it can be a fun thing to do together.

Check a phone book for a scuba shop. Shops generally offer lessons or will be able to tell you where you can get them. They can also tell you about scuba destinations in your area, as well as upcoming trips to dive sites in other areas.

Basic certification courses require classroom work and pool sessions, as well as four or five open-water dives. The cost will run about $350.

When you decide to become certified, find an instructor you're comfortable with and trust, because you're putting your life in that person's hands. Instructors can be certified by various agencies. The largest is the Professional Association of Diving Instructors (PADI), followed by the National Association of Underwater Instructors (NAUI). Your instruction may take place in a swimming pool to which the shop has access.

If you decide you like diving and want to continue doing it, it's a good idea to invest in these items, to suit your size and preferences:

- mask: $50 to $60
- snorkel: $30
- wet suit: $100 and up
- fins: $50 and up

You can continue to rent the rest: tank, regulators, weights, buoyancy compensation device (BCD) vest.

If you're a fan of the old Lloyd Bridges TV show "Sea Hunt," you may be surprised to hear that a long dive lasts

I Actually Tried Scuba Diving

One year our then-26-year-old son, who's a certified diver, offered a resort dive to members of the family going to Florida for a vacation in January. Our younger son's fiancée and I accepted the offer and had an experience we'll probably all long remember. The day before our dive, the resort diving instructor gave us private instruction in the resort's pool, which made learning to use the equipment fairly easy, since we could stand up in the shallow end of the pool any time we wanted to.

The following day we joined a group of people for first a snorkeling stop: swimming with manatees in a large lake near Florida's west coast. Snorkeling was a lot of fun and helped us get used to breathing through the snorkel and swimming while wearing the fins and wet suit.

After a quick lunch we traveled a few miles to a river site where we took a river scuba dive, going down about 25 feet. I found the sensation of the dive much different from snorkeling. Once I overcame a bit of panic and remembered to breathe I was fine, and the dive was incredible, as we explored interesting fish, plants and underwater topography, with an instructor always near. It was a gift I'll never forget.

about 1 hour. Your first dive will probably be half that long, depending upon the depth you dive.

Shuffleboard

METs: 3.0

Skateboarding

METs: 5.0

Skiing

METs: water ski 6.0
ski downhill 6.0
ski cross-country 8.0

Snow Shoveling

METs: 6.0

Soccer

METs: coach soccer 4.0
play soccer 7.0

Softball

METs: catch 2.5
game 5.0

Around the country, men and women ranging across a wide spectrum of age and ability levels enjoy playing softball. Slow-pitch softball is the most common, while college women athletes and teams of younger, quicker adults play fast-pitch. Fast-pitch softball is a pitcher's game, with the greatest challenge being to hit a ball that's coming very fast. In a slow-pitch softball game, on the other hand, you're much more likely to hit the ball, and the fielders have a lot more opportunities to field hits than in the fast-pitch version.

You can find teams of many different ability levels—from the less competitive mixed leagues to the men's-only industrial league or city teams. Softball is still a great game for neighbors and friends to play on a weekend afternoon or in the evening in the summer, as well. All you need are some softballs, a glove and a bat. If you've played before, but you don't feel that you can keep up with the level of play anymore, look for a team in a league that's less competitive. It's a great way to have fun—and it's something you can even do with your kids and grandkids!

Stair Climbing

METs: walk down 3.0
walk up with 1- to 15-pound load 5.0
walk up, carrying moderate load 8.0
walk up with 25- to 49-pound load 8.0
use stair climber 9.0
run up 15.0

Surfing (Body, Board or Wind)

METs: board or body 3.0

Humans have probably tried to capture and ride the waves forever. "**Bodysurfing** is just plain dangerous," says Ryan, an employee of a reliable surfing supplier in California. Although he notes that people do bodysurf at nearby Newport Beach, Ryan adds that the lifeguards there are "forever pulling out people who literally break their necks doing it. The ocean's a lot more powerful than you think." Ryan notes that the waves on California's coast can easily pick people up and throw them indiscriminately. If you do try bodysurfing, it's best to try it where the tide's tamer. It's not unusual to see people bodysurfing on the East Coast, for example, in areas and weather where the tide and wind don't support surfing with a board.

Windsurfing, on the other hand, is something you can do on an inland lake, river or bay in light to moderate wind. It originated in the late 1960s, became an Olympic sport in the 1980s and combines the skills of sailing and surfing. Over 1 million people go windsurfing, 40 percent of them women. The average windsurfer's age is 37, although about 10 percent are over 50. The equipment includes a synthetic sail that's attached to a pivoting mast that rises from the center of an 8- to 12-foot-long plastic or fiberglass-covered board. The windsurfer holds a chest-high boom and inserts his or her feet under straps at the rear of the board for improved stability and maneuverability in high winds.

Surfboarding can be done anyplace on a major ocean. Most common areas for surfing in the United States are the coasts of California, Hawaii and Florida. According to Ryan, it's challenging to learn to surf as an adult, because paddling a board out requires having a fair amount of upper body strength and knowing when to get up—called "pop up" in surfboarding. Doing it at the right time requires a fair amount of balance and quick reaction. However, Ryan notes that the shop has one older female instructor with 30 years' experience teaching adults. He says that in one lesson of an hour or so, she could get most adults up and riding a wave.

A lesson includes the fundamentals of water etiquette, a brief explanation of the mechanics of riding a planing device on a moving piece of energy, work on the mechanics and balancing for paddling (which Ryan says is trickier than

Kathy: There's Nothing Like Being Out in the Ocean

Because she grew up in California, Kathy is intimately familiar with the ocean. Although she now lives in the heartland, when she, her husband and their young adult daughters visit California, Kathy loves to go surfing. She believes an adult with adequate upper body strength and desire can learn to surf, and recommends going to a beach with fewer hotdogging kids to get started. "The beginner spends most of the time trying to get up," she says. "Once you get standing, you can control the board, and it's relatively easy."

Kathy's been around the ocean enough to know the shape of the waves and how the landscape of the ocean floor affects them. "There's nothing like being out in the ocean," she says. "Feeling the waves going up and down, and feeling the peace. It's more than a physical activity or a sport—it's a soul-making experience."

you'd imagine) and learning how to perform a proper pop-up—what you do to end up standing on the board as you ride the wave. According to Ryan, lessons cost about $50 an hour and you can rent a board for $20 to $30 a day. He notes that the skill of surfing is having a lot of water and wave knowledge—"knowing how to catch a wave and position yourself."

The shop, located at Dana Point, California, also offers a new device the shop's owner invented, called the Wave Ski, which basically combines a surfboard with a kayak, so that you can paddle out as you would a kayak and ride the surf back from a sitting position. Invented to aid people with lower body injuries, the Wave Ski also offers older adults the opportunity to get the sensation of riding a wave without needing the same amount of skill and balance that a regular surfboard requires. (You can read about it at the shop's Web site: www.infinitysurf.com.)

Swimming

METs: swim or tread water, moderate effort 4.0
swim for leisure in a pool, lake, ocean or river 6.0
backstroke 7.0
sidestroke or slow front crawl, 50 yards per minute 8.0
freestyle laps, fast 10.0
front crawl fast or butterfly, 75 yards per minute 11.0

Can't swim? Of course, you're not the only adult who can't. In fact, there are a lot of adults who can't swim—some because they never tried or had the opportunity, others because they had an experience earlier that turned them off to the water. If you're now interested in trying this terrific physical activity, there are ways you can easily do that, whether you sign up for a "Swimming for 'fraidy cats'" course, private lessons or an American Red Cross course for adults. Incidentally, private lessons may be more affordable for you if you talk with someone at your local college or university about having a collegiate swimmer help you learn.

There are lots of pools in most areas, and swimming is still one of the most affordable types of exercise beyond walking and running. If you live near a body of water, swimming may cost you absolutely nothing. Community centers, schools and colleges also frequently offer affordable swimming.

Swimming is the ideal sport for all-around fitness, as well as for releasing stress in your lower back. It engages all your large muscle groups, builds stamina, can help retain flexibility and improves your heart and lung function. It's a good idea to balance a variety of strokes, as the different strokes work different areas of your body: breaststroke for your upper arms, chest, inner thighs, hips and knees; freestyle for your arms, shoulders, stomach and legs; backstroke for your shoulders, upper arms and legs; and butterfly, which strengthens nearly your entire body.

You may be more tempted to give a water workout a second look—whether it's swimming or standing upright and moving in the water—when you know about a recent study. The Japanese study found that fitness levels in participants in a 12-week basic water workout group that met three times a week improved in all areas of fitness tested: aerobic capacity, flexibility and strength, body fat and cholesterol. In fact, working out in the water can be more effective in many ways than working out on the land, if you think of the water as a piece of exercise equipment.

Consider this, for example: if you do a leg lift on land, the pull of gravity that causes your leg to go down easily means that the lift really only works your muscles in one direction: the ones that cause your leg to lift. However, in the water, resistance means that you need to put more effort into moving your leg in any direction, meaning that you're working several different sets of muscles, versus mainly one set, when you do the exercise on land. This means that your legs can get a very good workout simply by kicking in the water, either while you hold on to the side of the pool or a kick board.

Incidentally, if you're fearful, try wearing a life vest, which will keep you afloat.

Swimming offers the additional benefits of protecting your joints and providing resistance in all directions. If you're overweight or pregnant, the buoyancy that water provides is a great equalizer that can provide tremendous relief. Many of the injuries people encounter while swimming are a result of poor technique or overuse of one stroke. If you often swim freestyle (also called front crawl), intersperse or finish off your swimming session with some backstroke swimming. And it's also a good idea to learn to breathe on both sides, instead of always turning your head in one direction.

There are several ways you can vary

You can learn to swim at any age.

a water workout to improve its effectiveness. You can step up your speed, as you see in the MET rates for various speeds listed above. You can add resistance and build extra strength by wearing webbed gloves or using handheld paddles now available—but be careful of overdoing it and injuring your shoulder. Or, you can add swim fins, which add resistance to your kicking and help work the muscles in your legs and back more thoroughly. Incidentally, your heart rate will be lower when you work out in the water—probably by about 10 beats per minute.

Other creature comforts also make swimming more doable. Water shoes (or, if you prefer, cotton sneakers) protect your feet from rocks, sticks or shells when you're not in a pool and provide traction when you're in a pool or shower or on a pool deck. Goggles help keep water out of your eyes and make it easier for you to see what's underwater. Now you can even buy corrective lenses for goggles or face masks that approximate the vision correction you need. And if you're afraid of the water, there are many different flotation aids now available that can help you feel secure.

Table Tennis (Ping-Pong)

METs: 4.0

T'ai Chi

METs: 4.0

T'ai Chi, of which there are several styles, is known for helping reduce stress and promote relaxation. It has also been shown to bring a significant improvement in physical function, abdominal muscle strength and balance in people who have osteoarthritis, although not necessarily in flexibility or strength of knee muscles. Studies have shown that T'ai Chi can also improve balance in older adults.

A key component of T'ai Chi, as with other mind-body exercises, is awareness of your body and your thoughts. Like yoga, it uses slow performance of unique movements, regulated breathing and imagery. You can learn T'ai Chi in a class at a recreation center, community education program or health club—or, if you prefer, you can learn it from a book or video.

Tennis

METs: doubles 6.0
singles 7.0

Tennis is a sport that adults can enjoy learning while getting a good workout. Many communities offer instruction through park and recreation departments or through school district adult education programs. Depending upon how rigorously you play, tennis can give you a very good cardiovascular workout.

If you played tennis as a younger person and have continued to play through middle age, you may be interested to learn that playing tennis is more likely to provide cardiovascular protection than playing golf, basketball, football or baseball, according to a recent study. Of 1,000 men surveyed, only 12 percent of those with strong tennis skills in their 20s developed cardiovascular disease during the next 40 years, versus 28 percent of those who had not played tennis when they were younger.

Here are some tips from the American Academy of Orthopaedic Surgeons for enjoying tennis without injuring yourself:

- Warm up with a slow jog for 5 to 10 minutes, until you start to sweat.
- Drink plenty of fluids before, during and after you play.
- Look for playing surfaces that aren't rigid. If less rigid surfaces aren't available, wear shock-absorbent heel inserts.
- Reduce your risk of ankle injury by wearing a tennis shoe with good support. Many people also use two pairs of socks or support socks.
- Dry your racket handle and dab sawdust or powdered chalk on it to prevent blisters.
- Don't unnecessarily arch your back on serves or overhand shots. Rather, bend your knees and raise your heels to balance your upper body weight over your heels.
- Try to avoid the quick stops and starts that cause ankle sprains. Try also

to avoid landing on the ball of your foot, which can injure your Achilles tendon.

■ Prevent tennis elbow by doing stretching exercises for your wrist, starting backhanded swings from your shoulder, bending your arm on forehand shots and not putting excessive topspin on the ball when you hit ground strokes.

Volleyball

METs: 3.0

The familiar game of volleyball has been around for over a century. All you need is a ball and a net. Lines are optional. You can play it indoors, outdoors, on hard courts, grass, sand—even in mud. For more information on the six basic skills (serve, pass, set, spike, block, dig); to see adaptations of the game for 2, 3, 4, or 6-player teams; learn some new variations—or for the particulars of beach volleyball—check out the USA Volleyball Web site at: www.usavolleyball.org.

Walking

METs: around home, under 2 mph 2.0
moderate pace, 3 mph 3.3
very brisk pace, 4 mph 5.0
uphill, 3.5 mph 6.0
5 mph 8.0

"When women tell me they can't walk a 5K distance (3.1 miles), I have to disagree with them," says Kathrine Switzer, author of *Running and Walking for Women Over 40: The Road to Sanity and Vanity* (New York, NY, St. Martin's Press, 1998). Switzer, who's also global director for Avon's running programs and director of women's health and fitness for Rykä shoes, is passionate about walking.

"I say, 'I know you can walk 5K, which is just over 3 miles. You can walk 1 mile comfortably in 20 minutes, right?' To which they answer, 'Well, yes.' And then I say, 'I know you can do three of those, because I've seen you shop, and I know you can walk 60 minutes—even with your arms full of packages.'"

As an advocate for physical activity, Switzer's also tenacious. "I tell people to get out and walk with their partner a couple of miles every day—that it'll make the difference of dying of a heart attack or not."

And, if you're not yet convinced, she has the clincher: sex. "I cite studies that show that walking improves your sex life, which isn't surprising, because it raises endorphins," she says. "Couples attribute it to being magically attracted to one another, but it's probably the first time in a while that they've actually talked to each other."

Start Small

If you're wondering how to incorporate more walking into your daily life, Minot Cleveland, M.D., practicing physician and evangelist for an active lifestyle, suggests starting small. "Instead of driving around at the mall, looking for an open parking place next to the handicap parking, park a little farther away in the lot and spend that time walking in," he says. "Find little ways to incorporate walking into your daily life. Goals are helpful, but you need to realize that it'll take time to reach them."

Cleveland talks of the 5- or 10-minute rule. "Start with a modest goal. Give yourself permission to start below the recommended level of 30 minutes most days of the week. Decide you're going to get 5 or 10 minutes of walking in, three times a week. If, after that amount of time, you don't want to continue walking that day, that's fine. But once you get out there and moving, there's a good chance you'll want to keep it up. Find someone that you enjoy being around, and walk with them."

Walk the Malls

Malls are great places to walk. Switzer notes that every day thousands of people participate in mall walking programs. "A lot of people are worried about safety, air pollution, very hot or very cold weather. The malls are climate controlled," she says. "And, they also have toilets."

While mall walking is free, for $14 annually ($20 per couple) you can join the Mall Stars Walking Club at the Mall of America in Bloomington, Minnesota. The program offers an electronic tracking service that tallies mileage, a frequent-walker rewards program, free body composition, height, weight and blood pressure checks, as well as monthly health seminars with guest expert speakers. More than 750 of the Mall Stars members are over age 50.

Mall walking programs around the country offer exercise seminars, climate control—even rewards programs.

And walking programs exist at malls all over the country. The Town and Country Walkers club at Kendall Town and Country Mall, Kendall, Florida, averages 75 walkers a day and offers 15 minutes of warm-up and cool-down exercises, with a 30-minute walking session. Check out the mall near you!

Promoting Walker-Friendly Communities

Cleveland is also active as an advocate for making neighborhoods more walkable. "We need to create places where it's easy for people of all ages and abilities to walk in their daily lives—to and from work, on errands and for recreation," he says, noting that communities need to remove barriers to choosing healthy physical activity, like walking. "We need to create environments where healthy choices are the easy choices."

"I try to speak for the everyday athlete," Cleveland says, noting George Sheehan's comment that we're all athletes—some in training and some not. Cleveland, who's chair of the Oregon Coalition for Promoting Physical Activity, was a Torchbearer in the 1996 Olympic Torch Relay and is 2003 president of the National Coalition for Promoting Physical Activity.

Pedestrian activist and architect Ellen Vanderslice became a radical pedestrian in 1985, as she was nearly run over by a motorist as she crossed the street with her two small children. After she bopped the car with her diaper bag, the driver got out and threatened her. About 13 years and many umbrellas later, she realized she "wasn't raising civility by giving in to road rage." So she learned to "smile like the front end of a 1948 Buick Roadmaster," which is what she advises any pedestrian to do if placed in a similar circumstance.

Vanderslice is president of America Walks, the national coalition of pedestrian advocacy groups. "Walking is magic," says Vanderslice. "Walking on two legs—without a tail for balance—is something that only humans do, and it's a bit of a miracle." She points out that walking uses nearly every muscle in your body, makes you breathe deeply and makes your brain work in a way that no other activity can.

Make Walking a Regular Part of Your Day

Walking with regularity offers many health benefits. For example, if you weigh 200 pounds and don't change one thing about your diet, but walk 1.5 miles briskly each day, you could lose 14 pounds in a year. If you don't want to pay attention to mileage or time, try tracking your steps with a pedometer. The average American reportedly walks between 2,500 and 5,000 steps a day. Track your number of steps and challenge yourself to beat yesterday's or last week's total.

The American Heart Association offers these suggestions for starting a heart-healthy walking program:

- Pick a time of day when it's

Switzer: Maybe a Tad-Bit Slower—but Still Quite Active!

In addition to writing about and promoting walking and running, Switzer, who lives in New York, does a lot of walking herself, noting that it's faster than just about any other mode of transportation there. In 1967, Switzer was the first woman to officially finish the Boston marathon. A veteran of 35 marathons, she won the New York City Marathon in 1974, and in 1975 was ranked the sixth fastest woman in the world and the third in the U.S. in the women's marathon. Now, at 56, in addition to walking a lot, she still runs, although she terms it "shuffling" or "lumbering" rather than running—about 30 miles a week.

Switzer also stresses that for most people, walking is as good as or even better than running. "You still get the full cardiovascular benefit, the movement and improved circulation," she says, noting that 1 mile burns the same amount of calories, regardless of whether you walk or run. "Everybody says they can walk, but a lot of people don't like to run, because it hurts their knees or thighs, or women complain that their breasts jiggle. But walking is easy and it's cheap, and people will do it. And heart disease is our number one killer."

convenient to walk—early in the morning as a way to prepare for your day, as a refreshing break from work over your lunch hour, at the end of the day to relieve tension. Plan on walking at least 3 days a week.

- Pick a place where you can walk year-round—your neighborhood, a local school track, a shopping mall—someplace that's safe, well lighted and has a walking surface that's fairly smooth.
- Decide if you want a walking partner, and if you do, find one.
- Get a decent pair of shoes that are comfortable and, if you're walking outdoors, wear comfortable, breathable clothing that you can remove if you become warm.
- Warm up by beginning slowly and, when you're finished, cool down by gradually slowing your pace. For the bulk of your walk, find a pace that allows you to converse comfortably. Walking at 2 miles per hour uses 160 calories if you weigh 100 pounds, 320 calories if you weigh 200. If you increase your speed to 4.5 miles per hour, those hourly totals rise to 295 and 590, respectively.

Relax in a comfortable, erect position as you walk with easy strides, letting your arms swing at your sides. As you take a step, land on your heel and roll

How About Walking a Marathon?

Carol, a mother and family practice physician interested in staying healthy herself, decided she'd make a dream of hers come true—doing a marathon. That doesn't sound so unusual—laudable, but nothing particularly unique. Nothing, that is, until you know that she was the only person doing a marathon on that route on that particular day—and that she walked it, rather than ran. Here's how it played out, beginning early on a recent Saturday morning.

Before the day of the marathon Carol trained by walking 50 miles a week. She mapped out her route, using the neighborhood park as the warmup loop. On the day of the race, Carol began her marathon at 5 a.m., did the park loop and paused at her home to pick up her water bottle and leave her sweatshirt. Then the route followed 12.5 miles along a paved, regional trail. At designated spots along her route, friends of Carol's met and walked with her for several miles. One brought lunch, and they paused at a rest area along the path to eat. At the halfway point Carol turned and followed the trail back, again joined by friends at designated points along the route.

Proud of her accomplishment, she arrived back at home just in time to resume her role as mom and ferry her kids to their afternoon's activities. Several months later, as she told this story, Carol clearly had found a degree of personal accomplishment in her feat—and rejoiced that she was able to do it without the pressing crowds of a regular marathon, at a pace that was comfortable for her.

forward to drive off the ball of your foot. If it's more comfortable, breathe deeply, with your mouth open.

Switzer notes that the biggest motivator for many people is to have a walking buddy—a friend, neighbor, your partner. "You start talking and you end up talking about everything. Walking suddenly becomes much more than exercise," she says. "You'll probably never need to see a psychiatrist. You'll become rejuvenated, especially if you're older and alone. It's great for the social life."

Can You Improve the Aerobic Value of Walking?

Yes, to a point, according to Ray W. Squires, Ph.D., director of the cardiovascular health clinic, Mayo Clinic, Rochester, Minnesota. If jogging and running—which burn more calories than walking—are not something your joints appreciate, you can do several things to improve the aerobic value of your walking.

First, pick up your pace. Notice that you can increase your MET level from 2.0 to 3.5 by moving from a casual stroll at the level you'd use around home (less than 2 miles per hour) to a rate of 3 miles per hour (20 minutes per mile). And, if you can manage to walk 4 miles per hour (a mile in 15 minutes), you can bump your MET rate up to 5. However, Squires notes, your body's biomechanics do limit how much you can increase your pace—a level that varies from person to person.

You can only walk as briskly as your body's mechanics will allow. After you reach that level, you must do something else to improve your aerobic workout. Squires suggests adding hills to your route, or, if you use a treadmill, increasing the incline or resistance.

Squires also says you can increase your energy expenditure by swinging your arms while holding or carrying weights. "This involves the muscles of your arms, chest, back and shoulders," he says. Mayo Clinic's Web site recommends doing that, noting that exaggerating your arm swings while carrying weights can enable you to double the number of calories you burn while walking. You do need to be careful, however, not to add weight too quickly or to fling your arms in uncontrolled movements, so that you end up injuring yourself. "Start conservatively," says Squires. "And swing your arms so that you have about a 90-degree angle at your elbow—not above your head."

Furthermore, Squire says, simply carrying or wearing the extra weight doesn't necessarily increase the aerobic value of your walk. The increase in energy expenditure that you expect, simply from adding weight, doesn't necessarily occur all the time, according to the American College of Sports Medicine.

While energy cost is directly related to total mass carried—regardless of whether it is body weight or externally added weight (ankle or wrist weights, a backpack or a weighted vest)—it all depends on whether the same movements are carried out at the same velocity for the same amount of time, according to Kirk Cureton, Ph.D., professor and head, Department of Exercise Science at the University of Georgia, who has researched this area. If you do manage to have the same movements at the same velocity, more energy is used. However, because this requires a greater metabolic expenditure, you'll perceive (correctly) that you're working harder, and probably slow down your pace a bit to keep the perceived rate of exertion constant.

However, Cureton says there's still the advantage of greater loading on your skeleton to help prevent osteoporosis—a reason for which you may opt to carry added weight. You can check whether you're slowing your pace by walking at a constant rate on a treadmill, both with and without the added weight.

"Any physical activity improves your cardiovascular health," says Squires. "If your goal is to increase your cardiovascular health and fitness level, you need to challenge your system. Runners can go faster or find hills. Walkers can use weights. But you may not notice a big difference, other than being able to walk farther—or do it without becoming fatigued."

Yoga

METs: 2.5 (hatha)

A meditative activity that's 5,000 years old, yoga helps you achieve union of mind, body and spirit through a series of postures, during which you pay attention to your breathing and movement, inhaling at certain positions, exhaling at others. It can help you relax and manage your stress, as you develop physical flexibility, strength and endurance, and—along with T'ai Chi—it's recommended by some of the best medical experts in the world.

The most common style in the United States is hatha yoga, which usually combines gentle breathing with a series of movements in postures called asanas. Although you can learn yoga from videotapes or books, it's probably easiest to learn from a qualified instructor. You can locate classes in larger cities at health clubs, Ys, churches or community education classes.

Research has established yoga's effectiveness in controlling pain by relieving stress and anxiety, as well as by slowing your heart rate and breathing. It's commonly used to relieve the pain of osteoarthritis and carpal tunnel syndrome (an overuse injury). Yoga should not be painful, so be sure you stop any movements before the point of pain to avoid injury.

Minot Cleveland, M.D., reviewed chapter 7 except for the travel section. Cleveland is an internist, and president of the National Coalition for Promoting Physical Activity.

The reviewer for the travel section is Marvin A. Brooks, M.D., a family practice physician.

CHAPTER 8

Avoiding & Dealing with Injuries

When you're injured, the injury you care about is the one you have. Most injuries, according to David Poulter, P.T., Dip. M.D.T., physical therapist, clinic director and international lecturer on conservative, patient-centered treatment, occur when you do too much too quickly, too far, too often. The President's Council on Fitness and Sports confirms this, noting that overuse injuries are the most common ones you'll encounter.

Poulter doesn't naively believe you'll always be free of pain as you undertake a fitness program. Rather, he says, "Expect some pains and strains. But don't work through pain. Look at pain as your friend. It's your only friend that warns you that you're about to do damage. It's your body's warning system that tells you when you've done damage or that you're about to do damage. Ignore it at your peril."

Poulter talks of different kinds of pain—and describes how pain can tell you various things. It's an effective warning system. If a movement causes pain, but the pain stops quickly when you stop the movement, your body's warning system has turned off and the pain leaves because you've done no damage. "Hurt, not harm," says Poulter. Many trainers recommend taking a stretch to the point just short of pain—and that's not harmful or injurious. Cardiovascular conditioning, on the other hand, should not cause any pain, and most people can safely do strength training just to the point bordering on fatigue, but not pain.

If you have done damage, that pain—your warning—carries on. For pain that lasts beyond your exercise session, Poulter notes that general muscle soreness frequently occurs most severely on the second day following overexertion. And he suggests discussing with your doctor any pain that doesn't improve after 24 to 48 hours.

As you recover, pain also tells you where you are in your recovery process when it's decreasing or intermittent. This type of pain doesn't warrant inactivity, however. "If you sit around waiting to become pain free before you begin movement, you'll have a worse recovery," says Poulter, who advocates movement in the presence of healing, rather than immobilization. "No one gets better sitting," he says.

A Lengthy Lesson on Overuse Injury

I'd been doctoring for several months to no avail to discover the source of shooting pains down my right arm that frequently went from my ear to my little finger. Finally, in a last, desperate attempt to learn the source of my pain, I agreed to see a rheumatologist, not because I actually thought this person could identify the source of my problem, but just to satisfy the other puzzled physicians I'd seen and my family, who were growing tired of my complaints.

To my surprise, after asking just a few different, quite specific questions about my activities, this excellent diagnostician told me I'd sustained an overuse nerve injury while swimming. Finally, the puzzle pieces all fit together.

Yes, I routinely swam for 2.5 hours a week in several sessions, always front crawl ("freestyle")—anywhere from half an hour to over an hour, sometimes 2 hours. I swam at a moderate pace and felt that I could easily continue swimming for hours on end. One day I decided to challenge myself by swimming my weekly distance in one session—2.5 hours. Yes, I recalled having some sort of cramp toward the end of my swim, but I simply decided to swim through it and promptly forgot it had occurred.

When I expressed surprise that I could actually injure myself in this way, the doctor said it was not an uncommon injury for people who move weight repeatedly above their heads—bricklayers, for example. And, as he pointed out, in the amount of time I'd repeatedly pulled water from above my head, my arms and hands had moved many pounds. He wasn't at all surprised that I'd injured myself, and he suspected I'd never be able to swim any sizeable distance again.

Fortunately, in that regard he was mistaken. I was able, over 6 years, to come back to swimming 2.5 miles or more each week. However, I've learned to vary my strokes and limit the distance I swim at one time.

However, there are some times when Poulter definitely recommends refraining from exercising—when you're physically tired and run down, for example, although exercising is fine if you're mentally tired. He also recommends backing off when you have a fever or feel like you're coming down with the flu—or when you're taking antibiotics. "Ask your doctor," advises Poulter, who notes that exercise can cause a localized infection to become systemic and dangerous.

When it comes to strength training, Poulter and most trainers advocate allowing at least a day for the portion of your body that you work in a session to rest and recover before you work that part of your body again. This doesn't mean that you shouldn't exercise at all, but you can vary your activities to work different parts of your body on consecutive days.

Poulter offers these additional tips for avoiding injury:

■ Warm up your muscles before any intense exercise. Stretching may or may not be helpful, depending upon the type of activity you'll do. Poulter suggests warming up with activities that resemble your planned activities, gently and gradually picking up your pace.

■ Learn to use equipment properly. If you're into heavy weight lifting, Poulter suggests using free weights—not the heaviest weights you can lift, but something closer to 70 percent of the maximum weight you can handle and lifting it more frequently.

■ Use protective gear designed both for the activity you've chosen and your skill level—especially wrist guards and helmets. Wear appropriate shoes, too, and replace them when they're worn. (See pages 147 to 149 for buying tips.)

■ To avoid injuring your shoulder's rotator cuff, work that part of your body either without adding weight or with weights no heavier than 1 pound. Any time you have a shoulder injury, Poulter suggests seeking medical care.

The U.S. Surgeon General Weighs In

Similar themes occur in *Physical Activity and Health: A Report of the Surgeon General.* You can avoid many musculoskeletal injuries by simply increasing the intensity and amount of your physical activity gradually. And, although it's possible to experience adverse cardiac events when you exercise, the report notes that regular physical activity lowers your risk of dying of a cardiovascular event, compared to inactive folks. The report advises caution when you undertake an activity well beyond your usual level of exertion and suggests beginning new activities moderately and gradually. And, not surprisingly, it recommends consulting your physician if you're over 50 and beginning a new program of vigorous activity or if you have preexisting health conditions or are at high risk of cardiovascular disease.

According to the Surgeon General's report, these are the most common adverse effects of physical activity:

■ musculoskeletal injuries, many occurring during repetitive motion or traumatic contact with the ground or other playing surface, or a ball or other equipment; areas most likely to be injured include your knees, ankles or feet

- strains, tears and fractures arising from sudden, forceful movement
- injuries incurred in collisions with other participants, equipment or surfaces

In addition, many other sport-specific injuries can occur—shin pain from aerobic dance or leg and foot injuries from long-distance running, for example. Activities that involve movements in several directions are particularly apt to cause injury—even doing something no more strenuous than making a bed, for example. Each year American adults sustain over 2 million sprained ankles and over 100,000 torn anterior cruciate ligaments (ACL, a common knee injury).

Advice from the American Heart Association

Three important factors affect your risk of injury or adverse events during exercise, according to Gerald F. Fletcher, M.D., cardiologist at Mayo Clinic and professor at Mayo Medical School, Jacksonville, Florida, and other experts who authored *Exercise Standards for Testing and Training: A Statement for Healthcare Professionals from the American Heart Association.* Those risk factors are:

- your age
- the presence of heart disease
- the intensity of your exercise

However, these experts point out that the benefits of exercising greatly exceed the risks. They encourage prudent exercise, noting that you're least likely to experience major cardiovascular complications—estimated to involve one in 60,000 participants—during controlled activities like walking, cycling or using a treadmill. In fact, studies strongly suggest that your risk of experiencing sudden cardiac arrest while exercising is quite similar to the risk you face simply by chance alone, except for a slightly increased risk for jogging—probably because, if you're untrained, even a slow

Don't Stop—Just Slow Down!

You can dramatically reduce your risk of injury—or re-injury—simply by modestly adjusting what you do. According to the Surgeon General, runners experience musculoskeletal injuries in direct proportion to the mileage run or to the frequency or duration of running. And previous injury also increases your risk.

In one study, joggers' injury rates hovered around 5 percent, while that of runners approached 57 percent. If you take aerobic dance classes, your risk of injury increases when you attend more than four sessions per week. But don't stop exercising! People who exercise regularly still have a lower risk of exercise-related sudden death than sedentary folks who suddenly begin exercising vigorously.

pace may cause you to exceed 80 percent of your VO_2max. Fletcher also coauthored a booklet, *Exercise for Heart & Health* (Atlanta, Georgia: Pritchett & Hull, 2000), that's specifically designed to help individuals with heart disease to exercise safely.

The authors say you can reduce your likelihood of musculoskeletal injuries—those to your bones, muscles, tendons and ligaments—by selecting low-impact activities, like walking, cycling and swimming, over high-impact ones that involve repeated impact to your knees, ankles and feet, like running and aerobic dance. They also advocate doing resistance training with less weight and more reps and say that people who face the greatest likelihood of a musculoskeletal injury in resistance training are those who have previously been injured.

Here's how these experts recommend you avoid exercise-related injuries:

1. Only exercise when you feel well. Wait until you're free of cold or flu symptoms for at least 2 days before resuming physical activity.

2. Don't exercise too vigorously after you've just eaten. Eating increases your intestinal tract's blood flow requirements, limiting the amount of blood available to your other organs during exercise. To avoid cramps, nausea or faintness, wait at least 2 hours after you've eaten before exercising.

3. Drink plenty of fluids—especially water—before, during and after exercising, especially if you're exercising at least moderately intensely for 30 minutes or longer. Water is the best sports drink there is. This is especially important if you're elderly, obese or take diuretics. And remember that adding alcohol to exercise can actually bring on heat stress, because of alcohol's effects on your body. If you're a man, take note: according to some experts, fluid loss and replacement needs are twice as great for you as for women.

4. If you exercise outdoors, adjust your exercise plans to suit the weather conditions. Once the air temperature exceeds 70 degrees Fahrenheit, slow your pace, drink adequate fluids and be alert to any signs of heat injury. It actually takes 12 to 14 days for your body to adjust to a warmer climate, and your body truly can't adjust to extremely hot weather. However, you'll tolerate physical activity more easily if the humidity is low and there's a breeze. When daytime temperatures exceed 80 degrees Fahrenheit, your best bet is to avoid the heat by exercising early in the morning or later in the day—or seek out an air-conditioned shopping mall. Be alert for these symptoms of heat injury: headache, dizziness, faintness, nausea, chills, cramps or heart palpitations.

5. If you're concerned about overexerting, slow down when you climb hills.

6. Wear loosely fitting, comfortable clothes made of a porous material and appropriate for the weather. In cold weather, dress in layers that you can remove as you warm up. Never exercise in rubberized clothing.

7. Know—and heed—your personal limitations.

8. Select exercise that's appropriate, and make endurance exercise a major component of your exercise program. If you're over 40, you may decide to avoid high-impact activities. If you opt for

them, begin slowly and increase your intensity gradually. Give your body time to adapt to the stresses and strains of your exercise program by building in sufficient rest periods or days.

9. Be on the lookout for these signs that you need medical attention:

- burning, tightness, a sensation of fullness or any other discomfort in your upper body (including your chest, arms, neck or jaw)
- faintness brought on by exercise
- wheezing or breathlessness that's uncomfortable; it should only take you 5 minutes to catch your breath after you stop exercising
- any discomfort in your bones or joints during or after exercise that exceeds slight muscle soreness

10. Start your activity slowly, and gradually pick up the pace as your body adjusts.

Additional Tips on Preventing Injury

You can avoid many injuries simply by using common sense. Injuries frequently occur when "weekend warriors" set out to do too much too quickly without prior conditioning or warming up.

Your likelihood of being injured increases substantially if you've been injured in the past. Your lower extremities are prime targets. One survey of 6,298 adult exercisers, ages 20 to 85, found that over two-thirds of activity-related injuries involved the lower extremities. While a previous injury to

You Know You've Overdone It When...

According to the experts who collaborated on Exercise Standards for Testing and Training: A Statement for Healthcare Professionals from the American Heart Association, these are signs that you've exceeded desirable levels of exercise:

- **You can't finish what you set out to do.** Experts say you should always have some energy left as you complete your exercise session. Don't "do it 'til you drop."
- **You exercise so strenuously that you can't carry on a conversation.**
- **You feel faint or nauseated after exercising.**
- **You continue to feel exhausted throughout the remainder of the day.** Exercise should stimulate you to complete your day's activities, not leave you feeling exhausted.
- **You can't sleep.** A program that's suited to your needs should help you sleep more easily, rather than leaving you unable to sleep.
- **You have persistent aches and pains in your joints that exceed mild muscle discomfort.**

the lower extremities was the strongest predictor of another similar injury in men, two factors top the predictability list for women: having had a lower extremity injury previously and amassing 20 miles or more of walking, jogging or running per week.

Yes, you may have some generalized muscle aches and pains as you start a new activity or increase the duration of your exercise. However, a proper warm-up program can help you avoid many of those aches and pains.

Here are some additional ways to avoid injury:

1. Start exercising slowly, gradually build up the speed, intensity and duration of your activity and work on maintaining flexibility—throughout the entire week. Never increase your routine by more than 10 percent a week. If you've had a soft tissue injury, stretching is doubly important, as scar tissue has the tendency to shrink and shorten as it heals and stretching it can help restore its preinjury flexibility.

Carolyn: Avoiding Those "Last Run of the Day" Injuries

It happened, as many downhill ski injuries do, during what Carolyn figured would be her last run of the day. The tip of her ski caught in the snow and she fell. She recalls hearing a sound like a gunshot and thinking that she'd broken her leg. Actually, the healing process would have been faster and less complex if it had been a broken leg.

Instead, the doctor identified Carolyn's injury as the common and severe complete anterior cruciate ligament (ACL) tear, an injury that makes the knee very unstable. About one in every 3,000 Americans—three to four times more women than men—suffer an ACL injury each year, the majority severe. Although many people injure their ACL while skiing, other common culprits (especially for women) include soccer and basketball, according to the American Academy of Orthopaedic Surgeons.

Because she wanted to remain active, Carolyn opted for reconstructive surgery. But she had to wait 2 weeks for the swelling to subside before having the surgery, during which a graft from one of her knee ligaments was used to replace the torn ACL.

The day after surgery Carolyn had her first physical therapy session. "It was important to start moving right away. My physical therapist said that aggressive rehabilitation was the key to dealing with this injury," Carolyn says. "He advised that the sooner you start moving the joint, the faster you regain full range-of-motion and muscular control." Carolyn was inline skating just 6 weeks after her surgery, although it took several years before she dared to ski downhill again. In the 4 years since her surgery, Carolyn has regained most of the function of that knee and now enjoys a full and active life.

2. Schedule days off; rest when you're tired.

3. Avoid exercising near heavy traffic, as the carbon monoxide levels can reduce the oxygen supply to your heart.

4. If you're particularly interested in avoiding pulled muscles, choose controlled, continuous action activities like walking, running, swimming or cycling over start-and-stop activities like racquet games or basketball.

5. Avoid locking the joints of your arms or legs while exercising.

6. Stop as soon as you notice signs of fatigue. Injuries are more likely if fatigue affects your concentration, coordination, endurance, speed, judgment and alertness.

7. Carefully consider your exercise environment to save harmful stress on your body. If you want to start running, for example, look for a surface with more "give" than concrete (a school track, for example)—and don't start by running downhill, which can stress your knees.

8. Continue to exercise, but don't push yourself when you're under emotional stress. Exercise will help you deal with stress, but pushing yourself too hard at this time is much more likely to cause back injuries, according to the American College of Sports Medicine.

9. Technique matters. For example, you'll put much less stress on your shoulders and reduce your chances of an overuse injury when you use pruning shears, if you hold them close to your body and pause a few seconds to rest every several minutes.

10. Avoid many biomechanical problems down the road by seeking advice from someone who's quite experienced at a sport that's new to you—before you begin.

11. If you enjoy seasonal sports, get back into them gradually, and remember you can't just pick up where you left off at the end of last year's season.

Don't believe, "No pain, no gain." It simply isn't true.

How to Deal with Injuries You May Encounter While Exercising

The most common injuries you'll encounter while exercising include:

- hypothermia
- hyperthermia
- injuries to your knees, elbows and shoulders
- shin splints
- dehydration

The pages that follow suggest effective strategies for dealing with them when they occur. You'll also learn about how to handle muscle pain and cramps and find a bit of general advice on bone injuries.

It's important to remember two things that will supercede any information you find here. First, listen to your body. What constitutes a serious health situation for you may not be the same as something that's serious for a friend or neighbor of yours. You know your body better than anyone else, and it provides good information about what to do and when. Second, this book cannot begin to replace the care and advice of professionals concerned specifically with your health.

When in doubt, seek competent medical advice. You're worth it!

Now that you know some of the most helpful ways to avoid injuries related to physical activity, let's discuss how to deal with hurts and pains when they do occur. Again, when in doubt, see your healthcare provider. And, even though you may find yourself dealing with some new physical challenges once you become more active, don't forget that statistics say your chances of avoiding many kinds of illness and aches are much greater if you're physically active than if you're inactive.

Two helpful books to have on hand as you become more physically active are *Mayo Clinic Guide to Self-Care* (Rochester, Minn.: Mayo Clinic Health Information: 2001) and *Treat Your Own Strains, Sprains and Bruises* (Robert Lindsay, Grant Watson, Donna Hickmott, et al. Waikanae, New Zealand: Spinal Publications, Ltd.: 1994), written by five physical therapists from New Zealand. Before you even get to the title page of the second book, it opens with what's called a "Panic Page," with first-aid instructions for strains, sprains and bruises: the familiar RICE method (see sidebar on the next page). The book also includes a warning after you're injured to avoid applying heat, massaging the injury or drinking alcohol—activities that can increase bleeding and swelling.

Signs That Say "See the Doctor"

You can treat many minor exercise-related injuries yourself, without seeing a doctor. However, it's important to know and be alert to signs that it's time to seek professional help. Here are some of the most common clues that it's time to see a physician:

- when your pain is extreme or persistent
- when you've suffered trauma to a joint, possibly affecting the underlying connective tissue
- if an injury doesn't seem to heal in a reasonable amount of time (the amount varies for different people; you'll notice, as you get older, that it generally takes longer for your body to heal)
- if you develop a fever or infection after you've injured yourself

Some symptoms require care more urgently than others. These include:

- if you feel tightness, pressure, fullness or discomfort in your chest that lasts more than a few minutes, especially if the feeling follows exertion
- if you have pain that moves from your chest to your arm or jaw—again, especially if it follows exertion
- if severe shortness of breath you experience after exercising doesn't improve in a few minutes
- if you have persistent, unexplained dizziness, faintness or nausea
- if you're suddenly weak or numb on part or all of one side of your body

RICE, PRICE or MICE—Cues to Some Generally Good Things to Do

If you encounter aches, pains—even injuries as you become more physically active, it's likely many of them will be muscle and joint injuries or pain. Common—and generally, good—advice for dealing with these injuries is summed up with the acronym RICE.

- **R:** stands for rest from the activity you were doing as you became injured in order for your tissues to heal. Resting also slows your blood's circulation, reducing bleeding and swelling.
- **I:** is a tip-off to apply ice or a cold pack immediately to the injured area, even if you plan to get medical help. This helps shrink blood vessels, reducing swelling and inflammation. To avoid damaging your skin by frostbite, place a damp towel between your skin and the ice pack, and only ice an area 15 minutes at a time. Repeat the process every 2 to 3 hours while you're awake during the first 2 to 3 days after your injury.
- **C:** stands for compression and reminds you, after you remove the ice, to apply an elastic bandage or cloth to the area—firmly, but not tightly. This helps reduce swelling. Loosen the bandage if your pain worsens or if the blood flow to the area beyond the bandage becomes restricted, indicated by swelling or numbness beyond the bandage.
- **E:** tells you to elevate the injured area above the level of your heart, especially at night. This enables your body to enlist gravity's help in reducing excess fluids at the site, further limiting swelling.

Several slight variations on RICE are helpful. Mayo Clinic uses the acronym PRICE, which begins with the advice to protect the area from further injury by using a sling, splint, elastic wrap, crutches, cane or air cast to avoid further damaging it. David Poulter, P.T., Dip. M.D.T., physical therapist, clinic director and international lecturer on conservative, patient-centered treatment, follows RICE with MICE, as pain lessens after about 48 hours. (And if your pain is not abating, talk with your physician.) The M is for movement. Poulter talks of healing in the presence of movement—not movement that increases your pain or further injures the area, but gentle movement that helps retain mobility and speeds recovery. Initially, Poulter recommends moving your injured joint in a so-called unloaded position—that is, without placing any body weight on it.

Muscle Pain

Not unlike Eskimos selecting which of many words for snow to use in their conversation, you may find you'll talk about different kinds of muscle pain, once you start exercising. That's reasonable, because there are different kinds of muscle pain, a variety of causes and some differences in how you handle the pain. Carol Torgan, Ph.D., exercise physiologist and fellow of the American College of Sports Medicine, distinguishes three kinds of muscle pain associated with exercise:

- muscle cramps
- pain that occurs as you near your maximum possible level of exertion
- pain that occurs a day or two after you've exercised in a way or to a degree that's new for you

Scientists are still researching and learning about many aspects concerning muscles and muscle pain.

Muscle cramps, or involuntary muscle contractions, occur not only during exercise, but frequently after you've exercised—or apart from any exercise that might have caused them. As Torgan notes, it's not always clear what causes cramps. "Charlie horse" is a term often used for a severe, isolated muscle cramp.

Sometimes cramps appear to result from muscle overuse and stress, especially if you exercise in warm weather when you're not well hydrated. Holding a muscle stretched tight in one position for a long time can also cause cramps. Scientists believe some cramps may result from a shortage of potassium, which is necessary for optimal nerve function and muscle contraction. Others say muscle cramps may be related to insufficient magnesium or calcium, as well as pregnancy, kidney disease, underactive thyroid, inherited muscle disease and hyperventilation (breathing too rapidly).

According to Torgan and Rob Johnson, M.D., director of primary care sports medicine at Hennepin County Medical Center in Minneapolis, Minnesota, current theory suggests that cramps may be a result of muscle fatigue affecting the muscle spindle (which causes your muscle to contract) and the golgi tendon (which helps your muscle relax). Fatigue is frequently a factor. Johnson believes that only rarely are shortages of potassium, magnesium or calcium involved. "It's not simply a matter of eating more bananas," he says. Torgan notes that cramps are most likely to occur as you finish a long or strenuous period of exertion—or if you're an older person with poor stretching habits. She also says there may be a hereditary component.

Many experts say that staying well hydrated and sufficiently stretching your muscles will help you avoid muscle cramps. Be sure you consume 8 to 10 cups of liquid each day, more if you exercise vigorously. Drink at least 2 cups of water a couple of hours before you plan extended physical activity, and take a break to drink at least half a cup more every 15 to 20 minutes as you exercise. Pay particular attention if your cramps follow the introduction of a new medication or a change of dosage, and talk with your doctor about altering the dose or trying a different medication.

If you frequently get cramps in your legs at night, stretch your calf muscles before you go to bed (see the calf muscle and Achilles tendon stretch, page 137).

Many people find that quinine—either consumed in tonic water or taken by prescription—relieves their cramps. Medications used to treat cramps include vitamin E and amitryptline (Elavil). And stretching, Johnson notes, although not proven to prevent muscle cramps, helps treat and reset crampy muscles. In Johnson's opinion, warming your muscles prior to strenuous exertion is key. Torgan also recommends regular stretching and good hydration.

Pain that occurs during or immediately after exercise is another type of muscle pain commonly associated with exercise. You can bring it on by exerting at near-maximal effort—sprinting in a race, for example, or swimming as hard and fast as you can until your muscles yell "Stop!" and force you to back off and recover briefly, as you continue moving more slowly. Researchers believe this pain may be caused by disturbances in your body's metabolism of calcium or in the production of other substances in your working muscles. This type of muscle pain lasts only briefly, but can be severe enough to temporarily stop you from continuing your activity. Consuming a diet rich in antioxidant vitamins C and E may help prevent this pain. Unfortunately, Torgan notes, massage hasn't been shown to relieve this type of muscle pain, improve the flow of blood to your muscles or help in the recovery of strength.

A third type of muscle pain Torgan discusses, **delayed-onset muscle soreness (DOMS)** and stiffness, typically occurs 1 or 2 days after you

What to Do if You Get a Cramp in Your Calf Muscle

Calf muscles are frequently the site of muscle cramps. Like his mother, my husband occasionally gets leg cramps at night—sometimes even while sleeping. Unlike his mother, who was certain that aloe vera relieved her cramps, my husband has found one solution reliably helpful. He pinches, hard, between his thumb and forefinger, the piece of skin in the bottom and center of his nose. He doesn't know why it works—it just does.

More traditional solutions recommended by experts include:

- holding your muscle in a stretched position until the cramp passes
- gently massaging and stretching the muscle
- sitting with the affected leg extended in front of you and grasping and pulling that foot towards you
- putting weight on the cramped leg and slightly bending that knee
- applying heat or cold to the muscle or soaking in a hot bath
- applying acupressure to the affected muscle

Incidentally, the hard pinch is one remedy also mentioned at the American College of Sports Medicine Web site, where you can also find suggestions like consuming calcium-rich foods at least twice a day, ingesting more sodium (if cramping follows heavy sweating)—or drinking 2 ounces of pickle juice 10 minutes before exercising, a remedy used by some football players and trainers.

engage in a new form of exercise, especially if the activity involved movements that cause your muscle to lengthen as it contracts—as you lower a weight during a biceps curl, for example. In addition to being sore and stiff, you may also notice that you lack strength in that muscle for a few days. You can gain some relief by gently stretching the affected muscles and using nonsteroidal anti-inflammatory medications (NSAIDS) such as Bayer, Advil and Aleve. Some people also find icing, soaking in warm water or balms and creams helpful.

Bone Injuries

Although estimates of the percentage of athletic injuries that involve bones vary widely, it's clear that bone injuries are more likely to occur during activities that involve running and jumping than during other types of exercise. But you can avoid many of those injuries if you:

■ wear appropriate shoes for your activity and replace them at recommended intervals

■ begin an activity gradually and increase your levels in a gradual way over a period of several weeks

■ be sure your diet includes plenty of calcium—at least 1,200 mg per day if you're under 25 or 800 mg per day if you're older than that; this helps prevent thinning of the bones (osteoporosis) that can often occur as you get older, especially if you lack sufficient dietary calcium

■ develop strength and flexibility in the muscles that support your bones—especially in any areas that you know from previous injury experience are particularly vulnerable

■ avoid running on surfaces that are uneven or squishy—or surfaces that include a mixed terrain, such as rocky, grassy areas

The classic symptoms of a bone injury are pain when you apply pressure and localized tenderness, especially pain that occurs as you bear weight on a bone. If you suspect that a bone is broken (fractured), it's best to use PRICE and seek medical help.

Some bone injuries may not show up on a regular X ray. Your doctor may request an ultrasound exam of the bone or a magnetic resonance imagery (MRI) test, depending upon which bone is involved and your activity level. For example, a hairline fracture that may not be visible on an initial X ray may become more apparent when your doctor compares a second X ray with the first a number of days later.

A bone injury does mean you should alter your activity as it heals. It's still important to move your body, but to do so without hindering healing. For example, while it's important to strengthen muscles adjacent to an injured bone, don't stretch them excessively so that they can't support the bone. Depending upon the injury, you may also need to alter your aerobic activity, to reduce the weight you place on the healing bone. Rather than running on land, for example, ask your doctor about swimming or running in the water, where your buoyancy will reduce the weight load on the injured bone. Cycling is another aerobic activity that you may be able to do for aerobic conditioning, if you have a bone injury. Be very careful about loading weight on an injured bone in resistance work. When in doubt, ask your doctor for advice. Just like any other injury, you should resume your activity gradually and include rest days. By now you can probably guess the advice: listen to your body.

Shin Splints

Pain at the front of your lower leg, between your knee and ankle, is often referred to as "shin splints." It may occur as you begin a new activity or an activity that you haven't done for a while. Although most of our tissues adapt and become stronger in response to gradual increases of work, this sort of injury occurs when the tissues can no longer keep up. What we commonly call shin splints is actually a variety of injuries to soft tissues or bones. Some experts no longer even use the term shin splints.

Initially, experts thought this pain in the lower leg results from an injured tendon, which may actually be the case sometimes. However, the most common source of this pain is inflammation of the thin covering that surrounds bones that bear weight. Generally, when your bones are stimulated by exercise, they lay down new bone cells. But if the stimulation occurs faster than your body can keep up by making new cells, the area becomes inflamed, possibly red and warm. It may hurt when you put weight on it, especially if you run. This injury is

Movement in the Presence of Healing

My husband and I have seen illustrations of David Poulter's "movement in the presence of healing" in our own bones in recent months. As I biked home from an early morning swim one day last summer, I took a corner a bit too fast, slid on the sand and fell. Fortunately, I was wearing my helmet, but I bruised myself rather severely and cracked a couple of ribs—a first for me.

Following Poulter's advice, I kept my lungs clear with deep breathing every day, while my husband held a towel wrapped snugly around my rib cage. I also was able, within a day or two, to resume swimming, listening to my body's messages about moving my arms. While my arm movement during swimming was limited for a while, I could still get a good workout by kicking vigorously with my legs and feet. As my ribs healed, the water's buoyancy enabled me to gently ease back into full range of motion in my arms and upper body.

My husband recently discovered what Poulter calls "the most classic example of movement in the presence of healing" while he recovered from coronary artery bypass surgery. Although his breastbone had been sawed in half and was healing, his heart still had to beat and he had to breathe deeply in order to keep his lungs clear—both causing movement in the sore and inflamed part of his body. And, even as his sternum mended itself, he began a therapist-directed program of calisthenics.

probably most common among people who become active after a period of inactivity or runners who overdo their training level. You can also injure the muscle in the front of your leg by over-stretching it—running downhill repeatedly, for example. Sometimes the pain may actually result from an incompletely cracked bone—tiny and nearly invisible breaks that may become an actual broken bone if you continue the activity that caused it.

The best thing you can do to prevent this injury is to keep increases in your exercise level under 10 percent per week. You can also lower your risk by wearing appropriate footwear and consuming at least 1,000 mg per day of calcium. If you have this type of injury, take a break from the activity that caused it and only return to it very gradually as your body attempts to heal itself. It may help to use heat on the area before you exercise and ice afterward. And use ibuprofen or aspirin for pain relief.

Meanwhile, select an activity that's less weight-bearing and doesn't stress the affected area, in order to keep moving. Aerobic conditioning exercises that may work for you include cycling, swimming or pool running. Don't place any weight on that area while doing resistance exercises until the pain is gone. Incidentally, while evidence doesn't really point to the condition of the arches in your feet causing this injury, some people find that wearing specially designed inserts for their shoes helps them avoid it. After you have this sort of injury, return to your activity level very gradually. And again, if your pain isn't reduced after resting your leg for several days, check with your doctor to be sure there isn't a break.

Knee, Elbow & Shoulder Injuries

Joints are common sites of injury, especially your knees, elbows and shoulders. Your shoulder, which enjoys a wide range of motion, is the most flexible joint in your body. Activities that involve doing things over your head or heavy lifting are the most common ones to injure your shoulder—tennis, golf, throwing a ball or lifting, for example.

If you injure your shoulder, rest for a day or two and use an over-the-counter pain reliever. Acetaminophen (Excedrin, Tylenol) may help your pain, but won't affect inflammation, while aspirin, ibuprofen (Advil, Motrin-IB) and naproxen (Aleve) are designed to ease both. For the first day or two, apply cold or ice packs. After that you can try heat and use whichever best relieves your pain. If the pain isn't better after several days of treating it at home, see your doctor. Although your doctor may suggest surgery if you've injured your rotator cuff, you may want to first ask for a referral to a physical therapist to try exercise.

Your **knees** are amazingly complex joints that enable your lower leg to move in a variety of directions. Your knee joint is also the largest joint in your body. Unfortunately, it may also be your most vulnerable joint. As you walk down the street your knees bear from three to five times your body weight—and up to seven times your body weight as you climb stairs. No wonder knees often seem like the focal point of injury!

Knee injuries fall into two categories: those that happen with a single event and those that occur over time. Single-time injuries are traumatic injuries, like the ACL injury Carolyn experienced while skiing (see page 203). Often the result of accident or impact, these injuries may involve the tearing or rupture of a ligament, part of your body's passive restraint system that holds the parts of your knee in place. You'll likely encounter an injury like this when your knee is twisted or turned beyond the position where supportive tissue can secure it and pull it back. Injuries that occur over time are often a result of repetitive movements that overstress your normal tissue, perhaps due to a sudden increase in your exercise level—running a marathon when you've only trained at a much lower level or playing twice as many tennis games as usual, for example.

The best thing you can do to avoid knee injuries is to build up the soft tissues that support the various parts of your knee. This is especially important if you participate in a seasonal activity that demands a lot of your knees—downhill skiing, for example. And it's important to realize that you can't expect to immediately resume your participation in a sport like that at the same point where

Shoulder Strengtheners

These exercises may strengthen the muscles in your shoulder—or promote healing, if you're already injured.

Behind-Your-Back Towel Stretch

1. Grasp one end of a bath towel with one hand and toss the rest of the towel over your shoulder.
2. Reach behind your back near your waist with your other hand and grasp the towel's other end.
3. Pull up with the hand above your shoulder, but not to the point of pain. Hold 10 seconds and repeat.
4. Switch hands and repeat on the other side.

Behind-Your-Back Towel Stretch.

Lying Strengthener

1. Lie on your stomach on the bed with one arm hanging down over the side of the bed.
2. With the palm of your hand facing out, hold a small can of food or a light weight and slowly swing your arm straight back and upward (a controlled movement). Hold briefly then lower slowly. Repeat 10 times.

you left off at the end of the previous season, unless you've had activity in the meantime that maintained and strengthened your knees' function in the same sort of movements. Surgery may be an option your doctor will recommend if you rupture or tear tissues or if a cumulative injury becomes disabling.

Elbow pain can be a real nuisance, especially for golfers and players of racquet sports. The most common elbow injuries are overuse injuries that cause pain in your forearm muscles and the tendons that anchor those muscles to your arm bones.

One of the two most common elbow problems produces pain and inflammation in the outer part of your elbow, the part that faces away from your body. You may notice this injury late in your swing as you grip a racquet or if you rotate your wrist to put spin on a serve. If you golf, this injury can cause pain in your nondominant arm or worsen when you swing at a "fat" shot or when the ground is hard.

The second common elbow injury causes pain on the inside of your elbow and affects the muscles and tendons that allow you to turn your wrists so your palm faces down. If you play tennis, you may notice it when you hit a forehand shot with topspin; if you golf, you may notice it in your nondominant arm.

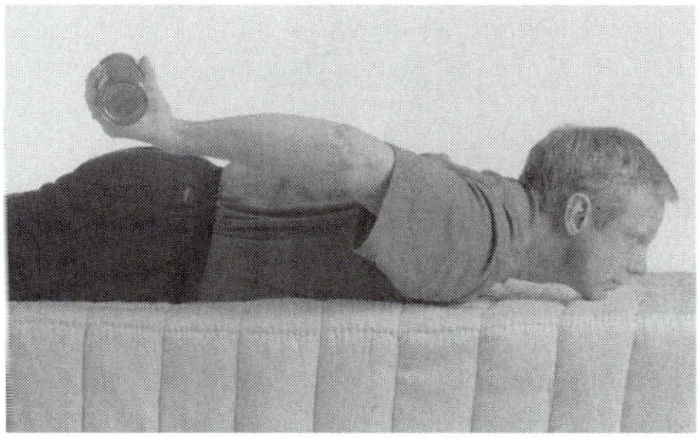

Lying Strengthener.

3. Now turn your hand inward and lift the weight forward; hold, lower and repeat.
4. Switch sides and repeat both forward and backward swings.

Resistance Band Strengthener

1. Securely anchor a resistance band to a fixed object (about the level of your elbow, if possible).
2. Stand, with your upper arm next to your body, your elbow bent at 90 degrees.
3. Grip the band and pull your hand across the front of your body slowly, keeping your elbow at your side. Slowly return to the start position. Repeat.
4. From the same position, grasp the band with the other hand and pull across the front of your body in a similar fashion.
5. Turn and repeat the exercise with each hand.

Resistance Band Strengthener.

Strengthen Your Knees

Bicycling, as well as rowing and cross-country skiing, offer good, low-impact strengthening for your knees. In addition, you don't need any equipment to strengthen your knees with these simple exercises at home.

Leg Lift.

Leg Lift

1. Stand with your hands on a counter or tabletop for support.
2. Bend one knee to bring the lower part of your leg up behind you (without using your hand to pull it up).
3. Hold briefly and repeat.
4. Add ankle weights (a little at a time) to increase your strength.

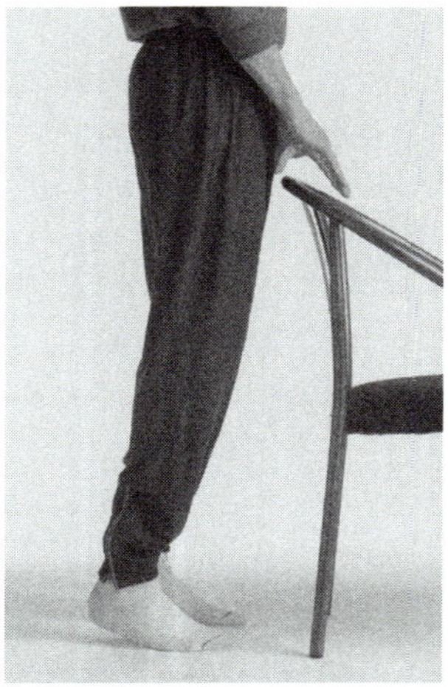

Standing Heel Raise.

Standing Heel Raise

1. Stand holding a counter or tabletop for support.
2. Lift your heels and stand on the toes and balls of your feet.
3. Hold briefly, ease down and repeat.

Semi-Squat.

Semi-Squat

1. Stand with your hands on a counter or tabletop for support.
2. Bend your knees and gently lower your body to a partial squat, with your back upright.
3. Hold briefly and repeat.

Wall Sit—a good conditioning exercise for downhill skiers.

1. Stand on a nonskid surface with your back against a wall.
2. Slide down the wall to a near-sitting position, keeping your feet in front of your knees.
3. Hold 10 seconds.
4. Repeat 10 to 30 times.

Wall Sit.

Regardless of which type of pain, you should always stop the movement that brought it on when the pain begins and don't resume playing until it has healed. (But don't discontinue your other physical activity!) Use over-the-counter anti-inflammatory pain relievers like ibuprofen (Advil or Motrin), aspirin or naproxen (Aleve). Once you've healed, loosen up the joint ahead of time with moist heat and take anti-inflammatory medication before you begin your activity. When you're done playing, use cold packs on your elbow for at least 10 minutes or gently rub your forearm muscles a few inches below your elbow for 5 minutes to relax the tissues and stimulate blood flow.

If your pain lasts more than a month, see your doctor. A physical therapist can also provide exercises to strengthen your wrists and hands. Sometimes orthopedic specialists suggest splinting your wrist to take some of the load off your forearm muscles. You can wear a splint at work or during the night, but not while you play sports.

You can avoid many of these injuries by developing and maintaining strength and flexibility in the muscles in the center of your body—your back, abdomen and hips. And, you can often avoid or remedy problems caused by improper technique by taking a few lessons in a new activity from a knowledgeable pro.

Dehydration

Dehydration is an injury you may not even see coming. Your body loses water at the rate of a quart or more a day—usually about 2.5 quarts, even if you're inactive. You lose 1 or 2 cups each day simply by exhaling. Your kidneys do a wonderful job of moderating your body's water level, sloughing water off in your urine when you have excess and hanging on to it when your body's fluid levels are low. But strenuous activity increases your fluid requirements, especially in hot or humid weather. And thirst—especially when you're older—is

Limbering up the arms.

Limber Up Those Forearm Muscles & Tendons

Simple stretching can help keep the soft tissues in your forearm limber.

1. Place your hand out in front of you, with your palm faceup and open.
2. Use your other hand to very gently stretch back the fingers on your open hand.
3. Hold for 30 to 60 seconds, relax and repeat.

a notably unreliable indicator of how much water you need.

Medications you take may also cause your body to excrete fluid. Diuretics, often called water pills, are commonly prescribed for high blood pressure and include furosemide (Lasix) and hydrochlorothiazide (HydroDIURIL). If you take these medications, it's important to monitor your fluid intake, because if you don't drink enough water or if your medication dose is too high, it's easy to become dehydrated.

When you start becoming dehydrated you may get thirsty and be able to head off dehydration by drinking some water and sitting down to cool off. Severe dehydration can impair your physical performance and cause you to have a headache, fatigue, flushed skin and a dry mouth. If you don't pay attention and drink some water, your blood pressure could drop dangerously low, reducing your body's ability to send oxygen and necessary nutrients throughout your body. Eventually, dehydration can cause dizziness, unconsciousness, a racing heart rate, kidney failure and death.

Some foods have high concentrations of water. Lettuce, watermelon, broccoli, grapefruit, carrots and apples are at least 80 percent water by weight. Low-fat cottage cheese, yogurt, potatoes and canned drained tuna are at least 70 percent water. And remember, caffeinated beverages cause your body to lose water.

Hypothermia

Hypothermia occurs when your body's thermostat can't maintain a temperature of at least 95 degrees Fahrenheit. This doesn't just occur in cold weather. It can also occur if, as a result of becoming

Dehydration Prevention Is Ongoing

Here are some easy ways to avoid becoming dehydrated:

1. From the time you get up in the morning, drink water:
   - a couple of glasses right away
   - every time you pass a water fountain
   - at your desk at work or as you sit at home reading or relaxing
2. Start your meal with a cup of juice, soup or water—it may even fill you up a bit, helping you eat less, if that's a goal. Drink water or another liquid with your meal.
3. Whenever you exercise, especially if it's hot and humid, drink more water or fruit juice that's diluted with water (one portion fruit juice to two of water). Drink one or two glasses 30 to 60 minutes before you begin exercising and another when you're finished. If you exercise for longer than half an hour, take a water break every half hour or so.

chilled by being in contact with wet, sweaty clothing or immersed in cold water, you cool off faster than you would in cold air. In fact, according to Johnson, a body immersed in cold water cools off 30 times faster than it does in cold air. It's also not unusual, he says, on the same day, to treat runners in the same marathon for both hypothermia and hyperthermia (which occurs when your body overheats).

Aging and being thin increase your risk for hypothermia. Some health conditions also interfere with your body's ability to regulate its temperature: cardiovascular disease, underactive thyroid or other hormonal disorders, severe arthritis, Parkinson's disease, stroke and other conditions that limit your normal blood flow. In addition, medications for anxiety, depression or nausea can interfere with your internal thermostat. And, although drinking alcohol may give you a warm feeling, it can lower your body's ability to retain heat, as well.

Hypothermia can occur in many different settings. The most common setting, according to Stephen G. Rice, M.D., Ph.D., M.P.H., F.A.C.S.M.; Ross Ellis, M.D.; and the American College of Sports Medicine, is when you're on a recreational hike in the mountains, where the changing weather conditions and the demands on your physical capabilities can exceed normal levels, making it much more likely to occur. When you're outdoors in cold weather, pay close attention to the temperature and the wind speed, which can remove that insulating blanket of warm air around your body very rapidly. Hypothermia also is common if you fall into freezing water while snowmobiling,

Father & Son Hang by the Nails

Larry, 66, son Monte, 42, and now grandsons Stefan, 11, and Cody, 13—all physically active—have had a few close calls with hypothermia. Every year, before the ice freezes very solidly, they're chomping at the bit to get out skating on it. Because they know they wouldn't last long in that cold water, they generally stay fairly close to the edge of the lakes and ponds early in the season, where they know it's shallow.

They also have a unique and handy safety tool: large nails. Larry carries two 6-inch nails in his pocket, to help keep a grip on the ice so that he can crawl out. It seems at least once every season, he ends up using them when he falls into the water. Monte, thinking he has a safer alternative, drives his nails into two blocks of wood (they float) and attaches them with a string.

Larry had a close call recently, when he and Monte were out skating and Larry went through the ice up to his waist. This was, of course, the one time Larry had forgotten his nails. Fortunately, he was able, using Monte's nails, to crawl out of the water in time to avoid hypothermia. Family members and friends just shake their heads and secretly rejoice that Larry has started lifting weights, so at least he's strong enough to pull himself out of the fairly shallow water.

skiing, hiking, ice fishing or skating.

Early signs of hypothermia include intense shivering and the inability to perform complex tasks. As it worsens, the person may begin shivering violently, slurring speech, and facing sluggish thinking and memory loss. If the shivering stops, that's a major red flag. It's important to recognize the early signs of hypothermia and to act quickly to prevent its progression to loss of consciousness or other life-threatening complications. Rather than treat this condition yourself, it's best to get the person to a medical facility, because the rewarming process can cause medical complications, including heart rhythm abnormalities.

If you fall into cold water, several factors affect how long you'll survive. If the water temperature is below 40 degrees Fahrenheit, you may survive less than 90 minutes. If, on the other hand, the water temperature is a bit warmer—between 40 and 60 degrees—you may live 1 to 6 hours. Other factors that affect your survival chances include whether or not you're conscious and your level of exhaustion.

If, during water activities, you fall into cold water:

- Keep your life jacket on, as well as any clothing you may have. Try to button or zip it, to benefit from the layer of insulation it can provide.
- Tuck your body together tightly to retain the heat you do have and limit the amount of skin that's exposed to the water.
- Only use your energy to swim if you're close enough to reach help; otherwise expending the effort can further lower your body temperature.

If you're with someone you think may be experiencing hypothermia, get medical help if the person has slurred speech and cold and pale skin or appears disoriented. Call 911 and move the person out of the cold. Remove any clothes that are wet. Try to insulate the person's body from the cold ground and share your body heat, if possible, by direct skin-to-skin contact. Warm beverages are only helpful if the person is alert and can swallow them, but don't give any alcoholic beverages. If medical care isn't available and you have access to warm water, place the individual in a bath that's warm to the touch but not hot. Do not place the person in a hot bath or apply heat to the arms and legs. Handle the individual gently and don't try rubbing or massage.

Hyperthermia

Hyperthermia is a problem of overheating. That's why in some sports, water breaks are mandatory.

While it's more apt to occur in hot weather, your body temperature can rise above the surrounding temperature at other times, as well, if your body doesn't cool properly. You're more likely to experience hyperthermia if you're older, obese, have been consuming alcohol or have an impaired ability to sweat. But it can also occur if you're younger, exerting heavily in hot weather and are dehydrated.

Hyperthermia is more likely if you're overdressed in bulky clothing, sleep-deprived, exercising in heat to which you're unaccustomed, confined to a poorly ventilated hot area or taking certain medications (including antihistamines, diuretics, laxatives, some heart medications, some types of antidepressants or medications for Parkinson's disease).

Elevated body temperature is the main sign of hyperthermia. You can experience heat exhaustion if your temperature rises to between 100.5 and 104.9 degrees Fahrenheit (98.6 degrees is considered normal). As your temperature rises you may become dehydrated, due to excessive sweating. You become fatigued, dizzy and have pale skin and shortness of breath. If it's warm and you're exercising and sweating heavily, this can occur in just 30 minutes.

If your body temperature hits 105 degrees or higher you may have heat stroke—which can occur within just a few minutes of beginning intense exercise, even if you're well hydrated. This is most likely to occur if you exercise vigorously in hot weather or if your ability to regulate your body temperature is diminished, something that usually occurs in older or very young people or people with chronic illnesses. In these people, it may not even require vigorous activity. At this stage your body generates so much heat that your cooling mechanism shuts down and you can no longer release the heat. Warning signs may include cramps, nausea, vomiting, headache, dizziness or weakness. You may sweat heavily—or not at all. Your resting pulse may exceed 130, your breathing may be shallow and rapid and

How to Avoid Hyperthermia

You're much less likely to experience hyperthermia if you're well hydrated. Remember, how thirsty you are isn't a good indicator of how much water you've lost. And don't try to judge whether you're well hydrated by how much you sweat. Any time your urine is darker than a pale yellow, drink at least a pint (2 cups) of water (unless your doctor has recommended otherwise). In addition, reduce your likelihood of experiencing hyperthermia:

- work out either early in the morning or late in the evening, when the temperature is lower
- wear light-colored, porous clothes that allow sweat to evaporate; avoid wearing heavy uniforms or equipment when it's warm outside
- drink water or diluted fruit juice as often as possible
- give your body several weeks to adjust to a move from a cool to a hot climate
- drink a lot of water—not caffeinated drinks—throughout the day when the weather is warm
- get out of the heat immediately and look for an air-conditioned building if you feel nauseated or dizzy; drink some water or cool yourself with a cool shower or garden hose

your skin may be hot and dry. You may be delusional or confused or show irrational behavior.

If you suspect that someone has hyperthermia, call 911 for emergency medical assistance and move the individual into shade or a space that's air-conditioned. Try to lower the person's body temperature externally:

■ remove tight or extra clothing

■ spray the person with water or cover him or her with damp sheets and blow the skin dry to increase evaporation

■ place ice packs near the person's neck, groin and armpit to accelerate cooling

■ put the person into a tub of cool (not cold) water

If you suspect a person may have heat stroke, don't give aspirin or acetaminophen (Tylenol).

Women & Men *Are* Different!

Until recent years, much of the research on physical activity focused on men. As a result, much of the exercise gear was designed to suit the male anatomy and didn't take into account a woman's biomechanics. But curves aren't the only things that differ between women and men, and some of those differences may affect your physical activity.

For example, a racquet that works just fine for a man may be too heavy for a similar-sized woman who may not have as much upper body strength and who may end up with tennis elbow by using it. Even if a woman and man are the same height, their leg length will likely differ: a man's leg length averages 56 percent of total height, while a woman's averages just 51 percent. This means, for example, that a man probably has a longer stride than a woman of the same height. Sometimes women become injured just trying to keep up with a man's pace. On average, men have larger lungs and hearts than women do, as well as higher blood pressure. Women, on the other hand, have wider pelvises, shorter legs, narrower shoulders and are more knock-kneed. Women's knees are also at a greater angle, which makes them more prone to kneecap pain and other knee injuries.

If you're a woman wanting to try some special exercises to help balance your strength with that of a man, experts recommend cycling as well as leg lifts and quad and hamstring stretches.

Alternative Medicine Remedies

It's not difficult to find many remedies touted for exercise-induced injuries. What is difficult, however, is finding good studies to support those claims. Here are several you may see promoted, and the latest word from Mayo Clinic's alternative-medicine expert Brent Bauer, M.D., assistant professor of medicine, regarding their efficacy:

■ Arnica: used widely in Europe to treat muscle pain following exercise. While one study suggests that components of the herb may be anti-inflammatory, arguing against any benefit is a systematic review of multiple studies that found no proven, demonstrable effect.

■ Echinacea: said to have a positive

What About Exercising During Pregnancy?

"I try to get to the health club three times a week," says Heather Koshiol, managing editor, North American Affinity Clubs, Inc., who edited this book. "I'm basically just walking, but I haven't gained as much weight as I did during my first pregnancy and I seem to have more energy this time around. And friends tell me that being more active throughout my pregnancy will make labor and delivery easier—and help me get back into shape, as well."

Koshiol is correct. Research shows that you'll have an easier and shorter labor and delivery, with fewer complications and less stress for your baby during delivery if you exercise while you're pregnant. That said, pregnancy is not a good time to go from seldom exercising to becoming a world-class weight lifter. Again, each woman is different, and your best advice will come from a health professional who knows you and cares for you on a regular basis. Here are a few general guidelines:

- Begin with the assumption that you can continue most of your pre-pregnancy activity into your pregnancy. Aerobic exercise is excellent, especially if you can continue on a regular basis the activities you've done previously. Most experts particularly recommend swimming, cycling and walking. This is not, however, a good time to start a weight-training program.
- As your pregnancy progresses and your body swells, avoid activities that have jerky or heavy bouncing movements, those that involve deeply flexing your joints, hard jumping, jarring motions or rapid changes of direction that increase your risk of falling.
- Consult your healthcare provider about how strenuously you should exercise if you have pregnancy-induced high blood pressure, an incompetent cervix, persistent bleeding or if it's hot and humid and you don't have a cool place to exercise.
- Don't exercise to the point of exhaustion.
- If your breasts are enlarged and tender, wear a good sports bra (some women wear two).
- Your joints and ligaments are more relaxed during pregnancy—especially in the later stages. This means you may be able to flex more easily, but it also means you're more apt to become injured if those looser tissues don't restrain movement they otherwise would. This is not a good time to start a rigorous aerobic dance class, for example.

After your baby comes, it's important to remember that some of the physical changes your body has experienced will take at least 6 months to reverse. Don't expect to get to your pre-pregnancy weight or to exercise at your pre-pregnant levels right away.

effect on immune system, aid wound healing and reduce inflammation. There's no solid support for it reducing inflammation, and it may actually have the opposite effect, as it stimulates white blood cell activity.

- Ginger: for reducing swelling and relieving pain. This does seem to have some anti-inflammatory effect.
- Turmeric: said to be a natural anti-inflammatory that relieves redness, swelling and pain when rubbed directly into a sprain. Bauer has not seen any solid literature on it and wonders if claims are based on lab test-tube studies, rather than on studies of human subjects.
- Vitamin E: said to speed the healing of microscopic muscle tears resulting from vigorous exercise. While Bauer says it may be a great antioxidant, he knows of no studies establishing its efficacy for muscle tears. Johnson, on the other hand, says there's never even been a decent study to establish the antioxidant effect of vitamin E, and he's quite concerned about the risks involved with vitamin overdoses.

As is always the case with alternative remedies: buyer beware. The National Institute of Health's Office of Complementary and Alternative Medicine is funding some studies that may provide answers over time. Meanwhile, remember that the United States Food and Drug Administration provides only very limited regulatory oversight of products of this nature, whether sold in health food stores or at your local pharmacy. Studies have frequently shown that you often don't get what's supposed to be in the package, and dosing is notoriously unreliable.

Johnson Fits Exercise into a Busy Schedule

As a person who treats many injured college athletes, Rob Johnson, M.D., director of primary care sports medicine at Hennepin County Medical Center in Minneapolis, Minnesota, doesn't shy away from exercise himself. "Because my days are unpredictable, I exercise early in the morning. Then I don't need to be concerned that I won't get it in," he says.

Although he doesn't remember not being active—he participated in team sports in high school and college—Johnson says he started running while in college in order to keep up with the athletes on his teams. "I did some triathlons, but I hate indoor swimming," he says. Now, at 56, Johnson runs about 30 miles a week in the winter and tries to ski cross-country 3 or 4 hours a week. In the summer he golfs several times a week and averages 50 miles running.

"I vary what I do," he says. "I may run 4 miles fast, and when I'm training for a marathon I may run 23 or 24 miles." Once, while running in Wisconsin, he got lost and ended up running 30 miles before flagging down a car and asking directions and eventually hitching a ride back to where he was staying.

Johnson's advice: "If it's expensive, don't use it. If it's inexpensive, remember that it's not proven and may have side effects, but if it works for you, moderate use may be OK. Just remember that none of these have been tested in reliable, verifiable double-blind, randomized control studies required by the FDA for their approval. And manufacturers aren't required to prove that what they say is in the product actually is in it."

Don't be surprised, in other words, if you find yourself asking, "Why should I use something that *may* work, when I could use something that's shown in scientific testing to work?"

Special Conditions

This chapter has not attempted to provide condition-specific advice. You can best get that advice from a healthcare professional familiar with your situation. Be sure, before you become involved in an extensively different exercise program, to consult your care provider if you have:

- diabetes
- heart disease
- high blood pressure
- arthritis
- asthma
- osteoporosis
- fibromyalgia
- implanted joints

You can also frequently find good advice from national organizations associated with your condition—the National Arthritis Foundation or the American Heart Association, for example.

Yes, you may become injured as you exercise, but the more fit you become, the lower your chances of injury. Unfortunately, may people who injure themselves stop exercising permanently, which can have much more dire consequences.

A reassuring word from Johnson: "Remember that the greatest predictor of all-cause mortality is peak exercise capacity. People who are more fit live longer. People who exercise longer or with more intensity live longer. The more fit you are, the more health benefits you realize."

David Poulter, P.T., Dip. M.D.T. and Rob Johnson, M.D., reviewed chapter 8. Poulter is a physical therapist, clinic director and international lecturer on conservative, patient-centered treatment. Johnson is director of primary care sports medicine at the Hennepin County Medical Center in Minneapolis, Minnesota.

CHAPTER 9

Overcoming Other Obstacles

When the Centers for Disease Control and Prevention queried people about why they're not active on a regular basis, the answers fell into seven main categories:

- lack of time
- social influence
- lack of energy
- shortage of willpower
- fear of being injured
- lack of skill
- lack of financial resources

Chapter 5 has already dealt with the most-cited reason: lack of time. This chapter offers help on some of the other obstacles. In addition to those listed in the CDC report, other common obstacles that may slow you down include:

- uncooperative outdoor weather—whether it's too cold, too hot or raining
- lack of noticeable progress toward your goals
- difficulty getting back up to speed, if you lose momentum or take a break for a while
- illness—and coming back from being ill
- holidays and other breaks in your routines
- newly postpartum—being a new mom or dad
- stress incontinence
- obesity-related concerns (sore knees, back, feet and other discomfort)

And of course, other obstacles will always arise—some you can't possibly anticipate right now. You will find, however, that, as you face up to and overcome these and other roadblocks, your determination will become stronger and stronger, until one day you'll be surprised to see how powerful your commitment to continuing a fit way of life really is.

It's likely, as you experience the benefits of an active lifestyle, that you'll find a similar sense of commitment. You'll face—and sometimes be stalled by—the obstacles mentioned above, and others as well. But the chances are good that once you've experienced the benefits of consistent activity, you won't want to go back, either. This chapter seeks to help you deal with obstacles—and you'll encounter obstacles beyond these, as well. But somehow, things look a bit different, once you become convinced that your body was designed for activity.

Social Influence

Face it. You're a social being, strongly influenced by the people with whom you come into contact. Sometimes that's a real "plus" that can contribute to your active lifestyle, especially as you become better acquainted with people who enjoy being active. Knowing that someone expects you to show up for your morning walk at the usual time can be just the nudge you need to get you out of bed on those mornings when it would be so much easier to just roll over and sleep.

Sticking with a program can be difficult, however, if the folks around you

Don Surprises Himself!

Two weeks into his new program, Don, whom you've already heard from several times as he began his fitness quest, was stunned. He'd worked out 10 of the last 14 days and still felt a strong sense of commitment—so much so, in fact, that it surprised him. His commitment went beyond the financial commitment he'd made, although that certainly helped drive him to keep going at times. But he'd spent money before and hadn't stuck with it. "I've unleashed a monster," he said of his determination to stay at it. He was nervous, however, that he might slip back into his inertia once school started, when he would again be in the classroom teaching all day.

Just 3 weeks later, all sense of doubt about hanging in there was gone. "I'm trying to do 6 days a week—I just *can't* do any less," Don exclaimed. In fact, as he returned to town at the end of a weekend away, he made a spur-of-the-moment decision. He'd skip the meeting he'd planned to attend yet that evening, in favor of working out. "It's that important right now," he said. "I have to figure out some way to do it. I really feel it if I miss my conditioning 2 days in a row."

hit the doldrums, activity-wise, and you slow down, as well. It can be especially challenging, as you get older, if people around you buy into the theory that aging is painful and inevitably involves slowing down or easing up on physical activity. This can become, for them, a self-fulfilling expectation. In the end, you're faced with a very personal decision that can dramatically affect your life: do you believe it's worth investing significant chunks of time—and other resources—in staying healthy? It's a decision each person must make for himself or herself—and one you can't force on someone else.

Sometimes, if people around you drift toward less activity, rather than more, you may decide you need to expand your circle of acquaintances to include more people who enjoy physical activity. There are several good ways to do that.

Look for, and try to hang out in, places where people are active. This can include parks and trails in your neighborhood or community, as well as community recreation centers, which often hold open-gym nights for adults—sometimes including hours designated for adults over 40 or 50. Check your city's newsletter, a local newspaper or call city hall to inquire. If you live near other cities, check with them, as well. Check postings in local libraries, bike shops and other sporting goods and outdoor gear retail locations. Sign up for a class in T'ai Chi, dancing or hiking, or show up for

Bike Trip Draws Participants Aged 3 to 70

When Judy's church group of young married adults decided to plan a low-cost weekend bike trip, they hadn't considered the possibility that anyone beyond the membership of their group would be interested. But they issued an open invitation to others in the congregation.

They were somewhat surprised at the intergenerational character of the group that ended up going. Several bikers were retired. The youngest participant, age 3, rode in a cart pulled behind parents' bikes. The oldest participant, a woman of 70, rode her three-wheeler. Everyone drove to and camped at a site near the middle of the trail. On Saturday, they headed one direction to the end of the trail and back. On Sunday, they rode the other direction to the end and back.

Each person did as much or as little biking as he or she wished. Each day teenagers rode one direction on the trail two times, while many of the participants covered the same ground once. As the first to finish, the young people were then responsible for building the campfire to prepare lunch. Those for whom 15 to 20 miles was a bit much for one day, did less, going part of the way out and back and spending the balance of the day relaxing or antiquing in the surrounding rural towns. The event was judged successful enough that it became an annual tradition. "My kids benefited a lot by getting to know the active older folks in a new way," says Judy.

Join others in your community for a class in yoga, T'ai Chi or another activity you haven't tried before.

an architectural walking tour of your town or another town nearby.

Intergenerational activities offer a wonderful opportunity for increasing your exercise level. One great way to do that is to get involved in activities with kids—whether your own, or others. Teams—basketball, volleyball, baseball, softball—always need adult coaches. Park boards, recreation departments, schools, places of worship, museums, zoos—all are frequently looking for adults who will help with kids' activities.

If your neighbors don't currently enjoy any activities together, consider starting a neighborhood croquet, badminton, softball, tennis, golf, Frisbee golf or bowling tournament. Or call a bowling alley and inquire about joining league play. You don't even need to bring a whole team—they'll connect you with teams looking for bowlers.

Boredom or Lack of Energy

Everyone gets bored from time to time. When that occurs, it's a good time to vary what you do or to find ways to make it more fun. For some people, biking around the neighborhood without a particular destination in mind is fine. Other people prefer to know where they're going and plot their route. Still others don't care which direction they head out, but want to know how many miles they've gone.

You will gradually learn what works best for you. If you're bored by the exercises you do at home, try doing your routine while listening to your radio tuned to a station with a peppy beat. Or, if you've been using a video—is it time to get a new one? Or maybe it's time to take an inventory of your interests and look into trying an entirely new activity.

One of the best ways to keep things interesting is by challenging yourself.

Buy an odometer for your bike and clock your mileage each day you ride. Record your total once a month and see how many miles you can accumulate in a season. Or buy a pedometer and try to increase your number of steps on a daily or weekly basis.

Regular exercisers use various strategies for overcoming the boredom of a treadmill or exercise bike. Some use a book—or even a trashy gossip magazine—as a carrot, only allowing themselves to read it when they work out. Others enjoy TV shows, either live or taped, or listen to CDs or their favorite radio station.

For some people, enlisting a family member, neighbor or friend as an exercise buddy livens things up, while others prefer the solitude of exercising alone on their own schedule. Why not set up a regular time to go to a friend's house and walk in that neighborhood, or pick up a friend and drive to an entirely new neighborhood that you'd like to get to know—and walk there? Inquire in your own and surrounding cities about bike or inline skating trails. You may be surprised at the large number that exist.

You may find another way to break the boredom of your exercise routine by going to a library or a bookstore that stocks magazines on your favorite activity—or on fitness, in general. Or look for role models, both at the national level

Give Me a Bike—and Flowing Water!

I've discovered that my love of water carries over to my favorite biking routes. Yes, I can work out at home on an exercise bike, but it seems unbelievably boring, even when I use a TV show I've taped or a favorite, peppy CD to keep me going—something I resort to, when I'm unable to get out on my bike for whatever reason.

But what I really have found that I love—and never even knew existed for the 30-plus years I've lived here—is a wonderful route, in the city, that goes to the river and follows it. After I ride several miles through quiet city residential streets and before I get to the river, I ride beside a creek flowing toward the river, and over a wooden footbridge by a small waterfall. No matter how stressful the day, that destination motivates me, with its reward of the bubbling water of the creek, the water falling over the stones and the quiet lapping of the river. And some days, when I have the time to bike a little farther, I'm treated to the joyful laughter of children playing in the spray at a water park along the river. Somehow it all nourishes my soul.

I can bike that route every day without becoming bored—and notice subtle changes along the route each day. After two seasons, I'm just starting to get to know my route and its two- and four-legged inhabitants, and I can hardly wait to get back there again in a few weeks for a new season.

I'm convinced that each of us has something that meets our needs in a similar way—it's just a matter of finding out what that is.

and in your area, of people who keep busy schedules and manage to stay fit. Don't be afraid to investigate or inquire about their fitness habits—most people are very happy to share their experiences with someone who's interested.

You might also be encouraged by checking your progress. Look at the earliest goals you set out and your initial results on any testing you may have done. Have you met some of those original goals? Have you rewarded yourself for meeting them? Do they need to be updated and revised? If so, why not do it now and consider adding in or swapping some new goals and activities? Cross-training with an additional sport may not only remedy boredom, but may also train new muscles.

Most people who are regularly active set aside a specific time each day for their minimum amount of exercise. Think of your exercise commitment just as you would anything else you regular-

Try a Triathlon!

Since the triathlon was introduced as an Olympic event in 2000, people are clamoring to get on board—many of them amateurs trying a triathlon for the first time. The full, Olympic version features a 1.5K swim, a 40K bike ride and a 10K run. Many Sunday newspapers carry notices of local triathlons in the sports section, or you can find the information at a local sports equipment retailer. If you're just getting your feet wet and that sounds like a bit much, you may be interested in the AARP Triumph Classic triathlon, held in numerous venues around the country.

Coming into its third year, each venue typically draws around 300 people. Although it's planned and designed for the over-50 crowd, you don't have to be 50 to participate. Typically, at least one of every 20 participants is younger than 50, often a spouse, child or grandchild of a participant who's over 50. The event features a 12.4-mile bike ride, either a 300- or 400-meter swim and a 5K run. At least one participant last year competed in four of the 14 races that were held, including those in Hawaii, Salt Lake City, Los Angeles and Phoenix.

The Triumph Classic is designed to be fun, rather than highly competitive, and awards go to participants over 50 (in categories of 5-year increments). After you submit your completed application (available at www.aarp.org/triumph), AARP will send you a registration and training packet that details a 12-week training program. Each venue has a coach who conducts weekly training sessions before the event, which you're invited to attend, once you've registered. Registration is $35. At the conclusion of the race all participants receive a T-shirt, finisher's medal and their official timing.

ly schedule and you'll be more likely to stick with it. Sometimes just trying a different time of day helps. Some people find extra motivation, just from getting up and sprucing up enough to go to a recreation center or local Y, while others go to those places without any fixing up and finish their workout with a beauty treatment.

You Lack Willpower?

Willpower is a challenge for many folks. Dealing with this issue depends a lot on where you're short of willpower. If you're frequently tempted to skip a day's workout—"It's too hot," "I'm too tired," "I'm too sore"—you probably would benefit from establishing a more regular schedule for getting exercise, just as you probably have a daily schedule for brushing your teeth or washing your face.

Don, who started his fitness quest as this book was written, frequently expressed his disappointment at his lack of willpower, when it came to food. He wanted to lose weight, but didn't want to stop indiscriminately eating freely whatever was placed before him. He did, however, have some strength and fitness goals beyond weight, and he focused on those, hoping that weight loss would eventually follow, as it most likely will.

Boost your willpower by remembering that doing something is much better than doing nothing—and that no one does what they're supposed to do all the time. If food is a problem, try keeping foods that are the most problematic out of your house—or in the freezer, where you need to go out of your way to get and prepare them. If it's a lot of bother to get something that you really want to avoid, you'll be less likely to get it. Limit some items to special events: favorite cookie recipes for the holidays and Grandma's brownies for family get-togethers, for example. And don't hesitate to freely consume plenty of fruits and vegetables!

Fear of Injuring Yourself

Want the bottom line here? The bottom line says that you're taking a much greater risk if you're inactive than if you

Your Inner Diet Voice

You may be able to avoid over-indulging in foods you'd like to limit by keeping the most tempting foods out of your house and rehearsing self-talk for times when you anticipate having difficulty passing up something particularly tempting. If I can pause just a moment, before taking that first bite of something I should pass up, I may be able to dissuade myself by asking, "Is this something you can eat any day? If so, why not wait until tomorrow, or another time?" This line of reasoning helps me distinguish special eating occasions that really only seldom occur, and then I try to convince myself that half a piece tastes just as good as a whole one, if I can savor it slowly.

participate in a reasonable level of physical activity. And you know the line: listen to your body. If you're currently participating in an activity that seems a bit too strenuous, look for ways to do it less strenuously. If, for example, full-court basketball or highly competitive industrial league softball are things you want to do and used to do, but seem to be a bit much now, seek out the milder versions—perhaps an over-40 or over-50 gym night or a less-competitive recreational or church softball league. You can find a variety of levels in just about any sport.

Similarly, if you're often in pain because of obesity-caused problems, get medical advice on the best ways to start tackling the problem with a program of physical activity. Health concerns may mean you'll need to adjust your expectations or technique for an activity that interests you, but your risk of injury with supervised activity is still much less than it is if you do nothing.

Understand that your limits may be much different from those of someone else, and don't let anyone convince you otherwise. Bodies are all different, and what's too much for one person may not be too much for another person. Don't be afraid to say you've had enough and need to back off or sit down. It may be time to revisit the Borg scale (see Chapter 4, page 88) and figure out where you are on the scale. Experts recommend aerobic conditioning somewhere between 12 and 14 for most people (11=light, 13=somewhat hard and 15=hard). If something has changed in the level you feel you can manage comfortably, it's a good idea to discuss that with your doctor.

Lack of Skill

Don't let anyone convince you that lacking skill is a good reason to walk away from an activity you'd be interested to try. You don't have to measure up to someone's expectation of being "good" at something to make it part of your repertoire—or at least to give it a try. Not only can you do your body a favor by investing the time and effort in trying something physically challenging or new, but you'll also help keep your mind young by tackling something novel. There are several good ways to do that, and what's best for you depends on how you best learn, what resources you have available to dedicate to it and the amount of time you're willing to spend. Take a quick inventory of resources available to you and match that with your interests.

If you're adept at researching and learning from your research, you may want to look into information available either on the Internet or in print at the local library. Although you can find some basic information in Chapter 7 on many activities, it's possible today, especially using electronic resources available at your public library, to find plenty of good information about nearly anything you'd like to do.

Depending upon where you live and what's available there, you may find many things covered in community education classes, usually offered at very reasonable prices. Sometimes you can even get free instruction. Another alternative is to find someone you know who does what you want to learn and ask that person for some helpful tips—which is frequently all it takes to master something you'd like to do.

Lack of Financial Resources

This book is dedicated to helping you become active and fit, even if your financial resources are limited. Many of the suggestions you find here don't require any financial investment—walking or jogging, turning on the radio and designing your own aerobic routine, for example. In fact, you have enough information here to create a fairly comprehensive, functional fitness regimen at little or no cost.

You may be quite surprised, once you start to investigate, how many resources are actually available within your own community. Community centers in many areas are underutilized and are a resource often overlooked. You may also want to go in with a friend to acquire a more expensive piece of equipment together—a canoe, kayak or snowshoes, for example. And chances are, family members may also welcome these gift ideas.

Need a spark that's low-cost? Try finding a new area for your workout.

Uncooperative Outdoor Weather—Cold

Unless your physician specifically tells you to discontinue outdoor activity in cold weather, there's no reason to do so, except in the most extreme weather. You do, however, need to use caution.

Continuing to exercise year-round puts you way ahead of folks who hang up their bikes or walking shoes and go into hibernation over winter. Besides keeping you in shape all year, exercising through the winter can also help you avoid the "winter blues" that affect so many people. It'll also help you avoid that extra layer of flab that many folks end up acquiring through inactivity over the winter months In fact, according to the American College of Sports Medicine, by staying active in the winter you may even lose a bit more body fat, just because it takes more energy to move over snow in heavy clothing and boots. And, as is true year-round, continuing to get a good amount of physical activity throughout the winter months also will help you be more energetic and sleep better.

There are several things to remember when you exercise outdoors in cold weather: stay dry, start gradually and work your way up to a comfortable level of exertion. It's also a good idea to avoid eating a big meal before you head out into cold weather. If you dress in clothing that provides insulation and protects you from the wind—and if you generate heat through physical activity, you can stay quite warm as the temperature plummets.

"There's no such thing as bad weather, only bad clothing," says Jim Gilbert,

Linnaeus Arboretum director and instructor in environmental studies at Gustavus Adolphus College, citing an old Swedish saying. On the January day he was interviewed for this book, Gilbert had been out walking in the southern Minnesota forest with his class for 3 hours in the morning on a deer study. The temperature was a balmy 10 degrees above zero Fahrenheit, the wind chill around 10 below, it was sunny and there was a northwest wind.

"No one was cold, because they dressed properly in layers," explained Gilbert, who frequently teaches two 3-hour classes outdoors on a wintry day (which keeps him outside for at least 6 hours), as students in environmental studies learn to explore and interpret the winter landscape. "These students will earn a living working outside, so we go out, unless there's a tornado warning or lightning," says Gilbert. "Our bodies can easily stand temperatures of 20 below zero if we dress properly."

So what constitutes "proper" attire, when you're outdoors exercising and the wind chill hovers near 40 degrees below zero? "Layers. You need to dress in layers," says Gilbert. "It's not hard to be comfortable. Your body generates warmth and layering helps keep that warmth from blowing away." Gilbert recommends an initial layer of polypropylene long underwear, which wicks moisture away from your body if you're active enough to work up a sweat. Then he adds a layer of wool pants or blue jeans, topped with snow pants. Any shirt is fine, topped by a fleece jacket

My Family & Friends Help Me Join the Y

For years, community center pools met my needs very well. Priced well below even the least expensive club, I found them fine places to swim, and not heavily used.

About a year before I began working on this book my local community center closed for remodeling and I needed to find another place to swim. The question was never whether I would continue to swim, but just where. After investigating my options, I settled on the local Y for the 4 months my community center would be closed. At more than twice the price of my community center membership, it was a bit pricey for me. But it was near enough to my home that I could bike there in decent weather, and the swimming hours were much more generous than those at the community center. Convinced that I was worth it, I decided to give it a try.

Now, over a year later, I'm still there. My community center has reopened, although the roads to get there are still under construction. During this time, on gift-giving occasions, I've asked family members to contribute money toward my membership rather than buy me other types of gifts. They've responded positively and generously. I've made their shopping easier and enjoy, at least for the time being, the luxury of swimming nearby at times that fit better into my schedule.

And, I've learned Y memberships are honored around the country, as well—a real bonus when I travel.

and a windbreaker. Boots with felt liners keep your feet warm, and Gilbert recommends both a stocking cap and a hood for your head to block the wind and hold in the heat that rises from your body, the most common type of heat loss. When it's cold outside, Gilbert never wears gloves, but puts ice chopper mittens over his warm wool ones, allowing his fingers to share their warmth and expose less area to the cold.

Experts disagree somewhat on fiber recommendations—many argue against wearing any cotton because it can absorb moisture, become wet and chill your skin. Experts split on their opinions about wool and some suggest not wearing down, but they're unanimous in their recommendations about layering your clothing and covering your head. Areas of your body most susceptible to frostbite include your fingers and toes, as well as male genitals and female nipples. It's also important to make sure your boots are loose enough to allow your blood to flow freely to and from your feet. And, if you're skiing downhill, it's important to wear protective eye gear to prevent frostbite of your cornea.

Both Gilbert and the American College of Sports Medicine recommend keeping an eye not only on the thermometer, but also on the wind chill, which is now calculated in a new way. Learn more about it at www.windchill.ec.gc.ca. Do your warm-up exercises and any preliminary stretching you plan to do

Check Out Indoor Options

Ask around about indoor options in your area when the weather's lousy outdoors. There may be more options than you realize. In addition to indoor shopping malls that now open early for walkers, some indoor professional ballparks open their concourses to inline skating, walking or running.

In Minneapolis, for example, the Hubert H. Humphrey Metrodome is open to inline skaters, walkers and joggers from November through April. Each year, over 50,000 people use the facility, paying $6 per time, for one adult, with season passes $169 to $189. Just 2.5 times around the concourse equals 1 mile.

If you don't know how to inline skate, it's no problem. Pay the admission fee, rent skates for $5 and take advantage of the facility's free lessons and free protective gear. One of the building's two levels is designated for fast-moving skaters, the other for slower moving skaters and walkers.

Another suburban city has an indoor park open 6 days a week. It includes a gym that's open for kids every day, with adult basketball time Monday through Thursday, from 4 to 6 p.m. The facility also offers an ice skating rink and a lap swimming pool. Single-time use runs $4, with season passes available.

indoors before moving outside, where the insulation and wind-protective value of appropriate clothing will combine with the heat you generate during activity to keep you warm. Multiple layers also enable you to remove clothing as you warm up and replace it again as you cool down. You're probably dressed adequately, if you feel cool as you start, rather than overdressing and sweating excessively as you exercise. When your hands and feet are cold and you start shivering, it's time to move indoors.

Experts also offer this additional advice for cold weather exercising:

- Be sure you drink plenty of water to avoid dehydration. In cold weather you lose more moisture as you breathe than you do in warmer weather.
- To reduce heat loss, plan your route so that you finish with the wind at your back, when you're the most sweaty.
- Use extra caution if you exercise outdoors in the dark, when it's difficult to spot slippery surfaces and when drivers can't readily see you.
- If you have cardiovascular problems, asthma or a medical condition that limits your exercise ability, check with your doctor before exercising in cold weather, as cold weather can exacerbate some conditions.
- You're more likely to stay warm if you avoid alcohol and tobacco products and consume carbohydrates—but not a huge meal—before going outdoors.
- Remember, if you'll be at high altitudes, you're at increased risk of frostbite there.
- Be sure to use sunscreen and a hat.

Environmentalist Takes His Own Advice

Jim Gilbert, Linnaeus Arboretum director and instructor in environmental studies at Gustavus Adolphus College, walks at least 2 miles with his wife every day—even after working outside all day. "We like to do 4 miles, but sometimes only get in 2, and then sometimes not until after the 10 p.m. news," he says. As he advises his students, Gilbert and his wife dress in layers that enable them to manage virtually any temperature that Minnesota winters offer.

"It's a frame of mind you have to set for yourself," says Gilbert. "We try, if we're going to visit someone, to walk there. When we have time, we walk the 10 miles around Lake Waconia [in the rural area where they live, west of Minneapolis]. "We walk every day, no matter what—if it's raining, if our feet hurt. My wife walked the other day with a stomachache and felt better when we were done."

Not that Gilbert doesn't put up with some flak. Staff at the car repair shop in town were surprised, when Gilbert said he'd walk the 3 miles home when he brought his car in for repair, and again when he turned down a ride back to the repair shop when it was time to pick up his car.

Uncooperative Outdoor Weather—Heat

While you can exercise outdoors in weather that's fairly warm, it's a good idea to try to avoid the hottest times of day, if possible. You should be able to work out at the same intensity as you would in cooler weather, but for a shorter period of time. And, if warm weather is new for you, give your body time to adjust gradually, and don't push yourself.

The most valuable tip for exercising in the heat is to drink. "Voluntary dehydration"—becoming dehydrated as a result of just drinking when you're thirsty—is a special risk in hot weather. Especially as you age, thirst is not an adequate predictor of the amount of water you need. And lack of adequate hydration adversely affects your heart's capacity for exercise. Imagine your car running with no oil—it's somewhat comparable. The best fluid to drink when it's warm is cool water, which is absorbed rapidly in your gut. If you'll be exercising continuously for over an hour, you may want to consider a sports drink that replaces the electrolytes you lose as you sweat. However, for most people, plain water is exactly what's needed. Even a 1 to 2 percent loss of body weight through sweat can impair your exercise performance.

Cardiovascular medications—including water pills and medications that limit your heart rate—as well as medications commonly used for allergies can increase your potential for becoming ill in the heat. Sunburn also decreases your body's ability to cool itself, so use sunscreen liberally before you go out in the heat. Normally, your body cools down as sweat evaporates in the air, especially if there's a breeze. Of course, your body will cool less effectively when it's hot and humid outside. Help your body get rid of excess heat by wearing porous, non-rubberized clothes when you work out in the heat. Wear a hat with a wide brim and seek shade from time to time.

Don't risk letting "voluntary dehydration" make you a victim of the heat.

Uncooperative Outdoor Weather—Rain

If you can't—or don't want to—exercise in the rain, you're best advised to have some fallback activities and locations in mind. Rain doesn't keep many diehard golfers off the course, although lightning certainly does! And, without lightning,

Whether in Colombia or Florida—Carmen Exercises in Hot Weather—with Care

Carmen lives in Florida but doesn't let the heat slow her down at all. Raised in Colombia by Colombian and Danish parents, Carmen says that both skin cancer and obesity were relatively unknown in her hometown of Bogota. Carmen says she's exercised all her life, wears sunscreen and always wears a brimmed hat when she's out in the sun.

Tips for exercising in the heat? That's simple, says Carmen, who lives 3 minutes from the Atlantic Ocean and loves walking on the beach.

In warm weather Carmen exercises early in the morning—around 6:30 or 7 a.m. She often walks on the beach at her 3 mph pace or takes the 3.5-mile loop on the street in her neighborhood. When several neighbors walk together—a group that has frequently numbered five or six in the past—they turn on their porch light in the early morning darkness to indicate their willingness to join in.

In rainy, exceptionally hot or chilly weather, Carmen exercises indoors, frequently with a videotape of aerobics instructor Denise Austin or another TV program to keep her pace lively. Indoor equipment includes a treadmill and bike, as well as free weights.

"I love exercising, because it makes my day. It makes me feel great!" says Carmen. "If I don't do it, I find that I'm sluggish and not fit for much of anything." After working out, Carmen eats a good breakfast. Then she's alert and ready to face the day's schedule. "In our home we have a very healthy diet consisting mostly of fresh fruit and steamed vegetables, whole grain, broiled or baked fish and poultry, low-fat milk and dairy products and a few vitamin supplements," says Carmen. "I've never taken any medication."

Lots of water and care when going out in the full sun are her secrets to healthy skin. "I don't want to look like I have alligator skin, like some people I see here," she says. Carmen also believes that it's good for her skin to perspire, and calls it "the eternal moisturizer."

"The bottom line, if you want to remain healthy, happy, vigorous and young at heart—regardless of age—is to do everything in moderation. Exercise, a healthy diet, fresh air, plenty of water and a very positive attitude will give you a very healthy, happy, meaningful life."

moderate rain also needn't prevent you from walking. You're drip-dry, remember! It is important, however, to remember that biking is difficult in the rain, because wet brakes simply don't work. Again, look for indoor locations to walk or otherwise get exercise.

Lack of Progress Toward Your Goals

This is a common problem that everyone faces at one time or another. The path to becoming fit isn't a smooth, even path. There will be times when you are doing great, simply to hold your own—especially if you're under one kind of stress or another. Remind yourself again and again that you're still ahead of where you'd be if you did nothing. Sometimes a real advantage to working out with a friend is being able to boost each other's morale when you hit the doldrums.

There are a couple of reasons for a seeming lack of progress that you may want to consider. Are you expecting something too soon—and do you need, perhaps, to put some incremental goals between your big goal and your starting point? Don, for example, wants to lose 100 pounds, which is overwhelming for anyone to consider. He needs some mile markers along the way, and he's developing those: deciding to work out 5 days a week, finding it easier to get in and out of the car, balancing well enough on one foot to be able to put on his trousers without sitting down, going up the stairs without becoming winded, doing 10—then 20—push-ups, seeing a leaner face when he looks in the mirror.

Don's now starting to date—which can be a goal as well as a reward for feeling better about himself. Not too far down the road, he's also looking at spring training with the softball team, and wondering whether his being able to take a more active role may mean he'll give some of the younger guys on the team a run for their money, as they defend their field positions. And he already knows that the run to first base will be easier. He hasn't mentioned it, but surely he also notices that he's now able to play the full 2 hours of volleyball on Friday nights—something that looked unmanageable just a few weeks ago.

No, Don may not have lost weight yet—although he may have converted some of his fat to muscle tissue. And he has noticed it's easier to pass up some things he'd have eaten without a thought not too long ago.

As you think about your goals, ask yourself if you can break them down into smaller increments that can help detect progress short of meeting "the big goal." Also treat yourself to something occasionally, simply because you're working on it. Just make sure that you're not rewarding yourself for losing weight or showing dietary restraint with a big meal or other counterproductive prize.

Getting Back Up to Speed, If You Lose Momentum or Stop for a While

Similar to the previous point, you need to consider your fitness quest an ongoing process, complete with ups and down and bumps along the way.

Remember that everyone falls back at times, and sometimes it takes a while to get back on track. Experts will tell you that you're actually coming out ahead, if you can simply maintain your position and not lose ground.

If you've been inactive for a while, don't forget that it may take a long time to get back to where you were before you lost momentum. Put in some interim, temporary goals. And don't be afraid they're too small! Remember, any amount of physical activity is better than none—you have to start somewhere.

When You're Ill

By now you could probably write this paragraph yourself. The cardinal rule: listen to your body. For additional help:

- It's best to avoid working out when you have a fever. This is simply a safety measure to avoid the possibility of an infection moving to different areas of your body, increasing your risk of complications.
- If you have a mild illness, such as a simple cold or sore throat, it's probably okay to work out, but feel free to cut back on the intensity and duration of your workout. Your body will let you know how much is too much.
- If you're coming back from an illness, injury or other limitation, remember that you'll need to do so gradually and gently. Don't push yourself, certainly not before you're comfortably back to where you were before you needed to take a break.
- If you have a chronic illness, such as exercise-induced asthma or unexplained chest pain, check with your healthcare provider to discuss what kind of activities are reasonable for your specific condition.

Most of the time, illness is a temporary state and after you recover you'll gradually work back to where you were before becoming ill. Sometimes, however, illness changes the parameters of what will be possible for you. In these situations, your recovery may include learning how to adapt your activity level to new limitations. While having to adjust your expectations may seem difficult at times, remember that you've done a lot of that since you were at the age when you expected to be able to jump off the fence, flap your arms and fly. Adapting is, after all, part of the secret of survival.

Holidays & Other Breaks in Your Routine

Holidays and other breaks are famed for challenging the best-laid fitness plans. Before your next major holiday, stop to think for a while about how you can improve the impact of the holiday on your fitness routine. Here are a few tips that can help:

- Try to be a bit less ambitious about what you take on at this time, so you'll have more time to continue getting the physical activity you're used to.
- If weight gain is a struggle for you over a holiday, rethink the significance of this holiday. Doesn't its significance truly go beyond food? Can you focus more on that perspective?
- If you plan to do a lot of cooking and baking, consider whether some of

your recipes could be adapted to be more heart healthy, perhaps trimming the amounts of cheese and other fats that are less heart healthy or substituting more heart healthy fats and oils—or pureed prunes for some of the oil.

■ Can your menu include more fruit and vegetable options that don't include high-calorie dips and sauces?

■ If Grandma's brownie recipe, laden with butter (and nothing else will do!), is vital to your holiday celebration, make a smaller batch and try to limit yourself to one reasonably-sized portion. Similarly, if you can limit yourself to one small serving of the rest of the holiday foods, it's a lot easier to keep your weight in check.

■ Respect the fact that others you know may also be trying to make their holiday traditions more healthful. Don't press someone who's trying to pass up the cookie plate to indulge.

■ If loved ones ask for gift ideas, why not suggest something that contributes to your goals—maybe money toward a membership, a piece of exercise equipment or a step counter, for example. Or suggest, instead of spending money, that they give you an I.O.U. for a walk with you every month for a year.

■ Why not start a new, active holiday tradition (or revitalize an old one)—sledding, skating or cross-country skiing, for example? Or, instead of an Easter egg hunt indoors, how about a more active one in a nearby park? Or a Thanksgiving family football game in the yard?

Once you start looking at holidays from this perspective, a lot of creative possibilities turn up. You'll feel much better, if you do nothing more significant than inviting those you're celebrating with to take a walk with you. And it may well be what you'll remember most vividly from the holiday, as you look back.

Special Challenges Face New Parents

For Mom. After you have a baby, you'd like to get back to your pre-pregnancy size and condition quickly, which is often difficult. Some of the challenges you'll encounter after giving birth include:

■ **Physical changes**—When you set up a postpartum exercise regimen, take into consideration that you may have become deconditioned in the later months of pregnancy and your ligaments will tend to stretch exceptionally easily for up to 3 months postpartum.

■ **Competing demands**—You may need to find creative solutions: swapping child care with another parent in your neighborhood or circle of friends while you each exercise; looking for a Y or a gym with child care available; buying or borrowing a jogging stroller; buying or borrowing from the library an exercise video for use at home or investing in home exercise equipment.

■ **Lack of good information about weight retention**—Changes in your body may persist for 6 weeks or more postpartum as you gradually return to your pre-pregnant state.

■ **Fear of interference with breastfeeding**—Breastfeeding has little effect on postpartum weight loss, and regular exercise has no effect on lactation. Be sure to drink adequate fluids, wear a good supportive bra (some women need two sports bras for adequate compression and stabilization) and nurse your baby or use a breast pump shortly before exercising.

■ **Stress incontinence** (leaking urine when you cough, laugh, jump or lift something)—a problem that's fairly common among women, in general (see next page).

For Dad. Becoming a parent is one of the most dramatic changes that occurs in the lives of many people. While the focus is frequently on the newest member of your family and on Mom's recovery, the event has a major effect on new dads, as well. It can be summed up in one word: chaos. Your orderly workout schedule is cast to the wind, and you may wonder if your life ever will regain a sense of order.

The challenges today's new dad faces are, in some ways, quite different from the ones your dad may have faced with the arrival of a new baby in the family, partly due to the expanded role of women in the workplace. Today it's not at all unusual for Dad to take on a much larger role in parenting and in household tasks. And, as a result, your own fitness habits may end up on a back burner, along with those of your partner, as you care for your newest family member.

Here are a few suggestions that may help you and your partner:

■ Babies are amazingly portable. If you're a walker or jogger, consider investing in—or borrowing—a good backpack or a jogging stroller.

■ Check out the latest options in baby front- or backpacks. Your body's closeness and motion can lull a wakeful

Thank Heavens for My Snugli!

Both of my children spent much of the first year or more of their lives snuggled close to me in a soft, sturdy cloth carrier that I wore on my chest. They thus accompanied me, riding downtown on the bus to swimming lessons (beginning, for our second son, at 2 months), vacuuming the carpet at home, shopping in the grocery store and picking strawberries at a local strawberry farm.

Apparently—judging from their delight fairly early on, every time I got ready to place them in the Snugli—it was a secure, comfortable spot for them, whether awake or asleep. Of course, cultures over the ages have secured their infants in a similar position with similar results.

I'm convinced that this well-padded carrier increased my core strength, as the babies added heft and I grew proportionately stronger. Many parents also find backpacks similarly comfortable for their tots. Either offers a great way for your child—even as an infant—to be introduced to an active lifestyle. Be sure to start placing your child in it early, so that your baby quickly becomes accustomed to being in it and you can adjust to the added weight gradually as your baby grows. A similar carrier is made by the BabyBjorn company.

child to sleep while you take a walk, clean the house, mow the lawn or do the shopping.

■ Some couples prefer to take turns watching the baby while their partner works out, while others prefer working out together and either taking the baby along, swapping child care with other parents, giving grandparents the opportunity to get acquainted with the baby or hiring child care providers—frequently a teenager in the neighborhood. Some Y facilities also offer cooperative child care, with parents taking turns assisting a person who's in charge of the child care area, in exchange for child care for their tot when they go to exercise.

Stress Incontinence

Nearly a third of women who exercise regularly—not just those who recently gave birth—report stress incontinence, especially during high-impact activities. Many stop exercising because of it. But there are ways to remedy the problem.

Try low-impact activities like walking, biking and swimming. Always empty your bladder completely before you start exercising. Avoid caffeine for several hours beforehand. Many women find it helpful to wear a tampon to increase urethral support. If you're overweight, you may dramatically improve the situation by losing a few pounds.

More than half of all women who struggle with stress incontinence find Kegel exercises effective in strengthening pelvic floor muscles, but most women don't do them regularly enough to realize the improvement. Here's how to do them:

1. Squeeze the muscles you would use to avoid passing gas. Hold for a count of three, relax for the same amount of time and repeat.

2. If you're contracting the correct muscles, you should sense a pulling feeling when you squeeze. You can check by placing a finger in your vagina and contracting your muscles to squeeze your finger.

3. Repeat this exercise frequently during the day—it's a great one to use while you're sitting in traffic. Do not use this exercise while you urinate. You should notice an improvement in your urinary control in 4 to 6 weeks.

Neither Rain, nor Wind...

The more accustomed you become to a fit way of life, the less distracted you'll be by obstacles along the way. Like other routines in life, you'll deal with the challenges and learn to be creative in tackling them. You'll get to know other active folks and learn from their experiences and share with others what you've learned. And soon, some of the roadblocks will look like minor ripples.

Marvin A. Brooks, M D., reviewed chapter 9. He is a family practice physician.

CHAPTER 10

Let What You Eat Work for You, Too!

When it comes to nutrition, it almost seems the more researchers study it, the more they realize they don't know about it. One fad follows another—frequently drawn from extremes. Like many people, you may feel you're getting jerked around by the so-called experts. So, what's the best nutrition advice for someone today who wants to become more fit? And what's the latest word on weight loss? Are carbs good, or are they horrible? Is protein in or out? And how can you avoid being jerked around by every fad that blows in the breeze? After all, it's your health that's at stake here.

"Current, up-to-date information needs to carry the message that a lot of things are still up in the air," says David McCarron, M.D., visiting professor at the University of California-Davis, Department of Nutrition. If they're honest, most experts today would probably agree with that statement. "In fact, in some ways," continues McCarron, "we've lost ground. Mineral intake by the average American today is about half what it was 50 years ago—and diners then had the basic food groups in front of them on the table. You could argue that the diversity of the American diet was better then, than it is now." Perhaps it's a question of whether today's shortfall is lack of diversity in what's available—or in what today's Americans actually eat.

You may be surprised at the simplicity of some very

sound advice that summarizes what you'll read in this chapter:

- Successful weight control is not a result of either diet or exercise alone—but both.
- Pay attention to portion sizes.
- You take a major risk by ignoring dairy products—or shortchanging water.
- Your healthiest eating comes from shopping the perimeter of the grocery store.
- Don't take seriously anyone who tells you that you can get all the nourishment you need from a handful of pills.
- Paint your food palette by color.
- Dining out can be healthful.

WIN the Rockies

WIN the Rockies illustrates well one of the latest commonsense approaches to eating. Wellness IN the Rockies (WIN the Rockies) is a community research and intervention program in Idaho, Montana and Wyoming, dedicated to the promotion of healthful and pleasurable eating, physically active living and respect for body-size diversity. The project is funded through a competitive grant award (#0004499) program of the United States Department of Agriculture.

Over half of the people in six communities who randomly received a mailed survey from the project responded, sharing their attitudes and behavior in the areas of eating, physical activity and body image. Respondents with a higher body mass index (BMI) were more likely to:

- drink sweetened beverages like soft drinks
- order super-size portions
- eat while doing other activities—watching TV, for example
- believe they got less exercise than they needed
- report a lower frequency of participation in physical activity

According to Sylvia Moore, Ph.D., R.D., professor and director of the Division of Medical Education and Public Health at the University of Wyoming, the object of this project is to help people develop life-long healthy habits rather than focusing on trying to achieve a specific body size.

The guiding principles of Wellness IN the Rockies are very straightforward:

- accepting and valuing every body, whatever size or shape

Moore Fits in Activity, Encourages Staff to Do So, Too

Regular activity is nothing new for Sylvia Moore, Ph.D., R.D., professor and director of the Division of Medical Education and Public Health at the University of Wyoming, and director of the WIN the Rockies health improvement project. Three mornings each week she does circuit resistance exercises, beginning at 5:30.

Moore also frequently walks to work—2 miles each way. "Our office is on the fourth floor and I take the steps—and encourage staff members to do so, as well," she adds.

■ helping people feel good about their bodies and about who they are

■ recognizing that people of all sizes and shapes can reduce their risk of poor health by adopting a healthy lifestyle

■ challenging size-prejudice beliefs

In the areas of positive self-acceptance, the project aims to help community members to identify and build on strengths and abilities, to be critical of messages focusing on unrealistic body images as symbols of success and happiness and to value themselves —regardless of size. WIN the Rockies encourages citizens to make physical activity fun and to include it every day. "Participate in activities for the joy of feeling your body move," the project urges.

Furthermore, WIN the Rockies' principles of healthful and pleasurable eating are surprisingly straightforward:

■ take pleasure in eating

■ take control—eat when you're hungry and stop when you're satisfied

■ follow the Food Guide Pyramid

■ honor the gift of food

Moore and others working on the project hope it helps communities stem the rising tide of obesity by helping individuals overcome real-life issues.

Lessons Learned from Members of the National Weight Control Registry

You'll find it difficult, if you understand the reason for this book's existence, to discuss dieting without talking about physical activity. Interestingly, that's also the consensus of a majority of the nearly 3,000 members of the National Weight Control Registry. James O. Hill, Ph.D., professor of pediatrics and director of the Center for Human Nutrition and the Colorado Clinical Nutrition Research Unit at the University of Colorado, and Rena R. Wing, Ph.D., professor of biomedical psychiatry and human behavior, Brown University, developed the registry to study a popular myth about weight loss: that everyone who loses weight eventually regains it.

The project began with an initial 784 enrollees: individuals who had lost an average of 66 pounds and had maintained at least a 30-pound loss for an

Earthquake Brings the Message Home for 36-Year-Old Woman

One of the National Weight Control Registry participants was at her maximum weight of 325 at age 36, when an earthquake brought the point home. When the quake disabled the elevator in her apartment building, she realized she couldn't climb the stairs to her apartment. It was time to do something.

By limiting the sizes of her portions, cutting fat and walking, she lost 160 pounds in the next 2 years. She's maintained that loss for the past 4 years with a combination of biking, weight training and yoga. Noting that acquaintances had told her that fat was in her genes, she now says, "My jeans are now size 11/12!"

average of 5 years. Nearly every original enrollee reported that a combination of diet and exercise not only caused the weight loss, but also makes it possible to maintain that loss. And—this may surprise you—42 percent reported that maintaining the loss was less difficult than initially losing it. Most also reported that losing the weight brought a significant improvement in their self-confidence, mood and physical health.

Defining successful long-term weight loss maintenance as "intentionally losing at least 10 percent of body weight and keeping it off for at least 1 year," Wing and Hill estimate that "perhaps greater than 20 percent of overweight or obese persons are able to achieve success. We found that in the National Weight Control Registry, successful long-term weight loss maintainers share common behavioral strategies, including eating a diet low in fat, frequent self-monitoring of body weight and food intake and high levels of physical activity." Wing and Hill also report that maintaining weight loss may get easier over time and that "once these successful maintainers have maintained a weight loss for 2 to 5 years, the chances of longer-term success greatly increase."

About half of the National Weight Control Registry members lost weight on their own initially, while the rest used formal weight loss programs or relied on the assistance of a healthcare professional. Those who lost weight on their own didn't differ from those using programs, in respect to total energy intake, percent of energy from fat or intake of a variety of selected nutrients. Both groups met the Recommended Daily Allowance (RDA) for most nutrients. Compared to the population at large, they consumed less energy—and a lower percentage of the energy they did consume came from fat.

Researchers concluded that, "despite using very different methods to initially lose weight, individuals who lost weight on their own, through organized programs or with liquid diets are all using similar strategies to maintain weight." Those who did regain weight reported greater increases in fat intake and reductions in physical activity.

Successful Losers Eat Breakfast

Breakfast was of surprising importance to successful losers in the registry. A recent update notes that 78 percent of the members report regularly eating breakfast every day—and only 4 percent report that they never eat breakfast. And, despite having an extra official meal, there was no difference in the energy intake between breakfast eaters and those who skipped breakfast. However, those who eat breakfast report getting slightly more physical activity than those who skip breakfast.

Although everyone is different, if you say that the road to weight loss brings emotional distress and depression, you don't get a lot of support from registry members. The levels of those conditions, as well as binge eating and self-induced vomiting among members is considerably lower than the levels of those behaviors seen among psychiatric patients—and similar to rates seen in a random sample of the general population.

Recent research compared members

who lost weight surgically with those who lost weight through nonsurgical means. While both groups, on the whole, continue to function well and maintain significant weight losses, members who had the surgery report that their diets currently include more fat than diets of the nonsurgical group. They also report, in comparison to nonsurgical registry members, much lower levels of physical activity.

Recently, researchers studied whether or not maintaining a significant weight loss becomes easier over time. Registry members who have maintained their new, lower weight levels the longest report that they use fewer weight control strategies—and that it takes less effort to keep it off and maintain their current weight than it took to lose it initially. And, whether members are newcomers to successful weight loss in the registry or are seasoned veterans, they seem to derive equal amounts of pleasure from exercise, low-fat eating and maintaining their weight losses.

Your Activity Level: A Key Factor in Losing Weight

Forget, for a moment, the wide variety of diets you've heard about. None of them dispute this truth: At the most fundamental level, your weight reflects whether or not your caloric intake exceeds your level of physical activity—your energy balance. If you eat more calories than your body needs to perform the day's activities, those extra calories are stored as fat. If you don't take in enough calories to meet your body's energy needs, your body goes to the fat you've stored to make up the difference. The most powerful weight loss formula combines the factors of energy output, and caloric intake.

Simply put, each pound of fat on your body is a storehouse for 3,500 calories of unused energy. Therefore, in order to lose 1

Most successful losers, 78 percent of those in the National Weight Control Registry, eat breakfast every day.

What Does It Take to Burn Off a Large Order of McDonald's Fries?

Have you ever stopped to consider, for one splurge item, what it takes to burn that extra amount of calories? Here's a good example. A large order of french fries (6.2 oz.) from McDonald's contains: 540 calories—as well as 26 grams of fat, 4.5 grams of saturated fat, 350 milligrams of sodium, 6 grams of fiber and 8 grams protein. Look at the chart below and consider how you would burn off an extra 540 calories.

If you're used to thinking in terms of calories rather than METs, here are some rough equivalents, based on a 150-pound person. (If you're heavier than that, it takes more calories to move the extra weight, so your hourly totals will be somewhat higher.)

Energy Expenditure Chart*

Activity	Energy cost (calories per hour)	Hours needed (to burn off fries)
lying down or sleeping	90	6.0
canoeing, 2.5 miles per hour	174	3.1
cycling, 5 miles per hour	174	3.1
walking, 2 miles per hour	198	2.7
light housework or cleaning	246	2.2
swimming front crawl, 20 yards per minute	288	1.9
tennis doubles, recreational	312	1.7
scrubbing floors	440	1.2
tennis singles, recreational	450	1.2
basketball, recreational	450	1.2
swimming, front crawl, 45 yards per minute	522	1.0
aerobic dance	546	1.0
racquetball	588	0.9
cycling, 13 miles per hour	612	0.9
cross-country skiing, 5 miles per hour	690	0.8

*source: President's Council on Fitness and Sports

You can lose about 10 pounds in a year by adding 15 minutes of moderate exercise each day, keeping everything else constant.

pound, you must expend 3,500 more calories than you take in. For example, if you add 15 minutes of moderate exercise each day—about what it takes to walk a mile at a moderately brisk pace—you'll use about 100 extra calories per day. Assuming your other levels of food intake and activity remain constant, those 700 extra calories of energy spent each week will amount to about 10 pounds of weight loss in 1 year. Similarly, an extra slice of bread or soft drink each day will put on 10 pounds in a year, if you don't increase your energy expenditure.

About three-quarters of the energy you use every day goes for your body's basic functions, like sleeping, breathing, digesting food. Not surprisingly, as you may have noticed from the MET chart (see pages 81 to 86), activities like sitting consume only small amounts of energy.

Exercise Alone Cuts Weight, Fat

Many researchers say that the best way to lose weight is to start a regular exercise program and increase the amount of physical activity in your daily routine. A recent 1-year study looked at the effect of exercise alone on postmenopausal women (studied at this stage of life in order to rule out hormonal influences). All participants were asked not to change their diets.

Members of an exercise-intervention group added 45 minutes of moderately intense exercise 5 days a week, for the year. Participants were closely monitored during the first 3 months, as they attended exercise sessions three times a week at a study facility, where they used treadmills and stationary bicycles and received optional strength training. They also exercised 2 days a week at home. For the next 8 months they attended one session a week at the facility and exercised on their own, for a total of at least 5 days a week. Meanwhile, members of the control group met weekly for 45-minute stretching sessions throughout the entire year.

After 12 months, with the only change for all participants being exercise levels, results were quite impressive. Exercisers lost weight: an average of nearly 3 pounds (1.3 kg), versus a 3.5-ounce (0.1 kg) weight gain for the control group. And don't forget that those exercisers also gained the other health benefits that accrue with physical activity, in addition to weight loss!

Exercisers also lost body fat rather than muscle, and there was a direct relationship between the level of activity and the amount of body fat lost. Women who were most active, exercising 195 minutes or more per week, lost 4.2 percent of their total body fat. This compares with about half that much loss (2.4 percent) of body fat in the intermediate group of exercisers (136 to 195 minutes per week), a much smaller (0.6 percent) body fat loss among low-activity exercisers

Healthy Community BMI Competition: An Idea Whose Time Has Come

Do you know your BMI? Do your kids or grandkids know their BMIs?

How about introducing a new kind of competition in your area? The U.S. Surgeon General, the Centers for Disease Control and Prevention and others—including family physicians all over the country—are becoming alarmed at the numbers of overweight and obese Americans. My family physician, Marvin Brooks, M.D., has a suggestion: How about initiating healthy community BMI competitions around the country?

Glance, for a moment, at the data presented in the maps below, provided by the Centers for Disease Control and Prevention. Note that in 1991, no states had 20 percent or more of adults obese. Then note the dramatic shift: by 2000, in only one state—Colorado—was less than 15 percent of the population obese.

Perhaps you could interest others in your community in changing that picture. How about initiating a competition to lower your community's collective BMI? Such a competition could be designed after models used for

Percentage of Adults Who Report Being Obese, By State*

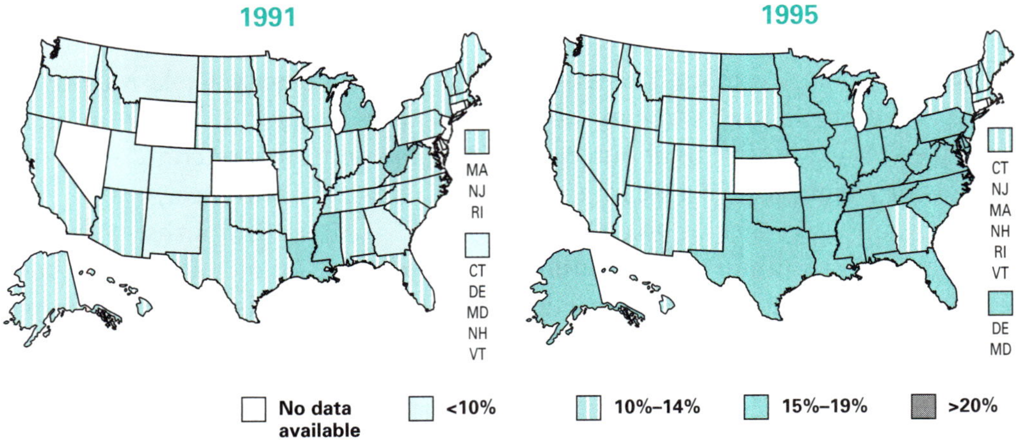

*Body mass index >30 or about 30 pounds overweight for a 5'4" person.
Source: CDC, Behavioral Risk Factor Surveillance System.

(less than 135 minutes per week) and a similar (0.4 percent) loss among members of the control group (the stretchers).

Furthermore, exercisers lost intra-abdominal body fat—the fat that puts you at the highest risk of cardiovascular disease, high blood pressure, high cholesterol and diabetes—at an even greater rate. Here again, the amount lost depended upon the amount of exercise they got. Highly active study participants lost 6.9 percent of their intra-abdominal body fat, while intermediate exercisers lost 5.9 percent, low exercisers lost 3.4 percent and control group members gained 0.1 percent.

Cardiorespiratory fitness improved in 84 percent of the exercisers, assessed by measuring their VO_2max at the beginning and end of the study. Authors of the study note that weight loss based on diet alone has not been shown to increase cardiorespiratory fitness levels. All participants in the study were overweight (defined as having a BMI greater than 25) or had BMIs from 24 to 25 with more than 33 percent body fat.

Of course, the scale and BMI don't tell the whole story. Contrary to what you may think, fat doesn't turn into muscle. They're two entirely different substances, as Gregory W. Heath, D.Sc., M.P.H., lead health scientist, Centers for Disease Control and Prevention, explains. "Generally, muscles are used for movement, even just sitting and fidgeting. Fat tissue, on the other hand, insulates, but doesn't do anything when you move, so uses very low amounts of energy."

Because muscle weighs more than fat, someone who's slightly overweight may not be overly fat, which you can see by observing some muscular athletes. Exercising appropriately may very well increase your lean body mass. That's also why participants in the study cited earlier lost a greater percentage of body fat than weight—and why you may lose inches with exercise, without losing weight.

other tallies that are kept for groups—and even begin with kids. Friendly competition could match school classes (with anonymous, mass totals used), entire schools, school districts or communities, much as reading competition has challenged many communities to pick up books. And no one can deny this sort of effort could have a major impact on a community's health, as well as on its economy.

Incidentally, you can learn your BMI (if you know your height and weight) by checking page 77 or going online at www.nhlbisupport.com/bmi/bmicalc.htm.

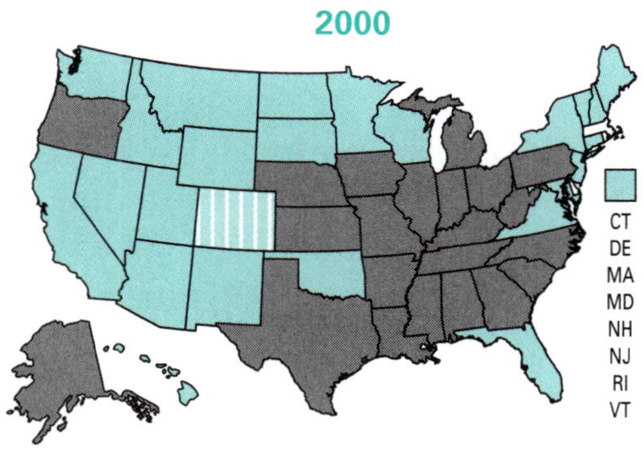

Studies also show that excess fat is more harmful around your abdomen than down around your hips and thighs. So being pear-shaped is healthier than being shaped more like an apple. In short, according to one study of nearly 15,000 participants, if you're a woman whose waist measures 34.5 inches or more, or a man whose waist measures 40 inches or more, you face an increased risk of high blood pressure, cardiovascular disease and diabetes. Another easy way to learn if you need to trim fat is with this self-test: pinch the thickness of the fat you carry at your waist and abdomen, where it most increases your risk of problems. If you can pinch an inch or more, you probably need to lose some.

There's another reason for trying to increase your muscle: muscle uses calories at a faster rate, which affects your body's energy requirement and metabolic rate, the rate at which your body burns calories in order to carry on everyday functions. People with more muscle tend to have higher basal metabolic rates, which means they use more calories at rest. Some studies also show that your metabolic rate stays elevated for some time after vigorous exercise, which means your body uses even more calories throughout an average day.

Effective Weight Control Weds Exercise, Reasonable Food Intake

As many as 25 percent of American men and 40 percent of American women are on a diet at any given time—not surprising, when you realize that about 34 million American adults are obese, which is defined as being 20 percent above their desirable weight. Yet, with that level of obesity in the population, you have to wonder how effective those diets are.

So, if you're convinced that you could benefit both from increasing your physical activity and eating more carefully, what's a person to do? You can find someone who's promoting just about any restrictive diet imaginable. But it's tough to argue with the results at the National Weight Control Registry—and fad diets aren't well represented there. And you may be surprised to hear some experts even talking of deficiencies.

"The problem with the American diet isn't one of too much in our diet, but one of too little. We have many people today promoting nutritionally inadequate diets, so that the problem becomes one of deficiencies in certain foods and nutrients, not excesses," says McCarron. "If we addressed American dietary deficiencies, especially in children and older adults, the rest of the diet would take care of itself."

Many of these restrictive diets, according to McCarron, are incompatible with getting adequate vitamins and minerals. "The issue isn't so much one of added salt and fat," he says, "but the foods people stay away from. Exclude dairy products, for example, and your mineral intake is deficient—period—unless you spend your whole day eating tofu. Dairy is where the minerals are."

To support this, McCarron cites the extensive recent CARDIA study of young adults who were followed for 10 years. The study looked for a relationship between intake of dairy

A nutritionally balanced diet is also intriguing, interesting ... and delicious!

products and risk for developing insulin resistance syndrome. Components of this syndrome include obesity, glucose intolerance, high blood pressure and elevated cholesterol—major risk factors for type 2 diabetes and heart disease.

Researchers concluded that overweight individuals consumed dairy products at a lower frequency than their normal-weight counterparts. They also found that dairy consumption was linked with consumption of whole grains, fruits, vegetables and saturated fats and inversely related to intake of sugar-sweetened soft drinks. The only other dietary habits with significant ties to insulin resistance syndrome are intake of fiber and protein: fiber intake dramatically reduces the risk of insulin resistance syndrome, while consuming a lot of animal protein in your diet dramatically increases the risk of insulin resistance.

Researchers concluded that the 10-year incidence of insulin resistance syndrome was more than two-thirds lower among overweight individuals in the highest category of dairy consumption than among individuals in the lowest category. They also concluded that the odds of developing obesity, abnormal glucose balance and elevated blood pressure were reduced by nearly 20 percent for each daily occasion of total dairy product consumption.

"We don't need a restrictionist view of the world," says McCarron, noting, that it's dangerous, for example, to lump all fats together and restrict them all. "If fats are tied with other key nutrients—rich in minerals, vitamins or high-quality protein—I'm not concerned about them, even saturated fats. And look at the healthful foods that have naturally occurring sodium. People who indiscriminately eliminate fat and sodium from their diets end up cutting things out of their diets that they need." To illustrate, McCarron notes the high levels of nutrients present in tree nuts, shown to be heart-protective. "And we don't say, 'Eat a ton of nuts every day.' You have to view the food in a context of all the nutrients that come with it."

McCarron also disputes the heavy burden placed on sodium by some. A cup of milk, for example, has 123 milligrams of sodium, yet he would not recommend eliminating milk from your diet. "Yes, sodium sensitivity is real, but the root of the problem isn't sodium, but a poor diet," he says. "What most researchers don't tell you is that for many people who don't have hyperten-

Don't Feel Guilty About Loving Nuts!

If you avoid nuts, due to their high fat content, you may want to revisit that decision. There's growing evidence, according to the United States Department of Agriculture Center for Nutrition Policy and Promotion, that nuts have bioactive constituents—including plant protein, dietary fiber and a number of micronutrients—that have a protective effect on your heart. Researchers looking at an assortment of nuts are finding an inverse association between deaths from stroke and intake of nuts, some of the most concentrated food sources of vitamin E. Nuts have also been shown, in studies of vegetarian foods, to improve control of blood glucose concentration, lower insulin requirements and bring better weight control for diabetic patients.

Although you need to plan for the calories that fats in nuts add to your diet, many seem to have a beneficial effect on cholesterol levels. Walnuts, for example, have been studied for their effect on serum lipids and blood pressure, and researchers now say that a moderate amount of nuts in a cholesterol-lowering diet decreases total cholesterol levels and favorably affects the lipoprotein profile of healthy men.

Nuts fall into two main groups. Peanuts, probably the first thing you think of when you hear the word "nut," aren't really nuts at all, although they're used in comparable ways and have a similar nutrient profile as tree nuts, a term that includes the rest of what you probably think of as "nuts"—almonds, pecans, walnuts, hazelnuts and others—including coconut. American annual per capita nut consumption went from 7 pounds in 1970 to nearly 9 pounds in 1997. Peanuts are by far the most frequently consumed (68 percent of total nut consumption). Tree nuts were fairly evenly divided: almonds (19 percent), coconuts (18 percent) and pecans and walnuts (tied at 17 percent each).

sion and consume a healthy diet, sodium is a nonissue." McCarron does not suggest heaping salt on your meal or looking for trans fats to devour. However, he notes that people who are in the lowest category of sodium intake are frequently way below the recommended dietary allowance (RDA) for calcium, potassium and magnesium, as well.

McCarron likes the DASH diet (see pages 260 to 261). "If you eat a well-balanced diet that includes five healthy-sized servings of fruits and vegetables and three servings of dairy a day, you'd probably get 90 percent of the nutrients you need," he says. "And it doesn't count as a dairy serving if you put milk in your coffee. I'm talking decent-sized servings of yogurt, milk or cheese."

"After the egg, the single best source of biologically active protein in your diet is milk," says McCarron, sounding like a commercial for the dairy industry. "Milk protein provides a wide array of essential amino acids and proteins that vegetable protein lacks."

Furthermore, once you get into exercising, McCarron says, you'll naturally seek more dairy intake. "Your muscles tell you that you need it to work," he says. "And many thin people have mineral-rich diets. The single best predictor of staying thin in America is whether you consume dairy products. With three to four servings a day, the data says you'll automatically gravitate to enough fiber. And a recent breast cancer prevention study concluded that a healthy diet includes a wide assortment of fruits, vegetables, dairy, lean meat and nuts."

Tufts University nutritionists, known for their dietary expertise, make these

Faced with Challenges, Nutritionist Manages to Exercise

David McCarron, M.D., visiting professor at the University of California-Davis, Department of Nutrition, was a long-distance runner from his late 20s to age 46, when childhood orthopedic problems finally got the best of him and necessitated a hip replacement. He tells of running a half-marathon in Paris at age 40, with 30,000 other entrants. "It got snug on the bridges," he recalls.

During those years it wasn't at all unusual for him to run 4 to 5 miles 5 or 6 days a week and 8 to 9 miles once a week. "It's a guaranteed way you can exercise," he says of running. "Unfortunately, I lost the possibility of doing much more of that after surgery, and now I'm close to needing two knee replacements."

Although he's limited in impact sports, McCarron manages to do a significant amount of cycling, noting that he had cycled 5 of the last 7 days. "It gets me outdoors, but unfortunately, I can't take my bike with me when I travel. So, when I'm on the road, I dream of biking, use hotel fitness centers and walk as much as I can. When I'm at home in Portland, I'm out on my bike for 35 to 45 minutes—and I do the hills here, which are substantial."

recommendations to help you enter a "slow food" state of mind, something they hope can counter Americans' recent urges to have everything fast—including food and drink. Remember, when someone else cooks your meal, they decide how much fat, sodium and fiber that meal will have. When you gulp a meal, you don't give your body the time it needs to tell you when you've had enough—an average of 20 minutes.

They also advise you to sit at a table to eat, and not to eat when you're not hungry. When you do eat, linger over the foods for a while in order to savor them. Although your taste buds can detect only salty, bitter, sweet and sour flavors, chewing your food thoroughly enables you to "taste" other flavors, as the smells of the food are released to your nose. Tufts' recipe also includes having the same standards for restaurant dining that you would at home—a leisurely, quiet meal—and getting vigorous exercise every day.

My, How the Portions Grow!

Portion control is a major problem for Americans today. According to a study reported early in 2003, Americans' portions for some food items grew dramatically between 1977 and 1996. Here are a few samples of increasing portion sizes:

- Mexican entrées: up 133 calories to 541 per portion (portions growing from 6.3 to 8 ounces)
- cheeseburgers: up 136 calories to 533 per portion (portions increasing from 5.8 to 7.3 ounces)
- hamburgers: up 97 calories to 486 per portion (portions growing from 5.7 to 7 ounces)
- salty snacks: up 93 calories to 225 calories per portion (portions expanding from 1 to 1.6 ounces)
- french fries: up 68 calories to 256 calories per portion (portions moving from 3.1 to 3.6 ounces)
- soft drinks: up 49 calories to 193 calories (portions increasing from 13.1 to 19.9 ounces)

It's not surprising that the prevalence of adult obesity also rose—from 14.5 percent in 1971 to 30.9 percent in 1999—since adding 10 calories a day to your intake puts on an extra pound in a year's time. Incidentally, the rising portion sizes of soft drinks (up 16 percent), coffee (up 22 percent) and tea (up 13 percent) also cause experts to be concerned about increased bone loss in the spines of women, due to the accompanying loss of calcium in milk that the shift represents. The problem is especially severe among people who consume more than 300mg of caffeine per day, or a little more than 2 cups of brewed coffee.

What *Should* You Eat?

"My advice about diet is this," says Heath. "Eat more fruits and vegetables, whole grains and cereals and several meals a week without meat or cheese. Don't pay a lot of attention to counting calories. Eliminate snacking and don't eat after 8 p.m. Most people aren't real active in the evening and go to bed between 8 and 11 p.m. Your body is extremely efficient and will store energy for later use. Besides, eating in the evening can also disrupt your sleep patterns."

"Remember, you put fuel in the tank at the beginning of a trip, not the end," Heath continues. And he takes seriously the role of the first meal of the day: breaking the fast.

The USDA's Food Guide Pyramid

You're probably familiar with the United States Department of Agriculture's food guide pyramid, and you won't go too far wrong if you follow the suggestions you find there, spelled out below. Note that the standard used is servings per day—and remember what you just learned about controlling portion size. Learn more at the United States Department of Agriculture Web site (www.usda.gov/cnpp).

Several recent adaptations of the food pyramid may be more helpful, especially if you want to get a good balance of nutrients while keeping your risk factors for cardiovascular disease,

United States Department of Agriculture Food Guide Pyramid

Food Group	Servings per Day	Serving size
Bread, cereal, rice, pasta	9	1 slice bread 1 cup ready-to-eat cereal ½ cup cooked cereal, rice or pasta
Vegetable group	4	1 cup raw leafy vegetables ½ cup other vegetables, raw or cooked 6 ounces vegetable juice
Fruit group	3	1 medium apple, banana, orange, pear ½ cup chopped, cooked or canned fruit 6 ounces fruit juice
Milk, yogurt, cheese group (preferably fat free or low-fat)	2 or 3 (3, if you're under 18 or over 50)	1 cup milk or yogurt 1½ ounces natural cheese (e.g., cheddar) 2 ounces processed cheese (e.g., American)
Meat (preferably lean or low-fat), poultry, fish, dry beans, eggs and nuts	2, total 6 ounces	2 to 3 ounces cooked fish, poultry or lean meat also counted as 1 ounce of meat: ■ ½ cup cooked dry beans or tofu ■ 2½ ounce soy burger ■ 1 egg ■ 2 tablespoons peanut butter ■ ⅓ cup nuts

diabetes, cancer and other major conditions in check. Incidentally, it's interesting to note that none of these guides suggest tallying daily calories. And, they may just hold more surprises for you.

DASH: A Proven Diet

Funded by the National Institutes of Health's National Heart, Lung and Blood Institute, the study that led to the DASH diet was conducted at four medical centers: Brigham and Women's Hospital in Boston, Massachusetts; Duke University

The DASH Eating Plan

Food Group	Servings per Day (except where indicated)	Serving size
Grains	7 to 8	1 slice bread 1 ounce dry cereal (check the label for the amount)
Vegetables	4 to 5	1 cup raw leafy vegetables ½ cup raw or cooked vegetable 6 ounces vegetable juice
Fruits	4 to 5	1 medium fruit ½ cup fresh, frozen or canned fruit ¼ cup dried fruit 6 ounces fruit juice
Low-fat or fat-free dairy products	2 to 3	8 ounces milk 1 cup yogurt 1½ ounces cheese
Meats, poultry, fish	2 or less	3 ounces cooked, trimmed of visible fat
Nuts, seeds, dry beans	4 to 5 weekly	⅓ cup or 1½ ounces nuts 2 tablespoons or ½ ounce seeds ½ cup cooked dry beans
Fats and oils	2 to 3	1 teaspoon soft margarine 1 tablespoon mayonnaise 2 tablespoons light salad dressing 1 teaspoon vegetable oil
Sweets	5 weekly	1 tablespoon sugar 1 tablespoon jelly or jam ½ ounce jelly beans 8 ounces lemonade

Source: National Heart, Lung, and Blood Institute

Medical Center, Durham, North Carolina; Johns Hopkins University, Baltimore, Maryland; and Pennington Biomedical Research Center, Louisiana State University, Baton Rouge, Louisiana. The diet was originally developed to address high blood pressure, and was shown to offer help in as little as 2 weeks. Since its original development, it's also been tested in a reduced-sodium version. In addition, many people have successfully used the DASH diet for weight control.

The DASH diet emphasizes fruits, vegetables and low-fat dairy products and is low in saturated fats, cholesterol and total fat. The diet is summarized by the chart on page 260.

Based on 2,000 calories a day, the DASH diet can be adapted to suit other intake levels, as well. For example, instead of a 6-ounce hamburger, substitute a 3-ounce hamburger and add ½ cup carrots and ½ cup spinach to save 200 calories.

The DASH Web site (www.nhlbi.nih.gov/health/public/heart/hbp/dash/new_dash.pdf) also offers helpful hints for gradually moving into the program. This not only helps you adjust gradually to the changes from what you're used to eating, but it also helps you avoid bloating and diarrhea that can occur if you add a lot of fiber to your intake too rapidly. Here are several of the helpful transition tips:

- Add a single vegetable or fruit serving to your meal.
- If you use canned fruit, look for fruit that's canned in its own juice.
- Cut back portion sizes gradually; for example, limit your meat to 6 ounces a day (picture 3 ounces as a deck of cards).
- Try adding one or two vegetarian meals (meatless) each week or reduce the amount of meat you use in a recipe.
- Use dried fruit, mixed raisins and nuts, yogurt, popcorn or raw vegetables as snack foods.
- If you have difficulty digesting dairy products, try lactase enzyme drops or pills or buy lactose-free milk or milk with lactase enzyme added.
- Check nutritional labeling on foods marketed as low-fat or fat free, because they're not always lower in calories than the original.

An update to the DASH diet also studied reducing dietary sodium—which affects some people's blood pressure. Find more information about that at the Web site, as well. Just be cautious, McCarron advises, and don't eliminate foods from your diet that naturally contain sodium, because you may unintentionally thereby eliminate other nutrients, as well.

The Mayo Healthy Weight Pyramid: Similar to DASH, but Less Extreme

You can find a variety of food pyramids at the Mayo Clinic Web site (www.mayoclinic.com), among them the Mayo Clinic Healthy Weight Pyramid (shown on page 263). While it strongly resembles the DASH diet, the Mayo pyramid has several key differences. Most obvious, when you look at the pyramid, is the Daily Physical Activity circle in the center—which communicates well the value of physical activity in maintaining a healthy weight and corroborates the experiences of members of the National Weight Control Registry. The chart below summarizes the Mayo recommendations. Note the doubling of vegetable serving size, as compared to the other diets.

Also note carefully the different portion sizes for various foods. You can eat virtually unlimited fruits and vegetables, although the daily serving targets (by number of servings) are slightly below those of the DASH diet. The range of daily servings of grain also has a lower minimum. And it's the only one of the three plans discussed here to lump dairy with meat, poultry and fish. Note that, although the number of servings for fats is higher than DASH's daily level, the Mayo pyramid includes nuts in that category, unlike DASH.

Disease Experts Care What You Eat, Too!

As debate continues over various diets,

Mayo Clinic Healthy Weight Pyramid

Food Group	Servings per Day (except where indicated)	Serving size
Vegetables	minimum 4	25 calories 2 cups leafy vegetables 1 cup other vegetables
Fruit	minimum 3	60 calories ½ cup sliced fruit
Carbohydrates (whole grains, including pasta, bread, rice, cereal)	4 to 8 servings	70 calories ½ cup grain or cereal 1 slice bread
Protein and dairy (includes beans, fish, lean meat, low-fat dairy)	3 to 7	70 calories ⅓ cup beans 2 to 3 ounces meat or fish 1 cup skim milk
Fats (especially olive oil, nuts, canola oil and avocados)	3 to 5	45 calories 1 teaspoon oil 1 tablespoon nuts
Sweets (candy and other processed sweets)	up to 525 calories per week	525 calories

experts concerned with disease prevention are concerned, in the same way as McCarron, about what your nutrition lacks, if you eliminate foods or categories of food from your diet. Here are a few facts noted by the American Institute for Cancer Research and the National Center for Chronic Disease Prevention and Health Promotion (part of the Centers for Disease Control and Prevention, Division of Nutrition and Physical Activity):

■ Only one in four American adults eats the recommended 5 or more servings of fruits and vegetables each day (a level that drops to one in five young people). Interestingly, men reportedly consume more fruits and vegetables than women. Eating those 5 servings of vegetables and fruits a day could prevent up to 20 percent of all cancers. Remember, vegetables become high-calorie when they're topped with cheese sauce, gravy, regular salad dressings or full-fat sour cream—or are fried in oil or butter.

■ Vegetables and fruits provide vitamins, minerals and phytochemicals (natural substances found only in plants) that protect your body's cells from damage by cancer-causing agents.

■ Variety in your diet is important, in order for you to consume the widest possible array of protective nutrients and phytochemicals—dark green and leafy foods, as well as shades of orange, red and purple.

■ Certain carbohydrates—especially fruits and vegetables—are clearly linked to lowering cancer risk. The sensible approach is to eat fewer refined carbohydrates and more of the carbohydrates that don't produce spikes in insulin levels (whole grains, vegetables, fruits and

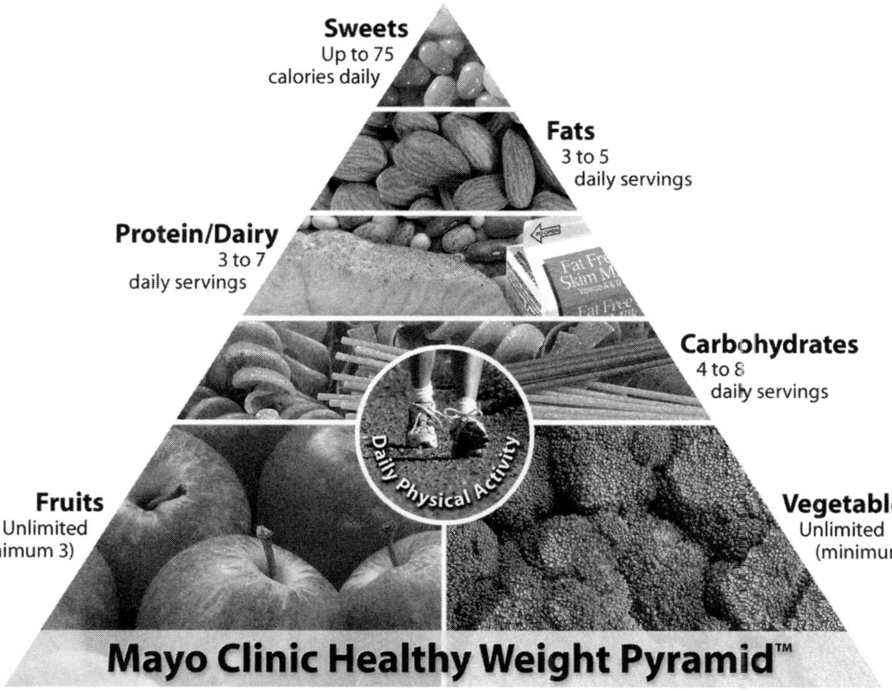

 See your doctor before you begin any healthy weight plan.

beans) in conjunction with small amounts of poultry, fish and lean meat.

■ Besides traditional fruits and vegetables, try to include 7 servings a day of other plant-based foods: whole grains (whole wheat bread or pasta, oatmeal, barley and brown rice) or legumes (dried beans and peas, including kidney, garbanzo, black beans, lentils and green peas). Whole grains are important, because they're higher in fiber and natural phytochemicals than refined white bread and rice.

■ If you like red meat, choose lean cuts and limit yourself to no more than 3 ounces (note the lower recommendation here) of cooked meat a day—a piece the size of a deck of cards. Diets high in red meat probably increase risk of colon cancer.

■ Certain fats are still linked to higher risk of chronic disease. However, researchers are beginning to see that some fats, used in moderation, may be beneficial: monounsaturated fats (contained in olive and canola oils, for example) may help protect against heart disease and the omega-3 fatty acids (found in fatty fish, soy and flaxseed) show some cancer-protective properties in the lab. This doesn't change the advice: to prevent chronic disease reduce your intake of saturated fats (the main fat found in tropical oils and animal products).

"If you want to lose weight and stay healthy, you have to eat less and exercise more, not simply cut whole categories of foods out of your diet," says Melanie Polk, R.D., director of nutrition education at the American Institute for Cancer Research. "People switching to high-protein and high-fat diets are damaging their health in the long term. The first step in any weight reduction program should be to reduce the amount of food consumed and increase the amount of physical activity. But remember, the right proportion of plant-based food to animal food is important to your long-term health."

Here are some additional tips from the National Center for Chronic Disease Prevention and Health Promotion:

■ Eat breakfast, and spruce it up with a banana or a handful of berries.

■ Drink 100 percent fruit juice, rather than punch or fruit drink.

■ Keep bowls of fruit on the kitchen table and counter.

■ Corn on the cob, baked potatoes and bread are nutritious foods—but beware of what you put on them.

■ Use low-fat dairy products, and drink 1 percent or skim milk.

■ Try 1 tablespoon of dressing on your salad, and the same with mayonnaise—or use light or fat-free versions.

■ You don't have to give up meat, but buy lean meat (cut from the loin or round), trim all visible fat and drain any grease.

■ Fried foods are not good for you. Bake chicken without the skin and substitute a baked potato for french fries.

■ Ready-to-eat vegetables (celery sticks, cucumber wedges, cherry tomatoes) and pretzels make great snacks.

■ Cut down on dessert sizes, and substitute low-fat or fat free baked goods, cookies and ice cream—or eat fruit instead.

■ Remember that the typical restaurant serving is about the size of two single servings. Ask for a take-home container or share one portion with a companion.

The New American Plate

A new program of the American Institute for Cancer Research (AICR) introduces the New American Plate, an effort to:

▪ highlight foods that can significantly reduce the risk for disease,

▪ show you how to enjoy all foods in sensibly sized portions and

▪ promote healthy weight as just one part of an overall healthy lifestyle.

This effort is based on the review by an expert panel of scientists of over 4,500 research studies from around the world—the most comprehensive report done to date in the area of diet, nutrition and cancer.

The AICR notes that a growing body of research shows that what you eat and how you live is closely linked with your risk of developing cancer, heart disease, type 2 diabetes and other chronic health conditions. About 30 to 40 percent of all cancers could be prevented by changing the way Americans eat and exercise—a number that would rise to 60 to 70 percent, if tobacco were eliminated.

Check out the traditional American plate and the new one at the AICR Web site (www.aicr.org). Traditionally, the American plate looked like this: a slab of meat that filled two-thirds of the plate, a small serving of a vegetable and some potatoes, white rice or pasta. It had too many calories to help maintain a healthy weight and too few nutrients to prevent chronic illness.

The New American Plate changes the proportions. Meat becomes a side dish, rather than the main ingredient. Two-thirds of the plate is filled with vegetables, fruit, whole grains and beans, while the other third is occupied by meat, chicken or fish. Vegetables, fruit, whole grains and beans contain phytochemicals, some of which eliminate the free

What Does a Serving Look Like?

No, it's not a stupid question. As the average number of calories consumed in a day has gone from 1,854 to 2,002 in the last 20 years, American have found it difficult to judge what constitutes a portion. Here, from the American Institute for Cancer Research, are some visual guidelines:

▪ The 2 cups of spaghetti on your dinner plate is really 4 servings.

▪ Small bagels in the grocery store are about 2 servings each, while the bagels you find in a shop are closer to 4 or 5 servings.

▪ Your breakfast bowl of cereal may be 2 or 3 servings.

Learn to eyeball your portions. Most servings are half a cup, or a rounded handful. Servings of leafy vegetables (1 cup) are twice that large, or the size of your fist. A serving of dried fruit (¼ cup) is a scant handful, while 3 ounces of meat, poultry or seafood look like a deck of cards and cheese (1½ ounces) like 4 dice.

When in doubt, consult the nutrition label for serving size.

radicals that damage DNA (genetic material), while others help rid your body of substances that cause cancer. Plant-based foods are naturally low in calories, so you can eat larger, more satisfying meals for fewer calories than is typical in the American diet. The AICR Web site also features some tasty one-dish dinner recipes.

The AICR says this is not a program about deprivation and that the food industry has confused Americans about reasonable portion sizes—shown by the fact that Americans consume about 148 more calories a day than was true 20 years ago.

Shop the Perimeter of the Grocery Store

Today many nutrition experts recommend that you spend most of your time grocery shopping in the perimeter of the grocery store—the aisles on the edges.

DASH: A Diet You Can Love

Okay, I admit I'm extremely prejudiced. I love the DASH diet. I can't help it. I've loosely used it to guide my personal food choices for several years, and I think it's unbeatable—although the Mayo Clinic Healthy Weight Pyramid comes close.

I'm only puzzled by DASH's lack of rabid adherents (besides myself). I'm convinced that this is because it doesn't offer traditional food product manufacturers a lot of profit, primarily because you end up eating a lot of fresh and minimally prepared foods. So, why would food processors advertise it? And I'm guessing that growers of fruits and vegetables don't have huge advertising budgets, either.

Originally attracted by its properties for reducing high blood pressure, I was also drawn by the encouragement at the DASH Web site (www.nhlbi.nih.gov/health/public/heart/hbp/dash/new_dash.pdf) to ease into what, for many people, is a dramatically different way of eating. I don't really consider it a diet—just a guide. Because I've always enjoyed fruit, vegetables and dairy products, DASH was not as big an adjustment for me as it would be for many other Americans—including my husband. And, I confess, I've committed an abbreviated version of its recommendations to memory, but I don't consider myself a slave to it. I basically use it as a guideline that has made me feel healthier than I've ever felt before. And it's helped me lose weight handily—and painlessly.

Here's how I do it. I'm probably closer to the Mayo pyramid by focusing on fruits and vegetables every day: I aim for 4 to 5 servings of fruits and 4 to 5 servings of vegetables each day. I try to eat at least 1 serving—often 2—of each at each meal. I keep in mind that, for many of these foods, half a cup constitutes a serving—except leafy vegetables, which, of course are less compact, so a serving is twice as large.

That's because the fresh and refrigerated food—and frequently the frozen food, as well—is located in or near these aisles. By focusing on fresh, unprocessed foods, you avoid many of the impossible-to-pronounce additives that concern experts—and you consume many of the nutrients that are destroyed by processing. You also avoid many empty calories that weigh down those foods preserved in cans and packages in the center aisles of the grocery store.

Buying, preparing and serving foods that are fresh shortly before you eat them isn't really that difficult, if you realize that many foods taste very good with minimal preparation. Many vegetables are quite tasty raw. And, with a microwave oven or a pressure cooker you can cook many vegetables in about the same amount of time it takes to open and prepare the same food that you buy in a can, package or frozen food container.

I'm not at all surprised now to hear experts talk about phytonutrients and the fact that foods are naturally so much more complex than we'd ever imagined. Yes, perhaps I could absorb as much calcium from a Tums as I do from skim milk, but I'm not convinced that calcium is the total picture of the benefits gained from milk, just as I'd say that it's inaccurate to limit your thinking of oranges as nothing more than a good source of vitamin C. I'm still fairly convinced, as are more and more experts, that we stand to gain from whole, fresh foods a huge variety of nutrients that simply haven't been bottled—or even discovered yet. However, I do also take a daily multivitamin—just in case.

Incidentally, besides the fruits and vegetables, I also aim for at least 3 servings of milk (and, because I want to avoid osteoporosis, frequently 4 servings) or milk products a day, usually skim; a few servings of grain products (I probably seldom reach DASH's recommended 8), and many days I also enjoy a small portion of fish, poultry or lean meat, as well as a handful of nuts. One way I've limited the amount of meat I use is by using half of what a recipe calls for in soup or stew. I also try to make at least one, quick meatless meal a week—enchiladas with a filling of refried beans, for example.

I haven't given up butter, but if that becomes necessary, I'll use one of the newer functional food spreads (Benecol or Take Control) that my husband uses. While they taste tolerable—and, incidentally, can be combined very successfully with just a bit of butter for baking—I still prefer the flavor of butter on bread and potatoes.

True confessions: I love some sweets, and indulge regularly in good dark chocolate. I've eliminated a lot of baking I used to enjoy. However, in recent years I've also lost my taste for most fried desserts, candy bars, store-bought bakery products—and I generally look for low-fat mixes for brownies and cakes. And, when I do succumb, I try to limit myself to a small portion.

Many experts also recommend that you buy foods grown locally, in season. This may seem confining, especially if you live in a climate where foods aren't grown outdoors year-round and grocery stores offer a huge array of foods during every season. But try shopping farmers' markets when you can, and you'll probably conclude that there's no taste quite as good as that of a recently harvested, fully ripe fruit or vegetable that's grown near enough not to require refrigeration before it's on its way to your home.

Fruits and vegetables are complex foods that supply an array of protective nutrients.

Paint Your Meals with Lots of Vibrant Color!

Researchers are just beginning to learn about the phytochemicals and micronutrients that occur naturally in foods. They're seeing, for example, that a vitamin C pill falls far short of providing all the nutrients that you can get from a simple orange—in addition to vitamin C. While they've discovered and begun to explore scores of phytochemicals, some researchers assert that there are hundreds more out there and that they've only begun to scratch the surface.

Two new books recommend increasing colorful produce consumption dramatically, in order to include a wide variety of nutrients in your diet. Apparently, many of these phytonutrients provide a distinctive color to foods when they're present. Thus, by selecting a wide variety of colorful produce, you ensure yourself a similarly wide variety of phytonutrients in your diet.

The following chart illustrates the concept. Note that some foods are shown several times, because they contain a variety of known phytonutrients. A few years from now, this list will probably be even more extensive. And that's why you should be skeptical, when someone claims you can get all the nourishment you need from a pill or artificial preparation. It's highly unlikely!

Currently Known Phytonutrients

Food	Phyto-chemical	Possible Benefits
guava, grapefruit (pink), tomatoes, watermelon	lycopene	may reduce prostate cancer risk
beets, cranberries, kidney beans, plums, pomegranates, raspberries, red apples, red cabbage, red onions, strawberries, sweet cherries	anthocyanins	may mop up free radicals, lower blood pressure, protect against circulatory problems caused by diabetes
chile peppers, corn, peppers, tomatoes	capsaicin	may block carcinogens from binding to DNA, relieve arthritis pain
berries, grapes, nuts, pomegranates	ellagic acid	may have numerous potent anticancer effects
apples, berries, cherries, red onions, red and purple grapes, tea, tomatoes	quercetin	may prevent cancer, benefit the heart through anticlotting action and lower blood cholesterol
peanuts, red and purple grapes, red wine	resveratrol	may promote healthy cholesterol levels, prevent cell damage and curb tumor growth
blackberries, blueberries, cranberries, grape juice, tea, wine	tannins	may protect against urinary tract infection
soy foods	isoflavonoids	may protect against cancer, benefit blood vessels, heart, brain, bones and cholesterol levels and may reduce menopausal symptoms
chives, garlic (not garlic supplements), leeks, onions, scallions, shallots	sulfur compounds (allicin, ajoene, allyl sulfide)	may reduce carcinogens and tumors and promote heart health

continued

Sources: United States Department of Agriculture, Ohio State University, Colorado State University, University of Illinois, Sheldon Margen's *Wellness Foods A to Z: An Indispensable Guide for Health-Conscious Food Lovers* (New York, New York: Rebus, Inc., 2002), *Consumer Reports on Health*

Currently Known Phytonutrients *continued*

Food	Phyto-chemical	Possible Benefits
legumes, nuts, oats, whole grains	saponins	may reduce blood cholesterol and neutralize carcinogens in the digestive tract
beans, flaxseed, wheat	lignans	may guard against cancer and heart disease
olive oil	oleuropein and hydroxytyrosol	may protect against cancer and cardiovascular disease
beans, figs, nuts, seeds	phytosterols (plant sterols)	may reduce cholesterol and hinder cancer
blackberries, black currants, blueberries, elderberries, purple grapes	anthocyanins	may reduce risk of cancer, heart disease, age-related memory loss
eggplant, plums, prunes, raisins	phenolics	may slow some effects of aging
citrus fruit	limonene	may block abnormal cell growth and neutralize carcinogens
citrus fruit	citrus flavonoids (hesperitrin, naringin, nobiletin, tangeritin)	may counter unhealthy free radicals and inhibit blood clotting
citrus fruit	coumarins	may have anticancer and heart-protective properties, although grapefruit may interfere with blood-thinning medications (Coumadin) and heart medications
apricots, butternut squash, cantaloupe, carrots, mangos, peaches, pumpkin, sweet potatoes, yellow peppers, yellow raisins	bioflavonoids	may reduce cancer and heart-attack risk and improve skin, bones and dental health

Currently Known Phytonutrients *continued*

Food	Phyto-chemical	Possible Benefits
apricots, citrus, peaches	beta-cryptoxanthin	may protect against certain cancers, heart disease, age-related macular degeneration
carrots, leafy green and yellow vegetables, broccoli, sweet potato, pumpkin	alpha- and beta-carotene	may protect against cancer, heart disease and vision loss
broccoli, green peas, honeydew melon, kale, kiwifruit, leafy greens	lutein	may preserve vision, reduce risk of macular degeneration and cataracts
arugula, bok choy, broccoli, brussels sprouts, cabbage, cauliflower, collards, kale, kohlrabi, mustard greens, radish, rutabaga, Swiss chard, turnips, watercress	glucosinolates (indoles, isothio-cyranates, sulforaphane)	may reduce risk of breast and prostate cancer
citrus, corn, eggs, most dark leafy vegetables	zeaxanthin	may enhance immune function, a strong antioxidant
artichoke	silymarin (milk thistle)	may reduce liver damage by certain drugs; occasionally has laxative effect
ginger	gingerols	may reduce nausea, arthritis, loss of appetite; may cause abdominal discomfort, heartburn, diarrhea and irritate the mouth and throat
licorice	glycyrrhizin	may reduce inflammation; may increase blood pressure, may inhibit menstruation or cause sexual dysfunction in men
purple grapes, many fruits, grains and vegetables	flavonoids	may make blood less likely to clot
apples, dark chocolate, grapes, pomegranates, raspberries, red wine	catechins	may reduce risk of certain cancers, may prevent heart disease

Water: Don't Wait Until You're Thirsty!

"For a substance that is so essential to life, water seems remarkably unremarkable: colorless, odorless, tasteless and ubiquitous. Yet, it is the magic elixir for learning, the 'secret potion' if you will," says Carla Hannaford, Ph.D., author of *Smart Moves: Why Learning Is Not All In Your Head* (Arlington, Virginia: Great Ocean Publishers, 1995). And it's so much more than even that!

"Water is one of the most important and most abundant inorganic substances in the body," Hannaford continues. "It makes up from 45 percent to 75 percent of our total body weight. Lean people have a greater proportion of water to total body weight because fat has very little water, while muscle has a lot. Water comprises more of the brain (with estimates of 90 percent) than other organs of the body, with muscles next at 75 percent, and then kidneys. Under normal conditions, it is recommended a person drink one-third of an ounce of water per pound of body weight (about a quart per hundred pounds of body weight) each day, with that amount doubled or tripled in times of stress."

None of the experts debate the importance of water to your health. Your body, after all, probably contains 10 to 12 gallons of water at any given moment. But when you exercise, it's easy to lose water quickly, and it's important to replace it as soon as possible, in order for all of your body systems to function effectively—and to avoid muscle cramping and the extreme of dehydration (see pages 215 to 216).

Sometimes the experts debate the amount you need to consume to replace

Being Well Hydrated Has Made a Difference for Me!

In the past few years I've noticed the differences of being well hydrated. Like many people, I previously only drank water when I noticed I was thirsty. But once I started drinking 16 ounces of water right away upon rising in the morning and drinking water frequently throughout the day, I noticed an immediate improvement in how I felt. I've also noticed that my skin, which tends to be dry, has become softer and smoother since I started drinking more water—and complete strangers have noticed and complimented me about my skin, as well.

I've also noticed the tendency of myself and those around me to become more constipated when we've had less water—especially while we're traveling or are otherwise distracted from consuming water conveniently. And I'm convinced that fluoride in my local water helps prevent cavities—even in adults. So, because my local water hasn't offered me a reason to change, I seldom drink bottled water. After all, I'm paying tax money for water processing that provides tap water that's more bacteria-free than most bottled water. I'm not adding to the environmental plastic problem by purchasing bottled water—and I'm saving money.

the 2 to 3 quarts a day you lose by perspiring, urinating, having a bowel movement, nursing a baby or sneezing —amounts that can go up very rapidly when you're exercising, especially in the heat or in a particularly dry environment. Harvard and Mayo Clinic experts suggest you need slightly more than the amounts Hannaford recommends: half an ounce per pound of body weight, rather than a third of an ounce. Others say 8 to 10 cups per day, or half a gallon. Recently, some experts say those numbers are a bit high and don't adequately account for the water in foods.

In any event, water is essential for many body functions. Thirst, especially as you age, is a lousy indicator of how much water you need to drink. A far better indicator is the color of your urine—if it's darker than the most pale yellow, you need more water (unless your doctor has advised you otherwise). It's a particularly good idea to drink water or juice right after you get up in the morning, since your body hasn't had any fluids for several hours.

Since many of the foods and beverages you consume contain water, you can count that as some of your total consumption. However, realize that caffeinated beverages promote urination and concentrated alcoholic beverages also have a dehydrating effect. Carbonation also interferes with fluid absorption.

In addition to replacing what you lose when you're exercising, drinking plenty of water helps prevent kidney stones by diluting the substances that spur formation of stones. It may also reduce your risk of colon cancer by helping move waste—including cancer-causing substances—through your colon and out of your body. Researchers also believe good hydration may lower your risk of heart disease, as your fluid levels may affect the thickness (technically termed "viscosity") of your blood, as well as other factors.

Dining Out—It *Is* Possible to Do So Healthfully!

Although it's more challenging to meet many nutritional goals when you eat out, it is possible to do a fairly good job, if you're deliberate and aware of some of the pitfalls. Many nutritionists believe that a major reason Americans struggle so mightily with obesity is because meals are frequently eaten away from home. Not only do you give someone else the opportunity to select the ingredients in your diet, but you may also not determine how those ingredients are prepared.

There is some very good information online about eating out. Most national chain restaurants—fast food, as well as others—provide nutritional information at their Web sites. Others have menus, which you can look over ahead of time, as you consider options that may fit into your eating style. Don't hesitate, when you know where you'll eat ahead of time, to call and ask about the menu.

Two good Web sites for information that's helpful when eating out are the Mayo Clinic Web site (www.mayoclinic.com) and the American Heart Association Web site (www.deliciousdecisions.org). The American Heart Association's site is particularly helpful with an online brochure that contains specific tips on ordering, according to the type of restaurant (American family, fast food, Chinese, etc.).

Here are some helpful hints for dining out, if you're looking for heart-healthy eating:

- Decide what you'll order before you go to avoid being tempted by a menu that has gorgeous photos of foods that may not suit your goals.
- If this is your first time at this restaurant and you know nothing about its food, take some time to study the menu and ask the server any questions you have about the food and its preparation style.
- Order first, so you're not tempted by hearing your companions' choices.
- Consider sharing a meal with a companion, since most restaurants serve double-sized portions. Or, if you're not sure that one portion will be enough, order it first and tell the server that you may want to order more, if you need more later.
- Drink a couple of glasses of water before your food comes.
- Beware of appetizers—many

It Doesn't Hurt to Ask—Before You Decide to Go!

Since I've started trying to eat in a more heart-healthy manner, I've learned to check before I go to a restaurant to determine whether it offers choices compatible with my eating style. Because saturated fats and cholesterol are the most frequent hurdle I encounter, I'll often call ahead and simply ask whether the menu has any low- or reduced-fat options. Frequently, the person who answers the phone doesn't know, but he or she can readily check with someone who does (unless you call during the lunch hour). If everything on the menu is laden with saturated fat and cholesterol, I may consider going elsewhere. Yes, you can vote with your feet and consumer dollars! I assume that, by asking, I'm letting the restaurant know that this is something I care about—and that it makes a difference in who gets my business.

If I don't have the opportunity to call ahead or find information at a Web site, I'll ask the person taking my order. Often, for example, it's possible to order something grilled or broiled (two processes that use little or no added fat), rather than fried, and it's also possible to order sauces and condiments on the side, where I can consciously add them to my foods with discretion.

Frequently, you can also ask to have foods prepared without ingredients you may not want: from a Whopper without mayonnaise to a Chinese meal without MSG (monosodium glutamate). (I must admit that I was less than satisfied the single time I've ordered a Chinese dish without the MSG—it simply didn't taste like much.) For other foods that are made while you wait, you can request less salt than would normally be used.

come loaded with saturated fat and cholesterol. Select raw vegetables, fruit or fish.

■ Eat your low-calorie foods first—the salad or broth-based soup, for example, then the vegetables served with your entrée.

■ If you're having pizza, consider ordering a veggie pizza (or select several vegetables of your choice) with extra sauce and half the cheese.

■ Be careful about toppers: high-calorie salad dressings or sauces on nutritious vegetables, butter and sour cream on potatoes, whipped cream on gelatin salads or desserts.

■ Select broth-based soups over creamy or cheesy ones. Many hearty vegetable or minestrone soups provide excellent nutritional value.

■ Avoid foods described as buttery, buttered, fried, pan-fried, creamed, scalloped, au gratin or à la mode.

■ Ask to substitute steamed vegetables for fries, fresh fruit salad for mayonnaise-laden coleslaw.

■ Choose fresh, raw vegetables, including a variety of leafy greens and a colorful assortment of other vegetables and fruit at the salad bar. Avoid cheese, bacon bits and prepared salads with mayonnaise or whipped cream, or take tiny amounts. Use a low-fat dressing (often available in separate packages) or limit yourself to one small scoop of regular dressing.

■ Your best bets from the bread basket include rolls and bread, rather than muffins and croissants—both typically high-fat. Skip the butter or margarine or opt for honey, jam or jelly.

■ When ordering pasta, stick with tomato, wine or clam sauces and avoid Alfredo and other cheesy, creamy

Fast Food Can Be Nutritious!

As more fast food chains respond to consumer demand for lower-fat foods, it's somewhat easier to find nutritious selections on a fast food restaurant's menu. Here are a few tips:

■ Grilled chicken is frequently the most nutritious, lowest fat and lowest cholesterol meat entrée.

■ Consider salads. Most restaurants that offer salad also offer fat free or low-fat dressings.

■ Skip the cheese, bacon and mayonnaise on your burger.

■ Skip the fried foods, including potatoes, chicken, chicken bites, fish or potato chips.

■ Limit your calories quite handily by ordering a small burger rather than a jumbo one.

■ Order milk or juice with your meal, rather than a carbonated drink or a milkshake.

sauces. Pass on dishes loaded with cheese—lasagna, for example—or share a portion.

■ When ordering Chinese dishes, avoid fried foods (including egg rolls or wontons) and choose dishes that are steamed, poached (Jum), boiled (Chu), roasted (Kow) or barbecued (Shu). Ask for sauces on the side.

■ Beware of many Mexican entrées. Look for items that aren't fried or cheesy. Fajitas enable you to select toppings yourself. Load on the salsa, which is fat free and has nutritious vegetables, and pile on grilled vegetables. Opt for soft tortillas over fried ones.

■ Remove skin from poultry and trim all visible fat from meat. Consider taking part of the meat portion home for another meal.

■ Share desserts with dining companions or order fruit, sorbet or sherbet.

The jury is still out on many issues regarding nutrition. A major goal of this chapter is to encourage you to consider the role your diet has in your fitness. Americans have an abundant food supply—which can be an asset or a liability. By selecting a variety of nutritious, fresh foods, you can use this abundance to enhance your health and well-being. Be wary of so-called experts who tell you to eliminate foods from your repertoire. You're probably better off eating a variety of foods in moderation, remembering that researchers haven't yet figured out how to get all of the nutrients naturally offered by food into a pill. And some of the very foods you avoid today may be the ones researchers will tell you to eat tomorrow, simply because they discover it offers some unexpected benefit.

The reviewers:
Sylvia Moore, Ph.D., professor and director, Division of Medical Education and Public Health, University of Wyoming, and director, Wellness in the Rockies (WIN the Rockies);

David McCarron, M.D., visiting professor at the University of California-Davis, Department of Nutrition;

Gregory W. Heath, D.Sc., M.P.H., lead health scientist at the Centers for Disease Control and Prevention;

Marvin A. Brooks, M.D., a family practice physician.

CHAPTER 11

Changes Aging Brings to Fitness & Fitness to Aging

"Old age isn't a painful disorder," says David Poulter, P.T., Dip. M.D.T., physical therapist, clinic director and international lecturer on conservative, patient-centered treatment. "Wrinkles don't hurt."

It's true. Many of the health problems facing aging Americans today are not inherent to aging itself, but are due to muscle atrophy, or shrinking, caused by a reduced level of activity. Yes, aging does typically bring some less than desirable physical changes. But regular exercise can have a major impact on those changes.

Absent Exercise—Aging Is All Downhill!

No matter what your age, you can hope Nolan Ryan is right, when he says, "You never reach a point where it's too late to start getting active. No matter what you've done previously, you can improve your chances for longevity and quality of life by getting into the habit of regular physical activity." Researchers are now convinced that many of the physical changes you may associate with aging are more a result of inactivity than of aging—or, at least, are worsened by inactivity. And they're also finding that it's possible—even at age 96—to positively influence those changes.

Aging can exact a high toll on your cardiorespiratory system. Maximum oxygen consumption generally goes down with age, and the heart may become slightly enlarged. On average, people tend to lose about half of their aerobic capacity between the ages of 20 and 80. Lung capacity declines, and systolic blood pressure (the top number) rises.

Osteoporosis causes bones to lose their density and to become weak and brittle, a key reason—along with balance problems—that a significant percentage of older people experience fractures. And, contrary to what many people think, osteoporosis is not just a problem for women, although bone loss does accelerate for women after menopause. Body fat may shift. Hearing—at least, in certain ranges—frequently declines. Changes may occur in the nervous system, slowing cognitive functions. Reaction times may slow down and sense of balance can worsen.

Experts tell us that, for the average person, strength typically peaks when you're in your 20s, stays fairly stable for about 20 years and then starts to decline in your sixth decade. They say you tend to lose more strength in your lower extremities than in your upper extremities. As a result, a healthy 80-year-old woman or man has about a third less knee strength than he or she did at age 70 and has lost some hand grip strength, as well. Range of motion is reduced as joint and ligament inelasticity reduce flexibility, affecting walking gait and balance.

Experts believe that undernourishment affects one in four older Americans. However, that's not the only problem with nutrition and aging. While caloric need generally declines by 2 to 10 percent a decade past the age of 20, intake often doesn't decline and physical activity frequently doesn't keep pace, either. As a result, the average American adult may lose 15 percent of lean body mass (muscle), while the percentage of body weight that's fat increases from 14 to 30 percent. So it's no surprise that excessive weight is a problem for many older adults—more than 40 percent of adults between the ages of 60 and 69, for example. However, experts report that this shift in body composition is not inevitable and can be reversed.

Physical Activity Can Reverse Grim News

Experts now believe that much of the decline attributed to aging is a result of inactivity. About a fourth of all elderly people are inactive, while another 54 percent are "sub-optimally active," according to the Centers for Disease Control and Prevention and the American College of Sports Medicine.

But, if you know any vibrant older adults—or if you are one yourself—you may know that some of the losses mentioned above aren't inevitable. Nor are they irreversible. "As you get older, staying physically active can help you decrease the aging process in many ways," says Gerald F. Fletcher, M.D., professor of medicine, Mayo Medical School, Mayo Clinic, Jacksonville, Florida, and lead author of the American Heart Association's recent scientific statement on exercise standards. "If you're physically trained, there's less decline in VO_2max—much less at age 85, if you've been active." An interesting study that followed members of the 1972 Olympic U.S. silver medal rowing team for 20 years found that the one member who continued training during that time retained 90 percent of his VO_2max 20 years later.

A 25-year study of 17,000 Harvard graduates showed that exercise can add a year or more to your life. And another study of 13,000 men and women found that the least-fit men died of all causes at a rate more than three times that of the death rate among the most fit—and for women the death rate was four times

"Hub" Defies the Clock

Hub ("Harold" to his parents) was active in his younger years—he'd played sandlot baseball until age 28, for example—but didn't have any particularly good aerobic activities in his repertoire. But when he was 42, a neighbor decided to start a neighborhood running club and invited Hub to join.

The group would run in the mornings before work. They started by running 2 blocks, then walked a couple of blocks and ran another one. By the end of that year, Hub and his neighbor Milt—the only two of the original 20 who stuck with it longer than 2 weeks—got their distance up to 1.2 miles. Hub continued running with Milt for several years. Then the race bug stung Hub.

"I guess it was the element of competition," he said. He ran his first race—7 miles—at the age of 51. And he's never looked back. Hub currently holds several state records for various distances. At the age of 54, he ran his first marathon, and now, at the age of 76, has over 40 marathons under his belt—and, he says, probably over 500 races of all kinds. After retiring from the insurance business at age 65, Hub continued running—and averaged a race a week for a number of years into his 70s.

Throughout the years, several injuries have sidelined Hub, but he's always worked his way back—most recently from a groin injury he suffered 2 years ago. Although he wasn't able to run consistently again until fairly recently, he continued walking every day for at least half an hour and did light stretching. Now he's running about 6 days a week again, and hopes to be ready for marathons soon. "When the weather's bad, I run by the watch," he says. "I did 75 minutes today. I usually do about an hour, once I get warmed up and into a rhythm."

Hub's kept his weight fairly stable over the years that he's been running, although he notes that he quickly put on 5 pounds seemingly overnight after his most recent injury—pounds he's since shed. Commenting that he's seen reports that most of what people today consider normal aging seems to be a byproduct of lack of movement, Hub says, "I guess I'd rather wear out than rust out."

as high among the least fit as among the most fit.

"You're only as old as you want to be," says Fletcher. "I have a lot of patients who decide that life is good. They maintain their weight and exercise well into their 80s, without much loss of capacity." And because he realizes that activity and attitude make such a big difference, Fletcher carefully takes the time to discuss lifestyle with his patients.

"Inactivity probably accounts for more muscular dysfunction than does the aging process itself," says Janie Clark, author of *Full Life Fitness: A Complete Exercise Program for Mature Adults* (Champaign, Illinois: Human Kinetics: 1992). "But there's a lot of research that shows that neglected old muscles can be revitalized with exercise."

Clark notes that exercise helps increase total blood volume, enabling more oxygen to move into your cells. It can enhance the mineral content of your spine and thighbone, an important contribution to maintaining bone health and strength as you get older. Studies show that you can reduce your risk of falling and fracturing your hip by 20 to 40 percent with a program of regular exercise. In fact, in numerous studies of older adults with osteoarthritis, exercise reduced pain and increased daily functions in people with osteoarthritis as well as it did in those who didn't have the condition—all without increasing the overall risk of injury among those who exercised.

Regular exercise reduces the likelihood that you'll develop diabetes by 36 percent, and has been shown to be as effective as tranquilizers—or more so—for relieving muscle tension. In addition, it also helps you fight depression and fosters optimism, positive self-image and confidence. It's been shown to help keep older adults mentally sharp and improve social adjustment, as well.

Resistance Training: The New Star of the Show

In the past few years, studies of the effects of resistance training for older adults have yielded particularly impressive results. While you won't increase the number of muscles you have, exercise can help reverse the trend to lose tissue in your muscles as you age. "If you don't keep your muscles strong by lifting weights, you lose about a third of a pound of muscle a year," says Miriam Nelson, Ph.D., director of the Center for Physical Activity and Nutrition, and associate professor of nutrition at the Friedman School of Nutrition Science and Policy at Tufts University, fellow of the American College of Sports Medicine and author of *Strong Women Stay Young; Strong Women Stay Slim; Strong Women, Strong Bones; Strong Women Eat Well* and *Women and Men Beat Arthritis.* Incidentally, Nelson, who's 42, has done a great job of figuring out how adults can get teenagers to exercise with them (see sidebar, page 179).

Resistance training can markedly increase the strength of your lower extremities, improve the speed of your walking gait and make it easier for you to climb the stairs. It also helps lower your risk of injury by strengthening the tendons and ligaments that stabilize your joints and is the most highly recommended way to deal with and reduce the pain of osteoarthritis. Here are but a few of the many impressive study results involving resistance training and older adults:

■ One study of 40 healthy, but sedentary, postmenopausal women, cited by Nelson in *Strong Women Stay Young*, found that those who did strength training twice a week ended up with bodies that were 15 to 20 years more youthful than those who did none—progress that was evident in just 4 weeks of twice weekly 40-minute sessions. In just 2 months, the participants typically doubled the amount of weight they could lift.

■ Several studies of older adults diagnosed with depression or other mood disorders found that participating in a supervised weight-training program significantly improved the quality of the participants' sleep, increased their strength (by 33 percent in one study) and improved their quality of life, while dramatically reducing their depression. And, according to the studies, the intensity of the resistance training was a significant predictor of the level of reduced depression, with more intense training reducing depression more dramatically.

■ In another year-long study of older women (average age 59), participating in a progressive resistance training program twice a week produced increasing and dramatic strength gains—over 70 percent for some body parts—although nearly half of those gains occurred in the first 3 months of the study.

■ In one 10-week study of elderly adults (average age 87), a progressive resistance program combined with a multi-nutrient dietary supplement

Weight training can dramatically improve your strength and walking speed—regardless of your age.

boosted muscle strength over 100 percent, walking gait speed by 12 percent and stair climbing 28 percent.

■ Even if you're an older adult with joint problems, strength training offers you impressive benefits. One study looked at men and women, ages 68 to 85, without neuromuscular or cardiovascular disease, and with below-average leg strength. Some participants used a strength-training regimen, others participated in endurance training, while a third group combined strength and endurance training and a control group had no intervention. Although joint symptoms fluctuated over time in all exercise groups, they didn't improve or worsen significantly in any group. Furthermore, participants with arthritis and joint symptoms gained as much strength as did those who had no joint symptoms.

■ And one of the most dramatic 8-week, high-intensity resistance training studies looked at 10 frail, institutionalized adults, average age of 90 (the oldest participant was 96). The nine individuals who completed the study saw strength gains average 174 percent and walking speed improve 48 percent. Another study of 100 nursing home residents, ages 72 to 98, found that a 10-week progressive strength training program increased muscle strength an average of 113 percent, while also improving walking speed and stair climbing.

■ You may be interested to know that new research shows that strength training can also improve the aerobic capacity of older, unfit adults. A 6-month study included men and women between the ages of 60 and 83, who participated in workouts three times a week. All of the participants saw their aerobic capacity improve and were able to work out longer on a treadmill at the end of the study. Gains between those who had fewer repetitions of a heavier weight were about the same as those who lifted lighter weights more times.

Trying a Triathlon at 71

Although he says he's always been active—"addicted to exercise," Bill, a cardiologist currently doing research on heart disease prevention, hasn't yet done a triathlon. Never having had swimming lessons, he's always been uncertain about being able to finish the swimming part of the event, which combines swimming, biking and running. But he expects to cast aside his uncertainty this spring, when he enters his first triathlon at age 71. The race he'll enter combines a quarter-mile pool swim with 8 miles biking and 3 miles running.

"Once I know I can do it, I hope to enter about one a month," Bill says. He has no illusions of finishing first, but will be happy just to finish and enjoys the camaraderie of working out with active people—many of them younger than he. Some of his workout buddies are serious triathletes. One has done the Ironman, which combines a 3-mile swim with a 110-mile bike ride and a full marathon, several times. But this senior has no interest in setting or breaking records other than his own. And, as he does successive races, he'll simply look for improvement.

Being accustomed to playing tennis several times a week, hiking, skiing and jogging—"I'm not a runner"—Bill had a ruptured disc in his back 4 years ago, which led to weakness in his right leg. After a neurosurgeon recommended surgery, he consulted with an orthopedic surgeon, a marathon runner himself, who told the cardiologist he had a choice in the matter: surgery or rehabilitation. He chose rehabilitation. And it's been

How You Can Realize Those Benefits

No matter what your age or physical condition, you can gain these benefits from regular physical activity, although you ought to take your individual needs into account. Here's some advice specially tailored to the older exerciser.

Make an Appointment to See Your Healthcare Provider

One of the first things you should do, especially if you've recently been inactive and if you haven't already done it, is talk with your doctor. It's also a good idea to do this as a safety precaution if you've been minimally active and want to ramp things up a bit. Your doctor may recommend that you take a stress test, in order to help establish safe guidelines for your exertion.

Ask if there are any special instructions you need to heed if you have heart disease, diabetes, high blood pressure, asthma, osteoarthritis or any joints that have been replaced. Also ask your doctor if any of the medications you take may affect your exercise or exertion levels. And follow the advice you're given.

If you notice that you have any discomfort in your chest when you exert, or if you find that you're short of breath, lightheaded or that you become fatigued easily, be sure to mention it to your

---

successful enough that he's hoping that his back will let him eventually do a full marathon.

Bill works out at a health club every day he's in town, probably averaging 6 days a week. His typical regimen includes a combination of activities: power pacing (variable- to high-resistance work on a stationary cycle), running (3 to 10 miles) indoors or outdoors, swimming, tennis and group-structured weight training. When I interviewed him for this book, Bill had just returned from a weekend of cross-country skiing and snowshoeing in the White Mountains of New England. He also enjoys climbing 4,000-foot peaks—even in the winter.

"Physical activity really gets into your blood," he says. "It helps calm you down and relaxes you, gives you a sense of fulfillment and control over your body's functions. And we're finding that the benefits of physical activity are incrementally more important in older people than in younger people—not only physically, but also mentally, and I'm guessing, in longevity as well."

"Balance training activities also have great value for older people," Bill adds. He particularly recommends one-legged dips (bending one knee and lowering yourself, while raising one foot behind, moving your arms above your head, then down to touch your toes) and balance board activities (movement done while balancing on a board with a hemisphere mounted on the bottom).

"The genes help," said Bill with a chuckle, when he learned that the friend who recommended him as a source for this book guessed that he was in his 60s.

doctor at this time, along with any other concerns you may have. If urinary accidents are a problem for you, mention it to your doctor, as well. You may be able to head off the problem by doing Kegel exercises (see page 243) and emptying your bladder immediately before exercising, or your doctor may also recommend a medication that can help. If you don't feel that your concerns have been adequately addressed, ask the question again or find another knowledgeable person to ask. Remember, you're the expert who knows your body better than anyone else.

Water Activities: Terrific for Many Older Adults

Many older adults enjoy swimming or water aerobics, because water activities spare you the weight-bearing impact of land activities. If you have osteoarthritis or fibromyalgia, the buoyancy water provides may make movement easier and less painful, although it's probably still a good idea to stick with low-impact movements. Because your body weighs only 10 percent of what it does on land when it's submerged in water, exercising in the water also makes moving much easier if you're overweight.

Although water temperatures between 78 and 84 degrees Fahrenheit are considered ideal for swimming and water aerobics, you may prefer temperatures at the higher end of that range as you get older, especially if you don't move very quickly. And you may notice, if the water is warm, that you'll have a wider possible range of motion once your muscles are loosened and warmed up.

Movement in the water can be as simple as walking for a given amount of time or as energetic and variable as you want to make it, if you and one or more other people toss around a beach ball—a great activity to do with kids. Many people also find that swimming or other activities in the water are great stress relievers. And it's something you can enjoy as many days of the week as you wish.

For water aerobic exercise, opt for water that's at least waist-deep for minimum impact to your joints. If you're judging your exertion by heart rate, reduce your training heart rate goal by 5 to 10 beats per minute for water aerobics. If you want to design your own water aerobic workout, check out Janie Clark's *Full Life Fitness: A Complete Exercise Program for Mature Adults* (Champaign, Illinois: Human Kinetics: 1992) for specific suggestions on how to put one together.

Add Some Aerobic Activities You'll Enjoy

If you've been active and need more of a challenge, first look at your aerobic program. Think about adding a new activity or working out more often or for a longer period of time—but not necessarily at a greater intensity. The simplest approach you can take is to beef up your walking—something that can nearly always be worked into your day. (Incidentally, did you know that the use of walking and biking as transportation has declined 40 percent in recent years?)

Walk after supper, instead of watching TV. Walk the dog. Walk to work or to the store. Take a long walk with your grandchildren or kids from your neighborhood. You'll gain the most benefit if you walk at a moderately brisk pace—not so briskly that you can't carry on a conversation, but briskly enough so singing is difficult. If walking doesn't appeal to you, pick another activity that you enjoy—perhaps jogging, swimming, playing tennis, cycling or dancing.

Researchers report that older adults are getting into sports and exercise programs at higher rates than any other age group—women more so than men. Are you interested in becoming more active, but stumped about what kind of activity to start with? Start out by making aerobic activity—one or several of them—the cornerstone of your fitness program and add in other activities as you wish. Aerobic activities are vital to keeping your heart strong and functioning well.

Cross-training—something you can do by adding a different type of aerobic activity—can condition a variety of muscles and help you get rid of excess fat. Aerobic conditioning also helps you build muscles, while you can use calisthenics to tone them.

Remember that doing even a little is better than doing nothing at all. If you take an invigorating walk, build up to a comfortably brisk pace gradually. If you're not used to walking briskly, you may be out of breath fairly early the first few times, and your legs may feel weak. When that happens, slow down a bit, and try picking up the pace again only when—and if—you feel up to it. Before long, you'll probably see an improvement as your body adjusts to the exercise, and you should feel better, both while doing it and afterward. Whenever you feel like you need to stop—do. And if you stopped sooner than you wanted to, try to fit in an extra session of physical activity sometime later in the day, if you're up to it. If you have osteoarthritis and are up to it, a swim or brisk walk will strengthen your cardiovascular system and help keep your muscles strong, which can markedly reduce the pain you regularly experience.

Remember, too, that you can get a very good aerobic workout on a flight of stairs—while also building muscle strength. The activity of climbing stairs is more intense than walking, so you can get more exercise in a shorter period of time. Use variations on a theme: go up and down the stairs normally several times, rest and then go up and down again. Or try one of these variations: step up one step with first one foot, then the other and then down again; go up and down sideways; jump repeatedly from the landing with both feet up to the step and then down again. Keep your hand near the railing—as insurance, in case you start to lose your balance.

Popular activities among older adults now include: fitness walking, cycling, running, calisthenics, aerobics, swimming, golf, bowling, camping, free-weight lifting, freshwater fishing, tennis and working out with equipment, according to Sheila Sobell, author of *Smart Guide to Sports Medicine* (New York, NY: John Wiley & Sons, Inc., 1999). If you opt for an aerobic dance workout, avoid any routines or groups that aren't low impact, and only move with controlled movements, avoiding slinging, jerking or bouncing movements. Eliminate extra wear and tear on your joints by not wearing or holding weights. If you select several activities to focus on regularly, choose activities that work different muscle groups.

Have Reasonable Expectations for Your Age & Ability Level

Don't expect to immediately function at the level of ability that you had when you were a teenager. Start slowly and progress gradually. Ease into a new activity gently, in order to avoid injuries—especially if you've been rather sedentary until now. Some experts suggest that it'll take you a month to come back for every year that you've been away from something.

If you want to try a new sport or activity, consider taking a class or otherwise getting assistance in learning to do it correctly. You may want to consider getting instruction, even if you're resuming an activity you had mastered years ago, because some of the techniques and equipment may have changed since you last participated in the activity. And sometimes you can

Design Your Own Low-Impact Aerobic Dance Routine

If you'd like to develop your own low-impact aerobic dance workout, all you need is some lively music that helps you start moving. Begin with a handful of steps forward or step in place to the beat, with your hands on your hips. Be cautious about including backward movements, if they make you unsteady. Substitute turning around, crossover steps, stepping in place or knee lifts. In low-impact aerobics you lift only your heels rather than run in place. If lifting your leg and kicking hurts, substitute knee lifts.

When you're comfortable with your foot motions, add arm movements. If it's painful or difficult to raise your hands and arms—or if you're not supposed to—move them out at your chest or to the side at your shoulder instead.

If you have a partner or friend who may also enjoy the movement—go ahead and ask him or her to join you. You don't need to have a professional instructor to enjoy movement together.

learn a new skill from a friend or acquaintance who's glad to share his or her expertise with you.

As you learn a new sport or activity, be especially attentive to information that can help you avoid and protect yourself from injury—information like how to fall to avoid injuring your wrists and fingers, how to stop, what kind of protective gear you'll need. Also learn to recognize what kinds of injuries are common to that activity and which ones are likely to need medical attention.

Incidentally, don't be afraid to ask the person who's giving you information to repeat it, if you have difficulty hearing it. And, if you sign up for a class, be sure that the acoustics in the room where the class will be held will allow you to hear the instructor. If it's a problem, try to place yourself as close to the instructor as possible, and let the instructor know that you have difficulty hearing, so that he or she can make a point of speaking clearly, projecting well and facing toward you when talking.

Keep Safety in Mind

Here are some general tips for exercising safely as an older adult:

■ Start slow and progress gradually.

■ Avoid cramps, nausea or faintness by waiting at least 2 hours after you've eaten a full meal, before you exercise. This enables your body to supply the needed blood to your digestive system before it sends blood to your muscles for exercising.

■ Always breathe in and out normally while you exercise. If a rhythm is helpful, exhale as you exert and inhale as you ease up. It's a good idea, when you're doing an aerobic activity, if you can work out long enough to have taken at least 50 deep breaths by the time you're finished.

■ Don't exercise to the point where you feel uncomfortable or awful—or where it becomes difficult to converse. If you start to feel shaky, short of breath, nauseous, light-headed or dizzy, slow your pace and, if it doesn't improve, stop. Don't begin again until you feel better.

■ If it's over 70 degrees and you're exercising outdoors, keep your activity at a slower, comfortable pace and drink plenty of fluids. Sometimes your body may not release internal heat as readily through perspiring, which may make you more susceptible to hyperthermia (see pages 218 to 220). If it's also humid when it's hot and there's no breeze, your sweat can't evaporate as readily to cool you, either.

■ Be sure to dress appropriately for the weather, at either extreme. As you get older—and sometimes as a result of medications or hormonal changes—you may find that it's more difficult for your body to adjust to sudden temperature changes. Use layers of clothing that you can easily slip on or off to help you adjust comfortably.

■ Don't skimp on 5 to 10 minutes of low-intensity warm-up and cool-down activity.

■ When you climb hills, reduce your speed, so your exertion level isn't greater than it was on the flat areas.

■ Check the surface where you'll exercise before you begin and avoid working out on surfaces on which you can't control slipping and sliding, as well

Warm-Up & Cool-Down Ideas

Warming up and cooling down helps you avoid injuring your muscles—including your heart. You'll fare much better in just about any physical activity if you can ease into it gradually and slow down gently. This enables your heart to keep up with increasing demands and helps ramp up the system of blood vessels that transport your vital, oxygen-carrying blood to the parts of your body that need it when you exercise—and also helps them send less of it there when you've finished the intense portion of your activity.

Beginning at a slower speed and very gradually picking up your pace of rhythmic movements over a period of 5 to 10 minutes is a great way to warm up—whether you're slowly pedaling a bike, dancing leisurely, swimming or walking at an easy pace as you swing your arms gently. After your muscles are warmed up you can add gentle stretches—up, down and sideways—to stretch the major muscles of your arms, legs and back. Save the longer, more intense stretches for your cool-down period.

Here are some other activities various experts suggest including in your warm-up regimen:

■ Sitting in a chair with arm rests, first move from a sitting to a standing position and back to a sitting position 12 to 15 times without using your arms. Then,

Stand-ups.

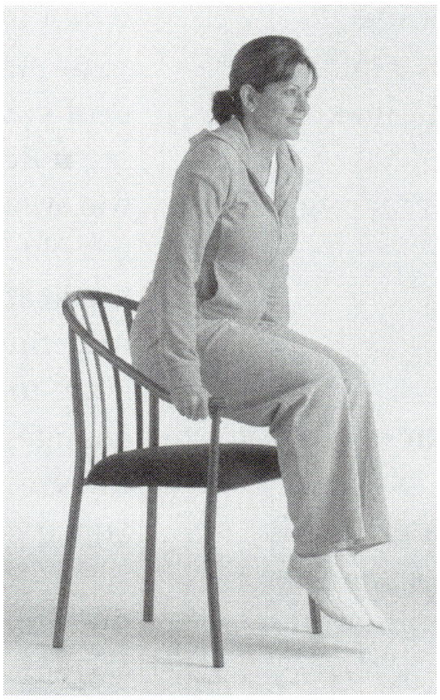

Sitting lift.

Knee hug.

with your hands on the arm rests, straighten your arms to lift your body from the seat and ease back down 12 to 15 times.

■ Hug, one at a time, each knee to your chest—while sitting or standing.

■ While seated, manually rotate your ankles and feet gently.

When cooling down, take at least 5 minutes to either slow down the activity you've been doing or use one of those listed above in the warm-up section. This is a good time to include any resistance work or calisthenics you plan to do, as well as some slow, gentle stretches.

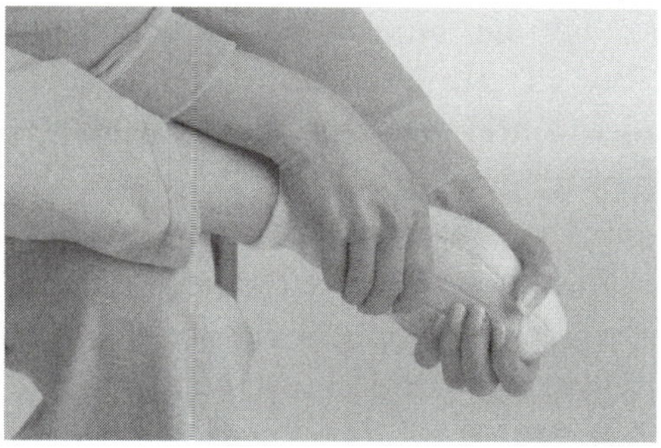

Ankle rotation.

as on surfaces with hidden bumps or holes that may cause you to twist an ankle or fall. Generally, it's fine to exercise on a carpeted floor, but less helpful on a soft bed. If it's difficult for you to get up and down, do so slowly to avoid becoming dizzy. And if one leg is weaker than the other, use the strong one to lower yourself.

■ If you have a hearing loss—or if you wear a headset or use a mobile phone while you exercise on public roads or pathways—be alert at the same time to sounds around you. This is especially important if you bike, walk or inline skate in places where you may encounter fast-moving or turning traffic.

■ Physical activity that's helpful shouldn't hurt. Learn to tell the difference between pain and muscular soreness. Avoid painful exercises.

■ Stretching often becomes more important as you get older—stretching the muscles in your chest as you breathe deeply, for example, seems to improve respiration. Maintaining flexibility of your feet's Achilles tendons is much easier than trying to restore flexibility when it's gone. When you stretch, extend the stretch to your full range of motion, but not to the point of pain. If you start learning yoga, look for a program tailored to older adults—one that has no unnatural stretches. Beware of bounces—they can often get you into trouble. And avoid locking joints—especially those in your knees or elbows.

■ If, at any time while you're exercising, you experience chest pain or pressure, dizziness, abnormal heartbeats or unusual shortness of breath, stop and rest. If it's not better in 1 or 2 minutes, seek medical help.

Be Sure You Include Resistance Exercises in Your Regimen

Although most experts don't recommend isometric resistance training for older adults (the type of training that doesn't involve muscles lengthening or shortening—standing in a doorway and pressing with your hands out to either side, for example), because it can increase blood pressure, they do highly recommend appropriate resistance training programs. If you have access to equipment that lets you know how much weight you're lifting or moving, that's a good way to start—especially if you have access to a trainer or someone else who knows the proper technique and can help you. Free weights, which can be as simple as cans of food or filled milk jugs, are fine, too, as long as you don't overdo the amount of weight in them. When you're older, it's safest to work with weights that may be a bit lighter, but to lift them more times. You can also get effective resistance exercise using resistance bands (see pages 145 and 213 for more information).

It's best to find someone who knows the proper technique and is willing to show you how to use weights properly, using your various muscles. Experts may suggest starting with only your body weight, then gradually adding weight, until you find an amount that you can lift 12 to 15 times. Avoid using weights that strap on, because it's easier to hurt yourself while using them, if you're older. Don't strain or hold your breath.

Here's a general pattern for lifting weights:

1. Take about 2 seconds to lift the weight, and gently lower it in 4 seconds.
2. Rest 1 to 2 seconds between repetitions and 1 to 2 minutes between sets.
3. Work up to 2 to 3 sets of each exercise, adding resistance only when lifting the weight 15 times becomes quite easy for you.

Only work until your muscle is tired, not until it hurts. Let your muscles rest and recover for 1 to 2 days between workouts. Meanwhile, continue to do your aerobic activity on most days of the week. Be sure to include some exercise for the muscles in your arms, shoulders, chest, abdomen, hips, legs, back and trunk.

Don't Forget About Your Balance!

A number of factors can affect your balance as you get older. Vision changes or difficulty adjusting to bifocal or trifocal glasses can make you unsteady or dizzy. Losing your balance as you get older can become a serious issue if you fall, as a fairly high percentage of older people do every year. If you're at all unsteady, don't close your eyes while you're standing, because much of your balance depends on visual cues.

One reason maintaining your balance becomes more difficult as you age is that doing so requires multitasking—doing several things at once. Add to that the problems caused by poor circulation or loss of sensation in the lower extremities, and balance becomes a serious issue very rapidly. "By the time you're 80, the rate of degeneration of balance is so steep that you'll have accomplished a lot if you can merely slow the rate of decline by participating in a serious balance retraining program," says physical therapist Robert H. Whipple, M.A., clinical assistant professor, University of Connecticut Health Center and physical therapist at Bethel Nursing and Rehabilitation Center.

"But aging is not synonymous with a sedentary lifestyle," says Whipple. "If you stay active and keep your body and mind alert, you can profoundly slow the rate at which you lose your ability to multitask." Whipple and other balance experts highly recommend T'ai Chi training as a valuable tool in improving balance and preventing falls as you age. Another thing you can easily do to improve your balance is to practice standing on one leg for a brief while each day, with your fingers lightly above the back of a chair, in case you need to steady yourself.

Drink, Drink, Drink—Water!

When you are physically active, you need more fluids than you require while sedentary. Thirst is not necessarily a reliable indicator of how much water you need, something that becomes even more pronounced with aging. In an interesting experiment, researchers withheld fluids for 24 hours from a group of younger and older subjects, causing, on average, a nearly 2 percent loss in body weight. At the end of the 24 hours, the younger subjects had much greater sensation of thirst and dry mouth than the older participants, and within a second 24 hours, the younger subjects had made up their bodies' fluid losses, while the older subjects had not.

Embrace Every Opportunity for Movement—No Matter How Small!

Even light physical activity is better than none at all. Don't hesitate to park a little farther away from the door to a store or building and walk a little extra. If you have a choice between pushing a button to open a door or opening it by hand—and you're strong enough to manage it by hand—do it, and be glad you're that strong. Look for stairs in buildings where you're used to taking an elevator and get off one or two floors early and walk the rest of the way.

Marge: Rolling, Now Walking & Stroking

Marge, now 84, is a vibrant, busy lady who gets to the pool early in the morning 5 days a week, before her day's activities are in full swing. A first grade teacher until she retired at age 62, she'd become a familiar sight in her mid-size town, biking everywhere she went.

Widowed for 9 years now, Marge experienced another life-changing event 4 years ago: she got a puppy. Now Marge bikes somewhat less, because she's added an hour-long walk with her dog every day of the week. And she's quite sure that her physical activity is what keeps her going, when a lot of her contemporaries are slowing down.

Physical Activity & Lifestyle Impact Each Other

You probably already realize many ways in which your other lifestyle choices affect your physical activity. Making sure that the food you eat is nutritious becomes even more important as you get older, for example, if you want to remain active and vital. Because your caloric requirements are reduced with aging, it's doubly important that the calories you consume have value, if you want to stay—or become—lean and active enough to fully enjoy your chosen activities. This becomes even more challenging, if you're dealing with chronic health issues, medication side effects and physical limitations. If you feel confused about what good nutrition means for you, considering your health issues, talk with your doctor about getting a referral to meet with a dietician.

Although it's true that sleep often becomes difficult as you get older, you should sleep better, once you're involved in an age- and condition-appropriate program of physical activity. And there's a good explanation for why you sleep better, after you've been physically active, according to Timothy Roehrs, Ph.D., director of research, Sleep Disorders and Research Center, Henry Ford Health System, Detroit, Michigan, who describes how a program of physical activity can improve sleep in elderly people. "Exercise, particularly in older people, increases the amount of slow-wave sleep, which is considered to be restorative sleep," says Roehrs. "As people age, the amount of slow-wave sleep normally declines. But for older people who exercise, their sleep is more like that of a younger person and it is restorative."

Although the long-range impact of some lifestyle choices is more difficult to offset with better choices as you get older, it is still possible. If you've smoked for years, you certainly know the hazards you face and you realize by now that some of the damage incurred by smoking may not be reversible. You can

Luther: More Vital Than Ever at 88

It might take a few tries to reach Luther at home, as he's busier than ever before, at age 88, taking classes, getting together with friends or family and volunteering at his church. And, although he says that getting his thyroid deficiency solved has also made a dramatic difference, Luther knows that his walking has had a major impact, as well.

The base of Luther's conditioning program is a walking program—at home on the treadmill in the winter, out and about in the malls and other Chicago-land areas in warmer weather. "I walk at least 5 days a week on the treadmill, at a 2 percent grade, at a rate of 2.5 miles per hour, for 30 minutes," he says. In addition, Luther also walks several blocks to the neighborhood grocery store about once a week. "I feel better now than I've felt in at least 5 years," he adds with enthusiasm.

still realize substantial benefits by stopping, however, and it's worth giving it a try. Similarly, if you've never used sunscreen and have had a lot of exposure to the direct rays of the sun, years of damage can't be erased. You can, however, avoid additional damage or complications by exercising caution even now and wearing sunscreen and a wide-brimmed hat when you're in the sun—regardless of the temperature, especially in high altitudes.

Inactivity magnifies the effects of aging—no matter how old you are. For one study, college students were forced to stay in bed for 3 weeks. Researchers found at the end of that time, that the students had undergone changes in their fitness and muscle mass comparable to what they'd be expected to experience in 20 years of aging. Exercise boosts the ability of even the smallest of your blood vessels to supply oxygen-enriched blood to all of your muscles and can dramatically reduce the loss of power you would expect to accompany aging. Experts at Harvard and elsewhere are now coming to the conclusion that the ability to perform physically doesn't inevitably deteriorate with aging, but is largely a product of inactivity.

So the best advice is to stay as active as you can. If you need help knowing how much and what kind of exercise to do, be sure that the person you ask to help you has had experience with older people. And listen to what your body—and your physician—tell you.

Timothy Roehrs, Ph.D., reviewed chapter 11. He is director of research. Sleep Disorders and Research Center, at Henry Ford Health System in Detroit, Michigan.

CHAPTER 12

Adjusting Your Goals & Keeping Momentum

By now you may have begun to experience some of the benefits physical activity offers—unless you're still in the "thinking about it" mode. If that's the case—jump in! It's fun! And it's an adventure that can lead you down some very interesting paths.

Hopefully, you haven't just responded, "But I don't have the time." If you've looked at anything else in this book, by the time you've gotten this far you could already have jumped in. One study of inactive young women in Belfast, cited in *Active Living Every Day*, a book recommended earlier, found that in less than 14 minutes a day of climbing stairs a group of women increased their fitness in just 7 weeks, evidenced by lowered cholesterol levels and improved ratio of HDL (high-density lipoprotein, the good kind) to LDL (low-density lipoprotein, the kind you want to avoid). If your first instinct is to say that there's no place in your day where you can find 14 minutes, stop and think for just a moment. Isn't improving your health worth at least 14 minutes a day?

And again, remember that it's easiest to make the fastest gains when you're deconditioned. It generally doesn't take long to see a change at that point, if you look in the right places.

Where Are You Looking for Results?

If you've worked on improving your fitness level for several months and can honestly say that you don't see any progress, pause for a moment to consider possible reasons why that's true. First, are your expectations reasonable? If you want to lose weight, but the only change in your life lately is some heavy-duty weight-training, don't be too surprised if you haven't lost a pound. Remember, muscles are heavier than fat. Hopefully, you feel better and can tell that you're firming things up. Do you notice that your clothes aren't as tight-fighting as they were? And can you move more easily? Those are results—maybe not the ones you'd expected, but they're positive outcomes, and they indicate that you're moving in the right direction.

Remember the fundamental fact that weight loss generally only occurs when your caloric expenditure exceeds your intake. So, if the effort you spend on weight training hasn't produced any weight loss, ask yourself what other ways you can find to either spend more calories or take in fewer of them.

Your best bet, as far as adding activities, may be to look over the activities listed in Chapter 7 (beginning on page 151) or to look at the MET table in Chapter 4 (pages 81 to 86). Try to locate one or several activities that you may enjoy that have a fairly high MET level and that you can do fairly often for half an hour or longer—in other words, a calorie-burner—that may be of interest to you—playing full-court basketball, tennis, racquetball, inline skating, jumping rope, climbing stairs, sawing wood or doing jumping jacks or other active calisthenics, to name a few. Or, you can burn more calories simply by stepping up the pace of your walking, jogging, swimming or cycling.

"Sticking with a program of physical activity has to do with perspective," says James M. Rippe, M.D., exercise adherence researcher and associate professor of medicine in cardiology, at Tufts University School of Medicine, and founder and director of the Rippe Lifestyle Institute, as well as author of 25 books, including *Fitness Walking, Fitness Walking for Women, The Complete Book of Fitness Walking, Fit Over Forty, Healthy Heart for Dummies, Healthy Heart Cookbook for Dummies* and *The Joint Health Prescription.* "You need to understand that you need a lifelong commitment and that, while there are short-term benefits, the key benefits from a commitment to fitness are mostly ones that you accrue over a lifetime.

"Don't limit yourself to short-term goals—although, every time you're physically active, you do get a short-term benefit. Close your eyes after you exercise and ask yourself, 'How do I feel?' In response to that question, most people answer, 'Calm, happy, like I've accomplished something.' Strive to make physical activity something you include as part of your daily life—like brushing your teeth or combing your hair.

"You also need to get away from thinking of physical activity as an 'all or nothing' proposition," continues Rippe. "Yes, there may be days when you have more difficulty finding the time to fit in your physical activity. It's not because you're a less worthwhile human being or have totally blown it. Get back into being active, and recognize that there

I Felt I Had to Add Exercise

It didn't make sense to me. I'd been very active for most of my adult life. Yet, I was sitting in a cardiology office, hearing an expert tell me that I had heart disease. Clearly, I needed to do something—and I did. In fact, I didn't feel I had time to do a scientific study, altering one variable at a time. I needed to see immediate results, so I immediately did everything the doctor and I could think of to improve the picture.

One of the things I did was ramp up my exercise level. I'd been steadily losing weight—and it keeping off—at the rate of about 5 pounds a year for over 6 years. But now I felt I needed to shed some more weight faster than that.

I already spent quite a bit of time each day in physical activity. I swam at a comfortable pace for half an hour 5 days a week, walked briskly 2 miles in the morning on weekdays and briskly again 2 miles in the evening every day. On weekdays I also took a 20-minute T'ai Chi break.

So then, in addition to more carefully watching what I ate, I decided to tweak my activities. I altered the half hour devoted to my morning walk, beefing it up by adding some time and expending some additional energy. And, for much of the year I started substituting about an hour of biking, frequently swapping morning times with my noon-hour swim. When I couldn't bike, I still walked, but tried to do it for 45 to 60 minutes, rather than 30 minutes, at a more vigorous pace. And, when I didn't manage to get in either that longer walk or bike ride, I used the exercise bike at my home for as intensive a workout (arms and legs) as I can get in about 30 to 45 minutes. I continued to do the T'ai Chi and added 10 minutes of relaxation meditation each day.

Although I'll always have heart disease (you don't get over that, unfortunately), the cardiologist was quite impressed with the improvement an echocardiogram showed 6 months later—and I hope good reports keep coming in for a long time. Yes, we don't know which of the six factors that I changed made a difference—or what percentage could be attributed to each. But I intend to keep following the cardiologist's advice: "Just keep doing what you're doing." And I must again remind women readers, who may tend to disregard their potential for heart disease, that heart disease kills half of all American women.

are infinite gradations and that you need to get started again where you left off."

Rippe recommends beginning slowly—perhaps with a 10-minute walk a few evenings after dinner, then gradually adding about 10 percent a week. He notes that you're more likely to turn gradual lifestyle changes into lifetime habits than you are to maintain dramatic changes.

Consciously add small amounts of physical activity into your day. Rippe mentions a study at the University of Pittsburgh School of Medicine that found that people asked to perform several 10-minute chunks of exercise during the day did more exercising than those who were asked to do the same amount of activity in one daily session.

How's your attitude? You're more likely to succeed, if you have a healthy attitude toward exercise and believe that you truly can stick with a long-term fitness plan, says Rippe. Start out small and gradually build up what you do—whether it's taking a short walk, jogging, swimming, cycling or some other activity. If you don't know whether your goals are reasonable for your current condition, check with your physician, who should be able to help you set reasonable goals. And be sure you've selected as the backbone of your program active options that are frequently available to you, not something you do a handful of times in a year—although you should feel free to add those in, as well, knowing that your conditioning the rest of the year will make doing them a more viable option.

Select something you can do nearly every day as the backbone of your activity program.

Rippe notes that a lot depends upon your personality type, as well. If you're highly competitive, studies show that you're more likely to stick with a program of physical activity than is someone who's single or less competitive. And a retiring, patient, calm individual may need more encouragement. Recruit your own fan club, whether it's a supportive friend, partner—or, perhaps, your healthcare provider.

Look for an inspirational role model—ideally, someone who's done what you hope to do, starting at a similar point. And remember that you have no choice but to start where you are—or not at all. And doing nothing certainly offers no better outcomes!

According to Rippe, lack of a positive body image also hinders many people. If that's your case, you'll probably be better off exercising in the privacy of your own home or with a trusted friend. Or how about trying to change your body image? Stand—or better yet, exercise—in front of a mirror and take a good look at yourself. Be honest about what you see—both the pluses and minuses.

You're more apt to omit your exercise during periods of stress. But don't torture yourself with guilt. Just resume your activity as soon as you can—even at a reduced level. Rippe notes that physical activity can help reduce your anxiety and tension, especially if you spend a few minutes when you're finished with your activity, eyes closed, focusing on how great you feel.

"Watch your mood differences, when you exercise, compared to those times that you don't," says Ann Webster, Ph.D., health psychologist at the Mind/Body Medical Clinic, Beth Israel Deaconess Medical Center, Boston, and instructor in medicine at Harvard Medical School. "Exercise is a very effective antidepressant and anti-anxiety agent, especially in these times of high stress. Just observe the differences you can see in yourself on days that you exercise, versus days when you don't. It affects how you feel, as well as how your body looks. Exercise is the perfect antidote for stress—no matter whether it's at home, at work, with your kids—whatever."

Webster also notes that it's much easier to stay committed to exercising if you find an activity that you like. "You have to find something that you enjoy. If it's not fun, people won't do it," she says. Webster also emphasizes the boost that you can get from finding a compatible exercise partner—whether it's your mate, a close friend, a neighbor—even your dog. "You end up motivating each other," she affirms.

Rippe: Physical Activity Is a Productivity Tool & Stress Reducer

Clearly, James M. Rippe, M.D., exercise adherence researcher, associate professor of medicine in cardiology at Tufts University School of Medicine, founder and director of the Rippe Lifestyle Institute, and author of 25 books, does have a life apart from working 80 hours a week—and it's a very active life. A married father of four, Rippe's personal regimen includes regular walking, jogging and weight training. He's also earned a black belt in karate and is an avid wind surfer, skier and tennis player.

How does he fit it all in?

"I used to say I could count on one hand the days in a year that I don't exercise. Now, I say it's less than two hands," he admits. "My mindset is that I'm always looking for ways I can be physically active. It's not a matter of fitting it in, but it's a priority."

"We know that the more hours you work, the more likely you are to exercise. Three-quarters of frequent exercisers say the main benefit of doing so is stress reduction. I plan my days so I don't miss my exercise session, because it's a key productivity tool for me. I'm less productive if I don't exercise, so it's a very high priority. Yes, there are occasional times when I don't get it in, but they're fewer than 10 times a year."

Webster: How Rare Are Mature Adult Gymnasts?

Aren't all gymnasts tiny, young girls? Have you ever known an adult gymnast? Yes, they do exist! Meet Ann Webster, Ph.D., health psychologist at the Mind/Body Medical Clinic, Beth Israel Deaconess Medical Center, Boston, and instructor in medicine at Harvard Medical School.

A perfect example of how loving an activity can motivate you, Webster has been interested in gymnastics since she took acrobatics lessons as a young girl. Now, living in New York, she's gone to the same gymnastics studio for over 30 years. "We do it all—swinging rings, trapeze, mat work," she says. And many of the others who go there have come for years, as well. Webster tells of one amazing professional model, well into her 80s, who goes there regularly for a gymnastics workout. After a good workout, Webster and her friends frequently reward themselves by going out for a skim latte or some soup—or they may take in a movie.

Webster and some of the other gymnasts and dancers have also become interested in gyrotonics, a whole-body-toning approach similar to Pilates, done on special machines. And for years, she's also enjoyed the benefits of yoga—"something anyone can learn—even from a video at home," she says.

Time for Taking Inventory

Regardless of how long you've made physical activity a key part of your life, it's a good idea to pause briefly from time to time, to see where you've been and where you're headed. If you made some notes or recorded goals as you began reading this book, pull them out again, and take a few minutes to reevaluate them. If you haven't really made notes, consider doing some journaling on a regular basis, so that you can more accurately follow not only the changes that occur as you become more active, but also your feelings about those changes. Have you met some of your goals? If so, did you reward yourself—or are you rewarded every day, because you notice that something that was previously more difficult is easier now? Note—and celebrate—those small victories!

Perhaps some of your goals look a bit lofty now, and you'll feel the need to adjust them to be more reasonable. Don't hesitate to do that. Remember, if you have no goals, you're likely to go exactly nowhere or backward. And if you haven't reached your highest goals, look for and celebrate any improvement at all. Did you have enough short-term goals? If not, add some. Take a few minutes, record the date, and update your list. Note the improvements you've seen—no matter how small—and set any new goals you'd like, whether it's an adjustment of a goal you had listed earlier or a totally new goal. Make some of your goals short-term goals, others longer-range.

If you want to keep your goals basically the same, ask yourself whether you

Don: The Cement Sack Goal

Two months into his program, Don, whom you've heard from several times throughout this book, looks at his progress differently than he did at first. No longer does he first bring up whether or not he's made a dent in his 100-pound weight loss goal. Instead, he talks of how he can tell, when he's missed a couple of days of working out, that he's really missed doing it.

Not that he doesn't notice improvements! "The main thing is how much stronger I feel," he says. "I know I look better and I've lost, maybe, an inch around my waist. A watch that used to fit comfortably had become impossible to put on, but now it's easy to get on. I can feel and see that my face, arms, legs, hips seem to be smaller and tighter."

Don realizes that he'll need to commit to reducing his food intake eventually. "My belly seems to be the last to fall into line. It seems that, as I got out of condition, I began by getting paunchy in the belly. Pretty soon, everything else around it just caught up with my belly. So now, maybe my belly's the last to shrink." Don does notice, however, that strengthening his abdominal muscles has meant that his belly doesn't protrude as much as it used to.

Don also notices that he's more agile and less prone to injury. "The last couple of years I've been leery about going for a walk when it's slippery outside, which is ironic, because I used to play hockey and was a good athlete. But recently I've noticed that my balance has improved, and I'm not afraid of walking on ice and snow like I had been. I can sense that I have better balance in my feet and body. I can even go down the stairs with a lighter step, rather than trudging down. And getting in and out of the car is now one move, not three, as it had been in recent years."

Don does have one very clear long-term goal, something he relates from his summers working on construction projects. "I look forward to the day when I've lost the weight and I can throw a 94-pound sack of cement over my shoulder and say, 'That's what I used to drag around.'"

To spice up your activity regime, set a date to exercise with a friend.

could reinvigorate them by adding or tweaking something. Consider some of these possibilities:

- Consider having a competition, whether it's with a stopwatch against yourself, with a friend or exercise buddy (if you don't have a buddy, think about whether you need one), a walk for a community nonprofit fundraiser whose goals you support or a low-level local competition (a triathlon, for example).
- Would you enjoy spicing up a current activity or trying a new one—whether it means learning and trying a new swimming stroke, walking in a new neighborhood, renting inline skates, a bike or a canoe or climbing a hill within driving distance on your next free day? Perhaps you'd like to try out the climbing wall at the sporting goods store. Maybe you could use a new pair of shoes or a new piece of equipment for an activity you already include.
- If you've had trouble sticking with a program, treat your workout times just as you would any other appointment, scheduling around them, noting them in your planner, if that helps. When you get up from the breakfast table, consider leaving yourself a reminder on a sticky note on the refrigerator door. If you've slipped away from an activity's regularity, set a date with a friend to exercise—a tennis date, perhaps. And don't shy away from paying a fee to rent court time. Remember—you're worth it! Don't beat up on yourself when you miss a day. Just set your mind to meeting your exercise goal tomorrow.

One thing that may help you stay motivated is to look for others who've sustained a level of regular physical activity over a period of time, despite having busy schedules that don't revolve around exercise. Try to hang around with them more and talk with them about how and where they find the time and what they do to stay motivated, when the going gets tough. It may be a good idea to expand your circle of

Nobby Cuts Himself Some Slack—but Not a Lot!

Having been a professional coach in Japan, Nobby, whom you met earlier, admits that he's compulsive about his workouts. But he's found a solution that works for him: he allows himself 4 days a month to miss his running. "Before, if I missed a day, I thought I'd stop working out entirely," he says. "But now, since I've started allowing myself to skip 4 days a month, I just remind myself that I'll be back at it tomorrow. And I am back the next day."

acquaintances, if everyone you know seems to be winding down, as far as their level of exercise. Try not to be judgmental, since each of us has different levels of motivation and focus at different times in our lives. Maybe seeing your commitment to physical activity will inspire your less active friends to bump up their own levels of activity.

Sometimes employers and coworkers are supportive; at other times, less so. Take every opportunity you can to help your employer realize that, in both the long and short run, employees who are physically active and healthy save them money, both with increased productivity and lack of absenteeism, as well as by helping keep insurance costs down.

Make it clear to those around you that your newly active lifestyle is one you expect will be permanent, and that it's for the long-term benefit to your health. Invite friends and family to join you, but don't hit them over the head with it. It's a very personal decision, and it's one each person has to make individually, when he or she is ready. If you're concerned about a partner or other loved one who isn't on board with a healthy lifestyle, it's nonetheless a good idea to mention it, not in a nagging way, but just as an expression of concern. Research does show that you can positively influence a partner, for example, to make significant—and needed—lifestyle changes in this way.

Updating Your Activity Goals

One way to expand your horizons is to add activities, as mentioned earlier. It's also a good idea, from time to time (perhaps every 3 months or so), to look at your exercise regimen and see if anything needs updating. Take a look at each component individually.

Beware the Big 5-0!

My husband and I found that as we and our friends began celebrating fiftieth birthdays, many of our friends suddenly became less active. They'd apparently decided that it's natural to wind down at that age. But we're not convinced.

Maybe we'll feel differently about it later, but for now, we're convinced that it's natural for us to be active. So we continue to play volleyball with our adult children and look for people with whom we can bike to Friday night suppers or walk after dinner. And, as we look at friends who are older than we are, it seems evident that the healthiest ones also happen to be the most active ones (and those who aren't overweight). The message seems clear: our bodies were designed to be active and moving—all our lives! So it encourages us to learn that 96-year-olds can substantially improve their strength with resistance training. And it reminds us to do a better job of tending to that part of our regular regimen.

And, guess what—an active life is a lot more fun, too!

Aerobic Activity. If, for your aerobic component, you've been doing the same thing—for the same amount of time at the same pace—for a few months, it may be time to update, whether it's taking a look at the same activity or activities or trying different ones. Two factors are crucial, when seeking aerobic activities that will work for you. First and foremost—it really makes things a lot easier and more pleasurable, if you can find something you love to do. You may find that you feel very differently about walking, jogging and running, for example—and only one of those activities may appeal to you. If so, then go for it! They can all be great aerobic activities.

But, suggests Marvin A. Brooks, M.D., family physician, don't overlook activities that you may have not considered in the past because they were out of your comfort zone. "For example, many adults have, for various reasons, steered away from water activities," he says. "It may be due to a bad experience earlier or because you've become convinced that it's something you can't learn. But think about expanding your comfort zone and giving it a try." Brooks notes that negative body image and fear of failure keep many people from trying activities that have the potential of offering excellent conditioning and becoming pleasurable, especially as you get older.

If you give inline skating a try, don't forget protective gear.

It'll be easier on your joints, if you don't limit yourself to high-impact activities—like jumping rope, running and aerobics. If you have one or more of these in your repertoire, consider adding swimming, cycling or inline skating. And remember that you need a solid base of something you can do year-round where you live.

Also consider how long it'll take you to master a new activity to the point where you'll be able to do it continually for a period of time, in order to see the cardiovascular benefit. Inline skating, for example, can take a bit of time to learn, which is fine, if you're willing to devote the time to doing that. (And please, wear protective gear, especially while you're learning.)

If you're happy with your activity, but want to know how to improve its aerobic conditioning value, here are some suggestions:

- Many experts recommend keeping your rate of exertion at a steady and fairly vigorous level, while extending the period of time you do it. Or, add another activity that works different muscles.

This approach makes it less likely that you'll incur bone or joint problems or cardiovascular complications, and you're more likely to be able—and willing—to stick with an activity.

■ Vary your routine. By limiting your aerobic conditioning to one format, one pace and one length of time, you're only training your body to do that single thing well. Vern Gambetta, the trainer you met earlier, whose clients have included numerous professional athletes over the years, suggests beefing up your routine by doing something as simple as adding stair walking to your day's activity.

Heath emphasizes creativity and fun in aerobic conditioning. "Be as creative as you want to be, in the context of your own enjoyment and preferences," he says. "Vary your program. Just as

What's Interval Training?

If you presently are doing endurance activities—distance running, swimming or cycling—you may want to include interval training in your routine. This is a method of challenging your cardiorespiratory system, using the overload principle, in order to improve it and cause it to operate more efficiently. You can also increase caloric expenditure. Before you can do this, notes Gregory W. Heath, D.Sc., lead health scientist, CDC Division of Nutrition and Physical Activity, you need to achieve an initial level of fitness that permits easily adapting to increased levels of intensity of effort.

To do intervals, you place several fast, "supermaximal effort" segments as Heath terms them, between stretches of slower aerobic activity. If you're a long-distance runner, you may intersperse quarter-mile stretches of all-out running between quarter miles of lower-level, yet aerobic running. Or you may simply try bumping up your level of speed between telephone poles several times along your route, as you feel able, returning to your previous level of exertion between spurts.

The period between the stretches of all-out effort is called the "recovery" period—when your body recovers after activity bordering on the anaerobic level, which occurs when your body can no longer supply sufficient oxygen in your blood to sustain the activity level and you tire quickly and have to slow down. "While this level of functioning is not necessary to your overall health," Heath says, "it does prepare you for that time when you need the extra spurt—sprinting to catch a bus or racing down the hill to grab your grandchild before he or she reaches the lake, for example. It helps your body adapt and become more efficient." Some experts, however, discourage interval work as a long-range approach and would rather see you simply ease into increasing your overall level as you can.

It's Fine to Substitute One Aerobic Activity for Another

One thing you'll notice, as you become more fit, is that you'll embrace opportunities for physical activity. While I usually try to add in additional activities, rather than substitute them for my usual aerobic ones, sometimes it just makes sense to substitute.

As I worked on this book, we had a snowfall that measured over 10 inches. And, as it happened, we were tending a relative's house at that time, as well. Most of my neighbors have snowblowers, but I've resisted that, preferring to celebrate good health by shoveling the snow by hand. And my area hasn't had that much snow in recent years, so no one is really tired of shoveling. In fact, I had missed having decent snow for cross-country skiing in town.

So, when 5 inches had fallen by 10 p.m., with predictions of 5 more by sunrise, I decided to get the jump on it, and clear the first half before going to bed. It was a lovely snow, sticking to the branches of the evergreen trees. It looked like a picture straight from a photo album. I shoveled for nearly 3 hours to clear driveways and sidewalks at both homes, and by the time I returned to my home, I removed another 2 inches from the front walkway. Soaked from the snow that had stuck to me and warm from the steady activity, I dried off and hit the hay, sleeping soundly.

A few hours later I was at it again, clearing the balance of the snowfall from both driveways and walkways. Interestingly, the snow had changed character in those few hours, so that it was now powdery and dry, not heavy and wet, like the snow I had shoveled earlier. Although I would have enjoyed making it to the swimming pool after shoveling, I knew that I didn't have time for both. But I had swapped another good workout at the end of a snow shovel for a swim. Because it was a steady, rhythmic, repetitive and energetic motion, I'd had a good workout—not a swim, but nonetheless, vigorous and invigorating in the beauty and quiet of the early morning.

And, when I was finished, as my neighbors were waking and dragging out their snowblowers, I glowed with the satisfaction of being healthy enough to move that much snow by hand, with no ill effects.

most people don't like eating the same thing day in and day out and find that variety makes life a lot more interesting, so it is with physical activity—unless you're addicted to one type of activity. I, myself, do a variation on a theme: I run, hike, bike and walk for pleasure. But I can't stand swimming in a pool, and I don't like stationary bikes or loud music and people jumping up and down."

"To improve your cardiovascular fitness, it's not necessary to do anything to the point of exhaustion," says Gerald F. Fletcher, M.D., professor of medicine, Mayo Medical School, Mayo Clinic, Jacksonville, Florida, and lead author of the American Heart Association's recent scientific statement on exercise standards. "Feel free to add additional activity that's comfortably strenuous until you're very tired. The duration of the exercise is what's important for cardiovascular fitness, although more intense exercise is probably more beneficial for your heart than less intense activity. And it's OK to rest between exertion—to run 5 to 10 minutes, then rest before doing it again."

Fletcher notes that maintaining a stable program will do a good job of keeping you at the same level of fitness, but not any better. If you're a runner, you can improve your cardiovascular conditioning by going faster, running longer or adding hills to your route. He also advises you to discuss any intentions of ramping up your program with a health professional—and increasing your program in moderation—never more than 10 percent per week. Fletcher also reminds you that if you've become deconditioned, it takes longer to come back—6 weeks to come back from 3 weeks of deconditioning, for example.

There is, apparently, some debate among experts as to the frequency of endurance training that's optimal, according to Jay Hoffman, Ph.D., associate professor in the Department of Health and Exercise Science, College of New Jersey, Ewing, New Jersey, and member of both the American College of Sports Medicine and the National Strength and Conditioning Association. In some studies, working out twice a week appeared to produce changes in VO_2max (the rate at which you extract oxygen from the air you breathe, a primary measure of aerobic fitness) that were very similar to those derived from working out 5 days a week, although Hoffman notes that the results may be closely related to the training intensity, and if you reduce the intensity, you would need to increase the frequency, as well.

Hoffman does note, however, that if it's one of your goals to reduce body fat, studies show that higher frequency is more beneficial, due to the greater caloric expenditure involved. So adjust your time, according to intensity of your exercise. Someone who's deconditioned could benefit from a fairly low-intensity 5 minutes a day, whereas the conditioned individual requires more time. Hoffman mentions that the general recommendation is still 20 to 30 minutes at a minimum of 70 percent VO_2max. Interestingly, one study of collegiate swimmers found that doubling their practice time from 1.5 hours per day to two sessions of the same length did not produce any greater swimming power, endurance or performance. Cross-training, or doing a different activity than you usually do, is good for maintaining general fitness, preventing boredom and treating or preventing injury.

Resistance. Depending on what you do for resistance training, there are plentiful opportunities for tweaking it. And, if you don't have resistance activity in your program, seriously consider adding it. Studies of its value as you get older just keep getting more and more impressive.

Vern Gambetta, who has coached at various levels for over 30 years and has served as the conditioning coach for several professional sports teams and professional athletes and who specializes in functional fitness, has some simple suggestions. "Look for total involvement. When we work out for an hour, we'll move the entire time. Switch exercises and keep a good pace. Change the direction you move the resistance, change your stance. Reach out instead of up, across your body instead of down." Gambetta notes that your pace will pick up, as your conditioning level improves, enabling you to fit more movement into the same time frame.

Many trainers recommend adding yoga or T'ai Chi to increase flexibility and balance.

Flexibility. Gambetta again emphasizes the need for controlling flexibility exercise, even when you're used to doing it frequently. "Keep doing it, and you'll see day-to-day changes in your range of motion," he says. Gambetta notes that you can gain more by doing the motions at a slower, more deliberate kind of rhythm, and suggests that you also consider adding T'ai Chi or yoga for increased flexibility and balance.

Balance. Gambetta suggests adding new movements to your balance regimen for fun and for increasing your balance ability. "Beef it up," he says. "Stand on one foot, add movement, reach up or out, dip down and hold your position. Then step to the right and to the left, sideways, backward and forward."

Fitness: A Goal & a Quest

For years, experts have sought to awaken Americans to the challenge of becoming a fit people. Some argue that it's the most patriotic thing we can do. The benefits have been well documented and approaches to becoming fit are constantly being explored and fine-tuned. Fitness does make a difference, as you will experience with your own increased activity.

For your information, the top health

Carmona: From Stickball to Surgeon General

"I've always been physically active," says Vice Admiral Richard H. Carmona, M.D., M.P.H., United States Surgeon General and Commander of the United States Public Health Service. "Growing up in a poor neighborhood in New York City meant there weren't a lot of organized activities," he said. "But I played stickball in the park with other kids from the neighborhood."

A high school dropout who later went on to become the top graduate in his medical school class at the University of California, San Francisco, Carmona played football and baseball in high school and was a swimmer. He didn't slow down after joining the U.S. Army, surviving the rigors of jump school and Special Forces training and becoming a combat-decorated Vietnam veteran. "Most of my jobs have required that I be physically fit," Carmona says, noting that physical fitness has enhanced his job performance throughout his career and has become a way of life.

"I incorporated physical activity into my life many years ago—and highly recommend doing that," he says. Although his current job keeps him very busy, Carmona makes time 5 or 6 days a week to work out. Now, at the age of 53, Carmona says he still uses a routine he established years ago, although he notes that, with each decade, he has to push harder to maintain the same level of fitness. "I have no choice: I have to push harder or let gravity and aging overcome my body," he says.

Noting that he rarely has the luxury of taking a break during the day for physical activity, Carmona says he frequently works out early in the morning, although sometimes it's midnight before he can squeeze in a workout. "But I'm determined to get it in, someplace," he says. Most of the time he's able to exercise in a well-equipped military facility, where his regimen includes 20 to 30 minutes of a variety of aerobic activities, 300 to 500 sit-ups, stretches and mild calisthenics. On lighter days he rounds out his hour-long workout with weight circuit training for his major leg muscles and may swim 500 to 1,000 yards. On alternate days, his aerobic activity is complemented by an hour-long weight circuit involving all his major muscle groups.

"When I travel, my staff works out with me," says Carmona, noting that he frequently conducts business with his aide as the two work out on adjacent treadmills. "If I'm not staying somewhere with access to the facilities of a military base," he says, "I stay in a hotel with a fitness facility. Or, if I don't have access to a facility, I'll run in an area park and use my body weight to work out." A survivor of numerous knee injuries and surgeries, Carmona now prefers the stationary bike or elliptical trainer over high-impact activities.

official in the country agrees with that assessment, and has found it to be true in his own life. Although he was not U.S. Surgeon General at the time of the report that alerted the nation to the need for concerted fitness efforts, Vice Admiral Richard H. Carmona, M.D., M.P.H., United States Surgeon General and Commander of the United States Public Health Service, is no less committed to the effort described in a fair amount of detail in Chapter 2. Not all of us have been as active as Carmona. But the benefits of physical activity are there for the taking.

Although you may not identify with the high level of fitness Carmona has attained in his 53 years, it's a level clearly attained through difficult and persistent effort. And, though you may never expect to become one of the country's leading health officials, fitness can, nonetheless, make a dramatic difference in your life.

While this book cannot be exhaustive in its coverage of what you may encounter on your fitness quest, it does seek to let you in on some of the very best advice that's out there—from some of the top experts. But remember, you're the expert, when it comes to your own body. You know how you feel, and you face the consequences of choices you make, regarding your activity levels. Celebrate the complexity and beauty of the masterpiece that's your body! Care for it and explore its potential. And enjoy a fit life!

Marvin A. Brooks, M.D., and Vern Gambetta reviewed chapter 12. Brooks is a family practice physician. Gambetta has coached at various levels for over 30 years, and is a conditioning coach for professional athletes and sports teams.

Fitness, a Continuous Process

As I set out to write this book, I decided that I'd know I was finished when I had all my questions answered, assuming that the questions I had were basically the same ones my readers have. As I finish this book, I have to report that many of my questions have been answered, thanks to the experts around the country who have been most generous in sharing their knowledge and experiences. I still have questions—maybe my name should be Curious George—and I shall continue to pursue their answers, as I would encourage you to do.

Life does go on, one way or another. I've made some changes in my exercise routine to reflect what I've learned—stepping up the pace of some of my activities to reflect the added cardiovascular value of vigorous exercise, renewing my determination to lose that additional weight I really don't need and including more resistance, flexibility and balance activities in my daily routine.

I've seen my husband survive a heart attack and open heart surgery, and I'm rejoicing to see him gradually—much more gradually than we'd expected—return to the good health he had enjoyed before. We share the hope that continuing to work on his risk factors and enjoying the benefits of his surgery will help him avoid additional health problems for many years.

I also just got some exciting news from a friend of mine who has fibromyalgia, whom you met in Chapter 3. I hadn't seen her for a while, having shared with her the chapter about three months ago. My physician, Marv Brooks, M.D.—who created the imagery exercise in that chapter—and I had wondered aloud just a few days earlier about how she was doing. Two days before I turned in copy for this book, I learned that my friend has shed 30 pounds and is well on her way to improving her health, although she still struggles with the effects of fibromyalgia. Not surprisingly, it's been a combination of improved diet and exercise that has made the dramatic difference, along with a very supportive environment. And my friend has every reason to believe that this will continue to be the case. It just had to be time to make the move, and she has done that.

You can, too, regardless of your age. Enjoy the benefits of being fit for life!

Acknowledgments

A project of this magnitude and with the various challenges I faced could only succeed with the help of numerous folks, to whom I am most grateful. With the hope that I haven't inadvertently omitted the name of anyone to whom I'm indebted, I first wish to thank and acknowledge the help of Claire Lewis, managing editor of the National Health and Wellness Club's *Today's Health & Wellness* magazine, who knew that this was a project for which I would have great passion. I'd also like to thank NHWC employees Heather Koshiol (managing editor) and Tom Carpenter (creative director), with whom I worked to develop the concept and direction of this book.

And I am especially grateful to six other people without whose extraordinary help this book would not have been completed:

Marvin A. Brooks, M.D., family practice physician and my personal physician

Gerald F. Fletcher, M.D., professor of medicine, Mayo Medical School, Mayo Medical Clinic

Gregory W. Heath, D.Sc., M.P.H., lead health scientist, physical activity and health, Division of Nutrition and Physical Activity, National Center for Chronic Disease Prevention and Health Promotion, Centers for Disease Control and Prevention

Judith K. Hinck, M.A., teacher and interpersonal communications specialist

Bob Madsen, proofreader, idea generator, cheerleader and my husband

David Poulter, P.T., Dip. M.D.T., physical therapist, center manager, international lecturer

I'd also like to thank the following people who provided original source information, referred me to additional sources and/or reviewed copy:

Brent Bauer, M.D., assistant professor of medicine and Mayo Clinic's alternative medicine expert

Vice Admiral Richard H. Carmona, M.D., M.P.H., U.S. Surgeon General and Commander of the U.S. Public Health Service

Minot Cleveland, M.D., internist and 2003 President of the National Coalition for Promoting Physical Activity

Andrea Dunn, Ph.D., exercise psychologist, Cooper Institute

Vern Gambetta, trainer and conditioning coach for professional athletes

Jim Gilbert, Linnaeus Arboretum director and instructor in environmental studies at Gustavus Adolphus College

Nobby Hashizume, founder and executive director of Five Circles, a nonprofit organization dedicated to enhancing and broadening the sport of running

Walter A. Hinck., M.D., family practice physician

Jay Hoffman, Ph.D., associate professor, Department of Health and Exercise Science, College of New Jersey

Rob Johnson, M.D., primary care sports medicine physician

Mike Killpack, director of sports, Amateur Athletic Union

Bess H. Marcus, Ph.D., clinical psychologist, Brown University Medical School, professor of psychiatry and human behavior and director of physical activity research, Brown University Center for Behavioral and Preventive Medicine at the Miriam Hospital

David McCarron, M.D., visiting professor, Department of Nutrition,

University of California-Davis

Lorraine Moller, 1992 Olympic women's marathon bronze medalist, four-time Olympian and coach of Wings of Mercury

Sylvia J. Moore, Ph.D., R.D., F.A.D.A., professor, Division of Medical Education and Public Health, University of Wyoming, assistant dean for WWAMI in Wyoming, University of Washington School of Medicine

Miriam Nelson, Ph.D., F.A.C.S.M., director, Center for Physical Activity and Nutrition, Gerald J. and Dorothy R. Friedman School of Nutrition Science and Policy, Tufts University

James M. Rippe, M.D., exercise adherence researcher and associate professor of medicine in cardiology, Tufts University School of Medicine, founder and director of the Rippe Lifestyle Institute, author of 25 books

Timothy Roehrs, Ph.D., director of research, Sleep Disorders and Research Center, Henry Ford Health System, Detroit, Michigan

Ray W. Squires, Ph.D., director of the cardiovascular health clinic, Mayo Clinic

Garen Stoehr, certified athletic trainer and regional educational coordinator, Northwest Athletic Clubs

Kathrine Switzer, author, global director of Avon's running programs and director of women's health and fitness for Rykä shoes

Carol Torgan, Ph.D., exercise physiologist and F.A.C.S.M.

Beth Warren, manager of Mayo Clinic's Dan Abraham Healthy Living Center for employees, affiliates and retirees

Ann Webster, Ph.D., health psychologist at the Mind/Body Medical Clinic, Beth Israel Deaconess Medical Center, instructor in medicine at Harvard Medical School

One aspect of this project that I found very enriching was discussing with many individuals their personal activity habits. I'm grateful to the following individuals who either shared their own experiences or helped me contact others who shared their experiences: Becky Anderson, Don, Darby, Larry, Chris Bopp, Lana, Christa Dickey, David and Grace Folkerds (for Helen Folkerds), Linda Ginenthal, Steve Gutmann, Tim Hensley, Chad Hoffman, Don, Harold, Betty, Valarie Kohn (for Gladys Skjeveland), William Kraemer, Bobbi, George, Dan, Tom, Lyn, Carmen, Kim Miller, Kathy, Carol Moreau, Kathy Nelson, Mia, Hazel Ouellette, Carolyn, Dan, Gay, Luther, Carrie, Francie Royce, Rebecca Seguin, Carol, Bill, Craig Stevens, Katherine Thiry, Howard Thomas, Lorna Tjaden, Mary Wagner, Michael Wattigny, Christine, Susan Wehrli, Ryan, Marge.

And I'd be remiss if I didn't thank my mentor, Dorrine Turecamo, who has always generously encouraged and counseled me; my mom, who instilled in me a love of the language and etched in my memory the phrase, "There's no such word as 'can't'" and my father, who urged me to believe I could turn dreams into reality.

—Lynn Madsen, Medical Writer

Index

D

E

F

G

H

O

P

Q

R